Scars Don't Hurt

MARGARET DAVIDSON
with Blake Davidson

CREATION
HOUSE PRESS

Scars Don't Hurt: A Story of Triumph Over Sexual Abuse
By Margaret Davidson With Blake Davidson
Published by Creation House Press
A Strang Company
600 Rinehart Road
Lake Mary, Florida 32746
www.creationhouse.com

Scripture quotations marked KJV are from the King James Version of the Bible.

Scripture quotations marked NKJV are from the New King James Version of the Bible. Copyright © 1979, 1980, 1982 by Thomas Nelson, Inc., publishers. Used by permission.

Scripture quotations marked NIV are from the Holy Bible, New International Version. Copyright © 1973, 1978, 1984, International Bible Society. Used by permission.

Cover design by Terry Clifton

Blake Davidson's photo by Ken Kenna

Library of Congress Control Number: 2004102753
International Standard Book Number: 1-59185-560-8

04 05 06 07 08 — 987654321
Printed in the United States of America

Acknowledgments

This book has been a labor of love and a team effort from the moment we began to write it.

Thank you Bill, my sweetheart. You are the love of my life, my soulmate, and my constant encourager. You have always believed in me, even when I didn't. I love you and thank God for you.

I wish to thank Blake, with whom I have spent countless hours talking, taping, writing, and editing, and with whom I now share an incomparable creative adventure. (Blake, I miss our special visits.) And also to my daughter-in-law, Christine, who is like my own daughter and close to my heart. Christine never once complained about the time Blake took away from the family to write, and committed countless hours editing style and content together with Jane. Thank you both.

To my girls, Shawn and Heather—thank you for being so vulnerable and for contributing to the authenticity of this book. Because you allowed your stories to be told alongside mine, many people will be helped and healed. Thank you to my understanding sons-in-law, Craig and Al, as well. I am privileged to have your unrestrained support.

To Marie Miller, who wrote the Foreword and never ceased to encourage me, and to the many who prayed over this project…thank you.

I'm indebted to my nephew, Rick Hiebert, who took on the massive responsibility of editing the manuscripts. Rick, thanks. My story is better written for passing through your hands.

Finally, I thank Jesus, my Savior, my Healer and my very best Friend—without whom there is no story to tell. I owe all to you!

Contents

Foreword

As a female evangelist, I am constantly pulled aside by Christian women who are scarred by an incident—or years—of sexual abuse. The wounds of the abuse are so real, the memories so haunting...and yet many do not know in whom they can confide.

It was only in the latter years of our relationship as prayer partners that Margaret unveiled her tragic story to me. I would never have suspected the extremity of it, as Margaret has been so completely healed that even the emotional scars do not show. Margaret revealed her story of restoration and grace one hot summer day as we were sitting on a memorable rock by a cottage interceding to God for our unsaved families.

Every person needs to read this book; not only to understand the deep issues of abuse, but more importantly, to sense the grace of God and to be encouraged in the power of prayer. Many women do not feel they will ever be totally healed. This story demonstrates the mighty and complete work of the Healer, Jesus Christ. As the story unfolds, families, pastors and counselors will gain a glimpse into the secret chambers that many are trapped in yet are too afraid to talk about. Some chapters may seem horrifying, but we are cautioned in the Word of God not to be offended by the truth. Both Margaret and her family have made themselves vulnerable in order to bless others and bring healing to many who are being held captive by their realities.

The title of this book is fitting: *Scars Don't Hurt*. As you get to know Margaret and follow the passages of her life, you can find strength for your journey of pain and find the courage to help others. Anyone who reads this book will gain insight they never had before and will better grasp the complexities of sexual abuse. I myself am able to serve others more compassionately after having read the story of how God took Margaret from pain and shame to peace and complete restoration.

—REV. MARIE MILLER

Introduction

BY BLAKE DAVIDSON

The first time I heard the story you are about to read, I was sitting on the kitchen counter beside the sink after helping Mom dry some dishes. We had been engrossed in a conversation about God and His grace, and how He can heal anything and make it new.

Mom and I often had these conversations, but this one was special. That day she told me that she thought it was about time I knew what her childhood had been like and how God had rescued and healed her. I remember sitting with fascination and curiosity, and thinking, *What does she need to be rescued from?* As she began to reveal what her family life was like, I soon realized it had been nothing like ours; the lady I knew simply as Mom was an incredible woman. In those moments as I sat on the kitchen counter, my mom became my hero.

A couple of years later when I was in my mid-teens, full of aspirations to become a writer, I told Mom that her story would make a terrific book. Then I took a presumptuous leap and shared that whenever she felt right about putting it all on paper, I would love to write it. She said she didn't know if God would ever lead her to do that; but if He did, she would certainly give me the opportunity.

During the years that followed, the urge to write Mom's story never left me. We spoke often about our special project—but the time wasn't right, the busyness of our lives and ministries didn't allow for it, and Mom didn't yet feel God nudging her in that direction. During the Christmas season in 1999, the subject came up once again. Mom had been having some heart problems and other health issues, and I said something I often said in passing: "Mom, nothing can happen to you until I get your signature on a book." Neither of us said any more about it.

Three months later Mom called me. She was very excited on the phone and said, "It's time Blake. It's time to write this book!"

She had been at a women's ministries meeting at her church, and Evangelist Peggy Kennedy, a special woman of God, was the speaker. After Kennedy shared, she began to pray with some of the ladies at the front and Mom went to look for a box of tissues. Suddenly, Peggy stopped praying and began looking for Mom. She said she had a special word from God specifically for Margaret Davidson, and she asked some others to find her.

As Mom reentered the room, Peggy said, "Margaret, I've never given a word like this to anyone before, but I feel strongly that God has something to say to you."

Mom was taken aback and wondered what all this could be about. As Peggy began to give the prophecy, Mom assumed it would simply be a word of encouragement regarding her health situation...and at first that is all it seemed.

Peggy continued, but this time in the first person, as though God Himself was speaking directly to Mom: "Margaret, I am not finished with you and I have a special plan for your life. I want to bless you and set you apart for this project—and I want your signature!"

When Mom heard the word *project* she got chills; but when she heard the last phrase, she knew instantly that God was directing her to write her story. No one else had ever used the word *signature* but me. The very next month we began the three-year journey together that would bring this book to you.

You know now why we wrote this book; I would like to tell you why you should read it.

I have been a pastor for nearly twenty years and I am constantly coming across hurting victims damaged by sexual abuse. While I was working in a newly planted church consisting of less than fifteen people, two different ladies approached me looking for God to heal them from their painful memories. As our churches grew, the scope of this problem became apparent, and I knew God could help.

Most of us do not know what it means to be a victim of sexual abuse. We want to reassure them that God can heal them, but we don't know what to say and we don't know how they feel. Anything we do say seems trite and can be dismissed because we don't truly know what it's like to be assaulted in this way.

Many times I wished this book were already written. Maybe I didn't fully understand a victim's pain or the various stages she must go through to finally receive healing, but I knew Mom did. I knew what God had done for her. I knew it because I lived with her and saw it firsthand. I saw God heal and restore someone whose childhood and life experience had been one of the most horrific I had ever heard of—so, when God healed Mom, I knew He could heal anyone.

This book then, is for every person who has been abused—physically, sexually, or emotionally. It's for everyone who *knows* someone who's been abused and wants to offer them hope. And it's for every pastor, counselor or elder who has had to sit across from a person in pain, not knowing what to do to help. *Scars Don't Hurt* is one woman's story. She isn't famous. She is not a celebrity. She is just one of the millions of people on the planet God has loved and restored.

This book is a book of hope and encouragement. It is, above all, a story—and a great one—that can inspire the entire human family, because Margaret Davidson is a triumph and Jesus Christ is the answer to any hurting soul.

Chapter 1

Journey to Sherbourne Street

During the last decade of the nineteenth century, Canada's West was being developed by Central and Eastern European immigrants—people from Germany, Russia and the Ukraine. My great grandparents moved from what is now the Ukraine (or western Russia), at the promise of low-cost land and prosperity, to what would ultimately become the breadbasket of the world—the Canadian Prairies.

German Mennonites, long without a home of their own in Russia and Ukraine, settled together and set up whole towns and farming communities. Such was the case in Gruenthal, Saskatchewan.

By 1908, Gruenthal was a community of 500, nestled into the flat countryside of central Saskatchewan. It was here, just twenty-seven miles north of Saskatoon, near the slightly larger town of Hague, that Katarina Thiessen's family made their home. Outside of town they had built a little house, joined hard against a bigger barn, and farmed the land. They grew grain and other cash crops, along with the vegetables they would need themselves to make it through the winter; then they hoped for a little extra to sell to their neighbors and those who lived in the village of Gruenthal itself.

In Gruenthal, everyone knew everyone else and, just as in all little villages, talked about each other's business. Though nearly all

1

were Mennonite, there were various sects, and each family took particular pride in the stream to which they belonged. Gruenthal's various Mennonite churches didn't always get along. Some Mennonites were very holy and righteous—others were less so. The Thiessens were of the "most holy" kind.

Mama Thiessen was all business. She was a no-nonsense mother of ten children, each of whom learned to do the work on the farm and in the house. There wasn't much time for fun or play, and those that engaged themselves in such were idle time-wasters, producing nothing of value and certainly not adding to the bottom line at the Thiessen homestead.

Katarina was born at the farmhouse March 4, 1908, the third of ten children and the second oldest girl. On December 18, 1907, less than three months earlier, the Hieberts down the street had just welcomed their new baby boy, William, to their crowded home. William had come into the world as part of a family of eight boys and eight girls. His eventual attraction to the cute little girl down the street at the Thiessen farm would create the home into which I would be born; but much would take place before that.

Little Katarina grew up and became part of the machinery that ran the family farm. The boys worked in the fields and the girls worked the garden, cleaned the house and prepared the meals for the men. Sometime in between all of those chores, the laundry had to be washed, rinsed and hung to dry—all by hand. The Thiessens managed to get by with everyone contributing, but had little to spare. They were poor enough that only the boys, who worked in the fields, were given shoes. Katarina and her sisters spent the summers barefoot, as did the girls in other Mennonite homes. Men provided for the home, and women sacrificed in order to allow the men to do their jobs.

Katarina was allowed to attend school for a couple of years, until she turned twelve and Mama Thiessen decided she was "of more value around the house." In her mind, boys were the ones that needed to go to school; girls didn't need an education to raise children. Before she left school, however, Katarina could read—only German, but she could read. Mennonite children were educated in German; that was why they had come to Canada in the first place—to forge out new communities where they would be free to be

Mennonite and German. Katarina's ability to read would later prove to be an important tool, helping her to overcome the huge obstacles she would face.

Besides work and home, Katarina's only distraction was church. The entire Thiessen family went to church. Everybody in town went to church. Church became part of the fabric of life; part of who you were and how you defined yourself. At church Katarina got the opportunity to sing—not merely in the congregation, but in a choir. Their little church choir excelled, and singing became Katarina's only relief from the drudgery of housework, cooking, and canning. As demand for the choir grew, she toured other churches in nearby towns. Katarina loved to sing; but more than that, Gerhart was in the choir.

No one in our family even knows Gerhart's last name, but in the last few years of Mom's life she told us his first name. She had carried it in the wound of a broken heart for over seventy years, knowing she would never be in the arms of the young man who was her first—and ultimately, only—love. It may have been a mistake to love Gerhart so deeply, but her second mistake proved even greater.

Soon after the First World War ended in 1919, the Canadian landscape began to change, including the tiny ethnic Mennonite towns in the West. The Canadian Parliament, fresh from their involvement as a country in the Great War, realized the value in being united as a sovereign nation. That ideal of sovereignty and unity would be impossible to maintain in a country where everyone continued to speak only in the languages of their countries of origin. Laws were passed to ensure that anyone going to school in Canada would now be taught in one of the two official languages: French or English.

German Mennonites vehemently resisted these laws. Where before they had been at each other's throats over the subtle differences in their copious governing rules and regulations, now they were united—united against the government of the very nation that gave them their new start. They fought valiantly and long, but eventually lost the language battle in their publicly funded schools. As a result, some in the community decided their freedom to live and educate their children as they pleased, would exist only if they lived somewhere else: Mexico, Central or South America. Families talked about leaving Gruenthal, and Saskatchewan, altogether. One of those families was Gerhart's.

They didn't leave immediately, but Gerhart and his family prepared to move to Mexico. Gerhart and Katarina were eighteen years old—old enough to be together; so Gerhart spent those preparatory months begging Katarina to come with them, to marry him and move with his family to Mexico.

Katarina was torn in two. She loved Gerhart dearly, but she knew innately, without the words needing to be spoken, that Mama did not approve—either of Gerhart or the move. Katarina loved her Mama; she was attached to her. Later in her life, many gossiping townspeople sarcastically referred to Mama and Katarina as the "hen and her chicks," because Katarina was forever going back to Mama Thiessen's house, hanging on her apron strings. She would go home every chance she could, until her own Mama would tire of her and send her off.

Katarina was looking for something in her mother that she never found. Katarina needed hugs and kisses, reassurance and love; but Mama Thiessen was always stern, unaffectionate, and businesslike. Good Mennonites were taught to work hard for God's affections: the better Mennonite you were, the better Christian you were, the more that God approved of you and loved you. Katarina longed to be loved by her mother—tenderly, affectionately—and she worked at it. She spent her entire life trying to please her mother. Mama Thiessen had her favorites, though— and Katarina wasn't one of them.

Because of Mama, Katarina couldn't accept Gerhart's proposal. She could not move to Mexico away from Mama! This was her second mistake and the worst of the two! It was one thing to be desperately in love so young; but then to deny yourself the opportunity for that love to blossom, to live with continuous thoughts of how things could have been with Gerhart, was too much. Katarina rarely spoke of him again.

When Gerhart and his family moved to Mexico, Katarina buried the pain in the deep recesses of her heart, shutting the door on those feelings for years.

A little less than a year later, Katarina married William Hiebert. William—everyone called him Bill—and Katarina had known each other for years. They were neighbors after all. What didn't she know about him? Mama Thiessen had said he would be a good provider, and with the Hiebert family farm just down the road from the Thiessens, she would be close to home. Little did it matter that Bill didn't attend the same Mennonite Church as the Thiessens—he was Mennonite, German, and nearby. Katarina no longer ignored her suitor.

William had been sweet on Katarina for some time, but to her he had always been the familiar neighbor boy. Bill noticed pretty girls, and Katarina was pretty. Modesty dictated that all the girls in their Mennonite town wore their hair braided, rolled, and pulled back into a bun, as the Scriptures say: "Whose adorning let it not be that outward adorning of plaiting the hair..." (1 Pet. 3:3). But not even that could diminish her obvious beauty. She had natural good looks and bright eyes; her neighbor had admired her for years.

Bill was delighted to finally have the girl on whom he had had his eye. Her mother had taught her how to keep house and take care of men, and she knew what it took to be a farmer. The two were married. It was August 1927, and Bill and Katarina were both nineteen years old. Gerhart hadn't been gone a year.

My future parents settled into farm work and moved into humble lodgings in a one-room storage area attached to a store in Gruenthal. They cooked, ate, and slept in that one room—much like a bachelor apartment, except without the modern amenities. For a job, Bill took the vegetables produced by his parent's farm and delivered them to people throughout the countryside. He would hitch horses to a wagon and travel a route where he knew the customers well—some of them too well.

Within ten months the Hieberts had their first child, initiating a pattern of one pregnancy after the other—a pattern which, over the years, Bill would come to resent. In those days you had sex and you either got lucky or you got pregnant...and Bill was never lucky! But he blamed Katarina.

Little Tina was born in June of 1928. She was the first-born and I was the second-to-last, but as I've grown up, Tina has become one of my closest friends. I love her deeply, though I never really knew what it was like to live with her; I turned two years old the year she was married.

Sixteen years and seven brothers separate Tina and me, and I often wonder what it would have been like if we had been born closer together. I wonder if things would have been different for me. I was a teenager before getting to know my sister, and she didn't have a clue about the trouble I was in at that time. If Tina had known, she would have rescued me much earlier. I'm certain of it.

Tina tells of happy times in those first five or six years. They certainly didn't have anything extra, but Dad had his vegetable delivery job and Mom helped out on the farms and raised the little ones. Mom just kept getting pregnant. She had Tina, then Isaac (Ike) and George, who were twins.

Even while pregnant, which was most of the time, women had to work—and not just in the house, but also in the garden and on the farm. (Mom never did develop much sympathy for the woes of expectant mothers—morning sickness and fatigue—because she never received any consideration while she went through it. Life just marched on. Being pregnant was not a terminal illness. The work still had to be done; grin and bear it.)

Mom was big on work. It's really all she knew as a child and it's what she expected from her children. In many ways she saw it as a blessing to have a large family, because all of the children would be farm workers. Boys worked outside, but girls worked inside and outside. Tina was the oldest and, since she was the only girl, much of the responsibility for meal preparation and clean-up, laundry and housework, fell to her, even though she was only seven or eight years old. Life was work and work was life.

Tina remembers those years as relatively happy—not because there was pleasure, but because of the absence of trouble. To Mom fun was a vice—idle time. Sometimes in the evenings Dad would begin to wrestle on the floor with Tina and the toddlers, but Mom would quickly put a stop to it, saying it was wrong and sinful, especially for a girl and a grown man. Almost everything was "sinful" to Mom. If you enjoyed it, it was fleshly and base; and the flesh was supposed to be suppressed and disciplined.

Sex, for example. Mom was no different from many of the women in Gruenthal who bound up their breasts and their bulging tummies when pregnant, so that others would not think about the possibility that they had sexual relations with their own husbands. To Mom, it was wrong to go out and be obviously "with child," or to be seen "in the family way." That was showing off your sexuality, admitting to the world what was actually taking place in bed with your husband. People had sex, but it was ignored, hidden, never spoken about. Mom would do nothing to bring attention to her sexuality and everything to deny it existed. The whole experience was shrouded in mystery and pretense. To her this was honorable decorum.

It's no surprise that this marriage would develop serious trouble before long!

Mom picked up where Mama Thiessen left off—raising her children the same way. Unaware of her aching need for her mother's affection and approval, she withheld the same vital gifts from her children. There were seldom hugs, and Tina and I can never remember, at least while we were growing up, ever hearing the words "I love you" from Mom or Dad. Mom was all business and work and piety; Mama Thiessen must have approved. I'm sure that was what Mom hoped.

In 1930 the first of several tragedies struck the young Hiebert home. Ike's twin brother, George, got pneumonia and couldn't recover. There were doctors in the area, but precious little medicine and science to help people who got seriously ill. Mom did what she could for her ailing son, but at eleven months old, George (the English translation of the German name Gerhart) died. The family of three children shrunk to two.

In those days there was little help to cope with tragedies. People buried their own dead, and little George was buried from the house in which he was born. Work was the only catharsis. The day after George died, there were still chores to do, still a farm to take care of. People simply carried on in a self-induced cocoon of detachment, a hypnosis that allowed them to make it to the next day. No one had grief counseling. Life was about surviving. Its urgency demanded the suppression of feelings. You couldn't just stop to recover emotionally, or the rest of your family would be in peril.

People comforted themselves in the loss of a child by telling each other "the baby is better off"—now he couldn't get sick anymore; he would experience none of the hardship of life, the pain of poverty, the work of survival; God had taken him. There was an assurance that babies were safe in death. Mennonites hoped they would be good enough to go to heaven, but they knew babies who died made it for certain. Babies were innocent. They couldn't intentionally sin or feel sin's guilt the way their parents did. God in His mercy had taken Katarina's baby George. It was Mom's view—and that of every other grieving mother following the death of her baby—that she really couldn't give him a good life anyway, and that it was better for God to take her baby, especially if he was weak.

This kind of thinking must have done incalculable damage to a mother's self-esteem. Losing a baby was accepted as fitting punishment for parents too poor to raise him. It was as if God were saying, "The life you are giving your child lacks opportunity; I'll take him instead; he's much better off with me than you!" The whole idea radiates condemnation and recrimination. People saw God as judge, but without the tenderness of grace and forgiveness. They saw God, but not Jesus. People didn't see the compassion of Christ, the way He was moved by the pain of people, the way He had intervened in Scripture, motivated by His great mercy. They saw pain and they saw the reason for their pain—themselves. They saw a righteous God ably administering the pain they knew they deserved. This was Mom's coping mechanism.

The Hieberts carried on. Soon another boy was born—William, named for his father but always called Willie. Following Willie came another baby who never really developed. He was probably severely retarded, though nobody ever diagnosed him as such; he just didn't grow. Mom and Dad named this baby Abe, hoping that perhaps he would be healthy. It wasn't to be, however; and after about a month Abe died as well.

Three years after Willie, Mom gave birth to another boy. Mom named him George. She must have been thrilled to finally have her little George, her little Gerhart. This child would grow up to be the central figure in the family's discovery of salvation. George would be the first to find Jesus and subsequently introduce our whole family to Christ, bringing the one Person into my life that could heal all the pain I would ever endure. My brother George was born with a God-breathed purpose, though nobody imagined it at the time.

After George, two more boys arrived: Henry (always called Hank) and Peter; so by 1940 there were six children in the Hiebert

8

household. (There had been eight full-term pregnancies in thirteen years of marriage, and two or three miscarriages in between.) The pressure to provide was wearing on Dad, and he was starting to dream of a place where some of his friends had gone—Ontario.

Mom told Tina years later that she and Dad had about six decent years of marriage. Those were the first six years, the only six that she believed Dad was faithful to her. Dad could always spot the pretty lady, and there were several along his vegetable delivery route. He had an outgoing personality and before long was engaged in one affair after another. Mom suspected there were affairs, but didn't know for sure until nine or ten years after they were married. About that time Mom stopped even the pretense that she loved Dad. Tina remembers the constant arguing and fighting beginning around that time, just before the family left Gruenthal.

Dad was tiring of the hardships of the rugged life in the West. Several of his friends and family members had moved to Ontario and had gotten jobs working in the factories there; they wrote back telling of the opportunities he could have as well. No one in the family spoke English. In many ways it would be like immigrating to another country, but the adventure intrigued Dad; he merely had to convince Mom it was a good idea.

It might have been the harshness of life in Saskatchewan, the promise of greater ease and wealth in Ontario or the fact that, in their small town, Dad was sleeping with too many women whom Mom had to face publicly. Maybe it was all of those things together, but Mom gave in and agreed to move to Ontario. She supported the move knowing full well she would be leaving behind Mama Thiessen. Maybe Mom just gave up trying to win Mama Thiessen's approval. Whatever the contributing factors were, the Hieberts decided to sell most everything they had, pack their suitcases and their six children, and board the train for the two-day ride to Ontario. The year was 1941.

Four families from Gruenthal decided to travel together, headed toward what they knew best, farming. The Gruenthal entourage arrived in Niagara-on-the-Lake, a small quaint town on the edge of St. Catharines; a town that had been the capital of Ontario before independence was granted to the Canadas. Niagara-on-the-Lake had held the seats of government for Upper Canada and was full of grand, Victorian style houses with intricately carved trims and lattice, painted white to accentuate their architectural excellence. It gave the small town a real feel of pomp and circumstance—a sarcastic irony to the living quarters Mom and Dad would find.

Outside of the town itself were fields upon fields of crops. The Niagara Peninsula had been blessed by the shelter of an escarpment, providing for a longer growing season than most other parts of Canada. The winters weren't as harsh, and the soil was rich from deposits left when Lake Ontario covered the whole region thousands of years earlier. Grapes and other soft fruits like peaches, plums, cherries, and apricots could be harvested here. The whole family—Mom, Dad, and all of the kids—could go to work picking fruit and tying grapes to the wires holding up the vines. And Dad ensured that they did.

The Gruenthal settlers decided their best chance to make it in this new place, where none of them spoke English or had any money, was to stay together. A storage warehouse at the regional airport on the outskirts of Niagara-on-the-Lake was secured and made into a makeshift apartment. Four small rooms in the building opened up into one large room. The four families settled into the warehouse in August 1941—without indoor plumbing, privacy, or the semblance of a kitchen. Tina was thirteen, Ike eleven, Willie eight, George seven, and Hank and Pete were three and one respectively.

Each family shared one of the small rooms; the large room in the center was for eating. In the "bedroom" was a double bed for Mom and Dad. The six children slept on blankets spread across the plank floor, without mattresses. At the top of each blanket sat towels or clothes for pillows. Dad and Tina worked each day picking fruit and all the money they earned went to support the family. When they got home each night, Dad and the other men and boys ate and relaxed before bed, but Tina's work continued. She washed and cleaned up after dinner. Woman's work involved everything inside the house, despite working outside in the fields too. The injustice ate away at Tina.

One particular day she had had enough.

After a tiring day working in the fields and orchards, the four families sat down to the communal supper, just as they did every day.

This time, however, when Dad told Tina to clean up and wash all the dishes, truth and fairness rose up in her spirit and, without thinking, she protested, "Can't the boys help with the clean-up? They ate too! Why should I have to do all the washing up by myself?"

It was a terrible embarrassment to Dad. Seething, he got up from the table and dragged Tina to the bedroom. He slammed the door and began to beat Tina with his fists. He punched and punched until Tina's face was covered in blood. Finally, Uncle Abe stormed into the bedroom and pulled Dad away, fearing for Tina's life. He held him while Tina slumped to the floor whimpering, her eyes blackened, her nose broken, and her body sore all over. Tina's rescuer turned to William, his brother-in-law, and yelled, "Don't hit her again, Bill, or I'll take her away from you forever!"

The lesson Tina learned that day was that nothing in her life was fair; nor was it ever going to be. But the spirit that she had exhibited at the table while questioning Dad could not simply be beaten out of her. Tina was a survivor—she would survive long enough to get out of Dad's cruel reach.

The fact that Mom didn't try to intervene troubled both Tina and me. She just sat there, listening to Tina's screams in the bedroom, knowing that Dad was beating her to a pulp. I cannot conceive that a mother would let this happen to her thirteen-year-old daughter without stepping in front of those blows. Mom thought differently. Tina had disrespected her father, and it was the husband's place to discipline as he saw fit. Thank God for Uncle Abe!

Those who had written Dad compelling him to come to Ontario implied that housing was supplied to workers and their families. This fallacious report became one of the Hiebert's major disappointments upon arrival. Housing was available only for veterans who had fought in the war. For farm workers, shelter consisted of a selection of shacks, trailers, or rooming houses; housing barely suitable for single transients, not families with six children. All of this only served to frustrate Dad and fuel Mom's complaints.

As their first winter in Ontario approached, a small house became available for rent in Virgil, a smaller hamlet within the borders of Niagara-on-the-Lake. Virgil was little more than a scant collection of houses grouped together on a main street, alone with some stores and businesses catering mainly to farmers. The townsfolk were mostly German Mennonites, so the Hieberts could get along quite easily speaking only German.

The tiny house had no inside plumbing or furnishings, but it was a house instead of a crude apartment, and it did have five small bedrooms. Knowing it would be warmer than their airport warehouse, the four families moved in before winter.

Soon afterward, Dad landed a construction job working on the Queen Elizabeth Way—a paved highway that was to replace a series of smaller, regional dirt roads and would provide a seamless link from Niagara Falls to Toronto. Workers were needed because many of the young and able-bodied men were fighting the Second World War in Europe. (Dad was a child during the First World War and by the time Second World War began he was in his thirties. He was simply too old and had too many dependants to serve his country overseas.)

To recruit men to build the highway, the government came up with incentives. Those building the Q.E.W., as it came to be known, were helping Canada at a time of need and would become eligible, like soldiers returning from the war, to government-sponsored wartime housing. As a result, Dad and Mom were able to get a mortgage at a reduced interest rate and purchased a quaint one-and-a-half story wartime house.

Wartime houses all looked the same. Row upon row of them were built in the Facer St. area of St. Catharines. Some had siding, but most, including the one we moved into, had a slate-like veneer.

The houses were packed close to the street and close to each other. Ours had a small patch of grass for a front yard—no larger than a bedroom in many homes today—and a four-foot-square wooden porch with three stairs that led up to the front door.

Once inside the front door, a small landing demanded that you make an instant decision as to where you were heading. Straight ahead a staircase led up to another tiny landing splitting two small bedrooms whose doors faced each other. A doorway to the left took you to the living room—an oblong room with an old couch at the near end and a huge dining room table in the center. Along the wall on the right was a wooden hutch; beside it stood the wood stove that heated the entire house. (A coal-burning furnace wasn't installed until years later.) On the other side of the room, in front of a small window, sat the ironing board which, for lack of storage, became part of the furniture. At the far end of the living area, a doorway led to a narrow galley-type kitchen where there was not space for a table, but where Mom put one anyway. A back door opened up into a shed attached to the house, and from there you exited into the diminutive back yard—a clothesline, an efficient vegetable garden and a swath of grass that took a mere five minutes to mow.

To the right of the dining room, a doorway led into a small hallway, two more bedrooms and a modest washroom. There was no basement.

The one, tiny washroom was shared by eleven people. Just inside and on the left was a wall-mounted porcelain sink with two individual taps. Next to the sink sat the toilet. The claw-foot tub lay across the back of the washroom, defining the little room's entire width of five feet. I still remember the carved toes and detailed toenails.

This house should have been a place of brilliant memories and nostalgic wonder, but most of those rooms hold visions of violence and pain for me. The house that Dad wanted so badly, the kind of house he and Mom had come to Ontario to live in, became a place he would rarely be—and a house of secrets, terrible secrets, that no one else would know about.

In November 1943 the Hiebert family, with their newest baby, Benjamin, moved into 17 Sherbourne Street, on a dirt road one block down from the Queen Elizabeth Way.

CHAPTER 2

Mom and Dad

Tina was fifteen-and-a-half years old when the family moved into the wartime house on Sherbourne Street. She couldn't speak English and hadn't gone to school since moving to Ontario. This would soon prove to be a contentious issue.

After the QEW highway was completed, Dad got a job at Conroy's, a local factory that manufactured car parts for the General Motors plant in town. This was the kind of job Dad had envisioned when he came to Ontario. No longer relegated to farm labor, he could earn a good salary and enjoy the protection of a union. Unfortunately, trouble was just around the corner.

Drinking alcohol had always been a part of Dad's life, even in Saskatchewan—only it was hidden. Dad's family made their own liquor and beer while on the family farm, and it became part of the fabric of their lives. But Mom hated drinking. Good Mennonites didn't drink; and if some did, they did so discreetly. Years later Mom talked about how she resented Hiebert family get-togethers even back in Gruenthal, because the men would separate themselves from the women and children and go off drinking.

While working on the farms in Niagara-on-the-Lake, money was scarce, language was a barrier, and living in a virtual commune made alcohol consumption impossible. Working at Conroy's changed all that. As part of the brotherhood of workers, Dad would join the boys

15

at the end of the shift for happy hour at the local "watering hole." With his outgoing personality and gregarious attitude, Dad made friends with his coworkers and later with the bar regulars. With a steady paycheck, Dad enjoyed a freedom that he hadn't known before. He got to the place where he spent his entire paycheck on drinking, carousing, and gambling, coming home only when the money ran out. Dad became a cyclical prodigal; but, unlike his biblical predecessor, he never learned his lesson in the pigsty.

He reveled in his newfound freedom while keeping the rest of his family in the chains of authority, intimidation, and dependence. Mom and the children spoke no English, had no money of their own, and were in a new neighborhood without friends or family nearby. Most of the families that came from Gruenthal had now returned to Saskatchewan—the combination of failed dreams and the culture shock of English Ontario were too much to endure. There was no peer pressure to keep Dad accountable; for the first time in his life he answered to no one.

His friends at Conroy's and at the bar knew little about him or his family, and Dad quickly learned an unabated power to manipulate—through secrets and ignorance. If no one *knew* about his domestic life, if he could just be the generous guy at the bar, buying rounds for the house, if he could be the life of the party, then nobody would really know about the abdication of his paternal responsibilities. At home the power of ignorance and secrets worked its magic as well. Dad never told Mom where he was, how long he would be out, or what he was doing—he didn't have to. What was Mom going to do? She had no money. She had no education. She didn't speak English. The children would keep her busy, and he knew she would never abandon them. Dad got so that he just didn't care; or, if he did care, he would drown his conscience in drunkenness. Mom had to placate Dad to get every cent she could from him. She would protest his behavior, but in the end she had to surrender to whatever he wanted so that he would give her at least the pittance dangled in front of her. If she didn't, there would be no food on the table.

Mom did fight for one concession: she permitted no drinking at home. When it came to the booze she hated, there was no compromise. It was the one scrap of power that she clung to, but it further polarized their fragile relationship. Since Dad couldn't drink at the house or bring his drinking buddies home, he just stayed away. Mom stayed at home with the kids and Dad was out after work with his drinking buddies. Dad didn't want to be there anyway—he preferred drinking.

Dad figured his money was his to spend in the bars and on the racetrack, and the children, starting with Tina, could work to provide money for bills and food. Tina got a job at Lightening Fastener, working a machine attaching stoppers to the bottoms of zippers. Tina didn't mind factory work; it got her out of the house during the day and she began to learn English. With English would eventually come independence.

Every Friday, payday would come—but not for Tina. Dad would go to Lightning Fastener and collect her paycheck for her. Tina did the work; Dad took the money. It could only get better once all the children went to work.

The plan nearly fell apart, however, when the local board of education got involved. With their own house and a permanent address, the school board soon learned of the house full of truant children. Dad and Mom were told that Tina would be tested and placed in school. She had been in Ontario nearly three years (since she was twelve), and prior to that had gone only to a rural German Mennonite school in Saskatchewan. Her developmental I.Q. test placed her at a fifth-grade level in most subjects, but lower in English—and she was unable to write and spell as well as she could read. Dad convinced the board of education that, at fifteen-and-a-half, six months before she could legally quit school, placing Tina in a class of eleven-year-olds would not be in her best interest. She had a job, she was contributing to the family's financial survival, and he needed her to keep working at Lightening Fastener. The board relented where Tina was concerned; but the boys—Ike, Willie, George, Hank, Pete, and Benjamin—would have to go to school. This was Dad's first introduction to governmental authority, and he consented. Unfortunately, it came too late for Tina.

As unhappy as she was, Mom could never divorce Dad. Divorce was a public disgrace in the 1940s. Only those in Hollywood divorced, and Mom wouldn't even have known about them, because going to the theater was a sin. She knew the Bible said God

17

hated divorce. If He hated divorce, it followed that those who got divorced were contemptible to Him.

Mom felt obligated to stay married in the legal sense—but she felt no compunction to stay married emotionally. The truth is she left Dad in her heart during his Gruenthal escapades, and maybe even before that. Perhaps she never loved him. Romantically there was nothing there; there never was. Mom always said, "Seck. All dat man ever, ever vanted was dat seck." Seck of course was sex. Her heavy German accent made it humorous, but her statement reveals how she viewed Dad and her duty to him. In her elderly years, when asked if she loved Dad, she would say, "Ya, like a brodder." Dad had sisters; what he needed was a wife—a woman who made him feel like a man. Mom eroded his *manness*—she pecked away at him, at every vestige of his being. Because of her attitude, Dad justified his sexual dalliances. Mom never saw her role in driving him away. To her it was that cursed *booze*. She was a good Mennonite woman and Dad was a drinker. God was testing her and she would just have to endure it.

Mom once told me that when she got married she still didn't know "how babies come." She understood how they were born—being the oldest she helped with some of the births of her siblings; but she didn't know what caused a woman to become pregnant. She didn't know what sex was, even on her wedding night. No one had explained or prepared her for what would take place the evening of her vows. Her ignorance ensured that her first experience with a man would be traumatic. In her time, sexuality was so hidden, that she was doomed to unpleasant, if not horrific, experiences in the bedroom. After she was married, Mama Thiessen merely told her, "Sleeping with a man is your marital duty. Men want it; you have to go along." Mom viewed sex as a conjugal debt. Men were owed it and women paid it—whether willingly or grudgingly, it didn't matter; payment simply was required.

It's entirely possible that Mom tolerated Dad's affairs, in some unknowing way, because it relieved the sexual tension between her and Dad. If Dad were sleeping with other women, at least he wouldn't be pressuring her. She would never have admitted that, but that's how she acted.

I don't ever remember seeing my Mom show any affection toward Dad. No playfulness. No hugs. No touching. She didn't learn these actions from Mama Thiessen; I don't think she thought demonstrations of affection proper. Regardless of the reasons for their absence, the fact is, they were missing. They were missing in her relationships with her children too. We never hugged in our family. Even babies were cuddled only while being nursed; other than that, Mom showed no tenderness, gave no loving caresses. It's possible she didn't know that she was supposed to.

I never once heard the words "I love you" from either parent. It's almost impossible for me to believe—having had children myself and having said that wonderful phrase to them every day of their lives—that it never occurred to either one of them to say it. And I never heard those precious words said between them, so I didn't know how a man and a woman were supposed to respond to each other in marriage. All I ever saw were battles. God had to bring other people into my life, years later, to teach me about love and tenderness.

Around the time Tina began work at Lightning Fastener, Mom was having difficulties with her health. The truth is Mom was always sick. She couldn't always convince a doctor, but whether they concurred or not, she was sick. She was especially sick on washday and cleaning day. It wasn't that she was lazy, just that she had Tina to do it—and, years later, me. Girls did the work in the house. On the farm, boys worked; in the city, they were merely expected to stay out of trouble. When they did get jobs, Dad picked up their paychecks.

As time passed, Mom missed her mother. When Mama Thiessen became ill, Dad got Mom a train ticket so she could visit. She left the children in Dad's care—which really meant Tina had to hold the house together.

One of the German women Dad had known back in Saskatchewan, who had been on his delivery route, had moved to Ontario with her husband and children. Tina knew her casually, having been asked to babysit her kids from time to time. The moment Mom got on the train, this lady moved in with Dad. With Mom gone, Dad was allowed to drink in the house; and drink he did, constantly. His lady-friend partied with him, picking up where they had left off when Dad had delivered her vegetables several years before. For three weeks while Mom was visiting her Mama out West, Dad and his lady drank, partied, and slept together under everyone's noses.

One day Dad came home with this woman while Tina was doing the wash by hand. She and Dad were exchanging affections on the front lawn—hugs, kisses, and flirtations that Tina had never seen displayed between her Dad and Mom. They were obviously drunk, but they didn't have the slightest concern about how they were behaving in public. They were two married people shamelessly flaunting their sexual tryst, worried not a whit that they would be caught.

The girlfriend came inside and addressed Tina with a laugh, "Are you washing the kids' clothes again? Don't they have another set of clothes—or do you have to wash the same clothes every night so they have something to wear the next day?"

She was mocking Tina, supposing that the teenager hadn't thought about the other clothes in their closets. The truth was, those clothes were the only set that the children had. If Tina didn't wash them, they wouldn't have anything clean to wear.

The woman's comment burned in Tina's spirit. How dare that woman come here when Mom isn't home and humiliate us! How dare she!

When Tina did answer her, the woman just stood there in drunken disbelief, saying nothing. What could she say? She was there partying with Dad, drinking and eating all the money that could have clothed the backs of his children. She just walked into the other room.

For at least a week, Tina worked at Lightening Fastener, came home and made dinner (first for Dad and the girlfriend, then for the children), washed the children's clothes, kept the house the best she could, then dropped into a heap on the bed to sleep. The whole time, Dad and the woman drank and ate, laughed and partied until they collapsed, finally blacking out late at night. Tina had had enough.

The next morning Tina told Dad, "That woman goes, or I'm taking the three youngest children with me and we're leaving."

Tina didn't even know where she would go. Possibly Dad thought she would go to the police or to children's services; either way, he didn't want the hassle and he relented. The woman left the house. With Mom two thousand miles away, Dad needed Tina around the house; he needed her paycheck too.

Despite the beatings she continued to receive, Tina was full of courage. That spirit would both help her and bring her greater grief.

At the factory, Tina's foreman recognized her dedication and hard work. He noticed that her pay envelope was picked up every week by her father and accurately sized up the situation. One day he took Tina aside and offered, "From now on, let me hold back a portion of your pay, not a lot, just a couple of dollars in cash. I'll save it up for you in little amounts, and when there is a significant balance, I'll give it to you."

Tina doesn't remember the man's name, only his generosity and kindness. Many people through the years became agents of help to members of our family. They left an indelible impact upon our lives and are likely unaware of the magnitude of that impact. One of the joys of heaven for me will be to personally express my gratitude to all of those who cared enough to intervene, at times rescuing us from our pain.

Before long, the few dollars deducted by her employer each week, grew. The foreman and his wife took Tina to a ladies shop and, for the first time in her life, she bought something new off the rack—a green suit! She purchased a blouse to go with it and felt wealthy and proud. The next day she was walking on St. Paul Street in downtown St. Catharines in her new green suit, feeling on top of the world. Dad hadn't even noticed the money missing from her pay envelope, and it felt rewarding to have something of such great value that she had earned.

In an instant though, her euphoria dissipated. Fifty feet ahead and walking toward her was Dad and a woman she had never met before, with three little children in tow.

Dad and the woman were walking arm in arm—lovers, a happy-looking family. Dad hadn't yet spotted Tina and just kept walking. As she moved toward him, all she could think to do was to embarrass him. She felt jaded and poor, neglected by Dad. There he was with this woman and these children—and they were all so well dressed. As she approached them, she noticed how much the children looked like her own brothers, how they resembled Dad.

"Hi Dad!" Tina fixed her eyes on Dad as he tried to look away. "How are you?" By now Tina's English had improved considerably from working at the factory.

Dad's face flushed. Not responding, he grabbed the woman's arm and hurried off. Tina says she still remembers the look of shock on the pretty woman's face. Tina thought, *She doesn't even know Dad has another family!*

It's strange, but in that moment Tina felt pity for the young woman. She's involved with a man she doesn't even know. He's duped her. He's lied about everything he is, everything he's done. It's obvious they've had children together, he's supported her to some extent, he's played the role of father and husband, and the whole time he's lived a double life! She fumed.

Then she remembered how well they all were dressed. She thought about the good things to eat that must be on their table, and her pity for the young woman quickly gave way to disdain for Dad. She hated him.

Dad's secrets—at least some of them—had been discovered, and Tina knew him for what he was. His other life with the pretty young woman and family in Port Weller (Tina found out where they lived) was over. When the woman found out her relationship with Dad was a mirage, she ended it. Afterward Dad was at home a little more often, though he was harder on Tina. He didn't like her strong will, the way she challenged him and spoke her mind. When he was drunk, his contempt for his oldest daughter was unrestrained.

Mom's health deteriorated for real during this period, and she had several surgeries. Each time she went into the hospital, Dad's brazen behavior intensified.

One incident stands out. No one can remember whether it was her gall bladder, spleen, appendix, a hernia, or some other ailment, but Mom was admitted to hospital again. (Mom had thirteen operations in all and a heart attack in her early forties.) At sixteen years old, Tina once again took on the mantle of household responsibility. She was washing the floor one night after supper on her hands and knees. (The floors were always washed by hand with a bucket and a rag. There were no carpets at 17 Sherbourne Street, only painted plank floors and linoleum in the kitchen, and they all needed to be washed every week. It's what Mom required.) Dad came in with his buddies from Conroy's. They had been drinking. Tina was at the front door, blocking the way in as she washed the landing.

"I'm washing the floors, Dad, and they're all wet," Tina told the drunken men. "Could you go around the back and come into the house through the kitchen?"

Dad flew into a rage and bowled past her, returning with a wooden chair from the dining room. He smashed it across Tina's hunched-over back while she knelt on the floor beside the bucket. The chair broke into tiny pieces. Dad moved her out of his way and walked into the house with his buddies.

Tina said nothing. Her greatest fear at that point was making him angrier. She grimaced in pain and waited for breath to return to her lungs, her ribs aching. She stayed there—a helpless heap on the floor.

As soon as she could, Tina went to bed. She shared a bedroom with her brothers. A sheet hung from the ceiling, separating her side from theirs; this was the extent of her privacy. But it was her sanctuary, her place of refuge. She prayed that night, as she did most nights, "God, please let me be dead. I want to be dead." There were never any prayers of thanksgiving or praise from Tina's lips, only desperate prayers to escape; and God never seemed to answer them.

Dad's fury did not only occur during Mom's absence. Often she was just standing there—silent. And though he did not explode in anger every day, it was unpredictable—that is what made it impossible to bear. The household lived in a state of suspended panic, wondering whether Dad was going to explode or not. His rages were infrequent enough that they shocked us when they occurred, and frequent enough that we could remember the previous incident vividly. We were apprehensive in his presence. Most times his anger came out of nowhere—as was the case at the dinner table one evening.

The whole family was sitting down together to eat—which wasn't often the case—when one of my brothers asked Dad for permission to finish the potatoes in the bowl. Tina objected, feeling entitled to at least half of what was left. Before she knew it, Dad's fist hit the plaster wall beside her head, leaving a gaping hole and a symbolic reminder that the desires and opinions of girls were not to be expressed. Tina had dared to question how Dad had ruled on the issue of the second helping of potatoes. Anything could set him off.

The walls of 17 Sherbourne Street bore the marks of Dad's fury in more places than strategically hung pictures could cover. I wonder what the neighbors thought when they visited.

Dad never hit Mom—at least that I ever saw—although he did shout at her, scaring her terribly. His favorite whipping posts were the children, and especially those who had spirit—who stood up to him and weren't intimidated. Dad didn't like to be challenged. Tina and Pete were the most vocal, and paid for it. Ike was a pacifier, a peacemaker who never spoke out of turn. It's as though he had wisdom beyond his years. He knew when to say something and when to stifle his words. Willie, Hank, and George were quieter—or more adept at getting out of Dad's way—incurring less wrath. Tina and Pete got most of the beatings. Tina was filled to the brim with justice and fairness. She was determined and refused to knuckle under, surviving by fantasizing about how and when she would get out from under his control.

Not all families were like hers, and Tina knew it. She remembered several large families in Gruenthal that were full of love and tenderness. They were poor. They had hard times. But there was laughter and freedom to be yourself, freedom to speak. Tina resolved to have a different family for herself. When she got married and had children, she would break the Hiebert mold and be like the parents she envied, the parents she saw as close as next door.

What's always puzzled Tina and me is that Mom and Dad had the same opportunities we had to change their family. If their parents neglected them, treated them with indifference, flew into rages and beat them, they could have determined to do things differently with their children—but they didn't. Possibly, they didn't realize the damage they were doing. All Mom ever said was, "Vee dit da best vee coult! Vee vere teached dat vay."

Breaking of the cycle of abuse in Tina's family, in most of our brothers' families and in my family years later, can only be the work of grace. God intervened in our lives. He changed us and rescued our children from the life their parents lived. For this, I am eternally grateful to God.

Within months of the time my family moved into the wartime house on Sherbourne Street, new neighbors arrived. Ed and Beatrice Oliver, parents of four children, were about the same age as Mom and Dad—but that's where the similarities end.

If you lived beside Beatrice Oliver, she was going to be your friend. The fact that Mom spoke no English and Beatrice spoke no German didn't phase her one bit. The concept that neighbors could be friends was truly foreign to Mom, but Beatrice's personality was infectious and impossible to ignore for any length of time—even for Mom.

Mom was intensely private. She was embarrassed by Beatrice's outgoing personality and rejected Beatrice at first. Beatrice, however, persisted. Every time Mom was in the backyard, Beatrice Oliver went outside too and insisted on speaking to her. Mom nodded politely, said hello, and then rushed back into the house as quickly as she could. This was the pattern for some time, until one day Beatrice refused to let Mom escape to the safety of her own house. When Mom retreated, Beatrice followed her inside, gabbing all the way and telling her that she would help her to speak English.

From that point on, they became fast friends. Mom relaxed and spoke over the back fence to Beatrice—German interrupted by broken English—while she conversed back in English and sign language until it was clear each of them understood the other. By 1946, they had spent enough time together that Mom was no longer a prisoner behind the locked doors of a foreign language and culture. This friendship would prove to be a great source of support, both to my mother and to the rest of my family in the years to come.

Tina quickly made a friend in Doris Oliver, Ed and Beatrice's daughter. Doris and Tina's bedroom windows faced each other across the driveway, so they tied strings between tin cans linking themselves together by their crude, but functional phone line. Doris would rattle the can in her bedroom with a nail and send vibrations along the twine to Tina's can twenty feet away every morning to wake her up. It was Tina's insurance against sleeping in and being late to work. Tina could not afford to get fired.

This was the first female friendship Tina had experienced since moving to Ontario. Teenaged girls talk a lot, and Doris soon had Tina speaking fluent English, with hardly a trace of German accent. Tina's confidence began to grow.

With all that she had been through, positive self-esteem was not one of Tina's strengths, though she was pretty. Curly brown hair hung long past her shoulders and her natural beauty went unnoticed by no one, except perhaps herself. She never received compliments at home, only insults and guilt trips. Having been trapped at home or on an assembly line for almost three years without the interaction of people her own age, she had no idea just how beautiful she was. That was about to change however, because Doris Oliver had an older brother.

Murray quickly noticed his little sister's new friend. Before long, Tina became aware of Murray's feelings for her and they began to date. *Dating* is the word others might have used, but Murray and Tina weren't dating, officially. They just spent time together, using clandestine maneuvers. Dad and Mom couldn't know about their relationship. Dad would forbid it, concerned he would be losing his control over Tina (and her paycheck), and Mom would just cry and make life miserable for both of them. Because Doris and Tina were such good friends, seeing Murray became easier. Tina spent as much time at the Oliver's house as possible.

Beatrice Oliver had a way of making everyone around her feel good and Tina loved the atmosphere at the house next door. To Mrs. Oliver, Tina seemed like one of her own children and she treated her that way. When Tina would come over, Beatrice would do what came most naturally to her—hug Tina. Mrs. Oliver was always hugging her children. It may have been natural for Beatrice Oliver, but it was anything but natural to Tina. She didn't know how to respond. There were no hugs from Mom and Dad at home. No kisses. No affection. When Mrs. Oliver threw her arms around her, Tina just stood there, stiff as a statue, not knowing she was supposed to return the gesture. But Tina liked the hugs and would linger there, taking in all of Beatrice's love. She felt valuable, and integral—something she didn't feel at the house across the driveway.

It seemed to us that Mom had little use for daughters. This may not have been the way she truly felt, but she did little to avoid sending that message. Sons were less trouble and easier for Mom to get along with. In Tina and myself, Mom saw clearly all of her own shortcomings. On June 16, 1944, when Tina was sixteen years old, I was born. Mom's eighth child would be followed three years later by her ninth—another boy she named David. Ben, David, and I were born into a very troubled house. We were the last children born to parents in a doomed marriage. Soon Dad would be almost completely missing from our lives.

At age seventeen, Tina was working at Hair Cloth Mill downtown and was growing tired of working for nothing. Murray held down a steady job and had proposed to Tina just before Christmas 1945. Mom and Dad were incensed and tried to force Tina to give back the ring and call off wedding. Dad made it clear that he would never give her permission to marry underage and would do everything within his power to prevent it. (Murray wasn't German and he wasn't Mennonite. Besides, Dad couldn't lose Tina's contribution to the survival of the family, or at least to his ability to buy rounds for the house at happy hour.)

Dad had continued to collect Tina's paychecks at her new job, just as he had done for two-and-a-half years from Lightening Fastener. Because she was under eighteen and living at home, her employer was obliged to give the paychecks to her father upon his request. Trapped inside 17 Sherbourne Street, working a full-time job and doing nightly the chores for a mother who claimed to be sick, Tina decided her only escape was to run away. The very next payday, she packed up her things, let Murray know where she would be and, with help from co-workers at the Hair Cloth Company, she moved out.

Dad arrived home furious that he could no longer lay claim to Tina's paycheck. (Tina had instructed her employer to deny Dad her check. She had an address of her own and would be collecting her own paycheck from now on.) Dad and Mom drove all over town looking for Tina. He was enraged; how dare Tina move out! How dare she tell her employer not to turn over her paycheck! Despite an exhaustive search, they never found her.

With the help of children's services, Tina was staying with the relative of a co-worker. For the first time in her life, she was free. She was out of her father's reach.

The stress of living at home and being engaged against her parent's will became so intense that Tina began suffering from terrible headaches. To cope with the pain, she literally ate Aspirin. She didn't eat properly and was anorexic in appearance. Her stomach, damaged by all the medication she took for the headaches, made eating painful. There hadn't been much food at 17 Sherbourne Street anyway, so it became easier to eat nothing. The woman with whom she lived noticed her emaciated appearance and began preparing huge lunches for Tina to take to work. At home she supervised breakfast and supper to ensure that Tina was eating. Tina slowly began to recover and put on weight. Color returned to her face and, for the first time in a long time, Tina looked healthy.

Dad had lost his second paycheck, Mom lost her eldest daughter and maid—and they were angry. It would be months before Mom, Dad, and Tina would speak.

Tina left home in the winter of 1946, several months before she would turn eighteen. She only needed to wait until then and she and Murray could marry, no longer in need of Dad's permission.

The wedding took place at St. Paul Street United Church in June of 1946. Both Mom and Dad were invited to the wedding, but said they wouldn't come. Dad showed up the morning of the wedding to give Tina away, but Mom stayed home—refusing to acknowledge her eldest child's marriage. She told everyone outside the family that she couldn't go because of the drinking and dancing; it was against her religion. Most things were.

On the day Tina got married, I was a two-year-old.

The Olivers had paid for the entire wedding—consequently, Mom wouldn't speak to her neighbor anymore. After the wedding, whenever Beatrice approached her in the backyard, Mom just gave her the silent treatment and walked back into the house. She turned her back on the only friend she had in the world, the one who taught her to speak English. Mom had spent countless hours talking to Beatrice, but now she couldn't even be civil.

Though Beatrice continued to reach out to Mom, Ed mostly ignored Dad. Ed was a family man. He took care of his responsibilities at home and had little respect for Dad.

Our house became the main subject of gossip on Sherbourne Street. My siblings and I grew up bearing the spectacle of shame, knowing that others were aware of Dad's drinking and philandering. Everyone on the street held an opinion. Some felt sorry for William, the victim of an overbearing and religious wife; she went to church and he went to bars. Others pitied Katarina, who was forced to care for nine children while her husband was off drinking and sleeping with everyone but her.

Despite all Mom's faults, I respect the fact that she never abandoned us—Dad did. She tried to provide the necessities of life for her children, she just didn't know how. Mom kept the family together the best she could. Dad could have made different choices. He could have provided for his family had he wanted to—he just preferred drinking.

Beatrice didn't give up on Mom, though she knew Mom was hurt and angry at Tina's leaving. Every day she continued to press for friendship. Several months went by. Tina and Murray began to visit as a married couple. Life didn't come to an end with Tina's marriage, and Mom relaxed her campaign of silence, slowly being restored to the relationship she had had with Beatrice. If there were any apologies from Mom to Beatrice Oliver for the way she had treated her, I never heard them. Mom just went on, letting things in the past remain as though they never occurred. Beatrice was as willing as Mom to bury the hatchet, and they became even closer friends.

By the time I was born, Dad didn't even try to hide his affairs. He came home when he wanted to and left for days and weeks at a time. At home he showed only contempt for Mom, deriding her for his own virility. "I just touch your skirt and you get pregnant," he would chide. Yet in the bars he would speak of her in glowing terms. Though he would never compliment Mom directly, he told others of her character and inner strength and that she was a good person. Dad never expressed a desire to divorce Mom; instead, he did what he wanted and rationalized his behavior with the belief that Mom didn't love him as a husband anyway. It just didn't matter.

My father had the potential to be a decent dad early on. He showed signs of that promise throughout my life, but unfortunately, the momentary glimpses of what he could have been were buried beneath the rubble of booze and self-centeredness. Drinking, carousing, and gambling blinded him to his responsibilities. His bar buddies were his family. His girlfriends took the place of his wife. He had left his paternal duty back in Saskatchewan, preferring the life of a carefree bachelor, despite the fact that he had nine kids.

By the time I was ten years old, Dad would rarely be at home. Only when he ran out of money would he come home for a couple of days. Mom got by on the part-time wages of her children and the pittance she could squeeze out of Dad. During canning season she tried to get ahead by working in the packing factories.

Dad and Mom began separating for significant intervals. At times months of separation stretched into years. A judge ordered

Dad to pay Mom support of twenty-five dollars per month, but he never paid. At one point Dad owed Mom two thousand dollars in back support. (He was in arrears an amount equal to more than six years of payments.) The oldest children—Tina, Ike, and Willie—were paraded before the magistrate and questioned about the conduct of their father. Tina remembers how devastated she felt being forced to publicly document Dad's negligence and irresponsibility, having to tell authorities how rotten he was, and wondering the whole time if there would be consequences to pay when he returned home.

Dad was not without cunning, however. A female judge he met at a bar told him to move back home temporarily, sleep with his wife, and the back support he owed could be legally cancelled. Dad schemed his way back into the house and into Mom's bed, and had his familial debt annulled. When they separated again, the record of his support delinquency started over, and Mom and the rest of us struggled on. Mom would not be duped a second time.

Shortly after Tina's wedding, George, who was ten years older than I, got an invitation that would change the course of my family's life. Leroy Baltus lived one block over from us on Cosby Avenue, and he knew George from school and playing in the neighborhood. Leroy's church, Elim Tabernacle on Queenston Street, was having a kid's hour on Friday nights, and Leroy invited George. George went to the kid's hour service and, from there, began going to Elim on Sunday mornings.

Elim Tabernacle was a little Pentecostal church that had started as a prayer meeting twenty-five years earlier. There were about a hundred people attending regularly. The church was born out of a wave of evangelism that started near the turn of the century in the Asusa Street revivals in Los Angeles and swept north to Canada, where newly planted churches from the movement formed the Pentecostal Assemblies of Canada. Forty years later, this church's passion to spread the gospel was evident. Leroy's invitation to George was the instrument God would use to reach me, and most of the members of my troubled home.

Every Sunday night, Elim Tabernacle held an evangelistic service. Members were encouraged to bring the unsaved—those they were trying to win to Christ. One Sunday evening, thirteen-year-old

George walked up the aisle and committed his life to Jesus. He was ecstatic as he returned home from the service, telling Mom that he was now a Christian; he had given his heart to Jesus. Although Mom was extremely religious, she had never heard that a personal relationship with Jesus was possible.

Before George began to attend Elim, the family had sporadically attended Scott Street Mennonite Brethren Church. The people there had been extremely gracious and helpful, many times bringing us grocery hampers and clothing. Mom hadn't connected with people or made any friends at the Scott Street Mennonite Church, however, and, wanting to keep all of her family together, decided that everyone would now go with George to Elim. Pastor Day welcomed our family with love and treated us with respect, uncommon to our experience. At Elim we felt better about the world; Jesus' love was evident there. The warmth of Christian people engaged the visitor, and powerful and anointed preaching compelled searching hearts to commit to Christ.

Mom was born again, though she remained shackled to many of the legalistic trappings of her Mennonite background. Still there was *something* different inside of her. She realized, because Jesus had died for her sins, that she didn't have to earn God's favor as she had tried and failed to do so many times before. The terrible emptiness of not measuring up to Mama Thiessen's ideal, and to God's standard, was gone. In its place was the knowledge of being forgiven—made clean by God's judicial declaration, "Righteous! Justified! Clean! Worthy! Saved!"

It was 1948. George had brought Mom, Ike, Ben, and the two youngest kids, David and me, into contact with the God of the whole universe. I didn't know it then, but I would need all of His strength and power to survive and overcome what was about to take place in my life.

I thank God for George. I thank God for Leroy Baltus.

CHAPTER 3

Willie

The following chapter reveals details of sexual abuse in my life. The descriptions of these events are quite graphic and could be disturbing to any who are too young or who have themselves suffered abuse. It is possible that reading about my pain could act as a trigger for those who have been abused and, if their healing is not complete, may cause a recurrence of their own trauma.

If you are a victim of abuse, read this chapter cautiously. My intention in writing the story of my life's experience, and in showing the degree to which I was damaged, is not to glorify the works of evil, but to let the reader see the magnitude of my deliverance and emancipation.

It wasn't long after the family began attending Elim Tabernacle that Ike, my oldest brother, married. Jackie, a wonderful French-Canadian girl, swept Ike off his feet and out of our house, leaving Willie as the oldest child at home.

I was four years old and Willie was sixteen.

Willie's personality and childhood is a mystery to both Tina and me. Tina was out of the house by the time Willie was thirteen, and I was too young to have known him as a child. He didn't stand out in a crowd or get noticed when the whole family was together. He interacted with his siblings as anyone normally would, so no one knew anything was wrong. But something *was* wrong—terribly wrong.

Perhaps because he was quiet and somewhat aloof, no one suspected anything was awry. I alone saw Willie's evil bent—his dark, cruel nature. For the next ten years, Willie became my tormentor.

Willie raped me—not once, not twice, but hundreds of times. I cannot remember a time as a child when I was not being sexually abused. Willie repeatedly, systematically violated me.

One of my earliest recollections is of Mom giving me a bath. (Because of our poverty, bath water became a precious commodity. Hot running water was unavailable, so we heated it in a large pot on the wood stove and then carried it to the claw-foot tub in the bathroom. To ease the workload on Saturday nights, at least two people bathed in each tub full of hot water. Usually I would have my bath first and then Mom would use my bath water for herself. Little girls didn't get as dirty as the boys, so it was the best option for Mom to bathe after me.) I started bleeding into the bath water from my vagina and the bath water turned red. Mom saw the blood gushing into the water and became upset.

"Vhat is dat?" she questioned, her harsh tone and German accent making it seem even more callous. "You're bleedink into da tub! Now I can't use your battwater for my batt! Vhy are you bleedink?" Those were the only words she said to me. I was bleeding into the tub from my bruised and swollen labia, and she was angry because she had to heat another pot of water on the wood stove.

"I was trying to ride one of the boy's bikes and I fell off the seat onto the cross-bar and hurt myself," I answered.

The answer satisfied Mom's curiosity. All she said was, "Girls veren't mate to ride bikes! Girls vere mate to learn how to vork. I have to teach you how to vork, not ride bikes." The matter was closed. This was Mom's tender response on an afternoon after I had been torn apart by Willie raping me. Mom believed my story and I remember being relieved that she did.

It seems incredible to me now, being a mother myself, that my Mom could have let the matter rest at that; that she could have believed the bike story. At the time I was only five or six years old and tiny for my age. Ben and Pete were two and four years older, respectively. Climbing up onto one of their bikes was an impossible scenario. I didn't have a bicycle of my own and didn't even know how to ride one. Whether Mom didn't reason her way through the story, or whether she was preoccupied with heating the water for her own bath, I don't know. She just accepted the explanation I gave.

The way in which I was able to lie so readily surprises me when I think back. It is entirely possible that Willie had given me the words to say should anyone question me about my injuries. He often instructed me very specifically on how to keep the whole thing a secret.

"Now, you don't tell anybody this!" he would say after he was finished with me. He didn't yell, but he spoke with the authority of an older brother, one who had been placed in an adult position over me. When I was six, he was eighteen. He had always been an adult in *my* eyes. I was just a little girl. I had to listen to him. He was in charge.

Being raped by Willie was a part of who I was. Since the time I could walk and talk, from four years old and up, every time Mom and Dad were gone, every time Willie was babysitting, every chance he could, Willie came for me. I didn't even know things were supposed to be different until I was older. To me, being hurt by Willie was an expected occurrence, a way of life. It was all I knew.

Every Saturday, Dad drove Mom to the meat market to buy some groceries. (Even after Dad wasn't living with us on a regular basis, he would come and take Mom to get groceries. If he didn't have money, Mom always did. After Dad left home, we took in boarders to make ends meet. In addition, Mom collected up to half of the wages the older children made in their part-time jobs, for room and board. Dad ensured that he could always come home when he needed to when his money was gone, and that there would always be a meal for him—by taking Mom for groceries. Everybody sacrificed because Dad drank and gambled away all his money.) Mom took David along in the beginning because he was a toddler and was too much trouble to leave at home with Willie.

Somehow Willie always found a way to rid the house of the other siblings. He would give them money for store candy, permission to go play in the neighborhood, or errands to run…something. I would be the lone child left in the house. I dreaded it!

35

Most of the times I was abused, events unfolded in the same way. Willie would force me into the bathroom and lock the door. He would strip off my clothes and stand me on the toilet, naked. He told me that if I stood on the toilet he could reach me better. He said he liked to view me, to see me naked, to see me at eye level, the same size as him. Then he would go to his knees with me still standing on the toilet, and he would fondle me and carry out cunnilingus on me. This would arouse him. His clothes would come off, and then he would sit on the toilet seat, making me kneel down facing him, and say, "Now, do to me what I did to you."

This meant he wanted me to put his penis in my mouth. I hated it! I would yell out, "I don't want to!"

He would growl back, "I said...you're *going* to! Now—do it to me!" His voice was mean and threatening. Then Willie would take my head in his hands and force my face down between his legs. I couldn't breath. I couldn't move. I squirmed and squirmed, but he held me there; he was so strong and I was just a little girl.

It couldn't end soon enough for me. The bathroom incidents made me feel worthless and humiliated—worse, if possible, than the inevitable penetration that followed. Even at that young age, I remember feeling stripped of worth, out of control, dominated, and powerless. He had been doing this to me forever. I couldn't remember a time, a Saturday ever, that Willie didn't take me in there! I felt trapped, as if I had no choice. Willie was babysitting me. Mom and Dad had left him in charge. I had to do what he said.

Aroused nearly to the point of ejaculating, Willie would carry me under one arm and my clothes under the other into the bedroom beside Mom's. Once inside, he would put me on the bed and close the door. Our bedroom doors had no locks, so he would always drag over the chest of drawers and place it in front of the door. If someone were to interrupt us unexpectedly, with the dresser blocking the door, he would have time to dress us both and make up some excuse as to why we were in the bedroom. But—in all the years Willie took me into the bedroom—no one ever came home; no one ever caught him in the act.

Willie had ropes from the shed by the back door, and used them to tie me to the four posts of the bed, my arms stretched out straight and my legs fixed, spread-eagle. The polypropylene cords dug into the flesh around my ankles and wrists, their coarse fibers irritating me, itching and hurting. Almost always he would gag me, tying a tea towel over my mouth and around my head. I couldn't scream, I couldn't bite—all I could do was cry. Before he could get me all the way tied, I would be fighting and wriggling all over, knowing what was coming. He would say, "If you fight me it will hurt more. Don't fight me. This is what little sisters are for. This is what you're supposed to do for your big brother!"

Next I would feel the pain of his penis penetrating my tiny vagina, ripping the tissue in a place not large enough to withstand that kind of assault. The pain was excruciating! Many times I bled. The whole time he laid on top of me, I would choke from the gag, feeling claustrophobic and panicking, thinking I couldn't survive another minute. It was suffocating.

Without fail, Willie would ejaculate inside of me. The mess of his semen mixed with my blood, and I would be so sore that, following his assault, walking was difficult. After what seemed like hours, it would end for *that* day. The ropes would be untied. I would get cleaned up and dressed, and Willie would threaten me, "If you tell anyone about this, I'll kill you! This is our secret Margaret," he said, passing on to me equal responsibility for his vile attack. "If you tell, I'll kill you!" Willie was violent enough, cruel enough, and angry enough—that I believed him. If I told a soul, I knew for certain, he would do what he promised.

Some days, if Willie thought he had the time, he would leave me tied up, go into the bathroom and clean himself up. Twenty minutes would go by and he would be able to get aroused a second time. Upon his return to the bedroom, I would be lying there captive for him to rape again. Once was horrible enough, but on those days when he would come back for more, I thought I was going to die! Willie only cared about his own gratification. Whatever it took to satisfy himself sexually, he did. He didn't care about my pain or the bleeding. He would just tell me, "Soon it will get better. It won't hurt as much. You'll get used to it the more that you do it! Just relax and don't fight so much and you might even enjoy it!" But in the ten to eleven years that Willie systematically raped me, it never stopped hurting. It never stopped hurting!

It was part of Willie's strategy to tie me up so that I would be as uncomfortable as possible. That way I would relax and stop fighting long enough for him to penetrate me sooner. "Lie there and let me get inside you and it will be over," he would say. I learned in time, after he had finally tied me up and was on top of me, to stop moving. The less I moved, as he thrust himself into me, the less pain I had to endure. I would lay there motionless, gagged and tied, crying and feeling like I was going to choke, waiting until it was over…waiting.

When he finally removed my gag, I would snarl, "I hate you! I hate you! I hate you!"

Willie would kind of smile and say, "You hate me? You can't hate me, Margaret, I'm your brother. You *can't* hate me."

I don't know why he did it—maybe to pacify his own conscience—but after he was through with me, Willie would throw a quarter on the bed. If I really fought him hard, sometimes it would be two quarters. In 1950 a quarter was a lot of money. (An hour's wages was still below forty cents.) He must have thought that if he paid me, I was getting something out of it—that somehow I was complicit in the act. He made a little prostitute out of me. It would be years before I would feel differently. I was Willie's little hooker. Though I was forced into sex, I always took his money.

On occasion when I was wriggling on the bed before Willie could get me tied down, he would threaten, "If you don't stop fighting me, I won't give you a quarter!" The only thing worse than getting raped as a little girl and getting a quarter thrown at you in the aftermath was putting up with the pain and degradation anyway and getting no quarter. In Willie's twisted way, he even made me want his lousy quarter.

Money was scarce in those days. There were times after Dad left when the hydro company would turn off the power because of unpaid bills. I remember being relieved when winter came, because they weren't allowed to shut off the power when the weather was so cold. At times when the water bill went unpaid, we were forced to get pails of water from our neighbors. Aware that Dad wasn't around, they graciously let us fill our buckets at their sinks, but the humiliation of asking neighbors for water was overwhelming. We always lived under threat of foreclosure, empty cupboards, and the loss of electricity, heat, or water.

We had no money for candy. With Willie's quarter, I could go down to the store and buy candy to comfort myself, pretending that things were okay. Every step I took on the way to the store throbbed because my groin was so ravaged, but I just had to get there. The candy helped ease my pain.

Pretending. I pretended all the time. Once the attacks were over, I just pretended they didn't happen. I compartmentalized the "Willie episodes" in my mind. I never spoke about them. There was nobody to tell, so I just buried each incident in my mind's tomb and made-believe it never took place. Willie never spoke to me about what occurred. He pretended too, never acknowledging the horror he brought upon me. He acted as if I didn't exist. Whenever our family was together, I ignored him and for the most part he ignored me. I don't know what other family members thought, or whether they even noticed. With seven siblings still at home, and the occasional boarder added for good measure, no one was very observant. Twelve years separated Willie and me and it probably seemed natural that we had few words for each other. Whatever the reasons, no one in my family ever suspected that Willie was abusing me.

But there had to be signs! My behavior was terrible. I was mouthy and angry. I often lashed out at people. I was always sore. I must have had constant urinary tract infections that went unnoticed, undiagnosed. There were no regular trips to the doctor's office. Until Ben was born two years before me, all the babies were delivered in the house, with at most the help of a midwife. This was well before universal health care in Canada, and we just never visited a doctor unless we were really sick. Mom was the only one who went to the doctor.

In those days, sexual-abuse awareness was non-existent. Teachers weren't cognizant of the signs. As far as society was concerned, incest and rape within families didn't happen. No one considered it possible. Healthy sexuality between loving spouses was never discussed; let alone the corrupted, perverted kind. Everyone in my life missed the signs of abuse. Margaret Hiebert was simply a poorly behaved, mouthy little girl.

❦

By the time Willie was sixteen he was drinking. Once he was eighteen, he went drinking with Dad. The pattern was the same for Hank and Pete. At one point Pete committed his life to the Lord and attended church regularly, even winning Sunday school contests; but in his late teen years he fell away, started drinking, and lived the rest of his days under the hard task-master of alcoholism. Hank, to my knowledge, never committed his life to Christ as a child. I don't know if he ever did. He too would be overcome by the plague of drinking. I regret that I do not to know where Hank stood with God. Of all my brothers, Hank was the sweetest, kindest, and gentlest by nature. He just never should have followed his dad's example and had that first drink. His life, and all of his potential, was wasted in a bottle. He ultimately died of alcohol poisoning at a relatively young age, having lost his family and everything he could call his own. I can only trust his soul to the care of the loving God who made him.

By the time I was ten, George was twenty and dating. He wasn't around the house that much. Soon he met Ruth, became engaged, and then married. From the first time he committed himself to Christ as a child, led by his friend Leroy Baltus, George fervently served God. He immersed himself in activities at church, became young peoples' president, and never became entangled in the life Dad lived. He and Ruth were like havens of protection from the storm of my life. Ike and Jackie also got saved early in their marriage and were super examples of a godly husband and wife. Ike would ultimately serve on the Elim Tabernacle board of deacons and was a leader in the church.

Ben was two years older than me and always worked industriously. He had a paper route that supplied him with money (and me, when he made me help him), and he was the first person in our family to graduate with a high school diploma. He was awarded an apprenticeship at General Motors and retired early to do missions work. Ben loves God and has always been a gentle witness of His grace. He was instrumental in the salvation of a man who I wouldn't meet for years, a man who would become my son's father-in-law. I am amazed at the intersections of our lives in God's plan.

My younger brother, David, got into trouble as a teenager and young adult; but he eventually came back to a relationship with the Lord. I have benefited from good relationships with five of my seven brothers throughout my life; but most of those relationships developed once I became an adult. Only Pete, Ben and Dave were at home by the time I was ten.

CB

Willie drank more and more. In his inebriated state he would tell his drinking buddies, how *easy* his little sister was. (How could a child my age be *easy*?) One of these drinking buddies and his sister lived on the opposite side of the street, up a ways from our house. He was about twenty years old when I had the misfortune of encountering him. Soon after we got our first phone, this man's sister, whom I barely knew, called our house and spoke to me. "Margaret would you like to go to the store for us? We need some milk."

Soon after we got our first phone, this man's sister, whom I barely knew, called our house and spoke to me. "Margaret, would you like to go to the store for us? We need some milk."

Her voice seemed friendly, and I hoped that after running the errand there would be some change left over for the faithful servant who ran it—an opportunity to buy a pop or get some candy. I leapt at the prospect and made my way up Sherbourne Street to her house.

As I approached the front door, I heard a man's voice: "The money for the milk is inside on the kitchen table." (I did not know then that Willie's buddy was the only one home. Since his sister had phoned me, I assumed she too was inside—so I went in.) When I got to the table, the money barely in my grasp, I felt the man grab my arm. "Willie's been talking to me," he said, "telling me how easy you are!"

I didn't know what it meant to be *easy*, but I recognized the smell of booze on his breath and I was getting an idea of what was coming.

"I'm gonna find out for myself," he snapped as he started dragging me into the main-floor bedroom. I started kicking and struggling, knowing all too well what awaited me behind that bedroom door.

"I'm here to go get milk—the lady—your sister, phoned me and asked me to go to the store for her!" I stammered.

"I don't need milk. I just had my sister phone you on her way out to get you here!" he said, a sly grin stretching across his deceitful face.

My worst fear was being realized. I was alone in that house with a man, and his sister was nowhere around. Nobody was. As he threw me into the bedroom, I saw that he had already removed his pants and he had an erection.

"Take off your clothes! Willie told me how you like it!"

"I don't want to!" I screamed back at him.

"I didn't ask you if you wanted to, I'm telling you. Take off your clothes!"

With that, he shut the bedroom door behind him, wrestled me onto the bed and tied me down. He was too strong for me. I couldn't fight him off. This twenty-year-old man raped me. He raped me the first time he had ever seen me! He lay on top of my ten-year-old body and he forced himself into me. Drunken, smelly breath mixed with his body odor sickened me as he had his way with a little girl too young even to have breasts; all because Willie had told him I was *easy*.

I was devastated. Willie was awful, but I was at least used to him. He had always abused me. I knew when to expect his attacks. This was so sudden. So arbitrary. So frightening. I told no one. Who was there to tell? I just went home and cried. Then I put the whole experience into another compartment of my mind and forgot about it—or so I thought.

I began to believe every man was like this…that every man who walked the face of the earth, if he had the chance, would force himself on me.

I became aggressive in the way I talked. I would be nasty and biting, using sarcasm to try to gain the upper hand. That's how I felt safe and in charge. I determined never to be that naïve again. I was mouthy and abrasive—not at all a cute little ten-year-old girl. I started protecting myself in the only way I could: I blocked everything out and pretended—pretended everything was normal, that I was normal and that nothing bothered me. I decided to be tough. If I was on the offensive, I couldn't be attacked.

That same year, somehow Pete found out about Willie's attacks. Willie must have told him while he was drunk about the things he did to me; but regardless of how the information came to him, Pete knew.

I already had enough problems with Pete. Fourteen at the time, he made the youngest children, David and me mostly, spit-shine his boots until he could "see his face in them." If we refused or put up a fuss, he would enforce his edict with violence. Once when I declined his command, he grabbed me by my two braided pigtails and dragged me from the front of the house to the back by my hair. Then I *still* had to shine his shoes. Pete had a cruel streak, and when he drank he became worse.

The boys' belief that girls existed only to "do their bidding" was reinforced by Mom. "Dat's your role in life. Little girls don't play in da streets, at least not da kind of girl you vant to be. They vork. Learn how to vork!" she would admonish. The boys had much more freedom than me. I was chained to that house.

Pete and I were home alone one day. "I know what you let Willie do with you," he said as he came toward me, grabbing me by the arm. He tried to get me into the bedroom, pulling me by my arms, dragging me. I kicked and fought. Being younger and smaller than Willie, Pete had a more difficult time handling me. "I don't care what Willie says, you're not touching me!" I snarled at him. "I'll scream! You think I won't scream? I'll scream and scream and all the neighbors will hear!"

With Willie, my prevailing thought was that I had little choice. Willie had always abused me—I expected he always would—and there was little I could do about it. Willie was confident that when he came for me he would subdue me. Pete, on the other hand, had never had me for his own gratification, and he somehow conveyed to me that he wasn't sure he could. It gave me boldness and I fought him.

"If you think I can't kick you really hard, just try me," I shouted at him. Pete threw me on the bed, shut the door behind him and took off his pants. His penis was erect as he moved toward me.

"Well I'll just tie you down then," he answered, like it was a game. "Besides, if you don't let me, like you let Willie, I'll tell Mom what you do with *him*."

"I don't care!" My words were not slowing him down. I lay there with my legs crossed on the bed. He hadn't tied me down yet and I still had my dress on. (Mom always made me wear a dress. It was a sin for a girl to wear boy's clothes, and pants were boys' clothes.) He wrestled with me to get my legs apart, but I held them clenched, intertwined at the ankles, with all my might. Pete hovered over me.

Suddenly, with everything in me, I swiftly let go of my ankle grip and kicked him as hard as I could in his exposed groin. The blow sent him reeling in agony and I ran out of the bedroom. By the time he recovered, someone had come home and the immediate threat had passed.

Pete hadn't known to tie me up before he struck; he didn't know to put the dresser in front of the bedroom door, and he didn't know that I would fight so hard. He never tried to overtake me after that; but I was always wary of him and avoided being home alone with him.

I had no such choice where Willie was concerned. In the early years, Willie was the one in charge; the one babysitting while Dad and Mom went for groceries. Later, even after he was married, I would have to be at home on Saturdays by myself, doing the chores Mom left for me to do. Mom would leave with Dad and say, "Have your work done by the time I get back!" If I didn't, then life took a turn for me that I couldn't bear.

Mom learned early that her best method of coercion was a guilt trip. If she came home and the house wasn't cleaned to her exact specifications, she would go into a familiar routine. Mom would literally become sick, to the point of death, right on the spot. She would get so upset that she would tell me she was having a heart attack—that my behavior and laziness was going to kill her. When I was young I really thought that she was going. Tears would flow. Pain would be displayed on her face and she would writhe about as though at any moment God would take her.

"Vhat kint of a daughter do I have? A lazy, no-good-for-nodding girl dat's going to be the deatt of me!" She would answer her own question. "You're going to kill me yet, because you don't do vhat I tell you! Do you vant to kill me? I vish I hat only boys; dey're less trouble! Margaret, you are so lazy and moutty, you're never going to amount to anyting! Now, go from here and do vhat I tolt you!"

Mom's idea of cleaning every Saturday was for me to wash all the floors in the house; then I had to wash out all the cupboards. There were no cupboard doors, and she insisted I take out every dish, wash it, wipe out every corner of the cupboards and then replace the dishes. Then I had to dust the rest of the house and clean the bathroom, floor to ceiling. If something wasn't done to perfection, she would make me do it over. I wanted to avoid her manipulative and demeaning tirades as much as I wanted to avoid Willie.

As I grew a little older, Willie wouldn't even be in the house when Mom and Dad left for groceries. Sometimes I would just be starting on the Saturday cleaning when Mom and Dad would leave without telling me. Usually Mom would come in to read me the riot act about getting my work done, but many times they just walked out of the house. It's odd, but Mom never ever said good-bye. There was no sensitive, "We're going now. We'll be back in a couple of hours." They would simply leave. It's hard for me to understand it now, even as I write this, because I never would have acted that way to my children. This was just how it was. They assumed Margaret, a ten- or eleven-year-old girl, would be fine at home as long as she had work to do. And they left.

On those Saturdays that I was alone and realized that Mom and Dad had gone, I would hope and pray that Willie wouldn't come home. Some time would elapse, and I would just begin to feel relief and hope, and then he would barge in. I wouldn't know which Saturday I would be all right and which Saturday I would be raped; and not knowing made it worse. I couldn't prepare myself. The anguish and uncertainty was unbearable, and nearly as debilitating as the attacks themselves.

On days when my hope was dashed, and my prayers for Willie not to come went unanswered, I thought God had truly forgotten about me. I believed He wouldn't answer my prayers because I was too bad. I was too mouthy and mean, and God had to punish me. I felt there had to be some reason God would let Willie do this, and the reason was *me*.

Willie's continuous abuse wasn't the only threat I faced. One summer day, a girl down the street asked me over to her place. When I got there I saw that her teenaged brother had set up a tent in the back yard. He invited us to go inside. The idea seemed fun, but when we went into the tent, he zipped the door-flap closed and began fondling me. I got scared. I screamed at him not to touch me. Somehow, I got out of the tent and ran home. I was a little girl—with no sexual maturity, no pubescent development, no breasts, no figure—and yet men and boys were always coming for me. I couldn't trust any male!

Being at home alone to clean left me vulnerable to others. One day a boarder who rented a room from Mom accosted me in the living room. Holding on to me, he began to grope me, putting his hands up my skirt and top. I turned and kicked him and, distracted, he let go of me. I ran out of the house and, because he didn't chase me, I got away.

After this particular attack, I finally reached out to someone; I told my Uncle Bill Thiessen, Mom's youngest brother. I loved Uncle Bill and I thought that, since the boarder wasn't family, no one would believe him and Uncle Bill would protect me. I thought for sure that he would go after the man. But all Uncle Bill said was said, "Okay, Margaret. If he does anything like this to you again, you come and tell me."

Uncle Bill didn't do anything! I don't know whether he thought I was making up stories to get attention or that there had to be a pattern of this behavior to take the matter seriously, but he took no action. I reached out for help and took the risk of telling an adult—and nothing happened. Society is more aware of sexual abuse today, but in 1955 these things were swept under the carpet. If Uncle Bill even talked to Mom about the boarder, she never mentioned it to me. Soon afterward he moved out, though; so I never brought it up to Uncle Bill again.

When Willie got engaged to Claudette, I said to myself, *Good! He'll be gone—out of the house and out of my life. I'll be safe now.* Such relief was misguided. All the time he was engaged, Willie still had me for his sexual pleasure. Once he got married, he came home less often on Saturdays—but he still came home. Things would get worse during Claudette's pregnancies. She had two children and, during each pregnancy, Willie's violent Saturday visits increased.

Willie was married and living out of the house at twenty-one years old and over the next four years his children were born. I was nine when he married and thirteen when the sexual attacks finally came to an end. The final rape I would endure would not be at my house at all. Willie wouldn't have to come home on a Saturday afternoon for me: Mom sent me to his house.

It was the summer I turned thirteen. Dad was on one of his furloughs from philandering and was temporarily living at home. He and Mom decided to go out West, back to Saskatchewan, to visit friends and family. They made plans to drive out, just the two of them, leaving the three remaining children with their older married siblings. Ike and Jackie, and George and Ruth split responsibility for Ben and David. Pete and Hank were in their late teens and working, so they stayed at the house on Sherbourne Street and I was sent to Willie and Claudette's.

I begged Mom not to send me to Willie's house. My skin crawled at the thought of living there for the whole three weeks Mom and Dad were away.

"Send me to Tina's house," I pleaded.

"You can't go to Tina's!" she said emphatically.

"Why not?" I asked.

"You're too stinkin' lazy! Dat's vhy! And you're so moutty and so bad dat Tina doesn't vant you! She has five children of her own; she doesn't neet you and da trouble you'd give her. She doesn't vant her moutty little sister arount," Mom scolded. "Besides," Mom paused, as though all the reasons given to that point weren't enough, "Tina lets you get avay vit too much and...and Villie and Claudette offered to take you."

I'm bad? I thought. What about Willie? Everybody thinks he's so great. No one knows what he's really like, the devil that he truly is! For the first time in my life, I really wanted to tell it all—to tell what Willie was really like. Mom thought Willie was better than me, and I wanted her to know who she had for a son! But I couldn't. I was still afraid of what he would do. I was sure Willie would kill me if I said anything. Besides, who would understand?

Suddenly Mom's words registered...*Willie asked Mom to send me there!* I went cold.

Then Mom's words about Tina began to cut me on the inside. Did Tina really hate me? She was always so nice. Was I really a bother to her and she just pretended to like me?

"But Mom, Willie's house is so dirty, I don't like it there. Please, Mom, please don't send me to Willie's!" I cried.

"It's too late now anyvay. I already tolt dem you vere staying vit dem. Dee arrangements are mate and I vant you to behave yourself vhile you unter deir roof!" Mom closed the discussion.

There was nothing I could do. I was going to stay at Willie's, and he had asked for me. But surely he wouldn't do anything to me when Claudette was in the house...surely.

Willie and Claudette lived in a two-story house on the west side of Twelve-Mile Creek in St. Catharines. Tina and Murray lived only about two miles further, out in the country, on the outskirts of town. I remember thinking as Mom and Dad dropped me at Willie's front door, *Tina's house is so close—why couldn't I stay at Tina's?*

The truth is, Tina *wanted* me to stay with her. Mom, however, was leery of Tina's influence. I was thirteen years old and Mom didn't want Tina putting independent thoughts in my head. She was already beginning to worry about losing her other daughter, like she had lost Tina to Murray. Her relationship with Tina was civil, ten years after the marriage, but she never forgot how Tina left her and ran away to marry Murray. To Mom, Tina had betrayed her. She didn't want me getting any ideas of leaving, so when Tina told her that I could stay with them, Mom said Willie asked first, and she didn't want to go back on her word.

Tina couldn't understand why Mom would send me to Willie's either. Willie, even then, was a drinker, and Mom hated drinking; but Mom was struggling to keep control of her children. If all of her children insisted on leaving, who would look after her?

The Saturday morning I arrived at Willie's house, Claudette welcomed me and I had no choice but to go inside. I watched Mom and Dad drive away.

Claudette had always treated me nicely. (I don't think she had a clue what Willie was like or what he had done to me.) I went in the house and pretended everything was fine, that nothing was going to happen. The first day and evening went all right, but I was uneasy and tentative. I felt safer that Claudette was always in the house and I stuck close to her.

Their house was modest, but newer than 17 Sherbourne Street. Willie earned a good living as a cement truck driver and they were able to live better than we ever did at home. The bedrooms upstairs were occupied by Willie, Claudette, and the two kids—I was to sleep downstairs on the couch in the living room. As I lay on the couch that first night, I felt somewhat relieved: Claudette was sleeping with Willie upstairs. *She would wake up if he left the bed*, I thought; but it still took me forever to fall asleep.

The next morning was Sunday and I wanted to go to church at Elim, but Willie refused to take me and I was stuck at their place.

I was angry and sulked; I began to think about being cut off from my whole world for three weeks. I wouldn't see anyone I knew. I couldn't believe Mom left me there. I was destined to be nervous and scared, hardly sleeping, unable to go to church, seeing none of my friends, for three weeks. It was hard to fathom how Mom could have been so stubborn. I knew there must have been some other place for me to stay.

As I prepared to go to bed Sunday evening, I comforted myself in the fact that nothing had happened the first night. *Willie wouldn't risk getting caught by his wife, trying to do anything with me*, I assured myself. My false sense of security would soon fail me, however, as I realized my greatest fear was about to become reality.

I woke up in the middle of the night with Willie's hands between my legs underneath my underwear. Groggy at first, I didn't know if I was having an all too familiar nightmare or if I was actually living a nightmare. When I realized what was happening, I screamed.

Instantly, Willie put his hand over my mouth, "Shut up! Do you want to wake everyone up?"

Yes! Yes I did! I wanted Claudette, and the children, and the whole neighborhood to wake up. I wanted them to come down those stairs and find Willie doing what he was doing and take him *away*. I hated him and I wanted him to stop. I wanted it all to stop.

As I fought him, he said, "This is my house. I can do what I want in my house!" His voice was angry and I knew I was in trouble.

He gagged me and tied a tea towel around my head to keep me quiet. He forced my hand over his, making me bring him to ejaculation. Then he stopped. He left me on the couch, gagged, and went into the washroom to clean himself up. I couldn't get the knot out of the tea towel; it was too tight. *Maybe that's all*, I thought. *Maybe he's done and he won't come back*. Within a few minutes though, he returned.

Back in the living room, Willie seemed happy. "Now I can go longer," he said. Willie was still erect and was pleased that he could be inside me for longer before he would have a second climax. For me, it meant the ordeal would be drawn out unbearably. He was going to drag me through a longer hell, so that his perverted thrills could be maximized. I didn't matter.

Before I could do anything, he was on top of me and then inside of me. I couldn't take it anymore. While he thrust his body against my little frame, all I could do was cry. I cried and cried, and Willie just kept hurting me. It probably took Willie twenty minutes to finish his assault, twenty minutes that seemed like two hours. Then he got up and went to bed, leaving me there, torn, bleeding, and crying.

This was the second night of twenty-one that I was supposed to stay at his house. I lay there for a couple hours, thinking of ways to get out of there. The next day, I did.

Tina says I called her at her house, early Monday morning, crying! "I hate it here! They won't even let me go to church. I can't stay here the whole three weeks. I don't want to stay here another minute! Tina, come pick me up! I want to stay with you!" (I have to defer to Tina's recollection at this point, because I have no memory of the next morning. I don't remember calling and don't recall saying anything. The events of the previous evening were so traumatic that I pushed much of what surrounded them right out of my mind. I only remember arriving at Tina and Murray's the next day.)

Tina remembers the phone call vividly. My crying struck such a strong chord in her that she immediately called Murray and went to pick me up. My reasons for leaving Willie and Claudette's didn't add up to the frantic state I exhibited, but Tina knew intuitively that she had to get me out of that situation. She told me years later that she thought something bad had happened as a result of Willie's drinking, and then she supposed I just didn't want to talk about it. She never pressed me about what had terrified me—she simply took me in.

At Tina's, I felt safe. I ignored the trauma Willie had put me through and pretended everything was fine. Tina says that by the second day I was acting like my usual self. I had accomplished another successful psychological burial; if I pretended all was well—then it was.

That second night I stayed at Willie's during Mom and Dad's trip to Saskatchewan was the last time Willie raped me, but his power over me, and the effects of his attacks, would last for years. The memories could only be buried temporarily. Soon I realized that those hurtful experiences demanded to be relived over and over again. Physically the abuse had stopped, but in my mind a war raged that I could not win. Only Jesus would be able to rescue me from my emotional hell; but it would be years before I would let Him.

50

CHAPTER 4

Life with a Secret

My pretentious life wore on. *Wore* is an apt description, because pretending became a burden I volunteered to bear. Life was lived in two spheres: a public and acceptable one that I carefully controlled and crafted, and a world totally out of my control, where I was overpowered and where everything that happened was unacceptable and shameful. I controlled the things that I could and tried my hardest to live in the "acceptable world."

Pretending promptly turns to lying, and lying becomes the primary method of controlling circumstances. I became a very good liar. I lied about most things; what I ate for supper, my birthday and Christmas presents, where I bought my clothes—they were all lies. If I lied, and I really believed my own words, my life would become anything I wanted it to be. It would be better than it was in reality.

I struggled at school. My ability to concentrate and care about homework assignments must have been affected by events at home, but at the time that rationale never entered my head. I just didn't feel very good about myself. Constantly abused, living in perilous financial circumstance, and being put down verbally by nearly everyone caused me to think that I just wasn't very bright. I certainly wasn't pretty or talented in any way. I had no idea why I was even here. God had forgotten about me, and I seemed to be important for little more than Willie's sexual gratification or Mom's house cleaning.

I would rarely invite friends over. Bringing someone from school into my real life would dispel the lies. My carefully crafted house of cards would come crashing down. I couldn't stand reality anyway. No one ever had to see that I really didn't have a certain doll, or that Christmas for me was only a hand-me-down dress, or that the meals we ate at our house were of the simplest and most basic kind. I let few people into my life to refute my stories. If they didn't come into my life, all my secrets would be safe. No one would ever really find out how very bad and awful I was.

The trauma children face while being sexually abused is intensified by the sense of ownership they feel. There is a perception, intentionally encoded by the abuser, that in some way the victim invited the abuse. I lived with the feeling that this wouldn't be happening to me unless I let it. For me that sense of ownership may even have been more acute because I took Willie's money. In some way I profited from his rape. These feelings destroyed my sense of value and I avoided any introspective thinking because the process of honestly looking inside myself was incredibly painful.

The road to recovery demands a relentless commitment to that very kind of introspection. The healing of painful memories and the after-effects of sexual trauma requires long, hard looks deep inside. Not ready to risk the inevitable pain of such activity, I harbored the hatred, scorn, and bitterness inside. I had earned the right to hate and vilify those who hurt me—that was my sense of control. I wanted to hate Willie. I wanted to hate my Dad. I wanted to hate, period. I was in charge of that hate. After all, I birthed it. I nurtured it. I stroked it. But the hate and anger I clung to was destroying me and making me into a person I didn't want to be—I just didn't know it.

With Dad gone for long periods of time, Mom was left to get by on the money she received from boarders and the jobs held by her children. During canning season she occasionally worked in the factories to bring in some extra money, but no one held Dad accountable—instead, we fended for ourselves, while Dad drowned his conscience at the bar.

In many ways, I was relieved when he was gone. Whenever he was home the house was full of fights and tears. When he would come home drunk, Mom would incessantly nag at him and cry. She would get sick with nausea and chest pain, and accuse him of killing her with his drinking.

"I'm going to die. I'm not going to make it trough da night," Mom would sob. "You're going to kill me vit all of your drinkin!" At eleven or twelve years old, I went to bed many times believing that Mom would be dead in the morning. I really believed she was going to die and there would be no one left to take care of me. It was emotionally devastating. I became ambivalent to Dad's long absences from home—at least his drinking wouldn't kill Mom.

And, when Dad wasn't living with us, I didn't have to face the shame of having a drunk for a father; it was easier for my lies to stand up. If Dad wasn't around, no one could deny what I said about him (the lies that made him out to be the man I wished he were).

Watching my parents go through the cycles of fighting, crying, guilt-tripping and death-threatening tantrums, hurt as much as anything that I went through. I lived with a feeling of dread. I knew what was going to happen, and I worried that it would happen that night. Constant tension was in the air because no one knew when all hell would break loose. There was nothing I could do to stop it.

If Dad wouldn't support our family, if he was drinking and carousing all the time, better that he didn't come around—life without him was more predictable. I longed for stability, to be able to predict with a reasonable degree of accuracy how a day would unfold. I never knew from one day to the next whether there would be huge conflicts caused by my Dad or older brothers coming home drunk, or whether Willie would be there, lying in wait. My entire life was uncertain, so I fought to control what I could. My first line of defense was sarcasm—if I could strike out first and hurt someone, I wouldn't be caught off guard by someone else's cruel words.

With Dad gone, the people at Elim Tabernacle really stepped in. Most of them were very loving and gave clothes and food hampers when needed. My sisters-in-law, Jackie and Ruth, gave us what they could, too. They were very good to me—always kind and generous. Years later, before I got married, Ruth would become a surrogate mother to me, helping me with the wedding and stepping in where my own Mom couldn't or wouldn't. I would eventually learn to trust her with my secret, and the integrity and the faithfulness with which she kept my confidence made her invaluable in my life.

I went to Sunday school and church twice each Sunday and began to learn Bible stories of times when God stepped in and overruled in people's lives. I knew that I was a sinner, that I was imperfect and flawed (if anything I knew it too well), and I committed my life to Christ, although I have no memory of the exact moment in time that I did so.

Church was another compartment of my life, another reality from my own. I loved how I felt in the presence of God and those loving people. Elim Tabernacle was a place where people praised and worshiped God with heartfelt singing and raised hands. People there weren't shy about their commitment and love for God. There were plenty of fiery preachers and evangelists that came through, too. They would preach about the coming of Christ and how we needed to be ready, that Jesus could come back at any moment and we needed to be looking for His return.

Legalism was prevalent back then, and legalists love to motivate through fear. Though Mom had learned the rudimentary principles of grace, her Mennonite background beckoned her at every opportunity to latch onto rules. Rules made Mom feel secure. With boundaries firmly in place, she didn't have to think or judge things for herself. She always looked to the preacher to give her rules to live by. It was easier than working out her own salvation with fear and trembling. External things, rather than the things of the heart, defined holiness for Mom.

She understood that salvation wasn't earned and that the true believer had to rely on the finished work of Jesus on the cross to get sins forgiven, but after that, Christians were supposed to appear different to a lost world—noticeably different. Rules made this possible: no makeup, no pants, only skirts for girls, and so on. In the 1950s, even bowling was worldly behavior, unbecoming a Christian. The theater was the playground of the devil, and so maligned was a movie house in Mom's eyes that, if it rained, she would rather get soaked to the bone and catch pneumonia than wait in its lobby until a bus arrived. Condemnation and fear invariably accompany legalism, and I lived in fear that I would miss the rapture or that I would be involved in some lie or sin and Jesus wouldn't take me when He came.

Somehow it never struck Mom that holiness is an inside-out proposition. Jesus said, "These people honor me with their lips, but their hearts are far from me. They worship me in vain; their teachings are but rules taught by men...Listen and understand. What goes into a man's mouth does not make him 'unclean,' but what comes out of his mouth, that is what makes him 'unclean.'" (Matt. 15:8–11, NIV). The predominant teaching of the day was one of being guarded and making sure you were ready, "should Jesus come back today," and few of us, including Mom, had any lasting assurance of salvation. The great hope and comfort of the Church, the rapture, was made out to be the big stick in the hand of God—a deterrent to keep the believer in line. I lived in mortal fear, not in faith that Jesus would return.

Others at Elim Tabernacle—those who lacked Mom's legalistic bent—freely demonstrated joy and love. In time their influence began to soften Mom's austere approach. She learned to pray and, toward those outside her family, she became more forgiving. Mom learned to read by reading the Bible, and within a few years she could read aloud quite fluently. She loved the Psalms and anything having to do with worship. Singing also seemed to soften Mom's tough veneer. Beatrice Oliver and Mom would walk home from church on summer evenings, Mom singing the great hymns she had learned and Beatrice whistling the accompaniment. One of the few pleasures Mom allowed herself was singing praises. The whole neighborhood listened to the two of them coming home from prayer meetings, Mom singing and Beatrice whistling, like birds.

Becoming a disciple of Christ is a lifelong process, and Mom learned more about forgiveness and the fruit of the Spirit later in life. When the marriages of the boys foundered and they subsequently brought home new girlfriends, Mom accepted them and made them feel part of the family without judging them. This was something that God brought about over time and in her older years.

When I was a teenager however, Mom was a relatively new believer, and it takes the Lord time to make us all new creations. (See Matthew 6:1–4.)

Though Mom was changing in small increments, she never arrived at a place where I felt comfortable enough to tell her what I had been through. Mom's way was to be focused on what was happening to her. If I told her about the evil perpetrated in her home by her own son, she would have seen the whole thing as some tragedy happening to her. Tina tells of Mom saying to her repeatedly as she grew up, "Someday you will know how I feel!" Tina would complain about the injustice happening to her, and Mom would discount any emotions Tina felt, comparing them to what she was going through. Mom's life centered on herself to the extent that she couldn't see past her own pain to the suffering of others. Her struggles were worse than anyone else's; she had to be in the most pain. In the absence of love, Mom craved pity; it was the panacea for all that ailed her.

Mom died without ever knowing what took place in my life—what Willie did to me. I always thought that it would break her heart, that she wouldn't be able to deal with it and that somehow it would just add to her own pain. The freedom to tell my story has only come since she has passed away.

While Mom, Ben, David, and I struggled at home to make ends meet, Dad lived his life as one big party. He had a reputation around the bars in town of buying rounds for the house. With a few drinks in him, William Hiebert became "Loganberry Bill"—in honor of the popular wine he liked to buy for everyone. He stopped giving us money for groceries—Mom had to come up with that herself—yet he was buying drinks for perfect strangers. Like my mother, I was fast developing a hate for alcohol and anything associated with it. Dad was the life of the party—just not our party.

From the time I was thirteen until I was fifteen, Willie's attacks stopped, except for the one time I was forced to stay at his house. Because Tina rescued me and let me stay with her, our relationship improved—I started to get to know my big sister. When I was fourteen, Tina was thirty and had a thriving family of five children. Mom, for the most part, was on better terms with Tina, and visiting her house was wonderful. Tina always treated me with respect and showed great interest in building a relationship with her little sister. I felt important in her presence. Her house was filled with laughter and affection. Murray, being brought up with Beatrice Oliver's hugs and open affection, brought that to his own family. Tina and Murray's kids were always hugging and kissing their parents, as if it were the most natural thing to do. It was foreign to my family experience, and to Tina's as well; but she was a quick study and made her home full of all the love that was demonstrated at the Oliver's. Tina had determined that the chain of neglect and abuse in the Hiebert family would stop with hers; and in so many ways she showed me that I could one day mother a normal and loving family. Tina's family gave me hope.

There are missing patches in the fabric of my memory of my public school years. Without question, my ability to concentrate on reading, writing, and arithmetic was severely compromised by the emotional and physical turmoil in my life outside school. In the third grade, I remember being slapped on the knuckles with a ruler because I couldn't spell the word *because*. I kept rearranging the letters and felt the pressure of everyone's eyes on me. Each time the teacher demanded I spell it again, I felt more inadequate. I was getting frustrated and I knew my teacher was nearing the end of her patience, too. She must have thought I was being lazy or clowning around and decided to bring the wooden ruler down on my hands. Though she vented her frustration on me, and doubtless felt better without all that pent-up anger, I still couldn't spell *because*.

That solitary moment from the third grade is all I can recall from that year, and the fourth grade is a total loss for me. I was ten years old and I think I simply went through every day in a fog, on autopilot—just trying to get to the end of the day.

By the time I was eleven and in fifth grade, I was clearly crafting my image as a tomboy. Boys had it so much easier than girls did. Boys seemed to be in charge of their lives and what happened to them. They played more, worked less, and seemed to please their mothers more easily than girls. I know Mom wished I was a boy…she told me, "girls vere much more trouble dan boys." When boys got in trouble, it seemed to be the kind they chose for themselves, whereas the trouble that came my way was out of my control.

The boys in my house, my brothers, refused to be told what to do. I admired that. They left when they wanted and came home when they decided. They never did housework. If I talked back to Mom, I would find myself lying over the toilet getting my lesson taught directly through the "seat of understanding." Mom had a leather strap—part of a horse's bridle—three-sixteenths of an inch thick that she would double up and use on my backside to emphasize her instruction to me. She couldn't spank the boys. They were too big and weren't afraid of the consequences of disobeying. I wanted to be a boy.

Mom insisted I wear only skirts and dresses; and what she wanted most, I wanted least. Several times I was sent home from Prince of Wales Public School because I wore jeans instead of the required skirt or dress. To me nothing seemed fair. Grudgingly, I would change into a skirt and return to school, looking like what everyone else wanted me to look like—a girl.

I did have two friends in elementary school. Typically any two of us got along well together, but when a third girl joined us, someone invariably felt left out, rejected. I hated feeling rejected and possessively demanded that each friend always choose me over the other. From time to time my two school friends would come to my front porch and yell through the screen in the front door, "Margaret, can you come out and play?"

Usually they were turned away, and Mom, waiting until they were out of earshot, would say, "Hmph! Girls out playin' in da streets! Girls are s'posed to learn to clean and cook and peal potatoes. Only da lazy girls play outside all da time, and Margaret you are not going to be lazy!" Most of our playing together took place in the schoolyard at recess or during lunch period.

I began to notice that my friends liked boys and had crushes on their classmates. Wanting desperately to fit in, I acted boy crazy, too. If it was normal to like boys, I wanted to be *more normal* than them. My life was so far from typical that I overcompensated, until there were no longer norms, only extremes. By sixth grade my behavior was so obvious that my teacher took decisive action. (This was the year I had my first male teacher and, as with most of the men in my life, I was wary of him.)

"You like Matty so much Margaret? You can just move your desk right beside his! Go ahead move your desk against Matty's!" His voice was stern and cynical. He came over to my desk and slammed it against the desk of poor little Matty, who was totally unaware of the distracting effect he had had on me. "Now you can look at him *all day long*!"

To an average child, the public humiliation would have been traumatic enough, but I was crushed. I was trying so hard to fit in, to be like my friends and the other girls, the last thing I wanted was to be centered out and made to look foolish. Another *man* had humiliated me! I hated men. Men were always humiliating me. I ended up failing the sixth grade. I should have failed the fifth; I couldn't spell, I couldn't do the math, and I was barely able to read. But Miss Dawson, my fifth-grade teacher, liked me. For some reason she had a soft spot in her heart for me and wanted me to pass into the sixth grade with my friends. It all caught up to me, however, and my first male teacher forced me to repeat the sixth grade while my friends moved on without me. I was a failure. Nothing I ever did was good enough. The more I wanted everything to be perfect, the worse everything turned out.

Mostly, I avoided men. At church, I sat with my mother during services. In Sunday school, there were only girls, so I felt more comfortable. Mrs. Pelissero made things special, and we got to do crafts and make things that tied into our lessons. The Bible stories came alive to me. Attending Sunday school, making friends, and doing crafts each week became my oasis in the desert. Occasionally, I was invited to go to the house of one of the girls from Sunday school. Their houses were perfect. They had nice things. It felt so different in their world.

One of the hitching posts to which childhood memories attach is a birthday celebration. These traditions occur from year to year and anticipation builds as the day approaches—the day that is only yours in the family, the day your family tells you that you are special. Birthdays were insignificant in my family. Not one of them is memorable. There was the vaguest of references made as I awoke on the morning of June 16 every year, "It's your birthday today, you know."

There was no, "Happy Birthday, Margaret"; no present, no card, and no big deal! My impact on planet Earth was negligible. The fact that I been here another year changed nothing and meant nothing, except that I had survived another year. Sure we were poor, but we could have celebrated birthdays. At school I heard about everything that happened to other kids on *their* birthdays— the presents they received and the cakes made in their honor. At our house my birthday was just like any other day, except worse, because it should have been something special and it wasn't.

Christmas was similar to a birthday, receiving only slightly more attention. Until I was a teenager, when my married siblings bought me presents, I never received anything wrapped up. There was usually a tree, but little tradition except that on Christmas Eve Dad usually came home drunk. On that tradition we could depend. On Christmas Day Mom tried to make it more pleasant than usual; and on Christmas Eve I would help her in the kitchen. If it were a good year, if there was a little extra money, Mom would make molasses cookies and a special dinner for the next day. Mom was strict about there being no alcohol or drinking in the house, so Dad would usually be sober all of Christmas day. Sober, but often hung over. The family would come over: Tina and Murray, Ike and Jackie, Willie and Claudette, George and Ruth and all the children—it was quite a full house then, and once I was a teenager, I did look forward to Christmas Day.

The Christmas Eve after I turned fourteen, I complained to Mom that I didn't have anything to open on Christmas. A few minutes later she came to me and said, "If you vant a present to open tomorrow, here you go, wrap dese up," and she handed me a pair of slippers. I took some newspaper that night and wrapped up those slippers for myself—desperate to have a present all my own on Christmas morning.

Once the gifts started coming in from my brothers and their wives—porcelain dolls and china tea sets—I never got to play with them. The day after Christmas, called Boxing Day in Canada, was literally that. The new toys I received were packaged up in boxes, or wrapped and put on a shelf. When I asked to play with them, Mom would always say, "You'll break dem! Ve'll put dem up dere on de shelf, and vonce every so often, ve'll bring dem down and have a look at dem." I never got to play with any of my toys. Once a year they were brought down from the shelf and cleaned; the rest of the year I could only look at them on a shelf, out of my reach.

I still have a toy stove, with little pots and pans, packed in the original box. It has never been opened, never played with, never enjoyed; it is stored in my attic. My daughters want it as a keepsake after I die, so I'm keeping it in the unopened box.

When my youngest daughter Heather saw my china tea set one day, I let her play with it. She was about seven or eight years old, and she loved the dainty cups and saucers. After a couple of days all the pieces were broken, but I was thrilled anyway; at least someone got to play with those dishes! Heather, as an adult, also claimed my china doll. She has it sitting in her bedroom as part of her décor. I'm glad she's getting some enjoyment from it—I never did. I never really got to be a kid.

After all of those disappointing Christmas mornings, I went to school with terrific tales of bounty. "I got figure skates for Christmas," I bragged to my friends. "They're white and shiny and brand new. I can't wait to use them!"

Within a few weeks my friends invited me to go skating. "I can't," I would say repeatedly.

"Didn't you get new skates for Christmas?"

"Yes, but well, they were too small, and they had to go back to the store—and then they didn't have my size in stock, so now I have to wait." The lie was well rehearsed and came off my tongue as naturally as though it were true.

Every year as I returned to school, each time following the Christmas break, the gifts would change but the lies remained the same. Whether I got a new winter coat or a nice pretty dress, no one at school ever saw them. They always had to be returned for some reason, they were too big or too small, or I was only allowed to wear them on Sundays. I received incredible Christmas presents that no one ever saw—not even me. My make-believe world was better than any real world could ever be; and the lies made me feel like I was important. I was worth the value of a Christmas gift. I was the same as all my friends.

People on our street had plenty of reason to gossip about us: they could hear us fighting and see the black and white police cars frequently parked in the driveway. The more Pete, Hank, and Willie would drink, the more problems we had with the law. Having police officers escort the boys home drunk or because they were driving under the influence, was a regular occurrence. At one point, David, my youngest brother, got in trouble with breaking and entering and on at least one occasion was sent to reform school for theft. At sixteen, Pete hopped a freight train and ran away out

West. Trouble was frequent; our family was reaping what years of alcoholism and dysfunction had sown.

That reaping was particularly difficult on Mom and me. Pete and Hank started to come home drunk as teenagers. Dad had started them drinking to make men of them. The first time Hank came home drunk, he vomited everywhere. Mom and I had to clean him up. "I'll never drink again! I feel so awful! Mom, I'll never drink again!" he vowed. (His words haunt me these many years later, as Hank died in his early sixties of alcohol poisoning. When he died, he was alone with no one to love him; his family long ago usurped by the bottle.)

Someone was always drunk at our house. I remember one holiday season Dad came home so drunk he passed out in our tiny washroom. Only Mom and I were home and we had to break into the washroom to get to him. He lay on the floor, covered from head to toe in his own vomit. Mom and I pealed his shirt and pants off, dragged his six-foot, 200-pound frame along the floor to the bedroom and got him into bed. The whole time, as we heaved, pulling on his arms in rhythm, Mom was sobbing. She heaved and then she sobbed, heaved then sobbed—it took twenty minutes to get him to his bed. The next morning, Mom was crying and telling him how awful the night before had been, and Dad denied the whole thing. He looked into the eyes of his wife and twelve-year-old daughter and said, "I wasn't that bad! You're making all this up!" Deny, deny, and deny...the creed of the alcoholic. I hadn't seen Dad that drunk and sick before, and I never wanted to again, especially around Christmas.

Besides bringing Christmas gifts for me once I was a teenager, my sisters-in-law, Ruth and Jackie, stepped in where they had to and helped me mature. They filled the gaps that Dad and Mom left. Clothes were given to me and altered when needed, so that I was better dressed. Even though they were used clothes, they were well kept and made my teenaged years more bearable. Jackie, not my Mom, taught me about personal hygiene, explaining the value of wearing deodorant each day and making sure that I had some. These were deeds of love and care, and, though I might have been somewhat embarrassed at the time, they helped shape me into a young lady. For their interest in me, and the time they took to show it, I am eternally grateful to both Jackie and Ruth.

While half of my family followed the influence of my Dad, drinking and hanging with those that did, the other half followed Mom's example and became involved in church. Ike and George, though married, helped influence Ben and me, and as I turned thirteen I started attending Friday night youth meetings. At first George drove us. He always went because he was young people's president, a position that in those days was filled by a layperson. Different people took turns sharing and teaching from the Bible and leading in worship, and everyone got the opportunity to develop latent gifts.

Being thirteen also opened up the opportunity to go to youth camp at Braeside. Braeside Camp was owned by the Western Ontario District of the Pentecostal Assemblies of Canada, and provided an inexpensive place for families to get away and sit under good teaching and preaching in revival meetings each summer. It was a dusty-road-camp, set amid mature trees, on the banks of the Grand River in Paris, Ontario, about an hour-and-a-half's drive from St. Catharines. Our family couldn't afford to rent one of the little cabins at Braeside, no matter how reasonable the rates, but some anonymous sponsor from Elim Tabernacle always paid for me to go to youth camp.

About 150 young people between the ages of thirteen and eighteen attended youth camp, led by counselors who were only slightly older. There were devotional services each morning where we studied the Bible and received teaching, and a big rally with a special speaker each night. The afternoons were spent in activities, crafts, and swimming, which was essential in southern Ontario's July heat. None of that really mattered to me. Braeside meant a whole week of heaven—away from Mom, 17 Sherbourne Street, and everything that was my life.

What I didn't count on was God getting ahold of my life. I found myself at the altar following the first service, seeking the baptism in the Holy Spirit. (Going to the altar—the steps to the platform at the front of the chapel—to pray following a challenging message, is a Pentecostal tradition to this day. Some of the greatest moments of my life have been spent in such a place.) I had never received the baptism, but had heard plenty about it. I longed for God to fill me to the point that the Holy Spirit would overflow in me and speak through me in a language I had never learned—a heavenly language, called tongues. I found myself inextricably drawn to the altar that night. As a counselor prayed with me, God began a healing and a cleansing through the Holy Spirit that would certainly not be instantaneous, but would start me on a path to total deliverance. The Holy Spirit gave me a few syllables of my very own prayer language and a greater sensitivity to all things spiritual. I began seeking Jesus and drawing close to him in a personal relationship, like never before.

This meaningful and integral moment in my life was made possible because someone responded to the urging of God's Holy Spirit and sponsored a poor kid to go to youth camp. Though I had gone through unspeakable horrors in my life, God had not forgotten about me. He was using people and circumstances to lead me, ultimately, to a complete inner healing. I didn't know it at the time, but in hindsight I can see His handiwork, His sovereignty, and His providence.

My life could have been so different if God had just intervened sooner. I could have been rescued from all the abuse I endured if events had unfolded differently. But God, in His sovereignty, allowed the evils of alcoholism and sexual abuse into my life. I don't know why, but instead of delivering me before, He chose to deliver me after. Because He chose to do things in His way and in His time, I've been able to help others in similar circumstances. My credibility with others who have been abused has been shaped by my own experience of rape and torture, but also by God's supernatural healing and deliverance from the prison it created.

One of the interesting turns my life could have taken, but didn't, involved the Andres. During one of Mom's many hospital stays, I was sent to stay at the house of a young couple from Elim Tabernacle. I was four years old. (If Willie's attacks had started by then, they had barely started.) Marge and Jack Andres were a Christian couple unable to have children of their own. They had volunteered to watch me while Mom recovered from one of her many surgeries. They fell in love with me and offered to adopt me, seeing that Mom had so many children and a husband who didn't support the family. Not surprisingly, Mom wouldn't hear of it and emphatically said no.

Years later, Mom would brag to me of how she was able to keep me. In those moments when she wanted to reassure herself of how great a mother she was, she would often say, "You know Margaret, dat Andres family vanted to adopt you vhen you vere little. Dey vanted you to be deir little girl, but I said no."

Though it made Mom feel better about herself, it made me seethe with anger at Mom and at God. Why was I not adopted out at four years old? If I had been a part of Jack and Margorie's life from the time I was four, I would have avoided most, if not all, of Willie's attacks; I would have been the only child of well-to-do parents who were enthralled with me. Things could have been so different! I resented Mom for reminding me of it. I spent a lot of time thinking about how I might not have been poor, abused, and the daughter of an alcoholic gambler; but, none of that thinking ever took my pain away. Pity parties never do.

Though I didn't have the Andres to live with, God brought another person into my life who proved to be a tremendous blessing—Ruby Ens.

CHAPTER 5

Ruby and the Supermarket

The Ens family, like the Hieberts, came to Ontario from Saskatchewan. Though not close, the families knew of each other while living out West. A while after their move to Ontario, Mr. Ens committed his life to Christ and the whole family became Christians, attending Elim Tabernacle regularly. It must have been there, at Elim, possibly in Sunday school, that we became acquainted. (Neither of us recalls the first time Ruby and I met—and that makes us feel as though we have always been friends.) Ruby lived with her parents and a younger brother a few city blocks from Sherbourne Street. It was a natural fit right from the start.

Ruby was one month older than me, but because of where she lived we attended different schools. Until I was a teenager, I would only see Ruby at church. Occasionally, I would go to her house following the morning service, or she would come to mine. After an afternoon spent together, we would return to the evening service at Elim, then go home with our own families. All week long we looked forward to being together at church and sitting beside each other in Sunday school. We never tired of being together and were the closest of friends.

Ruby's cultural heritage was similar to mine. She was from Saskatchewan, spoke German and her Mom was strict, just like mine. On Saturdays, she too had to scrub the floors and clean her whole house. We could share our complaints and feelings about the drudgery of our Saturday tasks, and each be comforted that we weren't the only children in the world chained to our houses by chores.

Because we wanted to spend the afternoons together, we raced through our Saturday cleaning. We usually rose earlier on Saturdays in order to finish house cleaning by noon. As soon as we each finished our chores, we started walking toward the other's house. Upon meeting each other, we would walk downtown to Kreskge's or Eaton's to buy nylons for Sunday. This became our weekly routine the summer I turned fourteen; each week, as long as the weather was fine, we would walk three or four miles downtown.

Those long walks were filled with great girly conversations, much giggling and secrets. Ruby had a wonderful sense of humor and I felt comfortable with her, as if she were my own sister—or better yet, my confidante. Ruby was someone I could trust. She was loyal and she liked me for who I was instead of trying to change me.

When the weather cooperated, we pooled our bus fare home and walked another mile or so to the Dairy Queen. The combined bus fare bought a foot-long hotdog and a Coke. We shared both, never minding the long walk back home.

Though scarce, money was available in small amounts. Both of us loved babies, and babysitting provided us with much needed pocket change. Mom never minded me babysitting. She encouraged it because she could go along with me and wouldn't have to spend evenings at home alone. As time went by—especially once Dad stopped coming home—Mom increasingly became fearful of being alone, especially at night. After giving Mom half of whatever I earned watching other people's children, I saved the rest for Saturday excursions and special events with the church youth group. Going downtown together empowered me; it was something I could do on my own.

As time went on, Ruby and I often slept at each other's houses. Mom always hesitated whenever I asked to stay at Ruby's, because then she would have to be by herself; she often countered by offering to let Ruby stay at our place. I preferred going to Ruby's, but staying at our house was better than nothing, so I rarely rocked the boat. Ruby and I slept in the room on the main floor right beside Mom's. Cramped together in a single bed, we exchanged secrets in whispers soft enough that Mom couldn't hear us. In the quiet stillness late in the night, we learned exactly what made the other tick.

On the rare occasion that Mom let me stay the night at Ruby's, I reveled in the privilege. Mrs. Ens had such nice things. With just two children, the Ens had much more money than we ever did. They weren't rich, simply middle class, but they seemed rich to me. Their quaint Dunblane Avenue home was decorated beautifully. Matching china was used only on Sundays and their cutlery was all the same pattern. Attractive wallpaper hung on some walls, and others were nicely painted and adorned. There were little figurines and knickknacks on coffee tables, and printed window dressings. At my house pictures weren't centered nicely on walls; they hung strategically over bruises in the plaster that had never been repaired. Since both of Ruby's parents were committed Christians, the atmosphere inside their home was one of peace. Even though Ruby had issues with her Mom common to most teenagers and their parents, and rebelled against how strict both she and Mr. Ens were, their home still felt different—safer.

I lived to get to the weekends. I endured the week so that, starting with Friday night's young people's meeting, I could be with Christians. Saturday I could spend with Ruby, and then on Sunday, there were two services and Sunday school to attend. Church and Ruby were my refuge from home.

Elim Tabernacle provided a ministry opportunity to a deaconess from a Bible school out West. A volunteer intern, she worked a secular job and gave many hours to the church in ministry. She had an apartment just down the street from the church, and many Sunday afternoons she would invite some teenaged girls to her place until the evening service. She was in her early twenties and had a large influence over the younger girls. Everyone who got the chance went to her place.

After the summer I turned fourteen, Willie never abused me again and my teenaged years became the happiest of my life. I loved spending time with Christians. Life wasn't perfect, but it was getting better. In those years, I discovered I had a sense of humor. It may have been a result of Dad's personality—he was well liked in his circle of bar friends—but more likely, I had been sarcastic for so long that people started to laugh whenever I vented. Whenever I teased or joked, and people laughed, I was affirmed and felt more confident. People thought I was funny. At last I had a gift; some talent upon which to hang my hat. I found that people liked to be around me because I made them laugh.

Laughter is a strange thing. We love it when people laugh with us, but hate it when people laugh at us. I liked it when I made people laugh. I enjoyed being light and frivolous. As long as I was joking, I never had to deal with the serious issues of my life. I had no idea as a teenager that soon the laughter would end, and that I would eventually have to deal with the mess that my sense of humor helped to bury. Being the center of attention in a crowd reinforced good feelings about myself, feelings that I was having for the first time in my life. Others assumed, because of my sense of humor, that I was strong and self-assured. It appeared that way and I liked the façade.

It's possible that no one ever suspected the sexual abuse in my life. Instead of sulking in the corner, I was always brash, sarcastic, and offensive. While many abuse victims become withdrawn, I developed into an extrovert—I acted out. I made up a world I could live in and a character that I could pretend to be. This was the key to my survival. The only problem was that the personality I was constructing wasn't really who I was, and no one knew the real Margaret Hiebert—not even me.

Two other girls that I met at church and hung around with were Alice and Naomi Davidson. Alice and Naomi were two of ten children, but the only girls, and I felt an affinity with them because I had seven brothers and only one sister. The Davidson family came into Elim after getting saved at a summer revival meeting at Braeside Camp. Robert and Daisy and some of their older children had visited the camp to make fun of the "holy rollers," a term many people used in the Fifties to describe Pentecostals. Sitting under the powerful preaching and conviction of the Holy Spirit, however, five of them rushed down the aisle to the altar, committing their lives to the very One they had come to mock.

Having experienced such a dramatic conversion, the Davidsons' lives changed forever and they immediately began attending Elim. Robert dug into the Bible, grew spiritually at an unbelievable rate, and became a deacon inside of three years. He loved to study, teach,

70

and expound on Scripture. Daisy was like everyone's Mom—a tenderhearted woman who made everyone around her feel as though they were the most important people in the world. She would sit down beside the one everybody else considered an outcast; it didn't matter if they were simple-minded or if they smelled…Daisy welcomed them. I was ten years old when the Davidson family became part of our church. By the time I was twelve, Daisy had been stricken by cancer.

For the next two-and-a-half years, Daisy was in and out of the hospital. The Davidsons lived about thirty miles outside of St. Catharines, near a little village called Caister Center. They had a farm and a trucking business, and, with five children still at home when the cancer struck, they needed help. Every weekend the girls in the youth group would hope to be asked by Alice or Naomi to go to the farm and clean the house with them. Many times Ruby and I would go and clean the whole farmhouse. Bob Davidson led a cottage prayer meeting there on many Saturday nights, so the house needed to be in top shape. Ironically, I didn't resent this housework. Not that my motives were purely to do a good deed for a sick lady; it was a chance to get away from the city and go into the country with Ruby. Alice and Naomi, and Ruby and I enjoyed our time together, even though it meant a boatload of work. Mom allowed me to go because I was helping someone in need—it was the Christian thing to do. It was more fun cleaning a house when it wasn't my own, and I was with friends and away from Mom's disparaging comments. At the Davidsons, no one criticized my efforts. I was even thanked.

To me the Davidsons seemed rich. Bill, the oldest son still living at home, had his own car and drove his siblings, plus any one else needing a ride, to and from young people's meetings on Friday nights. Afterwards we would often go for ice cream or floats, laughing and visiting—it was the best time in my life. At fourteen, my life was going along reasonably well—until one particular Saturday in December.

It was cold that Saturday, and Ruby and I were heading downtown on our customary trip to buy nylons, an essential item needed to complete our outfits for Sunday church services the following day. Once downtown, we cut through the Loblaws Grocery Store to warm up on our way to Kreskge's. We stood in the heated area near the exit, where shoppers collected their groceries and stayed while waiting for taxis to take them home.

Ruby and I sat down for a few minutes, watching the people come through the cash registers doing their holiday shopping. As we watched, I suddenly saw him. There at the cash register, with his grocery cart heaped and overflowing with food and all kinds of treats, was my Dad. He was with a woman! I had never seen her before, but there was no mistaking that they were together.

Mom had heard rumors that Dad had a girlfriend, but none of us had ever seen them together. Dad hadn't been living at home for about a year-and-a-half. We hardly saw him at all, except when he picked up Mom to take her somewhere. He wasn't paying support, and we were barely eking out a living at home. Ben, Dave, Mom, and I were the only ones left at the house. We didn't go hungry thanks to Spam, mushy peas, and canned soup. Here was Dad with another woman who wasn't my mother, *his* grocery cart filled to capacity, while we were eating scraps at home.

I burned with rage. That should be our grocery cart! That should be our food, our treats! I thought.

"Look! I think that's my Dad over there!" I said to Ruby. "It is! It's him! And look at his grocery cart—it's full!"

Leaving Ruby sitting in the waiting area, I approached Dad right at the checkout. "Hi, Dad!" I said with excitement, as if nothing was the matter and he should be thrilled to see me. I feigned friendliness, but I wanted to embarrass him; I wanted him to squirm in front of his girlfriend. I was sure he had never even mentioned us—his "other" family—and that he would start to blush at the sight of me. I felt crushed and angry—angry because he had deserted us for alcohol, because he didn't love Mom and, most of all, because of that huge, overflowing grocery cart.

Without flinching, my father looked directly into my eyes and said, "Who the hell are *you*?" Then he shrugged his shoulders and said to the woman beside him, "I don't know who the hell this kid is!"

I had wanted to embarrass and show him up—to let him know that I knew about his girlfriend and his heaping cart of groceries. I wanted him to know my pain, to feel what he was inflicting upon me. But instead of being embarrassed, he denied my very existence.

I backed up slowly, stunned by what had just taken place. (Tina never mentioned the similar experience she had with Dad until forty years later.) Tears welled up in my eyes and I hated him for making me cry—again.

"I hate you! I hate you! I hate you!" I screamed at the top of my lungs. I blurted out the words for the whole world to hear, but especially to remove any doubt in his mind that I *hated* him.

I turned and ran out of the store at full speed, sobbing, big tears streaming down my face. Ruby finally caught up to me and put her arm around me, but I was inconsolable. My own father, the one whose affections I had been competing for my whole life, denied that I was his daughter. I had feared rejection my whole life, but I had never experienced it on this level. More hurtful words I could not have imagined. All the pain of Willie's abuse could not compare to the pain in my heart at that moment.

In one second, all that made me feel special and wanted was wiped out. The progress that I was making with my self-esteem, because of the people at church and because of my relationship with God, was ripped apart. I kept hearing his words, "Who the hell are you? I don't know who the hell this kid is!" They rang in my head like a never-ending anthem. I wished he had beaten me, like he did Tina, rather than to hear him say those words. A beating would have been easier to forgive than what he said at the supermarket.

From that moment, I determined to hate my dad forever. There had always been disappointments with Dad. His never-ending promises were only outdone by the ever-missing results. "I'm going to take you guys to the beach," he would pledge. "But first, I have to go downtown and collect some money from a man who owes me, OK?" Ben, Dave, and I would be all ready to go, waiting for him to show up to take us to the beach—but he never came. He would meet his elusive creditor, Jack Daniel's, in a downtown bar, and never make it back in time to go to the beach. I could forgive him for that. I could forgive him for losing track of his promises in a bottle, but I could not—I would not—forgive him for rejecting me, for telling me that I didn't even exist to him. I would hate him instead. I would hate him for the rest of my life.

I was fourteen that day at the supermarket, and after that I barely spoke to my Father for five years, until I was married. I was civil, but avoided unnecessary conversation. If I were dead to him, he would be dead to me.

What I didn't know was that my hate and anger were really killing me.

Ruby finally caught up with me. She held me and comforted me in the cold, loving me through my lowest moment.

Later that night, in the dark, sleeping together in my single bed, in hushed whispers little girls use to tell their deepest secrets, I told Ruby about Willie.

I had never told anyone—not a soul. But I told Ruby. I trusted someone, and it felt liberating. I started and I didn't stop. I told her about the rope, the violence, and the terror—I told her and she listened. She didn't judge me. She listened and hugged me and said, "I'm sorry," and some of my hurt went away. I learned that night that some people *can* be trusted, that not everybody was out to hurt me.

I started to trust that night, and the long process of healing began. I started a journey toward restoration—a journey measured not in weeks or months, but in years.

CHAPTER 6

Bill Davidson

In the year the Titanic sank, 1912, another ship sailed from Great Britain. It set sail not from England, but from Ireland, and on that ship were Elizabeth Davidson and her children. Several months earlier, her husband, Tom, and their eldest son had left Ireland for the adventure of settling in Canada. He had found a job and then sent for his wife and kids to come and join them in what would be a new life in a different land.

Elizabeth and eight siblings crammed onto a ship. This vessel was the antithesis of the Titanic: not a luxury liner, but a crude and small ship, without the fanfare and the glitz. During the two-month sail, most passengers were sick most of the time. Too many people in a confined area, not enough fruit and vegetables and other nutritious food, and the tossing and turning of a little ship in the Atlantic Ocean, resulted in a three-fold assault on the passengers from Belfast. All anyone thought about was surviving the trip. To make it through, passengers dreamed about the promise the new land of Canada held for their families. It was their only motivation. They endured the voyage by thinking of the prosperity that inevitably lay ahead. Elizabeth's youngest son, Robert, however, seemed immune to all that ailed the others; he just played, oblivious to the discomfort gripping everyone else. Bobby (as he was called), was proving to be a strong and healthy child. He would need to be, for awaiting him was a life of hardship and loss.

At the Halifax harbor, Tom greeted the family he hadn't seen for several months. Amid the celebration frenzy, he hadn't noticed one of his nine children was missing. Finally he asked, "Where is Sammy?"

Tears welled up in Elizabeth's eyes. "He took sick before we set sail. He didn't get better, and I couldn't post a letter in time." Tom knew what Elizabeth was saying. Sammy hadn't made it, and Tom was only learning of his death on the day they were all supposed to be back together again. It was a day of mixed emotions: joy and sorrow cast together in the same moment, each fighting the other for dominance in the hearts and minds of Tom and Elizabeth Davidson.

The Davidson family had emigrated before. Earlier generations had moved first from Wales and then from Scotland, always searching for something better, an easier life. Tom and Elizabeth moved to Nairn, Ontario, in central Canada, soon after arriving in Halifax, and the older boys worked in the sawmills to provide for the whole family. Being the youngest, Robert went to school until age eleven, when it was determined he had benefited enough from school and could better help the family by joining his brothers at the sawmill. With the equivalent of a fourth-grade education, Bobby began his apprenticeship to life. He quickly learned the value of a good work ethic and the importance of community. For the next year he put himself to the task of milling wood and contributing to his family's survival.

One day at the sawmill, Bobby developed a toothache. As the pain became unbearable, he could no longer concentrate on his work. The abscessed tooth throbbed with pain until his whole head hurt. He decided he would go home. Upon arriving at the house he was asked, "What are you doing home in the middle of the day?"

"I've got a really bad toothache," he complained.

"Get back to work!" came the unsympathetic reply. "You can't come home for a lousy toothache!"

Robert left the house that day crying. The road back to the sawmill forked in two directions: one led back to the mill and the other led to the rest of his life. Twelve-year-old Bobby Davidson chose the latter. He didn't see the rest of his family, including his parents, until years later, just before starting a family of his own.

In 1920 things were booming after the First World War and Robert had little difficulty finding work. He quickly hired on as a cook's helper for a railroad construction crew. Canada, this vast wilderness of a country, had been linked from one end to the other by the railway; and much of the infrastructure supporting that system was waiting to be built. It was work geared to the young and adventurous, as work was found wherever new rails were needed. Bobby grew up quickly around these rough men and became hardened to adversity, taking it in stride as part of life. He learned the value of a hard day's work, eventually landing on a rail crew himself—the "extra gang"—under the leadership of one tough curmudgeon named George Thurlow. Bobby Davidson was a good worker and could toil all day doing heavy labor under tough conditions. George took a liking to the young man, though that wouldn't always be the case.

In 1926 Robert and others drank some of the cook's moonshine and ended up in the hospital with alcohol poisoning. The cook himself died, but Robert was nursed back to health. While in the hospital he shared a room with George Thurlow's son, who had been in for an operation. The young boy had a sister, Daisy, who came faithfully to visit. Daisy and Robert soon hit it off. To their delight, and George Thurlow's chagrin, love sparked between them. Daisy's dad made it tough for them to see each other. In later years Robert would often reminisce about walking for miles through the bush to meet Daisy at some clandestine location.

In 1927 Daisy discovered that she was pregnant and the decision was made: she and Robert would get married. George Thurlow found out about their plans for a secret wedding, and hurrying into town on the next Saturday afternoon, he came face to face with Bobby Davidson.

"Where are you going in such a hurry, Mr. Thurlow?" Bobby asked, with a touch of sarcasm.

"I'm on my way to stop this wedding. That's where I'm going!"

"You're too late," Bobby answered with an air of satisfaction. "We were married this morning, sir!"

George Thurlow looked at young Robert with an intense stare, his face becoming redder by the second. "You're fired!" he bellowed. And with that he turned around and promptly walked back in the direction from which he had come, leaving the new groom in stunned silence.

Daisy's dad was a tough man; a veteran of the Boor War, he had lived through much hardship. He was a man of authority, accustomed to being in charge. Unable to stop the wedding, he exercised control in the only way he could: he fired the man who took his daughter away from him.

Years earlier, while serving in the Queen's Army in India, Thurlow's entire outfit was stranded in the mountains of India and presumed dead. A dignified and proper Alice Thurlow did not give up hope, however, and miraculously, six years later, George Anthony Thurlow walked out of the mountains. The only change, aside from being six years older, was that his brown locks had all turned pure white. He was an adventurer, a soldier, a striking figure, and a leader of men. No young Robert Davidson was going to get the better of him.

As time went by, the chasm between George Thurlow and Robert Davidson narrowed, and, toward the end of his life, George lived with Robert and Daisy. The distinguished white-haired Englishman with the large handlebar moustache and the walking cane was ultimately treated better by the man he had rejected than by his own sons. George's limp worsened in his latter years, the result of a bullet wound he had received in the war. Eventually, since the bullet was never removed, gangrene set in and he died. George came to appreciate the treatment he received from his son-in-law and the respect Robert gave him. Ironically, Robert became—and everyone knew it—George Thurlow's son.

The monarchist pride and proper etiquette demonstrated by both Tom and Elizabeth Davidson and George and Alice Thurlow was not lost on Robert and Daisy. Whenever she could, Elizabeth would tell Robert's firstborn son, Bobby Junior, "Hold your head up, Bobby! We're their betters!" By that she meant that hanging his head in despair was not the way of a Davidson. A certain sense of English dignity pervaded the lives of Daisy and her children. Others might despair and wallow in self-pity, but not a Davidson. With that self-confidence came the belief that nothing was too difficult, that one need only apply himself and he could conquer whatever might present itself as an obstacle.

This sense of pride served Daisy well and was fortified by husband Robert. Robert's heritage had been that of the Orangeman—the Irish loyal to the King and Queen and to the Church of England; Irish monarchists. Though they rarely went to church, they held to the doctrine of the Church of England. "Surely the King and the Queen wouldn't have wrong advisors," became their simple philosophy. They took comfort in the *name* of the Anglican Church. They somehow reasoned that assenting to the dogma of the King and Queen would be enough to keep them in good standing with God, though they never practiced religion or attended worship. It was a form of godliness—if not in reality, at least in their minds—and it justified the way that they lived. The Davidsons were good people—hardworking and honest. Being religious, even if in name only, made them feel good about themselves in the midst of hardship.

As the Great Depression set in, Robert and Daisy started a family. By the time Daisy was twenty-seven years old, she had given birth to five sons. Robert, despite the tough times, always found work. In fact, he held down two full-time jobs to support his large brood. Like other families in that era forced to survive on whatever work they could find, they got by—until their house burned down!

Daisy Davidson faced the prospect of being homeless. By now the family had moved into the Niagara Peninsula, to St. Catharines, into a house that inexplicably caught fire and burned to the ground. Without insurance and struggling to get by in the latter part of the Great Depression, the Davidson clan moved into a barn, hip roof and all, that a Lincoln Avenue widow offered to rent to them. On weekends, Robert and the boys put up gypsum board to finish the inside walls. Daisy decorated the walls by pasting up sheets of old newspapers for wallpaper and painting them with a lacquer finish. Soon the barn began to resemble a house. "Home" was set on the edge of town, almost in the countryside, allowing the family to keep a cow for milk and a few chickens for eggs.

Living next to them were Eufrasio and Anna Pelissero, owners of a large chicken farm. They were intentionally friendly to Robert and Daisy, and the two couples formed a lasting friendship. Soon these neighbors would become integral to the transformation that would take place in all of their lives. The Pelisseros were born-again Christians and members at Elim Tabernacle, and they began to share their faith with family next door.

Since his time on the extra gang, Robert Davidson had been a chain-smoker. He would roll and light up his first cigarette in the morning, then light the next smoke from that butt, literally smoking one cigarette after another all day long.

Anna Pelissero would yell over the back fence, "Bob you let that little cigarette boss you all over the place!" Her good-natured teasing was sending a message that Robert Davidson was not in control of everything in his life; some things *had* him. Although he wouldn't learn the lesson until fifteen years later, the seed planted by the Pelissero family would eventually bear fruit.

The Second World War raged on and Robert tried to enlist, but was turned down because of the size of his family. He was disappointed, like most men of that time who couldn't serve in the defense of their country, but the war effort sparked the economy, and from construction to delivering milk, Robert was able to keep working.

Robert kept working—and Daisy kept having children. Ben, her fifth son, had a twin brother who didn't survive. After losing another set of twins, she and Robert decided she should have sterilization surgery. The surgery, not perfected at the time, worked temporarily. Seven-and-a-half years later, at thirty-four years of age, Daisy gave birth to Billy. Billy's arrival marked the beginning of Daisy's second family. The year was 1942.

Four more children followed. Daisy's first daughter, Alice, was born prematurely in January of 1944. Because Daisy went into labor so early, Bob rushed her to the hospital. Weighing only four pounds, Baby Alice had to stay in the hospital until she was stronger. When Daisy brought her home, her entire body still fit inside Daisy's hand. Bob and Daisy Davidson finally had a daughter and, after six boys in a row, Alice was their little princess. Everyone doted on her.

When Alice was just two months old, Daisy found out she was pregnant again. In December of the same year, Naomi was born. Two sisters, eleven months apart and born in the same year—this was Daisy's reward for raising six boys. After Naomi came Harry; and finally, in 1949, her last child, Kenny, was born.

The Davidson's landlady was fond of her tenants, and promised that when she died, they could keep the barn they had worked so hard to renovate. Robert and Daisy put much work into the house, knowing that someday it would be theirs. In those days, people were true to their word and verbal agreements were considered as solid as written contracts. When the old landlady died, however, her family sold her assets; and because there was no mention of her promise to Robert and Daisy in a will, their house was sold right out from under them.

Having gotten back on their feet after losing their first house, the Davidsons faced another move. All their work and investment into their rented house was for nothing. Robert worked even harder and soon they scraped enough money together to place a down payment on a 150-acre farm, forty minutes' drive from St. Catharines, in Caister Center.

In 1947, thirty-eight-year-old Robert, his wife of nineteen years, and their eight children started over.

Though the Davidsons moved away from St. Catharines, the prayers of Eufrasio and Anna Pelissero followed them. In just a few years, Robert, Daisy, and much of their family would be reunited with their former neighbors in a way they never dreamed. God had a plan and He orchestrated the events of all of their lives, bringing everyone to the same path—the path that led to Him.

The Caister Center farm was a dream come true for Bob Davidson. His whole life he had wanted to be independent, to work for himself and be the master of his own destiny. One-third of the 150 acres he bought was covered in forest and, for the first few years, logging would provide the income the family needed. Each day Robert, his older boys, and some men he hired trekked out to the bush to cut down trees. The Davidson's home business grew to the point that thirteen workhorse teams were required to haul the cut wood to the main road for shipment to sawmills. He made a business connection with Aldo & Muratori Sawmills, who would take delivery of the logs. Years later, the byproduct of the milling—sawdust—would ultimately provide a new business opportunity; but for the time being, logging paid the bills.

Shortly after moving to the farm, Robert's nephew, Andrew Gilbert, joined the family. To distinguish him from his cousin of the same name, everyone called him Gib (short for Gilbert), and he was taken in as Bob and Daisy's own son. Gib got along well with both Jack and Andy, transitioning from cousin to brother. Though they didn't know it, the Davidson clan was about to experience a life-altering change.

Neighbors offered to take the Davidson kids to Sunday school in Smithville and Bob and Daisy thought this was a great idea: the youngest children would be picked up and babysat for the whole morning each Sunday. Ben was twelve and could look after himself and, with Billy gone, Daisy could get a little peace. Billy was five when he started attending Sunday school at the nearby Free Methodist Church. For seven years people faithfully drove him and his younger siblings to church where they heard the gospel.

When Billy turned twelve, someone sponsored him to go to the Free Methodist's children's camp. Again God used an anonymous sponsor to impact a child's life forever. At one of the first services, Billy walked the aisle and gave his heart to Jesus. In that moment, God placed him on a path that would intersect mine. Much had to happen, however, before that great intersection would occur.

Three years before Billy went to camp, God was at work in another part of the family. Jack, while attending school, caught sight of a pretty Italian girl named Dinah. But Dinah flatly refused to date him.

"I only date Christian guys," she explained to Jack. "Now if you want to come to church and young people's group with me, then you can see me…but nothing else unless you give your life to Christ!"

If it took going to church to be with Dinah, Jack would go to church. Dinah's home church was Elim Tabernacle. Bob and Daisy had moved forty miles away from St. Catharines, but God was using people from the same small church to reach their family. Jack attended for a little while and then decided to commit his life to Christ. Jesus became Jack's Savior and, within two years, Dinah became his wife.

Back at home everyone knew Jack got *religion!* He became an instant missionary to his family, whose only reaction was to tease him—mercilessly. They believed that having gone head over heels for a girl, he had lost his mind in the process. But Jack hadn't just fallen in love with Dinah; he had fallen in love with the One who had died in his place 2,000 years before. Jesus so changed Jack, and filled him with such compassion, that he was consumed with the lost condition of his family. He began to pray earnestly at church for them. Those at Elim began to know the Davidsons vicariously, as Jack faithfully mentioned them by name at prayer meeting. By 1954, a spiritual conspiracy was taking shape—a calculated plan to capture the entire Davidson family for Christ.

Marge Andres and her husband, Jack, were asked to baby-sit the grandchildren on Braeside's campground. The plan was to whisk them off to junior church, ensuring their parents the freedom to attend the adult service. (Andy, Tom, and Bob, Jr., had married by 1954, and Bob and Daisy were already young grandparents.) The feeling prevailed that if all excuses were removed, including the need to watch young children, members of the Davidson family would say yes to an invitation to a revival camp meeting service. Others joined in to watch Billy and the younger ones at home, while Bob and Daisy and the older children made their way to Paris, Ontario, and Braeside Camp.

It was to appease their son Jack, and hopefully get him off their backs for a while, that Daisy and Robert said they would go. Five others from their extended family, plus Jack and Dinah, made the trip. Bob reasoned that, if nothing else, they would have a good time making fun of the "holy rollers." Ripping the crazies would be their entertainment. The Elim conspiracy was unified, however, and prayed earnestly that every member of the family would get saved that night.

Upon their arrival, Jack began introducing them to all of his friends and acquaintances from church, and the time was slipping away. As the service was about to begin, Bob whispered into Jack's ear, "Jack, I haven't had a smoke for two or three hours. You gotta get me to a washroom. I've gotta get a smoke!"

Jack moved toward the edge of the crowd entering the chapel, leading his dad to the washroom area for a smoke, but a few more people, anxious to meet his parents, interrupted them. Jack introduced Bob and Daisy to them and quickly got trapped in conversation. As Jack tried to politely excuse himself and his parents, slipping toward the edge of the throng, the ushers came into view and motioned for everyone to take their seats. Not wanting to be rude, Bob and Jack turned around and entered the chapel. Before they knew it, they were sitting on the bench and the singing had begun. Bob Davidson never made it to the washroom for that cigarette.

There was no laughing that night. No mocking, no jeers, no sneers as planned. Robert and Daisy and five family members came under something that they had never experienced before. A power moved in. The presence of God was thick in the room that night, and when the preacher spoke, conviction gripped their hearts. When the altar call was given, seven of them walked forward to give their lives to Jesus. Bob knew what this meant. Eufrasio Pelissero and others had told him about the gospel. His own son, Jack, had been totally transformed right in front of his eyes. He knew that this decision meant a radical change of lifestyle; and for the first time ever, that's all he wanted.

That night Robert and Daisy Davidson met Jesus. He entered their lives and wiped away their self-righteous feeling of superiority and the false comfort they had nurtured, numbering themselves among those of the Queen's religion. They saw themselves simply as sinners in need of a savior. They could no longer stand in the presence of a Holy God on the strength of their own righteousness.

Bob and Daisy were saved and filled with the Holy Spirit the same night. They lingered at the altar while God did a thorough cleansing of their lives, giving them a language they had never learned. They arrived back at the farmhouse in the wee hours of the morning, transformed into new creations. They had become followers of Jesus, and everything was going to change. Robert's telling of the story in years to come, usually included the phrase, "I never ever got to smoke that last cigarette!"

Prior to his conversion, Robert and his family lived by a kind of "Robin Hood" credo; only instead of robbing from the rich and helping the poor, they, being the poor, simply helped themselves. The Davidsons were good ol' boys; not bad by many people's standards—they would help a neighbor dig a drainage ditch all day in the hot sun or pouring rain—but if you had it and they needed it, they would find a way to take it. The cedar shakes on the chicken coop came from the construction site for the new school. Nobody guarded site supplies on the weekends, and the chicken coop did need siding. The steel gate to the pigpen took them two consecutive foggy nights to obtain. The first night, when it was dark, Robert and the boys stopped and loosened all the rigging until the gate just rested there. The second foggy night, it took only about sixty seconds to remove the bolts from the hinges and load it on the back of a truck. The family needed a mailbox. One was "borrowed"—once again, under cover of darkness—painted and put on a post in the ground by the next morning. They reasoned that they really needed it and the one they took it from didn't need it quite as much.

This moral code was innate. Every Davidson knew it. Be loyal to friends. Always put in an honest day's work. Be faithful to your wife. Don't swear around women. Steal only from the rich. But after his Braeside conversion, Robert Davidson's custom-made ethics no longer worked for him.

By 1954 Robert had partnered with Peter Grecco in a sawdust delivery business—Grecco and Davidson—that was often kept afloat via some shady dealings. The company supplied sawdust to be used in the purification process of abrasives. The sawdust was easily accessible, the result of all those connections with sawmills Robert had developed over the years, and Peter had the trucks. The business was mostly about loading and transporting. Peter lined up the end-users, and Bob oversaw the supply and delivery.

Peter and Bob saw the world from the same perspective—until 1958. That's the year Bob became a Christian. Shortly after his conversion, Bob walked into the office, shut the door behind him and announced, "Pete! I got saved! I'm a Christian now and, well, Pete, we have to straighten up the business! That's all there is to it. We gotta straighten things up!"

"Whaddaya mean?" Pete had noticed the recent changes in Bob and was nervous about what was coming next. He knew his partner. When Bob looked him square in the eye, he had made a decision; and when Bob decided something, little could be done to change his mind.

"The business—the way we do it! We have to do right by folks. No more going into a factory with a half-empty truck, giving the shipper/receiver a bottle and getting a signature for a full load. Stuff like that. If we deliver a half-load, we're gonna invoice for a half-load."

"We'll go broke!" Peter protested. But Bob was resolute and nothing was going to budge him.

Within three years business had doubled and they had purchased a whole fleet of brand-new dump trucks. God honored Bob

Davidson's stand and his unsaved partner was a joint beneficiary. Pete, to my knowledge, never gave his heart to the Lord, though he admired Bob tremendously, and was in awe of the changes God wrought in his partner.

The man who used to think first of his own needs and the needs of his family, made a 180-degree about-face. Bob Davidson became a caring and generous man, known for his benevolent treatment of others.

Years after Bob died, Billy, his son, met Mr. Atkinson, a former supplier to Grecco and Davidson. Mr. Atkinson had been the owner of a sawmill that sold sawdust to Bob and Pete. They struck up a conversation and Bill asked him, "Do you remember my dad?"

"Remember him? What a prince of a man. Do you know what he did? Robert Davidson offered to pay more for the sawdust when we didn't even ask for it. A prince of a man, that Bob Davidson! Always treated everyone fair."

Once he became a Christian, Bob couldn't give enough. Whatever he had on him when he sat in church, he would deposit into the offering plate. Most of the time he didn't even count it; he just gave whatever he had. He used to say, "Don't let your left hand know what your right hand's doin'." Having seen it in the Bible, he practiced it literally, deliberately refusing to acknowledge the amount given even to himself, so as not to take any glory or credit that otherwise belonged to God. Giving to God was Robert Davidson's duty and privilege; it was the least he could do for God who had done so much for him, and he didn't require any recognition for it.

Billy, being the oldest of the second group of kids, and the oldest of those still living at home, took on the mantle of responsibility. All of the kids walked to school—a one-room, eight-grade schoolhouse nearly two miles from the farm. This was the school they would know until high school. With the varied ages of the students, a lot of bullying and fighting often broke out. Many times Billy took the bloody noses for his younger siblings. Small for his age and skinny, he wasn't much of a fighter, but he scrapped when he had to. As it turned out, he had to fight more often than not. Talking his way out of altercations wasn't an option; for as long as anyone can remember, Billy stuttered. It wasn't a mild stutter either. He hummed and his lips shook. It didn't matter whether the word started with a consonant or a vowel; each was as difficult as the other for Billy to get out. To this day, he remembers driving with his older brother Jack all the way to church in St. Catharines, and for forty minutes Jack would try, unsuccessfully, to get Billy to say "cookie" without a stammer.

In winter, Billy would suffer the cold weather, having given away mittens, scarves, and sometimes his coat to the younger ones who had left things at home or at school. The impact of the gospel and Sunday school had left a positive mark on him, even before the rest of his family came to be Christians. His temperate and patient character, oft admired by those who came into contact with him, became his most endearing quality. God was, even then, enlarging Billy's capacity for empathy and compassion, knowing others lives would depend on it.

In many ways, Billy had an idyllic childhood. The economic hardship his parents endured was a reality only for the first part of his childhood. Once on the farm, things improved dramatically for the Davidsons. While his older brothers had to work in the bush, Billy played in the bush. He spent much time in the forest alone. And in the forest, it didn't matter if he stuttered.

Alone in the bush, there was no pressure to speak. He could play and pretend, all the conversations occurring merely in his head. As a result, he developed a great imagination.

Stuttering didn't affect his reading either…at least not if he read silently. Reading out loud was difficult, if not impossible; an egregious demand exacted by unsympathetic teachers. But in Billy's mind, words flowed unhindered. He escaped into books, reading all the classics and then acting them out as a great adventurer in the bush.

The only time Billy didn't want to be alone was if he could go somewhere with his dad. Billy wanted to be at his father's side at every possible opportunity and it often started a squabble between Bob and Daisy. Billy, just in from outside, would discover his father about to go out and beg to go along. Bob, frustrated that Billy would delay his departure, would look at his son and give some excuse, "You're not ready. I'd have to wait for you and I don't have the time!"

"Let him go, Bob; it'll only take a minute to get him ready," Daisy would usually pipe in. "I'll take a minute and spruce him up." Invariably Billy was shirtless and covered in dirt. Daisy would spit-bathe his face, put his shirt on for him and present him to Robert in about thirty seconds flat.

"Look at him, Daisy! He doesn't even have a clean shirt!" Bob would complain.

Daisy's retort was swift and cutting. "It's the only shirt he's got, Bob," she would say, her tone emanating from behind a sarcastic grimace. That would be enough to stop Bob's protests, and Billy would tag along with an impish grin on his face.

Billy watched his dad intensely. His dad was Billy's hero. Robert's self-assurance and confidence seeped by osmosis into Billy. Not bothered in the least by Billy's speech impediment, Bob encouraged him to be everything he desired to be. This assurance allowed Billy to become comfortable with who he was.

He learned how much his father loved his mother, too. Billy could feel the admiration and respect Bob held for Daisy. He learned to tackle problems. He learned that if you put your hand to a task, the sky is the limit; that there's nothing that *can't* be accomplished. Billy began to take on the positive qualities of his dad, becoming a likeable and positive young man.

Billy was becoming a solid citizen, except for his sticky fingers. Billy had a buddy, Johnny, and the two of them used to visit an elderly bachelor who lived nearby. The man had a habit of leaving his bulging wallet on the kitchen table. To avoid suspicion, Billy and Johnny would remove only a bill or two—no more than five dollars at a time. Five dollars went a long way in 1950, and the boys always had a hard time spending it all. A hot roast beef sandwich with all the extras, some dessert, and candy after, added up to only $2.50. One time the old bachelor caught on and accused the boys of stealing his money. Although they both initially denied the crime, Billy's conscience got the better of him, and before he thought about what he was doing, he offered the old gentleman half the amount back. When they got outside, Johnny nearly killed him. Though Billy's kind heart didn't do much for his friendship with Johnny, it probably helped steer him away from a criminal career.

Daisy was an amazing mom and made each child feel as though he or she was her favorite. She was loving and gentle, but always working. With ten children—and nephew Gib making it eleven—and none of the modern conveniences that exist today, Daisy was in a perpetual state of exhaustion; yet she always found time to spend with each member of the family.

Daisy never looked healthy, and for as long as Billy could remember she didn't feel well. She simply persevered despite how she felt, rarely stopping or withdrawing from the daily grind of laundry, cooking, and cleaning. Black rings always encircled her eyes, and her stomach was upset much of the time. She looked worn. Thirteen full-term pregnancies in a twenty-year span had taken a toll, and by the time she became a Christian at forty-six years old, she was feeling worse than ever. She began to drink castor oil as a laxative, straight from the jug.

Daisy was an uncomplicated lady who appreciated the simplest gestures like the time Bob covered the plywood floors at the farmhouse with linoleum tiles. Daisy was ecstatic. Bob knew how she hated the bare wood.

Daisy always did the little things for people that told them they mattered. The poor and less fortunate flocked to Daisy at church; she insisted upon sitting with those who made others feel uncomfortable: people with perpetual running noses and body odor; the less loveable.

From the time of their conversion, Robert and Daisy had a little less than two years to sit together in church. When Bill was fourteen years old he came home from school one day and the regular routine was broken.

"Son, would you mind if I didn't do your face right now? I'm really not feeling that well. I'll do it later, okay?" Every day after school, without fail, Daisy prepared hot compresses and applied them to Billy's face. In the throes of puberty, Billy had fallen victim to an aggressive case of acne.

"Sure Mom—no problem," Billy answered. He had no way of knowing then that she would never be able to help him with the compresses again. The next day Daisy went into the hospital and would remain there for the better part of a year, diagnosed with cancer of the bowel.

Much of the care of the smaller children at home fell to Billy. The daily grind of getting them ready for school, and later helping with the homework and laundry, became his responsibility; and he did his best to fill the gap. The girls, just two and three years younger, helped out as well. Every night Bob would come home from work and, after eating supper—or sometimes without eating anything—he would take Billy and drive the forty minutes to St. Catharines General Hospital to visit Daisy. They would arrive at six-thirty and stay until nine o'clock in the evening.

In 1956, there was no universal health insurance plan in Ontario. Some of the costs of hospitalization and taking care of Daisy were covered by independent insurance, but most were borne by Robert Davidson, though he never mentioned it. God had continued to bless his sawdust delivery business and, thankfully, there were sufficient funds to pay for Daisy's care and meet the needs of family members still at home.

During this time, Bob grew strong in his faith. Immediately following his dramatic conversion to Christ, he began to study the Bible. Bob had only the equivalent of a fourth-grade education, but his retention was good and he had become a voracious reader. Though lacking a formal education, he was a man of immense knowledge and he demonstrated great wisdom. By the time Bob was saved a year, he knew the Bible better than most Christians do after ten, and he became an enthusiastic evangelist—talking to everyone he could about what Jesus had done in his life. Most people were attracted by his easy manner and wanted to hear what he had to say. He was a gentle but confident witness for Christ. He had always seemed a confident man to Billy; but after he began to walk with God, all of his strengths became magnified. It was as though God took the little he had and multiplied it many times over—as in the story of the loaves and fishes.

Billy remembered Bob often saying, "Jesus said we're to be the light of the world, son, but He didn't mean for us to sunburn everybody." It was a good example of his earthy and practical wisdom. Bob Davidson knew God and he knew people—and that's how he got by. God gave him the strength to endure and overcome in the greatest trial of his life—the battle to save his greatest love, Daisy.

Part of the Pentecostal distinctive within the greater evangelical movement was the belief that God still performs miracles and heals people today, and that Jesus hasn't changed from the time He walked the earth. Bob, Daisy, and all of the children who had become believers, together with their Elim Tabernacle church family, were praying passionately, believing God for a miracle. Special prayer meetings were called, and many made it their business to encourage the whole family in this darkest of times.

Daisy had already been healed once since she was saved; she went forward in an evangelistic crusade to elicit prayer for a sinus condition that both she and her twin brother had had since birth. (Neither of them had been able to breathe through their noses effectively, and the sinus blockage had been the source of severe migraine headaches for years.) After prayer, Daisy breathed through her nose for the first time in her memory and never again suffered a migraine. (Her brother died years later, never having been cured from the same obstructed breathing; likely a severely deviated septum.) Everyone was hoping, including Daisy, for another miracle.

In December 1957, Daisy was sent home from the hospital in a severely weakened condition. The doctors had prepared the family for her imminent demise and sent her home for Christmas, to die.

She didn't die, however, and was home for a couple of months before being re-admitted to the hospital.

When Daisy was diagnosed with cancer, Billy had just entered high school in Smithville. School had gone reasonably well for him, and the forty-student-one-teacher-per-room schoolhouse had prepared him remarkably well. Because grades came easily, Billy had never really developed into a good student. There was always so much going on at home, in the bush and on the farm, that he rarely studied or did homework, preferring to fly by the seat of his pants—and for the most part it worked out. Billy passed with honors all the way through to high school. Maybe it was his mother's sickness, or the added responsibilities at home, but Billy's interest in things academic began to wane and he began doing only what was needed to get by.

In September of 1958, after the first month of the eleventh grade, he decided that he had had enough of school. His brother

Ben had joined the Air Force years earlier, and Billy told everyone that he was going to do the same. Daisy had taken a turn for the worse in the hospital and, if he wasn't going to school, he could help out more at home while waiting to hear from the Air Force. At sixteen, Billy quit school.

As soon as he could, he applied and took the test for acceptance into the air force. He got high scores on all of the written tests and needed only to take his medical exam to get in. Unfortunately, the first thing on the physical for an Air Force cadet is a color test and, since Billy was color blind, he failed. Though disqualified for the Air Force, he was told that he could still be accepted in the Army. Billy was devastated. He had bragged to all of his friends at high school that he was going to be a pilot, and he was ultimately too embarrassed to go back and face them. He remained a high school drop-out and took a job as a printer's assistant at *The Smithville Review*, a small community newspaper. The twenty dollars per week salary put gas in the car and, since he still lived at home, he could manage. As a journeyman printer he could become a printer's apprentice and learn a trade, so he stuck it out at the print shop on a promise of better things to come.

The trips to the hospital every day had gotten longer and more arduous. Daisy had slipped into a coma by the middle of December 1958, and in her semiconscious state and fading physical condition, she could no longer speak. Billy remembered one of the last things that she ever said to him: "I'm sorry Billy."

"For what, Mom?" Billy couldn't think of one thing his mother had done for which she could possibly need to apologize.

"Sorry, son; I never ever did do your face that day!" Her voice was but a whisper, her body fading quickly into death, and she was concerned about not putting the hot compresses on Billy's face two years before.

"It's okay, Mom. It's okay."

The last few days before Christmas 1958, the tone of Billy's prayers changed. "God," he started in a broken voice, "heal her or take her home…heal her or take her home!" By now she labored over every breath. Every time that she exhaled there was a long pause and those in the room looked up, surprised that she took another one.

At five o'clock on December 23, 1958, the nurses brought in soup for Bob and Billy. They were there faithfully there every night, many times without having eaten supper; and though the hospital food wasn't meant for family, the staff provided it to the father and son keeping vigil. As Robert said grace over his soup, Billy heard him say, "Lord, your will be done."

It was as if he was surrendering the love of his life to the care of his Lord. Within a few minutes, Daisy seemed to stir. The two left their soup and went to her bedside. For the next five minutes Daisy's labored breathing eased and she breathed normally, as if in a deep and peaceful sleep...and then one of those peaceful breaths was her last. She went to be with Jesus. At twenty minutes after five, Daisy Davidson passed away. She was only fifty years old and Kenny, her youngest child, was just nine years old.

Robert called in the nurse. "My wife is gone," he whispered gently.

"No! No! It can't be!" The nurse rushed to the side of Daisy's bed and tried to find a pulse. Realizing she was gone, she broke down and cried. "She never ever rang the bell," she said between sobs. "She was in all that pain, and she never ever rang the bell."

Robert went over to the nurse who was heaving, big tears streaming down her face, and comforted her. Robert knew where Daisy was. After the funeral, several of the nurses who cared for Daisy those two years in the hospital came to the church and committed their lives to Jesus; such was the impact of this suffering but gracious woman.

The ride home that night was quiet. Neither Bob nor Billy said a word. When they arrived at the farmhouse, Bob went upstairs, gathered the other siblings around and told them thier Mom had gone to live with Jesus. Billy watched his father that night as he always did. He still appeared strong, stoic. Billy saw no tears, in keeping with the philosophy he had lived by most of his life: men must be men; they must be strong and crying isn't an option. Billy didn't know how much his father hurt.

At fifty years old, Bob Davidson was still an attractive man and there were plenty of women anxious to be his wife; but he never married again. He would spend the next twenty-three years as a widower. Once Billy asked him why he never remarried, especially given all the opportunity. It was then that he fully grasped the extent of his father's grief. "I had thirty wonderful years with a great woman," his dad said. "And…and I never want to go through that kind of hurt again."

Following Daisy's death, Robert was home more. He made sure to buy good quality groceries and special treats for his kids to ensure their health. He did the very best he could to raise the three boys and two teenaged daughters without a mother…but Alice and Naomi struggled to reinforce their fragile self-esteem at so vulnerable an age. Harry, the second youngest, a straight-A student all through school, saw his marks sink in the absence of his mom and survived a somewhat turbulent adolescence before establishing himself successfully in adulthood. Kenny, who lived the fewest years with his mom, has some of the most vivid memories of the loving words and actions of a lady who, in her short life, personified the sweet and compassionate character of Christ.

Just as I did, Billy put his hurt in a box and tried to forget about the loss of his mom. Every year that goes by (by the time of this writing he's lived without his mom three times longer than he lived with her), he feels the loss a little more and longs for the day he'll see her again in heaven.

Despite his grief and the pain he was in, Billy was about to get acquainted with the woman who would become the next great love of his life—though at this point, I was hardly a woman.

CHAPTER 7

Things Get Serious

One of my first recollections of doing anything with Billy occurred right after Daisy died. Strange as it may seem, on Boxing Day, following the funeral, the youth went bowling. To take his mind off the previous few days, Billy drove a group of us there. He didn't seem to notice me in the car. Barely fourteen, I seemed young to him—just a friend of his sisters—and though he was nice, our conversation was limited to small talk.

The young peoples group ranged in age from thirteen to thirty-five and many married couples with small kids still came to mentor and support the younger teenagers. In the Fifties, "college and careers groups" were still unheard of, and it seemed natural to have older young people with us. Friday night meetings were the highlight of the week, and nobody had to be coerced into attending. Various people took turns running the meetings, leading singing and worship, and sharing from the Bible. The whole group voted on the office of "youth president." My brothers, George and Ben, had each taken a turn to serve in this capacity, and soon Billy would too.

The A & W Drive-in Restaurant was a hot spot in town and, after the meetings, most of us went there for ice cream, floats, or burgers. Because Billy had a car, I often traveled with him and his sisters, Alice and Naomi. He was popular and self-assured even then. Despite his stutter (which came to be accepted as a feature of who he was), Billy was a leader. He had charisma and people liked to be around him.

Only two months before his seventeenth birthday and working for *The Smithville Review* in the printing shop, Bill—as he now insisted on being called—was involved in a workplace accident. As he was feeding newsprint into the press, he momentarily looked away to speak to his boss. Without realizing it, he fed his fingers in with the newsprint. His boss watched in horror as Bill's hand was crushed between the huge rollers. The trauma put Bill into shock and he didn't feel a thing. His boss yelled, "Bill! Your hand!" and he ran over to the emergency stop button, slamming his hand down to stop the machine.

He reversed the machine and Bill's hand was released—a mangled, crushed mass of bleeding flesh and bones. As his hand was being freed from the press, excruciating pain hit him. He was rushed to the hospital where they cleaned his hand, wrapped it in a bandage and sent him away. No one knew whether Bill would regain the full use of his fingers. With the pain dulled somewhat by painkillers, Bill decided to drive to young people's group that night. He steered with his one good hand while holding the other above his heart to ease the throbbing. At the end of the meeting, Bill drove his sisters and a volunteer from Elim home to the farm to help with the housework.

Sitting beside Bill in the front seat that night was a skinny little girl he had hardly paid attention to before. She sat beside him and gingerly held up his wounded hand while he drove. Bill noticed how compassionate and caring she was and, even though she dressed like a tomboy, he noticed she was cute—but then he quickly put the thought out of his mind. That girl was me—Margaret Hiebert. I was only fourteen years old; too young to date, and definitely too young for him—he was almost seventeen.

The car curved around a bend in Highway 20. The country roads were dark so Bill drove with the high beams on. He maneuvered the car with his one good hand, while I tried to keep the throbbing in the other to a minimum, holding it up above his heart. When another car veered toward us, Bill thrust his injured hand into the steering wheel, preventing a certain collision. We avoided the accident, but Bill was in agony; he had to wait at the side of the road for a few minutes to regain his composure. I held his throbbing hand the rest of the way, gently rubbing his forearm and soothing his pain.

When we arrived at the house in Caister, I unwound his bandages, washed his injured fingers, applied salve and changed the wrap. It was a disturbing sight, and Bill's sisters weren't up to the task. He needed someone to help him, and it just seemed logical for me to be the one to do it. That night Bill took notice of me. He saw something attractive within me. He sensed my pity and compassion for him, though he indicated nothing to me. Years later he told me that February 12, 1959, the day he hurt his hand, was the day he first had feelings for me. A year would go by, however, before our first date.

By the spring of 1960, Bill had become the last man on earth I wanted to date...at least that's what I told everybody. Where other boys would succumb to their inhibitions, Bill confidently invited girls on dates. Looking at him from afar, it seemed to me that he thought he was God's gift to women and that no girl would dare turn him down if he asked her out. Of course, it was my own insecurity that caused me to feel this way. I hated rejection and believed that if I didn't *want* Bill to ask me out, he wouldn't be able to reject me by not doing it. It was my way of controlling the hurt.

Ironically, my aloofness was the very catalyst Bill needed. Intrigued by my ambivalence towards him, he finally asked me out. We went out a few times and had fun, but we weren't going steady. I was very fond of him but wouldn't let him know it. If he knew I liked him, I reasoned, he would dump me for sure, because it was impossible for anyone to *really* like me. I didn't like myself. I carried my big secret in the back of my mind, and I knew that if anyone truly knew what I had done (for I felt complicit in my own abuse) they would hate me as much as I hated myself.

We both still dated other people. Most times dates were really group gatherings, but when a boy asked you to go with him in his car, it was considered a date. Dates on Fridays with Bill included his two sisters in the back seat. On Sunday nights, his younger brothers, Harry and Kenny, tagged along, too. Bill and I dated casually during March, April, and May in 1960. I was about to turn sixteen in June, when things came to an abrupt end.

Bill would drive me home last so that we could talk and spend a little more time with each other. One night in the middle of May he drove me toward my house on Sherbourne Street. When we stopped at the edge of an intersection at a stop sign, Bill leaned over and kissed me. I sensed that it was coming and kissed him back.

When it dawned on Bill what he had done, he felt he had presumed too much. "I'm sorry..." he said. "I shouldn't have done that." (Most of the young men in that era felt that kissing a girl was a sign of a commitment. He figured that, if he was kissing me, I would expect to be going steady and would soon anticipate a marriage proposal.) We weren't a couple in the strictest sense; he hadn't given me his ring and we weren't going steady.

Bill drove home after dropping me off, thinking about the kiss. Concerned that I thought his commitment was greater than it was, and surprised by the strength of his own feelings for me, he determined to back off. Though he was nice to me at church following "the kiss," he didn't ask me out again for the entire summer. Bill's impulsive feelings scared him—but he wouldn't discuss that with me. I wondered what I did to offend him. I promised myself that if he asked me out again, I wouldn't let him kiss me. I believed that because he had gotten what he wanted, the kiss, the challenge had been met and he had moved on to a new one. Without knowing it, Bill had rejected me. I felt stupid and vulnerable, and I hated feeling that way. All summer I was angry with him. I felt sure he was ignoring me at church and felt awkward whenever he was near.

Bill, oblivious to my feelings, spent the summer of 1960 dating lots of girls and earning a reputation for playing the field. Nobody believed Bill could be interested in a steady girlfriend, and news of his dating adventures reached our church youth group before he did.

One of Bill's friends, Fred Gough, was about forty years old and, before finding Jesus as his Savior, was an alcoholic. Though Bill did not remember the incident that defined their relationship, Fred did. Often the young people would spend an hour or two after youth handing out gospel tracts on the streets. As he was exiting a bar, Bill handed Fred a tract. The tract convinced Fred that he was living a godless life and was heading for hell. On the reverse side of the literature was Elim Tabernacle's address, and Fred found himself there the next Sunday, walking the aisle and committing his life to Christ. His conversion was genuine and soon he was freed from the grip of alcohol. From that moment on, this older bachelor started hanging out with the young guys at Elim's youth group. Fred's apartment became a popular haunt for the guys, and Bill spent a lot of time driving Fred around. (Fred had had an accident while impaired and had spent a year in jail, in addition to losing his driver's license.)

In the fall of 1960, Fred needed to take a trip to Missouri and asked Bill to drive him there over the long Labor Day weekend. Bill drove and talked with Fred. It was a time for him to slow down and consider the things going on in his life, and he began to think more seriously about the girl he couldn't get out of his mind—me.

During the first two weeks of October, Elim held a two-week series of revival meetings. Revival meetings took place once a year or so, and the emphasis was firmly placed on inviting friends, acquaintances, and family members that were not born-again Christians. Usually there was a fiery evangelist preaching, and the congregation was encouraged to support the meetings with their attendance, finances, and prayers. Bill and I attended nearly every meeting and, following each service, we went out for Cokes and ice cream. Bill seemed different now. His attention was squarely upon me, and he didn't seem so distracted. We hit it off. But this time, true to the promise I made to myself, I didn't let him kiss me. When he tried, I turned my head away and said no.

Instead of being discouraged, Bill was challenged by my rebuff and determined to show me how much he liked me—just me. The gauntlet had been laid down, and Bill was compelled to pick it up. He was starting to figure out that I was not like all the others—he would have to work to win the affections of this girl.

Since the summer, I had been looking elsewhere for dates. My Uncle Bill Thiessen had a boarder staying at his house named Harvey, and I had implored Uncle Bill to set me up with a date. He wasn't a Christian, but I thought he was a nice fellow and Uncle Bill vouched for his character. By the time Harvey accepted Uncle Bill's proposal, however, it was too late.

On Friday evening, November 25, 1960, Bill, who had been doing much thinking about relationships since his summer ride to Missouri, confided in his two sisters on the way to young people's meeting: "I think I'm going to ask a girl to go steady with me tonight."

Alice and Naomi went directly to Judy, another girl in the youth group who Bill had dated casually during the previous six months.

"Judy! Bill told us! He's gonna ask a girl to go steady tonight after young peoples. Get ready! We think he's gonna ask you!"

It was a logical assumption in many ways, because Bill had taken Judy out a lot and others thought they would make a lovely couple. That night however, Bill asked me to go out after the meeting. At Mason's Restaurant he gave me his ring to wear. It was official—we were going steady.

The next day was Saturday and, after working in the National Bakery all day, I went babysitting. Uncle Bill phoned me: "Margaret, it's Uncle Bill. I finally arranged for you to go out with my friend, Harvey. How about tomorrow?"

"Oh, Uncle Bill! I'm sorry. I can't go out with Harvey now. Bill Davidson asked me to go steady last night and I said yes. I'm wearing his ring." I felt bad that Uncle Bill had gone to the trouble to set me up with Harvey, but the timing couldn't have been worse.

"He did what? You said what? Billy Davidson? You know he'll break your heart! If you're going steady with him, where is he tonight? How come he isn't taking you out tonight, eh?" Uncle Bill was flabbergasted. He knew that Bill and I hadn't been seeing each other since the spring. He was also aware of Bill's growing reputation.

"Oh, tonight he had to speak at his father's cottage prayer meeting at the farm," I answered, already having to defend the honor of my new boyfriend and my own decision to say yes to Bill.

"Speaking at his dad's prayer meeting! That's what he told you he's doing on a Saturday night? Margaret, c'mon! You believed him? He's probably out right now with another girl while you're home babysitting. I'm warning you, that Billy Davidson is a heartbreaker!"

"I'm sorry Uncle Bill, I am going steady and you'll just have to tell Harvey I can't go out with him."

"Okay. Okay. I'll tell him. But don't come crying to me when he breaks your heart!"

With that Uncle Bill hung up the phone and I was left to consider whether what he said was true. I just couldn't believe that Bill Davidson would ask me to go steady and then take another girl out the next day; nevertheless, I was sure Bill would eventually dump me. I thought about it every time we prepared to go out. *This could be the night, the night he tells me he doesn't want to see me again. When he finds out what I am really like, he won't want to have anything to do with me.* I prepared myself for the worst so that I wouldn't be shocked when I heard the words come out of his mouth. Even with the passage of time, a year later, I still believed Bill would ultimately reject me. After all, every man in my life—including my father—had.

During the summer of 1960, I had gotten a part-time job at the National Bakery and, heading into the fall, the cake decorator quit. The owner offered me the job. I had completed the ninth grade at St. Catharines Collegiate, but had trouble focusing. School officials recommended that I take a remedial class for grade ten. Already one year behind from failing the sixth grade, and never excelling in school, I brought up the job opportunity at the bakery with Mom. She encouraged me to take it. I would make thirty dollars a week at the bakery, with half going to Mom; my quitting school was a financial windfall for her.

Living at home, I could certainly survive on fifteen dollars per week, and I wouldn't feel like such a failure all the time. School frustrated me and added to the personal conviction that I was stupid. Because I could bake and decorate cakes, my self-esteem rose—I could provide for myself. Taking the bakery job made me feel adult.

Pocketing fifteen dollars for five and a half days' work made me think I had died and gone to heaven. I still had to clean the house and wash all the floors every Saturday afternoon, but I felt great having my own money. I could buy my own clothes and even save. I had never felt so independent.

Soon after I began work at the National Bakery, Dad returned home. Coming home—that was one of his schemes to weasel out of the money he owed Mom, and this time he even spoke of becoming a Christian. Since his denial of my existence that day at the grocery checkout, my relationship with Dad was barely detectible. I spoke to him when I had to, but was barely civil. My sincere hatred for him seeped out in unconscious sarcasm. I'm sure he felt the freezing cold breeze I emitted whenever we were together, but he never brought up what happened at the supermarket and I never forgot it.

"Whatever I've done," he would say, without acknowledging what both he and I knew was between us, "you have to forgive me. You know I've become a Christian and Christians forgive each other."

He mocked my Christianity. At the time I refused to believe he had actually committed his life to Christ. Nothing had changed. He still drank. He still went out with the boys. The only thing different was that he was eating our groceries again. My cynicism proved to be warranted as once again he left. He had stayed only long enough to realize that back-payments of child support were still due even if he moved back in.

On Friday nights Bill and I saw each other at young peoples, and Saturdays he usually picked me up for his dad's cottage prayer meeting. I would hurry to get my chores done so that Mom would have no excuse to keep me home. It didn't stop her from trying, though. In the first few months we were a couple, Bill would often come early, helping with the last of the floors so that we could get away earlier. Invariably when we were just about to leave, Mom would get violently ill. Every Saturday. Mom didn't want to be alone, and the only way she knew to keep us there was to have some angina or stomach attack. She would bring on legitimate symptoms and even look like she was close to death's door. She breathed heavily and clutched her chest as if she were having a full-blown heart attack. The first few times this happened, Bill suggested we stay with her and not go out. Curiously, an hour or two later, when it was too late for us to go anywhere, she would recover—miraculously. It didn't take long for us to recognize the pattern, and then, instead of staying home, we would have a word of prayer with her and leave.

As we walked out the door she would be yelling after us: "You shouldn't leave. I von't be here vhen you get back. I'll be dead! You vill see!" (Years later I saw my own mother's behavior acted out by Redd Fox on the television sit-com *Sanford & Son*. Mom acted exactly like Mr. Sanford did when his son Lamont didn't do things the way he wanted; right down to the way he clutched his heart.)

Mom was never in favor of my dating. She discouraged any and all boys who took me out. For her it was all about survival. Dating would lead to marriage and her abandonment. Her children would leave and she would be alone. Ben, Dave, and I were Mom's support, financially and emotionally. To her, dating represented the loss of her personal security. Besides that, she just hated to be alone.

The first time I brought Bill home to 17 Sherbourne Street, Mom met us at the door. She pulled me behind her and faced my bewildered date. She pointed her finger at him, looked him in the eye and said, "I don't vant you takink Margaret out anymore! Okay? You don't come here for her no more, ya?"

The whole time Mom was talking, I stood behind her using my best sign language, and motioning with my finger next to my temple that she was crazy. Though no sound was coming out, I mouthed the words, "Don't listen to her! It doesn't matter what she says. Everything will be all right." Bill realized from that first meeting that Mom was a desperate person, and he made it his mission to win her over. Eventually he did. In the end I think she liked him more than me—at least he didn't garner as much criticism.

From time to time we took Mom with us to Bob Davidson's prayer meeting. If we didn't have Harry and Kenny with us on our dates, shining flashlight beams on us as Bill walked me to the door, Mom was with us because she didn't want to be by herself. Though I complained at the time, Bill was showing me his soft and compassionate nature. "You shouldn't be so hard on your mom," he would admonish, "She's had a tough life." I was incensed, and hearing Bill tell me that Mom had had a tough life did nothing to ease my anger. In time I realized that Bill's mom was gone, and he probably would have preferred a bad mom, to no mom.

It was that nature that gave me the confidence to do what I always knew I would have to do. Even though Bill seemed like a gentle, understanding man, it would take all the courage I could muster to trust him.

We had been going out for a year-and-a-half and things were beginning to get serious. I started to test Bill. "Do you love me, Bill?" I would quiz.

"Time'll tell," he would say with a mischievous grin on his face. "Only time will tell!"

Needless to say, that was not the response I was looking for. *Time will tell*. I didn't have time. Before I would wrap myself up any tighter with Bill Davidson, I knew I needed to tell him my *secret*. Even though I knew there was nothing I could have done to stop Willie's attacks on me, the fact that Bill didn't know who he was dating bothered me. I felt dishonest. I was a fraud. If Bill knew I was *damaged goods*, at least he could make the decision to love me or dump me, having all the facts. As it was, I thought I was deceiving Bill, tricking him into loving someone who really didn't exist. Bill thought that he was dating a church girl, a *virgin*, from a Christian home.

He would sometimes bring up the subject of marriage. "One day I'm going to marry you," he would say, only half kidding.

"You don't want to marry me!" I always responded.

"Sure I do. Why wouldn't I? Why wouldn't anyone want to marry you? You wait. Someday we'll be married." The verbal sparring would dissipate into laughter or goofing around, and the subject would be forgotten until the next time.

One night in May 1962, Bill was driving me home after a Sunday evening service. He parked the car several blocks away so we could talk. He often did this, not wanting to pull right up to the house, knowing that Mom would be waiting at the door. "Honey, I do want to marry you." He wasn't joking this time. He sounded serious and passionate.

"Oh, Bill, you don't want to marry me." My tone was just as serious.

"Why? Why do you always say that? I really mean it. I want to marry you. We should think about when we can. We should make plans."

"Bill, stop." There was a long pause while I summoned all my courage. "I'm going...I'm going to tell you something now, and when I'm done, then you'll know why you won't want to marry me!" I quivered. The tears welled up in my eyes and forced their way down my cheeks. I spoke softly, my voice barely audible, afraid that if he picked up on everything I was telling him, he would bolt from the car.

"Bill, I'm not everything you think I am. I'm not a virgin." He just sat there in kind of a stupor, floored by what he was hearing—but not bolting; so I continued. "I'm not a virgin because one of my older brothers, my alcoholic brother, did things to me."

"What do you mean?" he asked, buying himself time to react. I could tell that in his innocent farm life, he had never imagined such things.

"He forced me Bill! He forced me!" As the words came from my lips, the dam broke; the pent-up tears I had been trying to hold back burst through, and I felt myself against Bill's chest, heaving with great sobs. "He forced himself on me for a very long time...I can't remember for how long...since I was three or four years old. It stopped a couple of years ago."

I thought for sure that by this point in my story, Bill would be pushing me away; unable to deal with the pain of losing the high opinion he had held of his girlfriend. Instead, he pulled me close and wrapped both of his arms around me. I sobbed and sobbed. Big spaces of time went by with nobody saying anything. Bill just held me and let me cry.

"I'm spoiled for you, Bill. I'm not a virgin. You won't want to marry me because I'm not a virgin!" My words were slow in coming out, halted with big involuntary breaths, the kind little kids make when they're trying to stop crying. I was trying not to cry, but I was scared. I was scared of losing Bill. I was full of shame. I honestly felt in that moment that, if Bill stayed with me, if he married me, he was being ripped off. He could have had any girl he wanted—a good one, not one as messed up as I was.

"I don't care if you're a virgin. I mean...I mean it doesn't matter to me. It doesn't make any difference to the way I feel about you. It's gonna be okay. It's gonna be okay, Honey." He couldn't have said anything more wonderful to me at that moment. I didn't believe him, but still, it was nice of him to say it. He was being so loving and gentle. He wasn't angry. He didn't get upset. All he did was try to comfort me.

After a long pause, he asked, "Which brother?"

"Wil-*ugh*-lie, my al-*ugh*-co-*ugh*-holic brother, Willie," I stammered.

Then Bill said something that he didn't intend to say, but that just seemed to surge up from the pit of his stomach. "I'll kill 'im! I'm gonna kill 'im."

It suddenly angered him that the young woman in his arms sobbing, the one he cared so much about, had been hurt. She had been hurt badly, and he knew who was guilty. After a few moments, his anger subsided. He stopped thinking about Willie and his attention turned to me: a heaving and shaking little girl in his arms. Then Bill began to cry with me. He cried with me. He didn't leave me. He didn't tell me what I should have done to fight Willie off, or how I should have told somebody or how I should have run to get help after the first time so that I didn't have to endure his rapes for ten years. He just cried with me.

For months I had wanted to hear Bill say the three words that I thought would make me feel secure, "I love you." Bill didn't think to say them to me that night—the words didn't come from his mouth—but every fiber of his being, every muscle in his arms that held me, told me that he did. His love was apparent from his actions, and his embrace communicated as much love as words ever could have. For an hour in the car, he just kept whispering, "I'm sorry, Honey, I'm so sorry! It'll be all right. Everything's gonna be all right."

After a time of silence, doubt would fill my mind again and I would say, "You're just saying it's all right *now*. It's gonna make a difference later. You're not going to be able to love me; you're just saying that now. When you really think about things, it's gonna matter. This is gonna change everything!"

I would finish and a whole new wave of tears would flow, and then Bill would say for the umpteenth time, "Margaret, nothing's gonna change. Everything's gonna be okay. Trust me, we're going to be okay." He never ran out of patience. As many times as I needed reassurance, he gave it to me—tenderly, lovingly.

At long last, I cleaned up my face and thanked him for being so understanding. He dropped me off at 17 Sherbourne Street and I cried myself to sleep that night, thinking that in a few days, when he came to his senses, he would break things off. I couldn't have been more wrong.

When Bill asked the question he had asked so many times before, he never dreamed he would be hearing the details of ten years of sexual abuse. This kind of thing was not publicized in newspapers or on television in 1960. No one talked about legitimate sexual behavior publicly; let alone this kind of horror. Even discussion about sexual indiscretion would be limited to an acknowledgement of a couple "having to get married." The subject was not expanded upon, and people spoke in hushed tones, ashamed of the sound of their gossip. Having to get married, with everyone knowing you were no longer a virgin, was the ultimate humiliation, especially within Church circles. If it hadn't been his girlfriend of eighteen months, if he had heard about this happening to someone he only knew casually, or even a perfect stranger, Bill would have felt devastated, sick to his stomach. The fact that it was Margaret who had endured such horrific treatment for the bulk of her childhood, and not some stranger, made the whole event surreal.

Bill drove the forty minutes home to Caister Center murmuring to himself, "I can't believe it! I can't believe this happened to Margaret. How could Willie, how could her own brother, have done this to her? How can she be so normal? God what am I supposed to do with this?"

All Bill wanted to do was protect me—to rescue me from my house of horrors. Besides the urge to protect me, he felt hatred for Willie. *The next time I see him*, he thought, *I'm going to want to kill him.* He knew it was wrong to hate, and thought of Jesus who prayed for those who crucified him. But his yearning for justice felt warranted. Our "talk" had deepened his love for me significantly. He felt closer to me than ever before. What I had entrusted to Bill in the car that night had elevated our relationship—things had gotten much more serious. He had yet to tell me that he loved me, though he knew he did. He realized he couldn't be careless with me; I was too fragile. It took tremendous courage for me to tell him my secret, and he wasn't about to leave me feeling insecure and dubious of our future. No longer indecisive about our relationship, he knew that he loved me and wanted to marry me, and he immediately began to confirm it with words.

Hearing him say "I love you" made me feel safe, and, wanting me to feel as secure as possible, Bill began to say those three words at every opportunity. He was tender and patient with me and, though he never brought up the subject of my abuse, he would talk about it when I wanted to. The truth is, I seldom brought it up again. The monkey was off my back. My secret was out. I had told a man my secret! I trusted Bill. To bring it up too often might just rock the boat.

Despite Bill's wonderful response to the secret, it was always a relief to get to the end of a night and discover he hadn't broken up with me. If he said my name with too long a pause following it, I would prepare myself for the blow: "*Margaret, I've tried, but I just can't deal with everything that's happened to you. I think of you differently now—maybe we should break it off...*" My body would tense, waiting for the inevitable moment when he would come to his senses and realize he could have a normal girl, when he would finally be sickened by the sight of me. I was perpetually insecure, despite the words Bill said to convince me otherwise.

It is difficult to explain the depth of shame that a victim of sexual abuse feels. My privacy, my soul, had been exposed without permission. The things we entrust to only one other person our whole lives—and then only through cautious courtship and the scrutiny of time—had been violently stripped from me, hundreds of times. The comfort that I should have had—that other people have—with their own nudity, was stolen from me. The violation and personal ridicule, the humbled, shamed feeling I had always felt, even while changing my clothes by myself, is indescribable. For Bill to know my secret and still love me was difficult to accept. My body had been raped, but the raping of my soul was much more difficult to overcome. God knew I needed a patient man, even more than I did.

Willie expressed no shame for what he had done, but I lived my whole life conscious of my heap of shame. Even though I hid it, I was sure people could see it. Paranoia surrounded my secret. Whenever anyone got too close to the box I kept it in and I feared its exposure was immanent, I lashed out, grasping at an ever-elusive sense of dignity. In sharing my secret with Bill, I risked everything. If he dumped me, he could tell everybody and the whole world would reject me. I walked through life fearing everyone could see the scarlet letter on my chest: not *A* for adultery, as in the nineteenth-century novel, but *I* for incest. Shame, shame—how would I ever be rid of it? I interpreted even perfectly normal behavior as rejection.

Bill was young people's president by this time, and though we were going steady and were quite serious, he felt obligated to set an example to the younger teens. When we were together in a group, he didn't publicly display affection: no kissing, no cuddling, and no holding hands. I took this to mean he was ashamed of me—and it made me angry. I wanted public affirmation. I longed for Bill to put his arm around me, hold my hand, and kiss me. Only a public demonstration of his love would do—affection he gave me when we were alone, I discounted.

Because I didn't truly believe Bill could love me, I looked for evidence to prove he didn't. I had lived with the belief that all men would eventually hurt me, because most of the ones I had known had. Men were fakers and con artists and their true nature would show after initial pretenses of sensitivity and kindness wore off. Bill was only the second person to know my secret and I wondered if I had made a terrible mistake by trusting him. It is difficult enough for well-adjusted teenagers to learn principles of love and trust, but with the baggage I carried, it was next to impossible. Bill couldn't do anything right.

Bill's continued silence about "our talk" had me convinced that my secret bothered him. In reality, Bill didn't obsess about it twenty-four hours a day—I did. He saw me only as the girl he loved, not as a spoiled virgin. Instead of a heap of shame, he saw Margaret Hiebert and all her good points. Still, my unpredictable outbursts and instantaneous mood swings troubled him. Willie's attacks had stopped, but the hurting had not. I desperately needed Jesus to heal me and to show me how to forgive...but it would be several years before I would realize it.

CHAPTER 8

Engaged

The summer of 1961 was especially difficult. In addition to bearing my soul to Bill and dealing with the myriad emotions that surfaced as a result, Ruby, my best friend and confidante, moved away. The Ens family had always dreamed of buying a farm and returning to Saskatchewan. At seventeen I was experiencing my first full summer without my only close friend, and I missed her terribly. Girls need other girls, and without Ruby nearby, I began to place Bill in an impossible position: I expected him to meet all of my emotional and friendship needs. I held him to such a ridiculous standard that he couldn't help but disappoint.

Experience had taught me that life was about levels. I had quit school and was working full time—level one. The next level had to be marriage. Marriage would solve all my problems. I would be rid of Mom and that house full of bad memories. Bill was telling me he loved me, but the real proof could only be realized at the next level—I needed the ring. Talking about marriage some time in the future wasn't enough. I wanted a diamond!

Bill and I were both working and I couldn't wait until we were working on a life together.

That fall, Willie's marriage finally broke apart. He had become a drunk and as irresponsible a husband and father as his mentor, my dad. Mom welcomed him back home and gave him a room upstairs. Five years after he left, Willie was back. Bill was concerned and warned me to be careful, and I was. Whenever I thought I might have to be home alone with Willie, I altered my plans. Thankfully he was out drinking most of the time and our paths rarely crossed. Nevertheless, a greater measure of stress and anxiety accompanied his return. One of the few times I spoke to him, it was to warn him of Bill.

"Willie, I have a boyfriend now, so you'd better watch your step! If you lay a finger on me, he'll be over here in a minute to lay a beating on you!" Willie heeded the warning and proved more a nuisance and a source of embarrassment than a threat.

At times Bill would drive me home to find Willie sprawled out on the lawn or laying across the entrance to our house, passed out in a drunken stupor. One wintry Saturday night around midnight, we found him laying face down in a snow bank. Concerned that he might freeze out there, Bill tried to drag him into the house. But Willie snapped out of his drunken fog and, not realizing Bill was trying to help him, started cursing and wildly throwing punches before finally collapsing. Unable to lug him up the stairs and into his room, we left him on the couch for the night. I was very embarrassed.

Bill wanted me out of that house. Hatred for Willie had turned to pity and disgust at how he was wasting his life. Sometimes Bill stayed the night to ease his own mind. He would sleep in my bed and I would sleep in Mom's with her. Mom believed he didn't want to drive back to the farm so late at night, but Bill couldn't bear the thought of leaving with Willie in the house.

Late in November of 1962, I finished up my shift at the National Bakery and made my way to the bus stop. Though not officially winter, it felt like it. It was already dark and I bundled myself up, looking forward to the warmth the bus would offer.

St. Catharine's city buses were the flat, snub-nosed types where the driver actually sat ahead of the front tires. Behind the driver was a regular two-person seat, but facing him, beside the door and across the aisle, there was a long four-person seat running parallel to the outside wall. If unoccupied, that's where I would sit. I felt safer looking at the driver. He had a uniform and looked like he was in charge. From this vantage point I could look to my right and see out the windshield, and to my left and see everyone that was on the bus.

I boarded the bus and sat down in my favorite spot. Behind the driver sat a middle-aged man wearing a long trench coat. I glanced over casually before looking away. From the downtown bakery to Facer Street, the stop nearest my house, was a ten- to fifteen-minute ride. About halfway home I looked up at the peculiar man across the aisle. Since he wasn't facing me, I took the liberty to look at him a little longer.

I guessed him to be in his mid-forties. He was scruffy, with at least a two-day beard, and was obviously inebriated. I recognized the all-too-familiar signs. I could smell alcohol and my instincts told me in an instant that he was wasted. I hated being around drunks. The only thing liquor had ever given me was heartache. Experience warned that the presence of a drunk meant something bad was about to take place. I sat uneasily in my seat, checking him out every thirty seconds or so.

As the bus approached my neighborhood, I looked up at the man and went white. He was staring straight at me with a wicked grin on his face. He had opened up the trench coat, and though he was shielded from the view of the bus driver, he was fully exposed to me. His pants were open and he was holding his penis! Pointing it in my direction, he motioned as though masturbating.

I was paralyzed in fear. I tried to get the attention of the bus driver, but my tongue was firmly stuck in my throat. I couldn't say anything. All I could think about was getting off of that bus! With one motion, I scooped up my stuff, jumped up, and rang the bell for the driver to let me out at the next stop. I waited by the door, my back toward the exposed man. As soon as the doors opened, I bolted. I started running and crying, too scared to look back to see if I was being followed. I felt that any moment the man was going to reach for me. I just tried to run faster.

It didn't take me too long to realize that I was still a half mile from home. The combination of darkness and my blurred vision couldn't slow me down. It occurred to me that if I zigzagged and cut through people's yards, I might be able to lose him. I plowed through shrubs, trees, and yards, strategically making my way home. Finally I got to my front door and burst inside.

"Mom! Mom!" There was no answer. "Mom! Are you home? Please answer me!" I pleaded.

It was Wednesday night and Mom had already left for the mid-week Bible study at Elim Tabernacle. No one was home. I was soaked with sweat and panting like a dog. I looked out the front door. I couldn't see the drunken man. I didn't even know if he got off the bus—I assumed he had. Relief began to assuage my hysteria; but then I realized something else…something even more terrifying. Willie could be coming home any minute! The immanent threat of Willie arriving plunged me back into wild panic.

I wasn't thinking rationally and believed that at any moment Willie would walk through that door and rape me as he had all those times before. Suddenly everything that Willie had ever done to me came back. All the pain and torture, all the fear and helplessness, rushed into my head. Weakened by the terrifying incident on the bus, I was ill-equipped to suppress thoughts of Willie. My mind, normally so controlled, was now left unguarded and every fear I ever felt was stacked one upon the other. The fear brought on by a flasher on a city bus became the more familiar dread I always felt when I knew Willie was coming for me.

What I was experiencing was a "trigger"—an event similar, but unrelated to abuse that throws the victim right back in thought and emotion to the center of a previous attack. The flasher, for all intents and purposes, was Willie. He triggered the buried memories of Willie's rapes and I was transported back to the point of being a helpless little girl. I had convinced myself that if I could just control my feelings and thoughts, and not think about the abuse, I would be okay. But an arbitrary event had triggered my memory and had taken me right back to the bedroom—tied up, fighting, and waiting for Willie to be done with me. I had had nightmares, but this was no nightmare! My fear was overwhelming and I couldn't simply wake up and escape.

Finally I rushed to the phone and called Bill at work. Through the crying and screaming, somehow, Bill got the gist of what happened.

"Stay in the house! Lock the door—I'll be right there! I'm leaving now, okay?" His voice was reassuring—but I couldn't stay in that house.

"I'll be walking up and down the street!" I said. "That way if Willie comes home I'll just duck into a neighbor's house. Look for me, Bill. I'll be walking up and down the street!"

The threat had turned from a stranger in a trench coat to Willie, and I would *not* be waiting in that house for him to arrive.

I had sounded so hysterical on the phone that Bill rushed out of the printing shop mumbling incoherently to his boss about an emergency. He raced down Highway 20 in the dark, aware of only one thing: I was in trouble. There was a paving crew on the wrong side of the road and Bill slammed on his brakes to avoid their truck. With all four tires locked and skidding, the car slid sideways, stopping inches from a telephone pole. For a moment Bill just sat there trying to regain his composure; then he nudged ahead, palms sweating and face ghostly white.

Calm down! He told himself. She'll be fine until you get there. As he drove he was thinking about what I had said to him on the phone and it all seemed inconceivable. Who were these people showing their private parts and playing with themselves? Margaret said she was sure the guy followed her off the bus! Oh, God, keep Margaret safe until I get there! Bill worried and prayed and told himself positive things the whole time he drove. Soon the pedal hit the floor again—he had already forgotten about the close call with the tar truck. I have to get to Margaret!

Although usually a forty-five minute drive from *The Smithville Review* to 17 Sherbourne Street, Bill made it in thirty. He pulled around the corner and saw me a few houses down the street.

I had been on the street the entire time, shaking both from cold and fear. It seemed an eternity since Bill had said he was coming. I climbed into his car and sobbed in his arms for half an hour. Bill just held me.

He held me and tried to get me to stop shivering. "Try to forget about it, Honey. It's okay. I'm here now. You're safe."

"Bill, I was so scared! He made me think of Willie all over again! Why does this keep happening to me? Why, Bill? Why?"

Eventually I calmed down and we drove to the A&W to get our minds off the night's events. At the restaurant we sat in the car as I talked more about everything that happened that night—and about Willie. Bill listened patiently, but didn't really understand why I kept bringing up the past. All he knew was that talking made me feel better, so he let me talk.

It might have been the times and the culture of the early Sixties, but neither Bill nor I even considered calling the police. (Today it would be the first thing I would do.) Back then such incidents weren't in the news. The media didn't report sexual assaults, and I had never even heard about flashers. The fact that the man exposed himself to me was a total shock. I thought no one would even believe me. I was so glad Bill did.

This stuff only happens to me! I kept thinking. *Why me? Haven't I endured enough of this?* I wondered what the next trauma would be and was constantly on guard. What was there about me that brought out this kind of behavior? *These deviants must see some weakness in me*, I reasoned. I lived in fear of the next horrible thing that would happen to me. There were times, moments, when I believed that God had truly forgotten about me. *How could He be concerned about me while letting me go through this hell?*

I loved God, but events like this caused me to hear voices—not literal, audible sounds, but sinister words in my mind: You're being punished, Margaret. God knows how bad you really are and He's punishing you. Every time you shoot off your big mouth, God is listening and He's trying to teach you a lesson. He's trying to get your attention. Margaret, you just aren't good enough!

I saw God as holding a two-by-four, waiting until I messed up and smiling with glee when He caught me in a wrong. I thought He took pleasure in punishing me. At this point, knowing God as my heavenly Father was a foreign concept. My only point of reference for a father was the one I had; and if God was like Dad, the two-by-four picture in my mind was an accurate one.

I learned later that the enemy, satan, is the "accuser of the brethren"; not God.[1]

God was waiting to heal me and make me whole, while the devil was intent upon my destruction. God wanted to show me how He

---

[1]Throughout this book, satan, or any of his aliases, will not be given the dignity of a capital letter. I will acknowledge him, in the least way possible, for he is ultimately the mastermind behind all the evil that came my way, and since all he seeks is glory, I will give him none.

could be my heavenly Father, how he could hold me in His arms and free me from my chains. First, however, I would have to see that I was in chains; and that revelation was still a few years away.

That night, Bill slept over. I slept with Mom, but felt safer knowing he was so close. I had survived my first trigger, even though at the time I didn't know that was what it was or to learn from it. As was my pattern, I buried this new trauma. "Just try to forget about it," Bill said. And that is exactly what I tried to do.

Willing myself not to think of these awful things became my focus. *Just don't think and you'll be fine. Get engaged, get married, and get out of this house; then, life will be perfect.* Even though I tried to make myself believe this, I lived in fear of the next time the poisons stored in that cesspool would boil uncontrollably to the surface and take over my world. I had to learn that I couldn't control everything; but I wasn't in the mood to be taught—not yet.

Within a couple of weeks, things returned to a semi-normal state. Still, the incident on the bus had its affect on me—triggering memories of Willie's abuse and undermining my confidence. I was unsure and wary. Riding the bus home was difficult and the internal pressure to move out of the house intensified. My relationship with Mom was deteriorating as she sensed the seriousness of my love for Bill. Wary of an imminent engagement, she became testy and difficult to live with. Though Mom saw it coming, each month that passed without a ring on my finger caused me to doubt Bill's intentions to marry me. The last straw was Rudy and Karen's engagement.

Bill had met Rudy Krulik the summer after he turned sixteen; the summer before his mom died. He had worked on the Pelissero chicken farm, catching chickens and cleaning cages. The Pelisseros had turned the farm over to their son Harry, who was as committed to leadership at Elim Tabernacle as he was to the family business. Each summer there was a job for any boy in the youth group who didn't mind hard work. Harry had married Hilda, Rudy's older sister, and so naturally she offered her little brother a job as well. Rudy and Bill hit it off almost instantly.

Rudy lived in Niagara Falls and went to an Alliance church with his family; but after meeting Bill, he began hanging out with others from his sister's church, Elim Tabernacle. In the summer, he and Bill would go to Braeside Camp—as much to meet girls as for the spiritual inspiration. They used to drive their cars slowly around the campgrounds looking for girls after services. While hanging out around the tuck shop, Rudy spotted a thin blonde talking to a guy in a car.

"See that blonde girl, Bill? Over there by that car? The one with the flowers on her dress! See her?"

"Yeah, I see her."

"Do you know her?"

"I know who she is. I've talked to her a couple of times. Her name is Karen Cowel. Her dad's Alf Cowel, a deacon at the Hamilton Bethel Tabernacle. He's come to speak at our cottage prayer meeting a few times. Once or twice she's come with him to play the piano."

Rudy couldn't take his eyes from her and he prodded Bill to introduce them.

Bill took Rudy right over and began talking to Karen, with the guy in the car still sitting there. "Hi, Karen. How ya doin'?"

"Hi, Bill. I haven't seen you for a while." Karen started talking to Bill right away and the guy in the car faded into the background.

"Have you met my buddy, Rudy?"

"No. Hi, Rudy. Nice to meet you." Within a couple of minutes, Rudy and Karen were engrossed in conversation and Rudy asked her to go out after the evening service. Karen accepted, and within a few months they were going steady. That was the summer before Bill and I started going out. By the fall, Karen and Rudy were double dating with Bill and me on a regular basis and the four of us became great friends.

After Rudy moved away in 1962, Karen and I got closer. I needed a friend and Bill and Rudy were such good buddies that Karen and I just seemed to fit. Karen was brimming with confidence and class. She played piano and sang, and was raised in a Christian home with godly parents, who, though they were just lay people, had started many churches and Sunday schools in the Golden Horseshoe (the area around the west end of lake Ontario, between Niagara Falls and Toronto). The Cowels were highly respected, and Karen seemed the perfect lady. She had impeccable etiquette and knew about "finer things" such as how to entertain and decorate place settings at a table—things I could have never learned at home. She was friendly and never seemed to be in a situation she couldn't handle. I admired her and it felt good to be around her, although I was sure she didn't need me as a friend.

Rudy proposed to Karen in the autumn of 1962. I thought for sure that my Christmas present from Bill would be a ring. We had talked much about being married, just not about the details, the time and place. My sister Tina had gotten married and away from 17 Sherbourne Street as soon as she could after turning eighteen, and by November I had already been eighteen for five months. I was ready for Bill to rescue me from that house. If he were serious about marrying me, if all he said about loving me was true, I would be getting my ring by Christmas. Rudy and Karen had set the precedent, and I couldn't wait for Christmas to arrive.

Bill Davidson did not like to conform to the actions of others, so for Christmas he gave me a hairdryer. A hair dryer! My disappointment was obvious. Knowing everyone, including me, was expecting an engagement ring, he didn't give me one. Between Christmas and New Year's I gave him the cold shoulder, and though I didn't come right out and say it, he knew I was upset. I had everything worked out; and when things didn't go as planned, I was livid. I took it as a personal slight and gave him a good dose of attitude.

Bill, unaffected by my behavior (having already purchased the ring), simply wanted to do things on his terms. He knew I would snap out of my miserable funk as soon as he gave me what he knew I wanted. Bill figured that when I saw the ring, I would instantly forget how mad I was at him. He was right—but first he made me just a little more angry.

On New Year's Eve, Elim Tabernacle always had a watchnight service from 9:30 to midnight, with a party afterward in the basement. I was looking forward to New Year's Eve as a date with Bill. We had made plans to go "over the river" (the Niagara River) into New York with Rudy and Karen after the party at church. The Christmas season had been especially busy at the bakery, and I needed a night out with Bill and our friends just to kick back and have a good time. When I got to church, I learned Bill had volunteered to run the film projector in the balcony for the special New Year's Eve movie; so there I was, stuck beside him in the balcony for the whole night, without our friends, distracted by the noise of the projector. Still miffed that I had no ring on my finger and that everyone knew "sensitive" Bill had gotten me a hair dryer for a Christmas present—after going steady for over two years—I was determined to make his night as miserable as I could.

All night Bill seemed to be egging me on, niggling me about every little thing and enjoying the rise he would get out of me. My bad mood seemed to entertain him. The movie ended, finally, and I stood up to go downstairs for the food and fellowship time—but Bill didn't move. The church had emptied and Bill was still fiddling with the projector.

"Let's go, Bill! Everyone is already downstairs! We're going to miss everything—there won't even be any food left!" I barked, letting him know how annoyed I was.

"Just a minute. I have to rewind the movie and put the machine away—then we'll go down." He seemed so dull and insensitive! It was as if he didn't even care I was upset. He fiddled around for another ten minutes, and I was getting madder by the second. Everything about him bugged me. I was sorry I had agreed to go to the watchnight service, about our plans with Rudy and Karen— everything. I just wanted to go home.

Finally he finished and we made our way down the stairs to the main floor, but instead of going to the basement, he said, "Let's go around outside. We can go into the basement from the entrance at the back, and we won't have to wait in line behind everyone else that went through the building."

"Bill, what's the matter with you? It's cold out there! Why would I want to go outside?" Bill, ignoring me, reached for our coats and headed out the front doors to the street.

We went outside into the freezing cold air and he said, "Oh! I left something in the car. Let's go to the car for a minute. I've got something I meant to bring in with me." Bill yanked me by the hand and started walking down Queenston Street to the car. (Elim Tabernacle had no parking lot to speak of; only a half-dozen cars could park behind the building. Most of the parishioners had to park on the streets in the neighborhood.)

"Bill! Just take me home! I've had enough! I'm tired. I'm having a lousy time. You can just tell Rudy and Karen to forget about going out after. Take me home!" Now there was no mistaking my emotional state.

120

"Look, just get in the car for a minute, let me get what I forgot, and then we'll go downstairs. If you still want to go home after that, I'll take you." We got into the car and Bill started fumbling around like he was looking for something. First he went through all of his pockets, and then he started with various nooks and crannies inside the car. I was livid.

"What are looking for? For Pete's sake, Bill, just take me home!"

He had put the ring in the compartment beneath the heater, and in the dark and cold, he was having difficulty finding it. At last he felt it, turned on the dome light and presented it to me. It was an engagement ring.

I was totally surprised. He had put me into such a lousy mood; I would have never guessed an engagement ring was coming. I melted into his arms and suddenly *nothing* bothered me. We rushed into the church, showed off the ring and then drove with Rudy and Karen to Niagara Falls, New York, where we attended an all-night gospel concert. After eating breakfast, Bill drove me home.

I was so happy that night that all my fatigue vanished. Finally I saw myself getting out of my life, leaving my troubles behind, leaving Mom behind, and dancing off into wedded bliss. I was euphoric!

Then I had to break the news to Mom.

We arrived back at 17 Sherbourne Street at eight o'clock in the morning, and I rushed into the house. Mom was already up preparing to go to Ike and Jackie's for the day. I hurried in, shouting, "Mom! Look what Bill gave me! Look what Bill gave me! It's a ring, Mom. We're going to get married!" I couldn't contain my enthusiasm.

It was the greatest evening of my life, but Mom couldn't bring herself to share in it.

"Huh!" she muttered with a disgusted look, as though the ring was nothing special. She wouldn't even look at it. I didn't care, though. I certainly wasn't going to let her rain on my parade. That I could see the end of trying to please her only affirmed the joy I felt. I was getting out.

The whole day at Ike and Jackie's Mom pouted. The more that people wanted to see the ring, the more she pouted and tried to rob me of my joy and enthusiasm. All she could think about was that she would be alone; Mom couldn't be happy for me.

We set the wedding date for August of 1963, seven-and-a-half months from the proposal. I wanted more than anything else to have Tina in my wedding. When we started to inform the family of our plans, we learned that Tina and Murray and their family had already made plans to travel out West during August. Murray's vacation time was set, and the arrangements were made. If Bill and I were to marry in August, Tina couldn't be a part of my special day, so we moved the date up to June 29, 1963—Tina and Murray's anniversary. How wonderful! Tina and I would forever celebrate our wedding anniversaries together.

It was bad enough for Mom that Bill and I were getting married in August. When I informed her that the date was being moved up to June, she became even more miserable. "Huh! You're moving da vedding closer? You're probably pregnant! Next ting ve know, da vedding vill be next montt!" Her tone was as harsh as it sounded, spoken bluntly in her thick German accent.

"No! I'm not pregnant! Bill isn't like that!" I said, annoyed.

"Ve'll see. Ve'll see vhen da baby is born, ya?" She was incorrigible.

As time went along and the wedding day was getting closer, Mom softened her rhetoric. "You coult live vit me. You and Margaret, you coult live here," she suggested to Bill one day.

Although money was going to be tight and paying a lower rent seemed attractive, Bill knew that living with Mom would be the death of our marriage. We had to get away, far away from that house and from Mom. We had set up our own life—together. Mom would have been a constant distraction and tension to us both.

"Mom," Bill said (calling her Mom by now), "you might live with me one day, but I'm never going to live with you." Bill had a way of being firm with Mom that she respected. He didn't say anything with the bitterness that exuded when I spoke to her; he was polite. Despite her liking Bill as a person, right up to the day of the wedding, she said she wasn't attending. I hoped she would honor her word.

Mom offered little help during the planning of the wedding and, to keep peace, I didn't bring up the subject. Bill and I had to save the money to pay for the wedding and then to set up an apartment with furnishings. Neither Bill's dad nor my mom was able to help financially and, even if she could have, I doubt Mom would have wanted to encourage us.

Thankfully my sisters-in-law stepped in and helped. Both Jackie and Ruth had always been very supportive of me. Ruth took special interest in the wedding and offered to help with the sewing of dresses and outfits. I was thrilled she was so enthusiastic, and in the final three months before the wedding I was at George and Ruth's house almost every day. She helped with my trousseau; she sewed my going away outfit and helped with the bridesmaids' dresses, too. During that time we became close and, since I couldn't speak to Mom and because Ruby was not around, I needed someone with whom to share my thoughts and doubts. Ruth proved to be a worthy confidante.

Though I was engaged and the date was set, I still feared that Bill would reject me—maybe even at the altar—that he would come to his senses and finally realize who I truly was. I know that all brides are insecure, but the extent of my doubts troubled Ruth. While trying to assuage my doubts and fears, Ruth began to probe for reasons behind my exaggerated jitters. Before I realized what I was doing, I told her about Willie. Although shocked, she believed me and kept my confidence. My brother George did not find out about my abuse at Willie's hand until years later. I had assumed, though I never confirmed it, that Ruth would eventually tell George what happened, but she never did. She felt that when I was ready to tell the members of my family about my abuse, I would. George only discovered the truth when an article was published in our denominational magazine, *The Pentecostal Testimony*, in the late Eighties. The names had been changed in the article, but I had told him my testimony was being published. When he read it, he came to me in horror and disbelief.

I have always felt bad about the way George learned about my ordeal. He was devastated and was hit by alternating waves of false guilt and personal responsibility. He had been totally unaware of Willie's attacks and wondered how, as my older brother, he had not been there to protect me. All of my siblings, upon hearing of my experience, expressed the same feelings. "Where was I? You could have come to me. I had no idea. I'm so sorry I wasn't there to help."

I've tried to explain to each of them that what happened to me was not their fault. It was the fault of a person giving himself wholly over to the evil that raged unabated in his mind. I didn't trust anyone with my secret, because Willie said that he would kill me if I told. If it wasn't me that he threatened, it was others in the family—I never had the confidence to tell anyone, until he stopped hurting me. It was not the fault of my siblings. I pray they don't feel the weight of a responsibility that is not theirs to bear. Willie—and more specifically, the demons that drove his compulsions—are to blame for the pain I endured. Unless you've been abused sexually, it's difficult to understand how trapped and limited the victim feels.

Sharing the secret with Ruth made her want to make my wedding day special. She was a refuge from the constant negativity at home and made planning the wedding a delight. Never complaining about the workload, Ruth made me aware of traditions and customs surrounding a wedding. I certainly could not have made it to June 29 without her.

As the big day grew closer, I had to start thinking about the honeymoon and birth control. The birth control pill had not yet been developed and a diaphragm was the contraception of choice. I booked an appointment with a gynecologist.

Dr. Mackenzie was recommended by my family doctor. He walked into the examination room with a nurse by his side. I had never had a pelvic exam, and though his manner was professional, I was nervous. I remember being relieved that a nurse was in the room. As he examined me to measure me for a diaphragm, his countenance began to change and a disturbed look came across his face. He left the examination room, motioning for the nurse to go with him, leaving me alone for a few minutes. When he re-entered the examination room, he was alone.

"Margaret, I've asked the nurse to give me a few minutes alone with you; I hope that's okay." His tone was slow and measured, and he paused between each phrase to find the right words to use next. Looking deeply into my eyes, as if looking into my soul, he asked, "Do you want to talk about this?"

The discomfort in the room by this time was palpable, and though he was ambiguous, I knew exactly what he was talking about. He knew that he didn't need to be more specific. His eyes told me in an instant that he had just seen a picture of everything I had ever gone through; my pelvic exam had told my ugly story. I

124

had no idea that an examination would reveal what Willie had done. At once I felt discovered. Though I had put on my clothes again after the exam, I still felt naked. Shame overtook me, and I could no longer look at him.

"No," I said sheepishly, "I don't want to talk about it." I didn't look up. My chin was planted firmly in my chest and I wanted to run—to run out of that examination room and out of his office. I wanted to run someplace safe, where no one could make me feel that shame again. I felt like a piece of garbage.

Fortunately the good doctor ignored my response. "Does your husband-to-be know about what has happened to you?"

"Yes."

"What kind of individual is he?"

"What do you mean?" I forced the question out. It was barely audible.

"Would you like me to speak to the young man for you, to prepare him?"

"Prepare him?"

"Margaret," he paused and gathered his thoughts like a gentle father might while explaining something delicate to a young child, "Margaret, this young man that you are going to marry...he need's to be...well, he has his work cut out for him." Doctor Mackenzie and I had only known each other a few minutes, and he was talking to me as though I was his own daughter. I knew he cared for me. He was concerned about what lay ahead. He knew that the pent-up sexual desire of a young groom might lead to aggressiveness in the throes of honeymoon passion—he knew that my ravaged vagina and cervix would not take the stress of an impatient lover.

Sensing my nervous tension, Dr. Mackenzie continued in a more "medical" manner. It made him more comfortable too. "Today when I examined you, I saw signs... signs of...well there was scar tissue. It is obvious that there has been ripping and tearing—that it partially healed, and then there was more ripping and tearing. Because things never got the opportunity to properly heal before more tearing occurred, there is a lot of scar tissue. Scar tissue has formed on top of scar tissue...many times. Well, there was no stitching on these tears as there would be when there's an incision for surgery, so the scars on your cervix and uterus…they're big! You have big, lumpy scars inside you."

I sat there ashen, looking at the floor. Dr. Mackenzie searched his mind for the words to tie things together. It was as if he felt the need to make some sense of it all, to my life and my upcoming marriage.

"Margaret, this man, the young man you're going to marry, he needs to be patient and gentle. You won't be able to withstand any kind of force or vigorous sexual relations. You're very torn, very damaged. Healed, then torn again…many times." He was starting to repeat himself. He kept talking, but I just sat there feeling worse. He tried to be gentle, but his words were cutting the hope and happiness right out of my heart. "You need to know one more thing. You both need to know… Margaret, I have never before seen what I saw today while examining you. The damage to the birth canal, the cervix, it's too badly damaged…you will probably never have children."

As he said those last few words, I knew his talk was over. He wanted to stop talking, and I couldn't have been more grateful he did. I gathered my things and walked slowly out of his office. For a few moments, I was numb—stunned by all he had said. Within a few minutes, however, the reality and hopelessness broke through and I began to cry.

No children, I thought. *I can never have any children! Bill wants children. He loves kids. I can't give Bill kids.* This was it. This would be the final straw. *When Bill finds out that I can't make him a father and knows that kids are out of the question, he'll walk out. Bill had been very loving and patient with me to this point, but what man wants a wife who can't bear him children?*

By the time I arrived home, I had prepared myself for his final words of rejection. I couldn't even blame him. I simply put myself in his shoes and justified the breakup. I steeled myself against the inevitable—it was the reasonable thing to do. Bill should be free to have a normal life. Marrying me would only hold him back, depriving him of what he deserved.

The abuse had ended nearly four years earlier, but I was still scarred by Willie. He had stolen everything from me. Everything that would give me back a reasonably happy life now seemed out of reach. It had never crossed my mind that bearing children would be impossible.

I had taken some comfort in the fact that, during the ten years I was being raped, I had never gotten my period. I developed physically rather late into adolescence, and was sixteen before my first menstrual cycle. I believed God slowed my maturation so that Willie could not impregnate me. Now I knew the truth: Willie, not God, was responsible. He had so scarred me that my womb couldn't even properly bleed and reline itself until two years after his last assault. Willie had taken my past, and now—at eighteen years of age and four years removed from his grip—I learned he had also taken my future. Thoughts of a happy marriage, motherhood, and a family were hopelessly gone. I went home and cried.

As soon as I could, I told Bill that I would understand if he wanted to cancel the wedding. He took me in his arms and gently scolded me. "I'm marrying you because I love you! If we never have children, I won't love you any less! Besides...we can just adopt."

He was so matter-of-fact about the whole thing that I doubted whether he understood what I was telling him. "It's not just children, Bill! I might have trouble making love. There's a lot of scar tissue. The doctor says we'll have to take it slow. I might not be able to...um...you know...our honeymoon night...we might not be able to...um..."

"Shhh," Bill whispered. "It'll be okay. We'll take it slow. It doesn't matter. We'll wait for as long as it takes to make you comfortable. I love you. It'll be all right. I love you! Now, enough of this talk of not getting married."

Who was this Bill Davidson? At that moment he seemed too good to be true. I was about to discover *exactly* whom God had sent into my life for me to marry. I was about to live with a man unlike most of the others I had lived with until then. A man who loved God—a man who loved me.

CHAPTER 9

Married

My relationship with Dad had been strained since the episode at the supermarket. He had been gone again since I was sixteen and I hardly spoke to him. That suited me just fine because I hated him. One day in June 1963, two weeks before I was to be married, Dad dropped in at the National Bakery where I worked.

I had no formal training, but took well to the creative outlet decorating cakes afforded. Dad had walked into the front of the bakery looking for me. The manager came into the kitchen in the back of the store where I was working, to let me know that a man was here asking to see me. I couldn't believe my eyes.

"Dad? What are you doing here?" Dad had never come to see me—anywhere, anytime! In my whole life he had never expressed an interest in where I was or what I did. For all I knew he didn't even know I worked at the National Bakery. Since I was fourteen I literally had spoken as few words to the man as possible. I hadn't the foggiest idea as to why he was here. I had sent him a wedding invitation out of courtesy or obligation—I don't know which—but I certainly didn't expect him to come or even to respond to it.

"I'd like to be able to give you away at your wedding." He seemed sincere and very serious, his eyes pleading for a favorable look from mine.

"Seems to me, you gave me away five years ago, Dad!" My retort was quick and sharp. I hoped it would cut him as deeply as the dagger he had plunged into me at the supermarket. The fact that we were at the front counter didn't matter. If he had enough nerve to come and talk to me after five years, and to do so in the lobby of a bakery, without the decency of a coffee or a lunch, then he deserved to be publicly humiliated. I laughed in his face.

He flushed and looked down at the floor, but he didn't get angry or upset about being publicly embarrassed.

"You remember that?" he asked sheepishly.

"Remember that? Do I remember that? How could I possibly not remember *that*?" I said. It was the single biggest blow I had ever received to my sense of personhood and worth, and he asked me if I remembered it. I was incredulous.

Now almost screaming, I must have been making the customers uncomfortable. Dad implied that my memory of the event was distorted. He wanted desperately to diminish its importance. It was as if he wanted to undo what he had said five years earlier, but didn't know how to go about it. He wasn't accustomed to apologizing. If he could have assembled the words "I'm sorry" at this point, it certainly wouldn't have done him any good. I would have thrown them back in his face. I had no respect for this man and I wanted him to know it.

I remember thinking how selfish and unfeeling he was. He cared only about himself. He wanted to take me down the aisle—as though he had really been a father to me, as though he had raised me perfectly. I would be his trophy on my wedding day. It would make him proud to give me away, and I wanted no part of it. I wanted him to ache in the deepest recesses of his soul; to feel the pain that I felt, to feel as rejected by me as I had been by him. Here he was, coming into my store without notice and ripping the bandage off an unhealed wound. How dare he! He didn't even have the decency to bring this up in private, instead forcing me to loathe him in front of total strangers. If he was embarrassed...great! It served him right.

Finally he said quietly, "Well, Margaret, despite all that—I'd still like to walk you down the aisle."

"You want to walk me down the aisle. That means that you're presenting me to my husband. You don't have the right! That's a privilege you should have earned a long time before now!"

Silence. Despite the raving tirade he had just endured, perhaps thinking I would give him one more chance, he simply stood there.

Unable to stand the strain of silence any longer, I said, "I tell you what, Dad. I'll make you a deal. I don't think that you can do it, but if you want to walk me down the aisle of that church in two weeks to give me away to Bill, you'll do it my way. It means nothing to me, Dad—either way." I was in control now and I loved wielding the power. "If you have anything to drink that day, and I mean any-thing, I won't let you. I'll get Ike to take me down the aisle. I'll kiss you when you arrive at the church and I'll smell your breath. You won't be able to fool me with vodka and orange juice either—I know that doesn't smell like booze—'cause I'm going to look into your eyes and I'm going to ask you if you've had anything to drink. I'll be able to tell, Dad. I'll be able to tell. One drink and Ike will give me away to Bill. That's the deal, Dad. Take it or leave it!"

"Okay, Margaret. I promise. I won't have anything to drink."

I didn't see him again until the day of the wedding. Just in case Dad couldn't deliver, I asked Ike to give me away. Dad had made another promise—like a thousand he had made before—and, like all the rest, I knew he wouldn't keep this one.

❧

I always dreamed of having my sister Tina as my matron of honor, standing beside me on my special day. I chose my matron of honor before there was a thought of a groom. Tina, my loving and special big sister, was more important than the groom. I was sure the groom would have to be special, and handpicked by God, but Tina *had* to be there standing up for me. When Bill and I moved up the date of our wedding and it fell on Tina's anniversary, I was ecstatic. Two sisters married years apart, but on the same date; it fit well into my fairytale wedding fantasy. What could be more perfect?

Unfortunately, during the summer Tina was horribly burned while preserving jam. The sealing wax exploded as she heated it, splashing all over the side of her face, neck, and left arm. The hot wax stuck to her skin and burned her flesh. She was rushed to the hospital, spending several days there to stave off infection. She had suffered second- and third-degree burns. Beautiful Tina, a young mother with five children, was horribly scarred.

Because her wounds had not yet healed, Tina approached me that spring and asked to be excused from our wedding. Her burns didn't matter to me, but Tina felt self-conscious and didn't think she could stand in front of all our guests. (Though her scars were devastatingly visible even a year after the accident, they did eventually heal...so well that, only a careful examination would reveal them today.) I understood Tina's feelings, but was disappointed that she would be unable to stand beside me on my wedding day.

When Tina excused herself, I asked Karen to be my matron of honor—and she graciously accepted. She and Rudy would be married just two weeks before us, on June 15. They would return from their honeymoon just in time to share in our day. As it turned out, Bill was Rudy's best man and I was a bridesmaid for Karen. It was a great time, that spring of 1963, as two couples who were best friends were able to stand up for each other.

Karen proved to be a generous resource to me. Not only could she entertain, she also knew proper etiquette and wedding protocol—unlike me. I felt ill equipped to plan even the simplest of weddings. Being so poor my whole life, I had been to very few weddings, and no social receptions (except those put on by the church), and they were planned by others. I had no idea how to coordinate events and make all the arrangements for our big day; but Bill was confident in me. He reassured me constantly that our wedding day would be a success, despite my feelings of panic.

The time flew by. There was so much to do. I was forever at my sister-in-law's house. Ruth and I worked on my going-away outfit and talked. When I wasn't at Ruth's, I worked as many hours at the bakery as I could, because we had targeted my earnings to pay for the wedding. Bill was working toward saving the first and last month's rent on the home we would share, and to pay down existing debts. I made an average of thirty dollars each week, half of which went home to Mom as room and board. With the balance I was able to pay for all of the wedding expenses, my dress, the reception meal and the hall rental—all without incurring any new debt. Jetting off on a honeymoon—that was a pipe dream.

Simple though it was, I was extremely pleased with how our wedding came together. My relationship with Mom during the engagement, however, fell apart. There was rarely a day during the whole six-month engagement that Mom didn't fight it. She was upset that Bill and I wouldn't be living with her once we married. As much sense as it made financially, it would certainly have been the end of any wedded bliss.

Bitter to the end, Mom made life miserable. "Vell! I'm not going to da vedding!" she would say.

My answer was always the same, "Fine! If you don't want to come, don't! It'll be a better day without you. If you don't want to come, then I don't want you there!"

I refused to show how deeply her comments hurt. Mom thought she could manipulate us through guilt into postponing the wedding or coming to live with her. I consoled myself, "She didn't go to Tina's wedding sixteen years ago and Tina survived. I don't need her there to have my special day. It will be better without her." She would not get the better of me.

People were so generous...giving me five bridal showers. The neighbors on Sherbourne Street, the Davidsons, my side of the family and Elim Tabernacle's ladies all gave me showers; then my bridal party, together with our friends, threw me a personal shower. Mom never attended a single one or seemed the least bit interested in the gifts I received. When I tried to show her all the wonderful things people gave us, she would just grunt and say, "Huh! Showing me all dat stuff just reminds me dat you're going!" Mom was determined to heap guilt on me for leaving her and marrying Bill. To her my engagement was not about my upcoming marriage but about her loss.

"How vill I ever make it? I'll certainly be deatt by da time you get back from da honeymoon!" These were the words constantly in my ears. "All you are talkink about is dat vedding! I'm not looking forvard to dat day—not at all! Kids only have vone modder. She raises nine kids all by herself, gives up her whole life for dem, and none of dem is villing to stay home vit her! No, I'm not looking forvart to dat day." Then she would shake her head and repeat herself, in case I had missed it. When June 29 arrived, I couldn't have run out of the house faster.

Friday, June 28, was wedding rehearsal night and it was nothing like I had imagined it would be. To me this night was all business—everyone else seemed to treat it like a joke. I had never known one special day that would honor me alone and wanted my wedding day to be flawless. Bill's brother Andy was clowning around, and Rudy, a recent groom himself, joined in. No one seemed to pay the slightest attention to where they should be standing or what they should be doing. Everyone was just laughing and joking.

Close to tears, I pulled Bill aside. "Nothing's going to go right tomorrow! They're all just goofing around! Everything's just going to fall apart...I know it!"

"Don't worry, Honey. Everything's going to work out fine. Trust me. They'll all behave tomorrow when it matters. You'll be surprised at how smooth the whole day goes." Bill was unflappable. Nothing seemed to bother him. While I was tied up in knots, he was going with the flow as if he didn't have a care in the world. At times I wondered whether he cared about the next day at all. Maybe it didn't matter to *him* either!

I was becoming a perfectionist. Having so little control in my childhood, I tried to control everything and everyone in my adulthood. Ridiculous as it sounds, I wanted to control the emotions and behavior of everyone in the room. I didn't realize it then, but I would never be able to control my life—in fact, Jesus was trying to let me know, even back then, that He was the One who needed to be in control of my life, not me. Unable to learn that lesson then, however, I just became frustrated and angry.

Our rehearsal party was planned for Ralph (Mac) and Jeanne McKinnon's house. Bill's dad had enough trying to raise five children without his wife, and so we involved him in the plans as little as possible. Jeanne McKinnon was my former Sunday school teacher. She and her husband hosted the rehearsal party at their expense and out of the goodness of their hearts—a goodness God placed there. Their only motive was love—love for a poor bride and a motherless groom. God has always blessed me with such people in my life. It was His way of telling me that He loved me. God was constantly reaching out to show me His great character and love—I was just slow to see it.

Following the rehearsal party, I stayed at George and Ruth's house while Bill slept at 17 Sherbourne Street, saving himself the forty-five-minute drive back to Caister Center. To keep with tradition, we agreed not to see each other on the day of the wedding until I would walk down the aisle. Ike had agreed to give me away. He knew about Dad's visit to the bakery, but, like me, didn't believe Dad could keep his end of the bargain.

The flowers for the bridesmaids and bride were to arrive at George and Ruth's, while the boutonnières for Bill and the groomsmen were sent to Mom's house. I wasn't sure that Bill knew these arrangements, so I called Saturday morning to make sure the groomsmen knew what they were to do with the boutonnières and the corsage for Mom. (Though she vehemently maintained that she would not attend the wedding, Bill and I sent a corsage for her, anyway.)

Bill was outside with my brother Ben, and Rudy, washing and decorating the cars, when the phone rang. Mom answered.

"Hello," she said weakly. I could tell that she had been crying. (Bill told me later that from the moment they woke up that morning, Mom had sat in the living room sobbing.)

"Hello, Mom," I said cordially but firmly. I didn't want to acknowledge her tears. "Mom," I continued, "the flowers for the guys are being delivered there and the corsage for your dress will be with them. Make sure Bill knows they're on the way."

"Vhy dit you buy me flowers?" Mom shot back. "I'm not going to da vedding, and I don't vant any flowers!" By now she was in full-fledged heaves and angry waves of crying poured over the telephone line. "I hate veddings! I hate dis day! I never, ever vanted it to come! I don't vant my flower—keep it!"

She had worked herself into a frenzy, a mass of hysteria. Anything I said from this point went unheard.

She was moaning and sobbing so loudly that Bill heard her from outside and went in to see what was wrong. He caught the last part of Mom's diatribe and rushed over to where she was. "Is that Margaret? Let me talk to her!" He took the receiver from Mom's hand, but didn't talk to me right away. Instead he covered the receiver with his hand and addressed Mom. It was muffled, but I heard what he said.

"Mom! Mom, listen to me!" He wasn't stuttering and his voice didn't have the usual soft tone she was accustomed to. "This is not about you. It's not your day! This day is Margaret's day! She has worked very hard to make this day come to pass and you are not going to ruin it! You are going to the wedding! If I have to physically carry you in, you will be in that church and you will see your daughter get married. Do you understand?"

I couldn't hear Mom's reply, but she must have nodded her agreement between giant sobs. I told Bill about the flowers and hung up. I was thrilled that Bill stood up for me and had put her in her place. My man had defended my honor—and it felt great!

Photos were taken before we left George and Ruth's and headed for Elim Tabernacle. About the only tradition that Bill didn't want to keep was the bride being "fashionably late." He prided himself on being on time, and was thrilled when I showed up at Elim right at two o'clock.

As I got out of the car, I saw Dad! He was dressed up and looking smart. I hadn't heard a word from him in two weeks—since our conversation in the bakery. Despite the nice clothes, I was cynical, assuming he was drunk. I steeled myself, preparing for the inevitable scene. I found Ike and motioned toward him. I wanted his emotional and moral support when I informed Dad that he couldn't walk me down the aisle.

"Hello, Dad," I said warily. "Have you been drinking?"

"No, Margaret," he answered softly.

"You haven't had *anything* at all to drink today?" I questioned a second time.

"No. Nothing."

I leaned toward him and looked straight into his eyes. They were clear—not red or misty. They looked different than they normally did. I moved toward him and kissed him. This was the final test; I could smell booze a mile away. I smelled nothing.

I couldn't believe it! My father had kept his promise. He was sober!

"Okay, Dad, you can give me away. Let's go."

Ike willingly faded into the background, and Dad and I walked into the church together.

When Reverend Earl Williams asked, "Who gives this woman to wed this man?" Dad spoke with a clear and resonant voice, "I do." My father had accomplished what for him was something incredibly difficult and novel: he had stopped drinking for a day. I can't recall valuing it at the time, but today it's one of the best memories I have of my wedding day—and one of the few cherished memories I have of Dad.

Working hard to compose my emotions so I could say my vows, I approached the altar. I couldn't see Mom as I walked down the aisle—but knew she was there. Everyone did. She was sobbing as though it were a funeral, not a wedding. She cried so loudly that, during the exchange of our vows, Bill and I had to speak up to be sure the other heard us. She moaned and groaned through the entire twenty-minute ceremony and Pastor Williams's charge to the new couple. When we left the building for our photos, the "grieving widow's" lament was still ringing in my ears.

I remember feeling relieved when we finally exited the church and could feel the gentle breeze—a brief respite from the ninety-five degree temperature. With the ceremony at two o'clock, and the reception at five, there was enough time to drive to the north end of St. Catharines, to a little park beside the Welland Canal. There we had some pictures taken, and hurried back to St. Giles for the reception. Two hundred invitations had been sent out, and about 120 guests attended. I was relieved that not all of our family members and friends could attend, as I had to pay for each meal myself. I had enough saved to pay for the entire reception.

The meal and the program at the reception were wonderful, and by seven forty-five, Bill and I were changing into our going-away clothes. While we dressed, the wedding guests passed the bride's shoe—a custom in our tradition—filling it with all of their loose cash and coins. That, added to all the money we got in wedding gifts, gave us four hundred dollars. It was the equivalent of two-and-a-half month's income; a huge blessing which allowed Bill and me to go on a honeymoon.

As we walked up the steps to the fellowship hall, Bill was busy stuffing his pockets with the loose change we received from the shoe. Suddenly a swarm of men, led by Harry Pelissero and others from Elim's youth group, grabbed Bill. They carried him off to a car idling nearby and threw him into the back seat. With tires squealing, the car took off toward the Welland Canal.

My new husband had been kidnapped in a practical joke, and all I could do was wait it out. My bridesmaids helped me pick up the money that spilled from Bill's pockets, now strewn all over the steps and parking lot of the church.

About a half-hour later a car came up Howard Avenue, the street adjacent to the church. "Get in the car, Margy! Get in the car!" Bill yelled, hanging out of the window of a car I didn't recognize. The car pulled into the church parking and parked briefly. Bill jumped out and rushed toward our old Ford with Rudy at his side.

I ran over to our car and got in. Pranksters had gotten to it earlier and it was now fully decorated by these unhired designers. The 1956 Ford had been jacked up on blocks so it rested an inch above the gravel, and the rear wheels just spun as we tried to make our getaway. Unsure whether we would be taking Dad Davidson's Cadillac or our own car on our honeymoon, Bill's friends had "redecorated" both vehicles. In shoe polish, the Ford read "mother-in-law in the trunk" and "just married—one dozen little Davidsons to follow," across the sides and back. Those guests still lingering in the parking lot helped us push the car off the blocks as Bill accelerated, the tires spitting stones behind us. We pealed away from the church watching our friends in the rear-view mirror; they were huddled together, congratulating each other and laughing hysterically. Once we were on the main street and heading for the highway, Bill told me how he escaped.

Startled when abducted from the steps forty minutes earlier, Bill didn't really know what the guys had planned for him or how long it would be before he could get back and leave for the honeymoon. Harry Pelissero had taken charge, and Rudy figured it was in his buddy's interest to go along. Bill fought all the way, but Harry, who weighed well over two hundred pounds, easily subdued him. In the melee, Harry inadvertently stepped on Bill's big toe. Though Bill didn't know it at the time, his toe was swelling as blood rushed beneath the nail.

The kidnapper's car was heading toward the Welland Canal and Bill realized he was about to take an unwanted swim. In the meantime, Rudy had an idea. While Harry held Bill in a half nelson in the front, Rudy reached over from the back seat and pulled the keys out of the ignition, throwing them out the open window. (Cars at that time did not have key locks on the ignition.) Gerry Baltus, the driver, slammed on the brakes, keeping his eyes fixed on the rear-view mirror, on the spot where the keys landed.

When Harry and his partners in crime got out to look for the keys, Bill made his getaway, bolting down the street. Several blocks away he flagged down a car, jumped in the back seat beside the driver's children, and frantically demanded to be taken back to St. Giles church. After listening to a brief explanation, the bewildered driver delivered Bill back to the church. Bill decided he and I should get away while the getting was good.

Pleased that he and Rudy foiled their abductors' plans, Bill spent the first part of our trip to the motel going over the story of their escape, laughing at how he had gotten the upper hand. As we made our way to the main highway, however, the pain in Bill's toe hit him and all the excitement of the last hour dissipated as the throbbing in his toe was punctuated with every heartbeat. Taking his shoe off, Bill drove the rest of the way barefoot, his blackened toe swollen and bleeding. Determined to enjoy the moment despite his discomfort, Bill and I cuddled together on the bench seat of our 1956 Ford, basking in the quietness that followed our frenzied wedding day.

We hadn't planned a formal honeymoon since, until the reception, we had no money. Now with two months salary in our pockets, we felt positively wealthy and set out for Toronto to spend the night. In the morning, we would decide where to go next.

As we made the one-hour drive from St. Catharines to Toronto, we talked about how the day had unfolded.

"Everything went so well!" I said to Bill. I rested under his right arm and, though I couldn't see his face, I knew he was smiling.

"Yeah, you planned it great, Honey." His voice was soft and complimentary. I remember thinking at the time, *That's right. I planned it, and it was great.* With no experience attending receptions or parties, let alone staging them, I had planned my wedding and pulled it off. I was proud of myself and it was one of the best feelings I had ever had. Bill's compliment boosted my self-esteem even more. God was letting me feel just how valuable I was, and He was using my new husband to reinforce it. Although I had felt like garbage for most of my life, in those few moments on the way to Toronto, I felt like a diamond instead of a lump of coal.

"God has really blessed us, hasn't He?" Bill said, always quick to give God praise.

"He sure has. He sure has," I repeated. My mind went back to the events of the past six months—the showers, the gifts, people's kindness. We had appliances and dishes and all kinds of gifts to make a new home. I thought of the McKinnons, the rehearsal party, and the extra cash at the reception giving us a honeymoon. "He sure has," I said out loud again.

"It would have been nicer though…if Mom could have enjoyed it!" I said, my tone mixing disappointment and sarcasm.

All the previous good feelings faded. There she was again. Mom was dominating the conversation on the drive to our honeymoon night.

I had been trying desperately to ignore her. For months all I thought about was getting out—getting out of that house and into my own with Bill. I figured my problems were all contained within that house and that Mom was the cause of ninety percent of them. As I drove away to my new life with Bill, something seemed to change inside of me. I had doubts that I was doing the right thing by leaving home. The thought of my ultra-dependant mother living by herself for the rest of her life bothered me. An odd sense of guilt swept over me. Within seconds I was bombarded by old thoughts: *I wasn't a good daughter; I was selfish; I didn't love my mother.* I had heard this my whole life. I thought I had left that world and wouldn't be hearing those words ever again. Now, suddenly, I wasn't sure. So often had Mom rehearsed those hurtful words that now I was hearing them in my mind without her being present to say them.

Bill consoled me, "Stop beating yourself up, Honey. Mom will be fine. Besides, your Aunt Anne is there."

Aunt Anne, Mom's sister, had traveled from British Columbia for our wedding and was staying at the house. It felt good that she was with Mom—that Mom wouldn't be left alone after the wedding. Aunt Anne was to stay a week. I thought that she would help the transition and would be a good distraction.

It struck me as odd at the time that I was sympathetic toward the woman who had given me nothing but grief. Mom had done everything in her power to make my life miserable and to frustrate the wedding plans, and here I was feeling sorry for her. Nonetheless, I felt pity for her. If only Mom had known—it would have made her happy. She loved people's pity.

"Hey, but how about Dad coming to the wedding sober? Wasn't

that something?" Bill changed the subject. He always looked for the positive.

"No kidding! I didn't think that would happen in a million years!"

CR

We learned sometime later just how difficult it had been that day for Dad to keep his promise. He had been sober all day. Between the wedding ceremony and reception, however, my brother Pete wanted Dad to go kill the two hours at a bar. He pleaded with Dad—but Dad wouldn't budge.

"Are you crazy? No way! I promised Margaret! No drinking for the whole day!" Dad didn't go with Pete or anyone else. He came to the reception and sat at the same table as Mom.

As things would turn out, this was the only wedding of his children that Dad attended sober. I remember warning my older brother, "Ben, you had better talk to Dad before your wedding or he'll come drunk!"

"No he won't! He'll honor my wedding just like he did yours. He'll be all right!" Ben brushed me off.

"The only reason he came to my wedding sober is because I made him promise. Make him promise. Ben, have a talk with him."

"Margaret, you're too outspoken. I'm not going to embarrass him. He'll be fine—you'll see."

Ben never did talk to Dad, and three months later, in September, Dad staggered into the church for their wedding—late and drunk. He stumbled down the aisle, needing its entire width to make it to the front pew where the family sat. He smelled like the bowery— alcohol and smoke mixed—and his appearance was shameful. In between the wedding and reception he went to a bar with Willie and Pete, and all three of them got even more hammered. By the time they arrived at the reception, Dad was so drunk he fell off of his chair during the meal.

I was a bridesmaid to June and sitting at the head table. I couldn't resist the urge; I leaned behind the girls' backs and motioned to get the groom's attention. "Well! I hate to say I told you so—but you're the one suffering now!"

Ben blushed. He was embarrassed, and after I opened my

mouth I felt bad for rubbing it in. The whole bridal party wanted to crawl under the head table with Ben leading the charge. Dad dishonored him. He disrespected Ben and June's day and made a mockery of it, embarrassing Ben in front of his friends and his new bride. It was awful.

We approached Toronto from the west and traveled along the lakeshore to the east side, an area called "the Beaches." Near the Greenwood Racetrack we found a quaint little motel and Bill decided that's where we would spend the first night of the rest of our lives. We didn't need a reservation and each room had air conditioning. That was enough to convince us.

Curiously, I never even thought about the honeymoon night and the fact that Bill and I would be making love—that is, until we drove up and parked at the motel. Then all at once, thoughts about having sex, and the doubts and fears that accompany those thoughts, swept into my mind. It hit me. I was scared to have sex. What would it be like? Would it hurt? Would I be responsive to Bill? These would have been legitimate thoughts for any bride, especially a virgin, but for me, when all of my experience associated with sexual intercourse involved violence and power, it was nearly overwhelming.

I remembered what the doctor had said: whoever my husband was going to be, he would have to be a special man, a gentle man. Everything Bill had shown me about himself reassured me he was that man. Still, I wondered, when it came to making love, what he would be like. Until Bill, every man I ever knew seemed to be something other than what they appeared. I secretly pondered whether that was true of Bill too! Was he feigning a gentle spirit for the three years we dated? Would he too change into someone I didn't know? Would he suddenly become rough and insensitive when it came to sex? I entered the motel room nervous and a little sick to my stomach.

It was between nine and nine-fifteen when we unlocked the door and entered the little room. Bill turned the television on—*Gunsmoke* had just begun. We were both feeling a little awkward and, strangely enough, that made me feel better. I wasn't the only nervous person in the room. We hadn't talked a lot about making love and sex while dating. It was like we had to put the idea of intercourse as far from our conscious minds as we could. Mostly we had spoken and dreamed about falling asleep in each other's arms, and how, after we were married, we would never have to leave each other and go home. For lovers, saying good-bye and going home is the most dreaded part of the evening; and the quickest part to arrive. We were frustrated though; holding our bodies back from expressing the deepest part of our love for each other proved to be a battle. That frustration often spilled into other areas, making each of us tense and petulant. Now all of that frustration was gone. This night would hold no more restraint. It was a great relief.

Bill and I always wanted to honor God and be virgins, at least in the context of our relationship, on our wedding night. This was not easy, especially after being together for two-and-a-half years. During our engagement we had rules—specific rules that we both agreed to, and for which we held each other to account. We decided that parking and necking were out of the question. We agreed to hold each other to "good-night kisses." Some of them were longer and more passionate than a typical good-night kiss, but for the most part we stuck to our commitment. The last thing either of us wanted was Mom's prophecy to come true: "You're probably already pregnant!" It felt great to present ourselves as gifts to each other on our wedding night.

Bill unwound watching television as I showered. When I came out of the shower, dressed in my new honeymoon nighty and matching nightgown, Bill decided to take action on his throbbing big toe. He entered the washroom, raised his foot to the sink and lifted the nail to relieve the agonizing pressure. Instantly blood covered the sink. With the pain lessened, Bill turned his attention toward me. He limped from the bathroom back to the bed, where we cuddled.

With the lights turned out, we held each other and watched the motel television. In no time we were bored with *Gunsmoke* and Bill hit the off switch. I was happy to be under cover of darkness. We had never seen each other naked, and I was glad that that tradition continued for at least one more night.

For four or five years I never fully undressed while making love. Completely nude, I felt uncomfortable and vulnerable. I'm sure it was because Willie always stripped me; I found the nakedness humiliating. Bill just lovingly accepted this idiosyncrasy and never pushed me where I didn't want to go. It's strange, but being totally naked made me feel like sex was being inflicted upon me; while partially clothed, I felt partly in control and secure. I didn't talk about it to Bill—he just seemed to know and always left me with the comfort of a nighty.

As we lay together in bed tenderly caressing and kissing, I felt safe. I knew Bill Davidson loved me and I loved him. I wanted to give myself to him, even though I didn't know what to expect. When the moment for intercourse arrived, there was no pain. There was no discomfort whatsoever, and the first time we made love that honeymoon night I enjoyed it immensely. Bill kept asking if I was hurting, but the wonderful thing was that I wasn't. I look back now and am amazed at my own ignorance that night. No one told me what to expect. I knew that men achieved orgasm, but I had no idea that women experienced sexual pleasure, too. God gave me a great gift that night and showed me what he had intended from the beginning within married intimacy. The pain and torture I had endured at the hands of those who took their sexual gratification at my expense, seemed a million miles away. It was buried. At that moment I was in the arms of a man who loved me; and sex with him was nothing but beautiful and reassuring.

I was married. We were finally together—never to be separated again. I was sure the wedded bliss would last my whole lifetime, and I set Bill up on a pedestal. He didn't ask to be put there—I put him there without his permission. Since he would doubtless fall in the future, I assured my own emotional devastation.

CHAPTER 10

Smithville—The First Year

On the second day of our honeymoon we drove down the road—the old life was gone and I was in utopia. Naïve as it sounds, I thought I would never have another problem. I had entered a new world. In my mind, my old world, centered in the house on Sherbourne Street, was the source of all of my problems. My new world, which I had entered through marriage, was totally different. Its center was Bill, and it seemed to me that nothing could ever bring those opposing worlds together. All the tension and resultant bickering that had marked the few weeks prior to the wedding melted away as pent-up frustration gave way to marital intimacy. As we sat beside each other on the bench seat of the Ford, we were as close emotionally as we were physically. I was with the love of my life.

The unplanned nature of the honeymoon helped us relax. We didn't have to be anywhere in particular, and we just made up our itinerary moment by moment. On Sunday we decided to travel to Halliburton, a little resort town two-and-a-half hours north of Toronto. Murray and Tina's lakeside cottage was nearby, and we thought it would be nice to visit them. (We always referred to it as Murray and Tina's cottage, but in reality Murray's father and mother owned it together with their four adult children.) Tina and Murray were due to leave with their family on a trip to western

Canada first thing Monday morning, so we thought it would be great to surprise them on Sunday. I knew my sister's generous nature, and suggested to Bill that we get a motel room in Halliburton and then make our way to the cottage. We arrived unannounced and Tina quickly offered to put us up over night.

"We already have a hotel room in the village—our stuff is there. We wouldn't think of putting you out," I replied. I loved my sister and her family, but Bill and I had only slept together one night in our whole lives, and we weren't ready to add a whole group of relatives to the mix.

Tina argued a little with us and tried to get us to cancel the room and save the motel cost, but soon gave up—realizing that money was not the issue. We sat by the lake Sunday afternoon and talked about the wedding and how well everything went and how wonderful it felt to be married. The conversation turned to Mom and how brutal her display of crying and moaning all day had been. The day after, it all seemed funny and we were able to laugh at her pathetic behavior. Even Mom hadn't been able to take away from the beauty of our day. We ate supper around the barbeque, and then, when we hugged and kissed each other good-bye, we headed back to the village.

Monday morning we checked out of the motel and decided to drive through Algonquin Park, a large Provincial Park in northern Ontario. In land area, it is the size of some countries in Europe, and is renowned for its wilderness preservation and wildlife population. We drove through on the main road from one end of the park to the other, hoping to see a bear, a moose, a deer…anything! It took a full day to drive its width and we didn't see so much as a bird. At the far end of the park, we stopped at a tiny motel late in the afternoon.

Since all of the wedding graffiti was still on the car (though now smeared), we drove down to the beach and washed the Ford. When the car was sparkling again, we made our way back to the motel. The drive and the carwash had tired us out and, wanting to get out of the muggy air, we immediately went into our room and flopped down on the bed. We laid there for about a half-hour, cooling down and napping in each other's arms; deciding that our suitcase and toiletries could stay in the trunk until later. It was time to eat supper when we awoke, so we walked down to a little restaurant we had

146

spotted on our way back from the beach. The heat had subsided, and the night air was perfect for a walk. We followed a little path in the forest past some railway tracks and down to the beach. We walked the shoreline and jumped between rocks, playfully risking a fall into the water. Once in town, we had a lovely meal and reveled in each other's company. We finished our dinner and walked, arm in arm, back to the motel, intent on unpacking our things and getting to bed early.

When we got back to the car in front of the motel, Bill reached into his pocket for his keys. No keys! We searched the motel room—nothing! We retraced our steps down the path in the forest, on the way to the village, past the railway tracks; we searched by the rocks we had leaped between. No keys! We went back into the restaurant. No one had turned them in. By the time that we returned to the motel, everyone staying in the other rooms came out to help us. All of them were nice, but despite the effort of more than ten people, the keys weren't to be found.

We had no clothes, except for the ones on our backs; no toothbrushes or toothpaste, no deodorant and, worst of all, no pajamas. The third night of our married life would have to be spent in our birthday suits! This fact was not lost on all of our new acquaintances from the motel and, as we looked for the keys, everyone laughed and teased the unfortunate newlyweds. Darkness fell and we had to give up the search for the night. Bill and I went to our room and wondered how many days we would be stranded there, or if a locksmith was anywhere near this corner of the Algonquin wilderness.

Thirty-five years later, the same situation might throw Bill and me into an agitated state; but that night we were so relaxed and happy, we just laughed and put off finding the keys until morning.

Despite the good-natured ribbing of the motel guests, there would be no sleeping in the nude. Bill was still quite shy, and I was nowhere near confident enough to let Bill see me in the altogether! We turned out the lights and slipped beneath the sheets wearing our underwear. Even having our pajamas locked tightly in the Ford's trunk was not enough to overcome our modesty. I'm certain that, in the dark, both of us were blushing.

The next morning we began to dress in the previous day's clothes. As we sat on the bed, we heard a metallic clunk beneath us.

The old-style bed in this motel had a large headboard and foot-board. When we had come in from the beach the afternoon before and collapsed on the bed, the keys must have slipped out of Bill's pocket and lodged between the mattress and the footboard. Now, as we once again flopped on the bed, the wedged keys were released. We were ecstatic. We rushed to the car to get our toi-letries and fresh clothes and, after showering, we checked out. It was Tuesday morning, July 2.

After a day and night spent at Bill's Uncle Ben and Aunt Sapphira's house in Bancroft, we were anxious to get home. On the way we stopped to visit some family in Manuth on Thursday, and then headed home on Friday. Having rented a little house outside of Smithville near the print shop where Bill worked, and having spent two weeks decorating it before the wedding, we were excited about getting home and setting up house.

I dreaded Friday—not because we were moving into our home in Smithville, but because we were stopping at 17 Sherbourne Street first. All the wedding and shower gifts were at Mom's house. We would have to stop there, pick up all of our belongings and then try to leave. I had been anticipating Mom's crying and guilt-trips for a couple of days. For the first time in my life, I had been a whole week without the tension Mom always produced, and I was less than thrilled at the prospect of listening to her caterwauling again.

Hoping for the best, I tried thinking positively: *Maybe Aunt Anne has been a good influence on Mom and helped her get used to the idea that I'm never coming home again.* Aunt Anne was always positive and cheerful. I wondered how they could be sisters at all.

I felt myself biting my bottom lip as we pulled in the driveway. Mom was sitting where we had left her the previous Saturday morning. She was in the same chair and she was crying. I wondered if she had stopped at all during the six days that we were away—it was as if she hadn't moved for a week. Sitting, moping, and weep-ing—that's how I pictured her spending our whole honeymoon.

It would have been nice to hear, "Hi, Honey! It's great to see you! How was your honeymoon? Oh, I missed you so much!" Instead Mom greeted me with, "You'll be sorry! You'll be sorry you treat your modder dis vay! I voult never tink children coult be so mean to dere modder! You vill be sorry…"

148

My mood changed in an instant. I had gone from Nirvana to Hades. Bill and I loaded up the Ford and got out of there as quickly as we could. When we arrived Mom was crying and when we left she was crying; in between she worked full time loading on the guilt. Try as I might to dissociate myself from that guilt, I couldn't. I carried it with me on the quiet drive to Smithville, like a hundred pounds on my shoulders: I was a horrible daughter. I ached to be in our new little house.

Outside Smithville proper is the township of St. Anns, a little farming community. Our two-bedroom home stood in the middle of a cornfield, and the closest neighbors were half a mile away in either direction. The only other building within eyesight was a tiny barn in back of the house.

The fresh paint and wallpaper gave the tiny bungalow a bright look, and we were proud of our first home. Though we had electricity, there was no indoor washroom or telephone. Attached to the barn behind the house was the outhouse. Because there wasn't a washroom inside, there was no tub, and at that time no one had showers. For the whole time we lived there, I managed, by some supernatural intervention, to avoid a nighttime trip to the outhouse. It was by the barn! I imagined that mice, rats, and other similar creatures were a major threat in the night. It didn't seem nearly as bad in daylight.

The rent was forty dollars per month—one week of Bill's salary. Because I was collecting unemployment insurance, we were actually able to bank some money. (I was forced to quit the bakery job; Smithville was a forty-five-minute car ride from St. Catharines, so it was impossible for me to keep working.) Bill came home from the print shop each day for lunch, and in the evenings he was home by 6:05 p.m. I didn't have a driver's license, so I walked everywhere. Two to three times a week we traveled down the road to Caister Center, to Dad Davidson's farm. They had indoor plumbing and a bathtub. I could do laundry there as well.

It might have been even lonelier for me, except that from August through September of 1963 I had little Christine to keep me company. My older brother Pete and his wife had separated. Pete was an alcoholic and womanizer, and did not support the kids after he left. His wife had to go back to work to feed their three children, so I offered to watch Christine, their two-and-a-half-year-old daughter. The kids lived with their mom, in St. Catharines, so we took Christine home with us every Sunday evening after church, returning her to her house every Friday night when we came in for young people's meeting. It must have been awful for Pete's wife—being separated from her little girl—but they were tough times, and she did what was necessary to survive. As newlyweds, we enjoyed "our little toddler" roaming around the house for five out of seven days each week. Bill loved having Christine there. I loved it, too; I was not by myself. But soon, my insecurity got the better of me. Each night Bill would come home and the first thing he would do was play with Christine. I had imagined myself totally captivating the attention of my husband when he arrived home from work—now I had competition. It didn't matter that I was competing with a baby for my husband's attention. I grew jealous. Bill seemed to want to play and talk with Christine more than talk with me! I had been without an adult to talk to all day, so by the time Bill came home I was dying to talk to someone—anyone who could talk back.

It was clear that Bill loved kids, and my insecurity may have been rooted in the conversation I had had with Dr. Mackenzie months earlier.

What if I am unable to have children? Will Bill continue to love me? He said it didn't matter—that if we couldn't have our own children, we could adopt—but what if he was lying or changes his mind down the road? Will he reject me because I can't give him his own child? These were the kinds of thoughts flooding my mind. Filled with self-loathing, I worked hard to give Bill reasons to stop loving me. Lost in my own unresolved issues, I began to resent little Christine's presence in our home.

Despite the doctor's poor prognosis for me getting pregnant, I used a diaphragm regularly. With money so tight and my unemployment insurance only temporary, there was no way either of us wanted a baby right away. We couldn't see ourselves living on one salary and adding a child to it.

On weekdays I looked forward to Bill coming home for lunch and supper. During the evenings, for entertainment, we would visit the Davidson farm or one of our neighbors for coffee. On Fridays, after dropping Christine off at her mom's, we would head over to young people's meeting at Elim Tabernacle. Bill was still young people's president and would often share the devotional. After visiting the ice cream parlor with friends, we would head back to Smithville. On Saturday evenings we would either go out with Karen and Rudy or go to Dad Davidson's cottage prayer meeting.

Karen and Rudy had moved to Fergus, about an hour's drive away where he worked at a bank. Some weekends we would make the trip down to see them and visit with their new friends. The friendship between Karen and me continued to grow. I admired Karen and how she used her gifts in hospitality. She was a classy lady, and emulating her seemed to me to be a worthwhile goal. I was careful not to reveal too much of the real me, however; I didn't want her to think less of me.

Most Sundays after church we went to visit Mom and spend the afternoon with my family. My brothers often came over with their wives and children, and at four o'clock in the afternoon we would get out buns and coffee and eat around the big table. This was when Mom was the happiest—her kids were home in her house again. She would revel in the attention and be pleasant. Once our light supper was over, we would all head over to Elim for the evening church service. After service, we would pick up Christine and head back home. Compared to the weekend, the weekdays were slow and uneventful.

Our first summer together was everything I hoped it would be. I loved being married.

Part way through October, Pete's wife made other arrangements for Christine, and she no longer needed me to babysit. Suddenly, I was alone every day—all day. Bill still came home for lunch, but the rest of the day I felt isolated. Going to Dad Davidson's farm to bathe and do laundry, and trekking out to the outhouse in the cold, had long since lost any romantic appeal. The weather was turning colder, and imagining myself alone every day all winter was more than I could bear. We were benefiting financially by living in St. Anns, but I was dying inside. Without a phone or people around, I felt sure I would lose my mind. November was gray and depressing, and many days when Bill got home from the print shop, he would find me crying.

After a few weeks of melancholy, Bill suggested I try to get back my old job at the bakery. He even suggested moving back to St. Catharines and said that he would drive back and forth to Smithville to work.

"You don't want to be on the road an hour-and-a-half each day," I said sheepishly, wanting Bill to refute it. "I'm just being silly."

"No really, it's no trouble. The extra money that you'll make working will pay the difference in the rent in the city, and the extra gas will be covered too. I can see how lonely it is out here for you. When we go in for young people's on Friday night we'll stop by the bakery." He had made up his mind and I was glad he cared about how I felt.

There had been a change in management at the National Bakery just before I quit four months earlier, so I took care to sell the new manager on who I was and how long I had worked there. "Is my old cake decorating job still available?" I queried.

His answer shocked me: "Sure, I can use you. Come in Monday morning."

"Monday? I don't think I can start that soon—I live in Smithville."

"Well you have to make up your mind fast. If you want the job, be here Monday morning—or else I got to look for somebody else." His voice was curt and no nonsense.

I couldn't believe there was still a spot for me and I didn't want to miss the opportunity. "Okay, I'll call you tomorrow and tell you if I can work it out."

As I was leaving the bakery he yelled after me, "By the way, I have a cake decorator, so you'll be working the counter. That's the job I have for you!"

"All right. I'll let you know tomorrow." I went to the car to tell Bill.

Bill agreed that I needed to take the job and, until we could find a place in St. Catharines to rent, I would return to 17 Sherbourne Street. That Sunday I moved in with Mom while Bill traveled to the little Smithville farmhouse. I was back in the house I had escaped only four months earlier and Bill and I were living in different places. I felt awful. For the next month Bill came and picked me up on weekends and I lived with Mom during the week. Without a phone at the farm, we hardly even spoke. We had gone from sleeping together every night to a situation worse than when we dated; at least *then* we could speak on the phone. Mom was as thrilled as I was horrified.

"I told you you'd come back home. You and Bill shoult live here vit me!" Daily I had to hear her comments. I felt like I would go nuts if I had to stay there for any significant amount of time. The only thing worse than *being* in prison, is to have escaped, tasted freedom, and then be captured again. It's a double hell! I felt trapped and desperately hoped we could find a place of our own—quickly!

By December, Bill and I had found a place in the south end of St. Catharines near Thorold. We moved into a second-floor apartment on Rowntree Road. It was a small place and we had to travel up wooden stairs at the rear to get to our door, but we were back together—and we even had an indoor washroom! Christmas was coming and all was well again in my little world. We decorated the place with some new furnishings and even purchased a brand new couch and chair set "on time"—after all, we were both working so the monthly payments wouldn't be a problem. I had hardly ever sat on new furniture before, and now I owned a matching set! I loved the little place and set about making it a home.

When we were first married, we lived in the glow of each other's company. Our devotional life was sporadic at best, and, even though we loved God, we weren't as committed and diligent as we ought to have been. I read the Bible and so did Bill, just not together and not every day. We had a loose connection to Christ, despite the fact that we were leading young people's meetings every Friday night. We knew all about spiritual principles—we just didn't discipline ourselves by bringing them into our daily experience. We were soon to realize the consequences of ignoring biblical truth.

I worked all of November, December, and January at the bakery, but in February my world began to crumble. I missed my period. (I hadn't begun having a period until I was sixteen years old; but once it began, it was regular. I could set my watch to it.) My period was late! I didn't want to mention it to Bill, so I just waited. Soon I began to experience morning sickness. I would start the day vomiting. As the nausea subsided, I would board the city bus from the edge of St. Catharines and commute downtown to the bakery. The whole time on the bus I would be swallowing, trying to stifle what was determined to come up. The bus would stop and I would run out the door and into the washroom at work, barely making it to the toilet where I would vomit for the second time. This pattern continued for several days, and I had an awful feeling that the worst was true—I was pregnant.

In those days it was common practice to wait until two menstrual cycles were missed before going to the doctor. I kept telling myself, *I'm not pregnant. How could I be? There were only one or two times I didn't use my diaphragm. I couldn't be that unlucky. Lots of people miss a period.*

Bill noticed how sick I was over a two-week span. "You're just having a bout of the flu," he reassured. "There's no way that you're pregnant!"

In the back of our minds, the doctor's pre-wedding speech kept playing over and over, like a recorded message: "You'll probably never be able to have children." To us, getting pregnant was a foreign thought—it would be a difficult thing, at best; planned, certainly—a goal to work toward. Getting pregnant accidentally was out of the question.

Bill was petrified at the thought that I wouldn't be able to work. We had moved back to St. Catharines on the assumption that I would have my job. "I hope you're not pregnant. I mean, how can we live on just my wages and then add a baby to the mix?" Bill would hope out loud that I was just sick, and I knew then that Bill didn't want this baby. Every insecurity imaginable flooded my psyche. All my childhood fears, along with thoughts of Bill's eventual rejection, flooded my mind. I imagined Bill would leave me. If I *was* pregnant, it was *my* fault—and that would give him cause to set me aside.

Two months before I was married, my longtime manager at the National Bakery, Harry McLeod, moved on within the company, and a younger man replaced him—the man who hired me in November. We didn't know each other, but being of Dutch decent, the new man ruled the bakery with an iron fist and austere demeanor, not at all like Harry. He really didn't believe married women should work outside of the home, but reluctantly hired me back because I didn't require training; besides, I was a good worker. I could work the counter and also fill in if the cake decorator was overworked or off sick. He hired me back because it made business sense—though he secretly feared I would get pregnant, proving to be unreliable.

By mid-March I was at the doctor's office, having missed a second period. My family doctor gave me an internal exam. "Yep! You're expecting," he said, using the socially acceptable term at the time. "Margaret it looks like you and Bill are going to have a little baby!" I'm sure he thought I should be pleased.

Bill picked me up from the doctor's office. "The doctor says I'm pregnant—almost three months." I said quietly.

"Well, he could be wrong! Doctors have been wrong before!" Bill was grasping at straws. As he spoke, I had to motion to him to pull the car over to the side of the road so that I could throw up.

At last after a long silence, Bill began to accept the truth. "What are we going to do, Margy? Do you think you can work for a little while?" His voice was gentle. He was trying to be sensitive; but I knew he didn't want to have this baby—not now!

"Yes, I can work! I'll keep working up until the baby's born, and we'll try to save some money." I felt the financial pressure like a car sitting on my chest. I decided I wouldn't tell my manager about it—not until the last possible moment. We needed the money.

The very next day I went into work.

"Margaret, can you go upstairs to the storage attic? We are out of cake and pastry boxes." My manager was asking me to retrieve packages of folded cardboard boxes. They came in groups of one hundred, and each package weighed about twenty-five pounds.

"Could someone else go up and get them? I don't feel that well today," I asked politely. I hoped that he would think that I was having my period or something and would get someone else to run the errand. I over-estimated his sensitivities.

"Are you employed here like everyone else?"

"Yes."

"Well then, if you work here, you have to pull your own weight. You gotta do what everybody else does! Now go get those boxes!"

I gave him the dirtiest look that I could conjure up and stormed up the stairs to the attic above the store. *I'll show him*, I thought. *I'll take him down two packages. Pull my own weight—indeed!* I piled two packages of the pastry boxes, two hundred in all, on my arms and struggled with the fifty-pound load all the way down the stairs. He had laid down the gauntlet and I had taken it up! My arms and stomach muscles ached under the weight, but I made it to where he was standing in the kitchen. I dropped the packages at his feet as if to say, "There you go, you big goof!"

As I dumped them on the floor, I felt a gush!

With a look of horror on my face, I turned and ran into the washroom. I was hemorrhaging—and not just a little. A steady stream of blood flowed from my womb, at twice the rate of my period's heaviest day. As the water in the toilet turned red, I started to cry, "Oh no! Oh no! I'm losing my baby!"

I cleaned myself up the best I could, put on a pad, and made it out to the phone in the front lobby. I called my doctor and told him what happened.

"Margaret, calm down and listen to me! Margaret, you have to get off of your feet. Lie down, even if it's on the floor, and put your feet up. Find a chair or something and elevate your feet. That should stop the bleeding. Do you understand me?" The doctor was very calm and didn't seem the least bit upset by my news.

I got off the phone and lay down on the floor in the back part of the bakery. I asked one of the other girls to call the home of Andy, Bill's brother. I knew that Alice, Bill's sister, was there. She had a car and would come pick me up. Andy and Jeanette's house was in Effingham, a community just outside the St. Catharines' boundary. Though it was March, it was snowing—a late spring storm—and I hoped that Alice could get there quickly despite the weather.

It seems strange to me now that I didn't phone Bill at work, but he was in Smithville. It was the middle of the day, and I didn't want him to worry. I couldn't believe that I might lose our baby by foolishly trying to get back at my boss. Despite my best efforts, my whole yellow baker's uniform was soaked with blood from the waist down. My manager came in the back to see what had happened to me. He looked at me lying there.

"I'm pregnant," I snapped.

He hit the roof. "Pregnant! You got yourself pregnant? Great!" His tone was sarcastic and mean. "I'm sorry I hired you back. Why did you return to work if you were going to get yourself pregnant? Look at you! What good are you to me *now*?"

I couldn't believe how crass he was. "I'm sorry! I didn't mean to get pregnant. I just am." I started to apologize and then this anger welled up within me, an anger from the deepest part of my soul. *Who does he think he is?* I was lying on the floor, bloodied and upset, with my feet elevated on a chair, listening to him ball me out for getting pregnant—as though I was solely responsible and did it just to make his life unbearable.

"If I hadn't had to carry the stupid boxes down, I'd have been fine!" I yelled back at him. "You're the one who sent me up to carry those stupid things down—even after I asked you nicely to get someone else to do it! This is all *your* fault!" I don't think he expected me to answer him back so forcefully. Normally I just did as I was told and wasn't a problem employee. He backed off when I answered his ridiculous accusation, sensing that perhaps he had stepped over the line of common decency, he didn't say another word.

In the snow, it took Alice about half an hour to get to the store. She was nervous—about me, about the baby, about the snow. Somehow we got into her Volkswagon Beetle and headed toward Rowntree Road, to our apartment. Just before getting there, as we were trying to get up the hill on Mountain Street, the car skidded off the road. There we were, nose first in a ditch. We hadn't been driving very fast, but the road was an ice rink. She checked to see that I was all right, then started to panic. Alice alternated nervously from giggling to crying.

"Marg, I'm so sorry! What are we going to do? Oh no! This is awful! Oh no," she giggled. Then, thinking it wasn't very funny at all, she broke into tears. "Oh, no! Marg! What are we going to do? What are we going to do?"

I wasn't in any shape to problem-solve, so ultimately she decided to leave me for a few minutes and knock at the door of a nearby house. As she left the VW, I just prayed that everything would work out and we would get out of this. At the first door she came to, without so much as a hello, she blurted out, "Uh, can you help us? Um, well, uh, I've got my sister-in-law in the car and she just found out she's pregnant. Uh, well anyways— that doesn't really matter—I mean, well, it matters but...she's bleeding! She just found out she's pregnant and she's bleeding! I picked her up from work. I was supposed to take her home—but the snow, and the hill! And well—we went off the road! The car's over there in the ditch! Margaret's there, too—in the car! Can you help? Can you help?"

Alice spoke quickly when she was *calm*. When she was excited, she could hardly keep any particular train of thought and her words tended to come out confused and choppy. Her emotions were wound up like a top. It's a wonder the lady at the door understood a word of what she was saying.

"Sure, no problem. Let me get my coat." This wonderfully kind lady came out in the snowstorm and, with Alice's help, got me into the house.

They got my coat off and, when they saw how much blood I had lost—my uniform was now bloodied from just above my waist down to my knees—they undressed me as quickly as possible, cleaned me up, and put me to bed. This lady whom I didn't know, whom I had never even casually met, dressed me in her own underwear and nighty and put me in her bed. This helpful lady turned out to be a nurse; God knew who we needed. She elevated my feet and made me as comfortable as possible, all the while saying positive and hopeful things to me: "Don't worry, Honey, you're going to be all right. You just need to lie down and the bleeding will stop. Don't worry. Everything's going to be fine. You'll see. Now try to get some rest." If I didn't know that she was a real person, living at a real address, I would have thought that God sent me an angel.

While I lay in her bed, exhausted and scared, she took my uniform and undergarments to her basement and laundered them. A distraught Alice phoned Andy and Jeanette. As soon as Andy arrived home from work, he came with some help and retrieved the car from the ditch. He made sure that I was fine and said that he would call Bill to let him know where I was. If I hadn't needed to lie down, Andy would have taken me to his house right then; but no one wanted to move me.

Lying there in that bed, I was sure my baby was gone. I had passed blood clots half the size of my fist. I was only eight or nine weeks pregnant; the embryo was less than the size of those clots. I just lay there and cried.

Andy phoned Bill, who left work as soon as he could and picked me up at the nurse's house. Though I'm sure Bill thanked this sweet lady profusely, in the hurly-burly of leaving and getting me out to the car, I didn't have the chance. I've always regretted not thanking that generous and kind lady personally for her help on that awful day. We arrived at our apartment shortly after seven o'clock and Bill and I slowly climbed the stairs to the apartment. Bill hugged me and put me to bed. I wanted to wake up the next morning and learn that all of the horrible events of that day were merely a dream. I fell asleep, exhausted—but when I awoke, reality hit me within seconds. It was no dream.

The next day I went to see the doctor. "Were you still sick, nauseated this morning?" he asked.

"Yes."

"Well that's a good sign. And what about the bleeding? It's stopped now?"

"Yes."

"Well, I don't think you lost the baby. I don't want to give you an internal exam—things are too sensitive, and if you haven't miscarried, I don't want to do anything that might bring it on. I think the best thing to do, Margaret, is just wait. We'll wait it out, see how you are in a couple days. Okay?"

I nodded my head.

"All right. Call me if you start to hemorrhage again. Now, no more heavy lifting. Stay in bed as much as you can; and you'll have to quit working."

His last statement was made in a matter-of-fact manner, as if it was an obvious, easy decision to make. I would have to quit working.

I had initiated the move back to St. Catharines, so I was responsible for getting the new apartment. Now I had to quit my job and have a baby. I felt like I was adding strain and pressure to our home. What were we going to do? I had lived my whole life in poverty and financial uncertainty. The last thing I wanted was for my marriage to be that way. It was as if all the walls of our new life together were crashing in on us. It was hard for me to breathe, just thinking about it.

Though we had spent several years under good preaching and solid doctrine, Bill and I were not regular tithers when we first got married. The scriptural principle of giving God one tenth of our earnings hadn't made it to the top of our priority list. We seemed to have so many other things to do with our money. In the back of our minds we knew better. We knew that it would be difficult to ask

God to take care of our needs if we weren't diligent about our responsibility to Him; but it didn't come up in our conversation at that time. Each of us felt somewhat guilty for being lax in giving to God, but with me having to stop working, there would even be less money. There didn't seem to be a hope of God getting what was His. We didn't yet know that if we fulfilled our giving responsibilities to God, we could pray with confidence—asking Him to help us out of our financial problems.

As I rode home from the doctor's office, my mind was preoccupied, not with the baby directly, but with how we were going to make it without my bakery job. *Now what am I going to do? I wondered. How am I going to tell Bill that I can't work for the next six months until the baby's born?* The figures leaped to the screen in my mind: our apartment rent was sixty-five dollars. Together Bill and I were making almost eighty dollars every week, but Bill only made half of that at the print shop. We have to make it on forty dollars per week, add a baby and all of the expenses that go with it, and Bill still would have to pay for all that gas traveling to Smithville every day. It cost us more to live than we were making.

"Oh, God, you have to help us," I cried. "You just have to!"

Two days after leaving work hemorrhaging, I went back in to speak to my boss. "The doctor says that I can't work anymore—that if I do I'll lose my baby for sure. I'm sorry to leave you stranded, but could you please sign that you laid me off for health reasons? That way I can claim unemployment benefits until the baby is born?" I was being as sugary sweet as possible.

"Collecting unemployment insurance means that you are available for work. If you can't work, you can't work, but I'm not going to lie for you. I'm certainly not going to *pretend* that you are available. As far as I'm concerned, you don't qualify. I'm stating that you quit."

He was so cruel! How could he be that mean? He simply wanted to get back at me for getting pregnant, for making him look for a replacement.

I stormed out of the bakery. Good thing we had six months of saving money when we first got married. At least that will help until the baby is born, I comforted myself.

For the next two months, Bill left the house each morning at eight o'clock and returned at seven in the evening. I was alone again all day, but at least this time, I had a phone. When he left in the morning, I was leaning over the toilet vomiting; and when he came home at night, there I was again. Bill would joke, "I'm going to rig some sort of harness over the toilet to hold your head up. Do you spend the whole day there? I can't believe you're so sick!"

"I'm not there all day, it just seems like it," I would reply humorlessly. In between episodes of being sick I would try to force down some dry crackers and a drink. I was losing weight by the minute, and I didn't even want this baby! I felt even worse knowing that Bill wished I had never gotten pregnant. I was miserable.

Bill started taking as much overtime at *The Smithville Review* as he could. On Saturdays he offered to help his Dad haul sawdust, and he started running a gasoline account at Garner's Service Station so that we had enough money to live on. If we didn't have to pay for the gas every week, we had more cash flow. We started to sink into debt. Bill had car debts before we were married, and then we bought that apartment furniture on time...and now we couldn't even pay cash for filling up the car!

By June of 1964, the morning sickness that had lasted all day was subsiding and, with the sunny weather, I began to feel better. We started to talk more about whether the baby would be a boy or a girl and began to daydream a little about how wonderful a new baby would be. Bill seemed happier about the thought of being a daddy. We were the first young couple in our group of friends to be expecting, and I became the center of attention on Sundays. I loved it. People at Elim seemed to be delighted at the prospect of a new baby in the church.

Right at the end of the summer, God answered my prayer for help. Bill got a phone call asking him to come in for one last interview at the Workman's Compensation Board. It had been five-and-a-half years since Bill's hand was crushed in the printing press, and he had yet to receive any compensation. They wanted Bill to settle the claim, and then a check would be forthcoming. Within six weeks we had a check for three hundred dollars in our hands—the equivalent of two months of Bill's salary. We were *wealthy!* With less than a month to go before becoming parents, it felt good to walk into Garner's Service Station and clear up Bill's entire account. Suddenly the pressure was off; God's timing couldn't have been better.

CHAPTER 11

Trouble in Paradise

The whole time I was pregnant, I could only imagine having a girl. I only *wanted* a girl. I couldn't visualize myself with a baby boy. As far as I was concerned, the baby I was carrying was a girl.

After the fourth month ended, I felt better and made up for all of the meals I missed due to morning sickness. I ate double portions every time I sat down. My appetite was insatiable, and I gained sixty pounds in five months.

From childhood, I had always hated milk, yet I knew that the growing bones and teeth of my unborn baby depended upon my consumption of calcium. Concerned, I brought up the subject with my family doctor.

"Do you like ice cream?" he asked.

"*Yeah!*" I said emphatically.

"There you go! Eat all the ice cream you like!"

It was the one prescription I filled diligently.

I would go for a walk nearly every day to the store, buy three ice cream bars and eat them all before I got back home. Most hot summer evenings Bill and I would go to Avondale Dairy and get triple ice cream cones. Bill didn't mind. We had no air conditioning and going to the dairy was a way to cool off. Conveniently, the three ice cream bars I had eaten earlier in the day failed to come up in our conversation.

I was due October 10. By Sunday the twenty-fifth I was fifteen days past due and desperate to have the baby. Bill and I went to Uncle Bill's house after the evening service at church and Aunt Anita served us coffee—and ice cream!

Uncle Bill said, "Ah! You'll probably have the baby tonight," teasing me at the table.

"I don't think I'm ever going to have it!" I said sarcastically.

At five o'clock in the morning on October twenty-sixth, I awoke with labor pains. I woke Bill up, all excited, "This is it! I'm in labor! We're going to have a baby!"

We had no television in the apartment, so Bill's nightly entertainment consisted of intricate jigsaw puzzles. After I woke him up, he occupied himself at the kitchen table where he had been working on a particularly difficult puzzle for the past three days. "Let me know when you have to go to the hospital," he said calmly. Bill has always been calm—too calm.

We waited until the contractions were five minutes apart—Bill timing the intervals while searching for elusive puzzle pieces—then we left for the hospital. On the way we confirmed the name we had picked out for a girl: Wendy Catherine.

Labor was long and difficult. We were at the hospital by seven o'clock, but by two in the afternoon the baby still hadn't come. The obstetrician would tell me to bear down and as I did they could see the baby's head; but something was holding it back, preventing the birth. Deciding things would be better with anesthetic, they put me under and prepared me for a Cesarean section. The anesthetic produced an unexpected relaxation of the muscles in the birth canal, and they were able to guide the baby out with forceps. It was then that they discovered the problem: the umbilical cord had been wrapped around my baby's tummy—not once, but twice—and every time I pushed, that cord would tighten, stopping any movement forward.

My little baby girl, weighing just six pounds and five ounces, was rushed away and placed in an incubator. There they administered oxygen and kept a close watch on her. Bill was in the waiting room, knowing nothing of the struggle our little baby girl had gone through to get into the world; and I was unconscious in the recovery room. (In 1964 fathers were not at all part of the birth process. Their role was to sit patiently in the waiting room reading magazines until the doctor brought them the news.) By the time Bill knew there was anything wrong, our baby had been born and things were under control.

I was dopey from the anesthetic for a couple of days and didn't remember much of what happened. I vaguely heard voices telling me that I had a little baby girl and that she was under the lights. (Our blood types were not an ideal match and the baby was considerably jaundiced.) On the third day, Bill brought little Shawn Marie into my room.

"*Shawn Marie?* You named her *Shawn Marie?* What happened to *Wendy Catherine?*" I couldn't believe that he had named her without even consulting me.

"Well, Honey," his voice was soft and apologetic, "you were in recovery...I couldn't talk to you and...well, with what she went through being born and the fact that she's okay...and you're okay now... 'Shawn' means God is gracious. She's a gift of God! I just really like what her name means!"

I should have been more upset than I was, but his explanation softened my response. I was so grateful that it was all over, and we were both going to be all right, that it didn't seem to matter. Whether her name was *Wendy Catherine* or *Shawn Marie*, she was mine. I had a precious little baby girl.

At the onset of labor my family physician had been attending. When a Caesarean section seemed imminent, the obstetrician/gynecologist on call was Dr. Wood, an associate of Dr. Mackenzie (whom I had seen for my premarital exam). It was he who came to check on me before I went home from the hospital. He sat down on the edge of the bed.

"Margaret, whatever did you go through in the past?" He was sincere and his face was full of compassion, as though I was a fragile little girl. His question caught me quite by surprise.

"Nothing."

"Well...it's just the things you said...coming out of anesthetic... You said things. You reacted so badly in recovery. It's like you've been through something traumatic...something awful, something scary."

"Well, I don't know what that could be!" I said as I looked away from his penetrating eyes. "Really, if something did happen, I don't know what it was!" By this time I was somewhat defensive and he stopped questioning me.

Deny. Deny. Deny. If I didn't admit it happened, I wouldn't have to think about it. In the two years since I had married Bill, I hadn't thought about the rapes—at least not consciously. Now this doctor suddenly brought it up. It was all I could do to push it back down, pull myself together and go home with my baby after eight days in the hospital.

I desperately wanted to breast-feed my baby girl, but Shawn was so placid and sleepy, she had trouble latching on. I had to set an alarm, even in the hospital. It would go off every four hours through the middle of the night so I could wake Shawn and feed her. Even after the eighth day, I wasn't convinced she was getting enough milk. I lacked confidence that I could look after this little baby. I didn't know how to be a mother. If I couldn't even feed her properly, how would she survive? I was plagued with negative thoughts.

When Shawn reached six weeks old, I thought, "Wow! She made it! She's still alive!" I was surprised she ate and grew. I didn't think I could keep her alive for that long.

Throughout my pregnancy, I had been convinced I was having a stillborn. Shawn was not active in the womb—she was placid even then. Shortly after I found out I was pregnant, we had watched a movie about a girl whose baby was stillborn. I figured, in my twisted thinking, that God was preparing me. He was using this movie to warn me that my baby would be born dead. I lived in silent dread.

It wasn't just the movie. About a month earlier, a salesman came to our door selling a special combination stroller-highchair. We listened politely at first, even inviting him in—we were having a baby, and we did need a stroller. Then he dropped the bomb.

"It's just six hundred dollars," he said, as if it were twenty.

Bill apologized for letting him think we could purchase such an expensive item and moved to show him out. When he got to the door he indicated that his manager was with him that night and there might be something he could do about the price. We were young and gullible. We let him excuse himself and he went to fetch his boss.

The hard-sell tactics of his mentor quickly replaced the quiet, unassuming manner of the young man we had spoken to at first. He laid it on thick. If guilt would move us to buy, he would employ it in truckloads. Frustrated at our constant refusals, he finally blurted out, "Well! You're not fit to *be* parents if you won't provide the necessities of life for your new baby! I wouldn't be surprised if something happens to that baby of yours—you're not fit to be parents!" Suddenly Bill was less polite, threw the two of them out and shut the door. But the damage was done; I knew it was another prophecy of doom from God. He was trying to prepare me. My baby was going to die!

Driven by my insecurity, I spent more time at home—my former home. Once Shawn was born, my relationship with Mom improved. Mom enjoyed the company, and she had an automated ringer washing machine that enabled us to avoid the laundromat. Perhaps because she saw me as an adult now, she treated me better. I had the choice of whether to come over to the house or not. I was no longer trapped at 17 Sherbourne Street, so she made my stays there more pleasant, hoping I would come more often. Dave was hardly there anymore, and she was almost always by herself. Being two years removed from living with her, I felt sorry for her; and, strangely, I missed her. Deep down I wanted a relationship with my mother, and now it seemed easier.

Mom loved Shawn. She was never a woman enamored of babies—presumably because she had eleven—but she did things with Shawn that she never did with her own children. She played with her and held her for hours. While I did the laundry, she watched Shawn without complaint, as if it were her greatest joy.

One day while I was doing my laundry, I lost my engagement ring. The semi-automatic, ringer washing machines had a tub and agitator, like machines today, except they were unable to spin. After the wash cycle was finished, we had to reach into the tub, pull out the articles of clothing and feed them by hand between the two moving rubber rollers. Excess water was squeezed out of the clothes that were then ready to be hung on a line. My hands were constantly in the water. With soapy, wet fingers, my engagement ring slipped off without my knowing. When I discovered it wasn't on my finger, I was frantic. Mom was on the floor of the dugout basement of her house for two hours, searching for my ring. When she found my diamond amid cobwebs, in the corner of the cellar, she was ecstatic.

167

"I found it! Margaret! I found it! It vas in da corner, by da oil tank." She had a huge smile on her face. Mom hardly ever smiled. I realized that day that Mom never had a diamond ring from a man who loved her—who genuinely loved her—and she was desperate to find mine. It was as though *my* ring was hers. As sick as I was at the thought of telling Bill I lost my ring, Mom was sicker. The joy I saw on Mom's face as she handed me that ring is seared into my memory. Without doubt, it was the best moment I had ever spent with her...ever.

After Shawn arrived, our one-bedroom apartment on Rowntree Road became cramped. We found a three-bedroom for nearly the same rent on the other side of town, only a couple of miles from Sherbourne Street, and moved to Niagara Street in St. Catharines.

Bill's work was not going very well. His boss had always assured him he was a printer's apprentice. Bill figured the pay was modest, but at least he was acquiring a trade. Once he was a *bona fide* printer, a journeyman, he could shop himself around and find better money elsewhere. After Shawn was born, Bill approached his boss about certification. He had been a faithful apprentice for five years and wanted his tradesman's ticket. As his boss applied for Bill's certification, he learned that his own journeyman's papers were not current; that in fact he was not even licensed as a journeyman printer himself. Bill's five-year apprenticeship had not been registered. It was meaningless. If Bill wanted to be a printer, he would have to begin the whole process again from the beginning. He had spent five years earning lousy pay to obtain a journeyman's ticket that was never possible from the outset. Bill was heartbroken.

Bill hardly ever gets discouraged. Positive and cheerful, he has always taken the lumps that come in life and put them in perspective; but when he lost the chance to be a journeyman printer, he was downright depressed. The motivation to go to work every morning was gone. He saw himself at a dead-end job, only putting in time to feed his family. He felt taken advantage of, duped, and angry with himself for not being more diligent, for not making sure things were done properly. He had trusted his boss and gotten burned. In one day, everything that he had been working for was gone.

He investigated a posted position at *The St. Catharines Standard*, our local daily newspaper, but the job was entry level; he would be starting again for dirt pay. At *The Smithville Review*, Bill set the type, arranged the columns, and even sold some advertising. It was a thinking and planning job. At the *Standard*, he would be taking a step backwards and be even less fulfilled.

Feeling depressed, we decided to drop in and visit Bill's brother Andy. Andy had a way of making Bill laugh, and we visited them often. Jeanette, Andy's wife, had a sister who lived a half-mile down the road. She and her husband dropped in soon after we arrived and, as Bill shared what had been going on at *The Smithville Review*, her husband, a foreman at General Motors, spoke up.

"I think I could get you into GM, Bill—if you're interested."

"Interested! Of course I'm interested. Could you really do that?" The thought of getting into General Motors was a dream. They paid great money, and Bill, at twenty-three years old, might even be able to apply for an apprenticeship. We were almost afraid to think it could be possible. GM had a great pension and benefits; we could go to the dentist! The only thing we feared was getting our hopes up too high, only to have them dashed.

The workers at General Motors were coming off a strike at the end of 1964. Armed with a new contract, management was ready to hire several hundred workers. Getting hired was more about who you knew, or were related to—as there were thousands of applications—than any qualifications you might otherwise have had. In January 1965 Bill got the call and began working in the factory. His paycheck went from sixty dollars to $115 per week, without overtime. After taxes, our take-home income increased by about eighty percent. The financial security was wonderful. I was set for the next thirty years: I had a faithful husband with a union-protected job, regular pay increases, group benefits, and a retirement pension. Everything that I lacked as a child became mine in the first two years of being married.

From Bill's first moments in the plant, however, he hated it. He worked on the assembly line, doing the same menial tasks repetitiously for eight-hour shifts...3,000 endless cycles. No thinking. No planning. No responsibility. And no reward for hard work. Within the first couple of weeks several men approached him and told him he was working too fast. He was told to slow down; he was making it harder on the other workers, making them look bad. Everything he had ever been taught about hard work and getting ahead worked backwards in a union environment. Slackers were protected and defended. Those who had a good work ethic were attacked and maligned. When better jobs were posted on the board, ability and prowess meant nothing. Bill would apply for a better job within the plant, only to watch someone with more seniority get the position. His thoughts of getting an apprenticeship quickly dissipated—those opportunities were given to the workers with a high school diploma.

Most of the time he had to work shifts. Sometimes they would rotate between days and afternoons, and at other times a night shift of eleven to seven was added. It was more difficult to plan ahead, or to be as involved at church as he once was. But it was the whole factory environment that disturbed Bill the most. He was surrounded by men whose personal drive and ambition had been ripped out of them, sold for the price of a healthy paycheck. Their language was bad, their talk was idle, and their minds had shrunk from years of thinking only about how little they could get away with doing while still keeping their jobs. The place was full of men whose purpose for living and working was reduced to bringing home money. There was little imagination and no reward for creativity. General Motors was a black hole that Bill entered every day, whose only escape was the double doors beside the time clock, accessible only after he had given away eight hours of his life.

Each day he went to work, Bill died a little inside. It was a slow death—almost imperceptible at first—but a death just the same. I didn't see it at all. Bill rarely complained; but even if he had, I wasn't listening. All I thought about was how good our life was, how secure I felt. It was great to have more money. I never wanted to worry about money again.

Shortly after moving to the Niagara Street apartment, we started thinking about having a second child. Bill's new job and the three bedrooms made it possible to think about more kids. I was grateful at the time that we could have children, but sort of took it in stride. The fact that we already had Shawn took the sting and the fear out of the dire warning Dr. Mackenzie had given me. It was evident that I could bear children, and it really didn't dawn on me to thank God for it. It's not that I wasn't thrilled; I just didn't attribute the gift of children to God. Having children hadn't been a pressing desire from the first moment we were married. We really would have preferred to be more financially set before having kids, and Shawn's conception was a surprise. I never got to the place where I had needed to pray to have children—and if I had been in that situation, I don't know that I would have thought that asking God for a child was a legitimate request. I know differently now, but then, that kind of request seemed selfish somehow. Stories of Hannah and Elizabeth from the Bible must have escaped my mind—or maybe they were just that, stories. I didn't see their practical extension; that God loves to give good gifts to his children, especially babies to barren mothers. Now, I thank God every day for my children.

When Shawn was six or seven months old, we started trying to have another baby. We thought that we would be able to afford just two children on Bill's wages, and if we were going to have only two, we wanted them close in age. Shawn had been a perfect delight. She hardly cried. She was cute as a button and everyone adored her. At only a few months old, she was living up to her name; she was God's gracious gift to us.

I got pregnant right away, without losing the weight I had put on carrying Shawn. I imagined what my new baby would be like: a little playmate for Shawn. In my daydreams, I once again envisioned a little girl. I saw an idyllic family: Bill and me and our two cute little girls. This time I was somewhat more disciplined and didn't fill as many ice cream prescriptions. I gained a modest twenty-five pounds, compared to the sixty I gained with Shawn. I was definitely less sick this time, and began to reflect upon the possibility that I would have a son. Being raised the younger sister of six older brothers, I was never enamored of having a boy. *What if I had a boy and he was like...* I never let myself fully form that thought. I knew that couldn't happen in *my* family—we were totally different. *We're a loving, Christian family; there's no booze—and God owes me big time,* I reasoned. That was how I felt. God had punished me and put me through horrific pain—I had suffered enough. I thought He couldn't possibly let that happen in *my* perfect little family. God owed me. He owed my kids a life free of pain and suffering. I had paid the toll for their free ride. That's what I thought.

And, I thought, if the suffering price I paid wasn't enough, God would spare me for Bill's sake. I had married honor, not wealth. My family was bereft of honor and full of shame, but Bill's family was a picture of integrity and love. I married into respectability. Bill was a smart, spiritual young man. He was a leader. He was popular and young people's president. I knew God might still have some punishment left for me, but certainly not for Bill. I believed that would protect me. I would be safe because of him.

That was it. I thought God allowed Willie to rape me for ten years because I deserved it. I was so bad that He had to let that happen to me so that I would serve Him. It sounds ridiculous to me now—but then, that was exactly what I believed.

As the end of my term approached, I began to feel guilty for only wanting a girl. *Maybe Bill would like a son. He would enjoy doing father and son things*, I thought. After all, I loved the thought of growing close to Shawn as she matured into a young lady. I thought it selfish of me not to consider that Bill might relish that same kind of closeness with a son. I began to warm to the possibility of having a baby boy. As my attitude changed about the possible sex of my baby, I started praying for my baby's future, that, whether a boy or a girl, my baby would love and serve Jesus.

April 15 was a Friday night. On Fridays, Bill would come home from work and lead the young people's service. (Despite the shift work, Bill was still young people's president. On nights he had to work, he would organize a replacement; but most Friday nights we were there—all three of us.) After Bill went into work that Friday, I called Alice, Bill's sister, to pick me up. We were going shopping. The baby was nine days overdue, but we were getting close to April 21—Bill's birthday—and I had yet to purchase his present. I was afraid I'd be in the hospital over his birthday, and I didn't want to miss giving him his gift.

Bill left for work before 7:00 a.m., so he was already up when I woke up that day. Just like the first time, my night's sleep was brought to an end by labor pains. When Alice picked me up, I made sure I didn't tell her I was in labor; she would have freaked out and cancelled the shopping excursion. I knew it would be a long time before the contractions were close together enough to go to the hospital, so I merely suffered the contractions in silence, turning my face away from Alice whenever I needed to grimace. We were home by early afternoon and Bill arrived by 3:30.

I brought Bill his supper of fish and chips to the table.

"Aren't you eating supper?" he asked.

"I'm not that hungry." I paused for a moment then said, "Bill, I'm not going to be able to go to young people's tonight."

"Oh, no? Why not?" Bill questioned between mouthfuls.

"I'm in labor."

Bill jumped up from the table. "You're in labor? Okay! I'll take you to the hospital first, and then I'll go to young people's meeting. I'll see if someone can take over for me; then I'll be right back over to the hospital." He was thinking out loud. "How far apart are they?" However tired he had been after work, he was now fully energized.

"Bill, really! I'm all right. The contractions aren't that close. Go to church and *then* you can take me to the hospital when you get home."

As I went into the kitchen, Bill watched me. He could tell by my breathing each time I had a contraction, and he timed them while he finished eating. "They're too close. I'm taking you to the hospital first. Let's go."

St. Catharines General Hospital was two doors down from Elim Tabernacle. Bill dropped me off to wait out my labor under the watchful eyes of the nurses and went over to lead the youth service. He rushed back as soon as the kids were dismissed, but he needn't have. My little baby boy wasn't born until one o'clock the next morning, April sixteenth.

This time there was no name controversy. Blake William was eight pounds, two ounces and healthy. There were no complications with the delivery and my little family was complete...at least, that's what I thought.

Following Shawn's birth, my world had gotten better: we had a new apartment, a new job, and my relationship with Mom improved. But after Blake was born, things started to unravel. Shawn was just seventeen months old at Blake's birth and was a busy toddler. Fearing I would have trouble nursing again, I put Blake on the bottle. I had two little babies, a boy and a girl, and everything in my life was supposed to be perfect; yet I felt down—really down. Post-partum depression hit me in waves; some days worse than others. I had no reason to be depressed, and still I was. I had feelings of lethargy during the day—but worse things happened at night. I started having nightmares.

For three years I had hardly thought about the sexual abuse in my childhood. Each time someone inadvertently caused it to come into my mind, as when Dr. Wood talked to me after Shawn's birth, I pushed it down into a dark pit. I kept a lid on that pit and I never lifted it off to take a look. I pretended. Just like when I was a little girl, I pretended it didn't happen. Bill and I never spoke of it. I never brought the subject up and, to my mind, that strategy was working. I was living the big lie. It was as though there were no repercussions. I was raped and molested for ten years of my childhood, yet I lived and acted as though I had a normal upbringing. To look at me, to listen to me, was to see what seemed to be an average young mother of two. Except for the fact that I was more defensive than most if cornered and that I possessed a sarcastic wit, most people whether they knew me well or not, wouldn't have clued in to what I had been through. I was a phony, but no one knew—especially me.

Every garbage dump has a maximum capacity, and the pit in my mind where I had stuffed all of my pain had reached its limit by the time Blake was two months old.

Willie's troubled marriage and subsequent move home to Mom's must have bothered me more than I had admitted. When we visited on Sunday afternoons at Sherbourne Street, Willie was there. No longer did I feel free just to pop over and do laundry at Mom's house. Soon Willie hurt his back and went on disability insurance. He wasn't going in to work every day, so we couldn't predict when he would be home. Bill felt the full force of my fears.

"Bill, on Sunday afternoons, if Willie is there in the living room and Mom calls me into the kitchen to help with the lunch, don't you let Shawn out of your sight! Don't go to the bathroom! Don't leave that room without bringing Shawn to me! Don't ever leave her alone with him—ever!"

I would sit on the couch and cringe as Willie played on the floor with my baby. Mom would call me to help her set out the food, and I would glare at Bill—he would go on alert.

Bill never had that much to say to Willie. Other than a passing hello and some idle small talk, he ignored him; much of the time Willie was sullen and moody anyway. He rarely came down from his room when the family visited on Sundays. Occasionally Bill and my brothers would break out the Monopoly board and play a game, usually around Christmas. Willie played in the odd game with Bill; that was the extent of their relationship. Other than saying hello when I entered the house, I ignored him completely. The rest of my family hardly noticed that we didn't speak, because my brothers' wives and their children were usually there; I was busy talking to everyone else. It was normally a very full house.

After seeing Willie on Sundays, I would often have a nightmare that night. I had two kinds of nightmares. Sometimes they were a fever-pitched collage of episodes with Willie I had actually lived through; but more often, they were a single experience repeated over and over. I would be walking from the bus terminal in downtown St. Catharines to the National Bakery where I worked. It seemed as though it was dawn or dusk; there was never very much light. A gray pallor made everything in the dream hard to distinguish. For some unknown reason, I would go to the back entrance of the bakery, in the alley. (I never went into the bakery through the back entrance in reality—but I would in this dream.) As I moved toward the door, I could make out the shape of a man. Someone was standing there—in the doorway—waiting for me. He would snatch me, put his hand over my mouth so I couldn't scream, and then gag me. He always gagged me! In my sleep I would choke, feeling that gag as if it were real. I couldn't breathe and I was suffocating. I was sleeping, but I was choking—choking and terrified. I knew he was going to rape me. I knew the feeling right before a rape and I knew this total stranger was going to rape me!

The nightmare usually ended there, in the anticipation of being raped. Rarely did I actually *get* raped in the dream. I usually woke up in terror immediately preceding it. Sometimes the nightmare would get stuck, the gagging and choking repeating incessantly like a broken record. I would live on perpetually in the moment of shear terror right before a rape. The rape wouldn't happen and the dream wouldn't end. I was frozen in that horrific, helpless moment, knowing what was coming and unable to avoid the inevitable. So surreal was the nightmare that, inside of it, I felt myself trying to wake up!

Then, with a start, I would awaken. The sheets were always soaked with sweat and I would be crying—hysterically crying. When I would wake up, Bill would too. For at least fifteen minutes, I would

175

be inconsolable. Bill would just hold me. Finally I would get up the courage and tell him what happened in the dream, sobbing between each sentence. He would always just sit there, with the lights on, holding me and listening. He would listen to everything in the nightmare. Every time I had the *same* nightmare, Bill listened.

Waking brought instant depression—the blackest, deepest, heaviest, most evil depression you can imagine. It was like demons were clinging to my heart, sinking their life-sucking talons into the depths of my soul, dragging me into that pit I had tried to keep closed and holding me there. The accompanying depression seized me once awake, just as the man in the doorway had held me in the dream. I couldn't shake it off. The nightmare had tentacles that reached from the subconscious into my reality. It was an abiding evil presence and it lasted for days.

The next day or two would be filled with crying. I could hardly look after my babies. I started having flashbacks. The nightmares left me vulnerable to images of the past. I would be transported back to a childhood experience of abuse, reliving it with all the same emotional anguish, as if I was physically there. Every time a scene with Willie flashed through my mind, the fear and terror I felt as a child overtook me like a cloud. It took my breath away. I would try to think of other things, but I was bombarded with memories of my abuse. During those times I thought I was going crazy.

As each day passed, and the distance between nightmares grew, my emotional state would slowly improve. I thought a little less about Willie and life temporarily returned to normal. The first time it happened, I thought the nightmare was an isolated incident—from time to time we all have nightmares; but I kept having it. It became more frequent and regular. Soon I was having the dream five or six times a year. Every couple of months I was sucked back into that pit. Different things began to trigger the night terrors. In the beginning, seeing Willie on Sundays or running into him at Mom's during the week would instigate the trouble; but eventually being around drinking became a trigger. Drunkenness and abuse were linked throughout my whole childhood. Neglect and violence were almost always perpetrated amid the stench of alcohol. The smell of it gave me flashbacks. I would see people in a restaurant drinking and my imagination would be engaged. I hated booze! I associated even social drinking with evil. I began to live in fear of when the next bad dream would come.

Going to bed was scary. Would this be the night? Would I wake up in a cold sweat? Even when more time elapsed between episodes, I was not relieved...I knew instead, I was just that much closer to the next dream. When I went out in public I was more afraid than I had been before. Suddenly my greatest fear was stranger rape. Possibly because I knew it would now be difficult for Willie to hurt me—whenever I saw him, Mom or Bill was nearby—or because the man in my recurring nightmare was someone I didn't know, I feared a stranger was going to rape me. I didn't go out at night if I could avoid it, and I didn't like being in unfamiliar surroundings by myself. I lived in fear that the car would stall—our vehicles were always old and unreliable. More often than I ever shared with Bill, I felt the cold shivers of panic creep up and down my spine.

The cycle was always the same: be near Willie, see a person drunk, or have an argument with Bill that left me feeling insecure, and that night the dream would come. Each time I would wake up drenched in sweat and crying hysterically. After half an hour of shaking while Bill held me, I would have to talk. I always had to *talk* about what Willie did to me. Then I would be filled with doubts. The instant depression made me feel absolutely unlovable—by Bill or anyone else.

"Bill," I would sob, "how can you stand me? I'm so much trouble! How can you be with me? How can you love me? You're going to get sick of this. I'm such a mess. You could have had anyone—a normal person—and you got stuck with me." Every ounce of self-worth was sucked from my being. For a couple of hours, nothing Bill said could soothe me. I was a seething caldron of self-loathing, fear, and insecurity. I was a giant heap of shame!

"I love you," Bill would say patiently. " I love you and I'm always going to love you."

"No, you don't," I would contradict. "How could you? How could anyone? You're just saying that to make me feel better. What is there about me that could ever make you love me?"

Self-deprecating insults would roll off my tongue unabated by Bill's loving assurances. My mind was so full of lies and deceit, I didn't know fact from fiction. Nonetheless, Bill listened to me talk.

He let me get out all the things I needed to say. It was the middle of the night, so he would lose at least two hours of sleep just calming me down, but he never complained.

"I don't know why you have to keep talking about it. Surely bringing it up all the time is making it worse. I wish you could just forget about all those bad things, Honey. I'm so sorry you had to go through all of that, Sweetheart."

Bill thought that talking about it made it worse. He didn't object to listening—he just didn't see how it helped. What he didn't realize then was that I *needed* to talk about it. I had been stuffing my memories down inside of me. They were coming up involuntarily from the internal pressure. He was the only person I could talk to. In 1966 there were no Christian counseling agencies, and secular psychiatrists were considered carnal and ungodly. Bill was my sounding board, my patient listener—if he hadn't listened as much as I needed to talk, I would have surely ended up in a mental institution.

The nightmare episodes were bad enough, but within a year the thing that had been so precious between us, the closeness and intimacy we enjoyed in our marriage, would be threatened. By 1967 demons from the past showed up in our sex life.

Sex with Bill for the three years we had been married had been beautiful. When we made love, I felt special and loved. There were no problems or difficulties. We had sex often, and it was mutually satisfying; and, other than the six weeks before and after our babies were born, there were no significant lapses. Bill waited out those times patiently, and we enthusiastically counted down the days until we could make love again.

Without warning one night as we were making love, something changed. My husband was inside me and a gap in my reality opened: it wasn't Bill anymore—Willie was on top of me!

"No! No! Stop! Stop! Stop! No! Get off! I can't handle this anymore! Get off!" I was screaming!

Bill rolled over thinking he was hurting me.

"I'm sorry, Bill. It's not you...I mean it was you...but then it wasn't," I stammered. "All at once I wasn't making love to you anymore—you changed into Willie and you were..." I couldn't finish my sentence. A flood of tears overtook me. Bill held me in his arms.

178

"It's okay, Honey. It's okay," he soothed. "Just forget about it. It's all right."

"What's happening to me? Am I going crazy? I'm ruining everything! Now I can't even make love with you! Oh, Bill, I'm sorry! You should have a normal wife." One sardonic comment after another flowed out of my mouth. Then, just like after a nightmare, I had to tell what happened, explicitly detailing everything Willie had done to me. It must have been excruciating for Bill to listen to—but he listened, hugging me, caressing my back as if I were his little girl. He listened and reassured me of his love.

The dreams were bad enough. Now my reality was being interrupted by terrors while I was awake! I didn't know whether I would ever be able to make love again. The question dogged me: "What if we try to have sex tomorrow or the next day, and the same thing happens? What if it's never Bill again? What if he always transforms into Willie in my mind?" Every light in the bedroom was on. I was hugging Bill, crying on his chest, every muscle in my body was trembling—and I was full of every fear and doubt imaginable.

The nightmares increased in frequency and the flashbacks during lovemaking repeated in a cycle, every couple of months. After an episode like this, and the long conversation that inevitably followed, Bill would have to roll over and try to get some sleep. Depression and after-shock flashbacks would fill the next few days, and then a shroud of normalcy would slowly emerge. Things would be temporarily forgotten, but the possibility of their return was in the back of my mind every time I went to bed. Most nights, going to sleep filled me with angst.

I didn't realize then how blessed I was to have Bill as a husband. In the throes of intimate passion, he had to abruptly stop making love; his once loving and affectionate wife transformed into a crying, trembling, pitiful heap in his arms. Where, only moments before, he had the expectation of climax and the rewards of romantic love, now he was thrown violently into emotional chaos. The situation demanded that he instantly move from intimate and tender caresses to soothing and comforting care. He never once complained. Never did he say that he was getting ripped off in his marriage. He never sarcastically brought the subject up later, complaining that he wasn't having his sexual needs fulfilled. In fact, he never brought up the subject of my abuse, nightmares, or flashback episodes—at all. None of the games that are often played between warring spouses were evident the day after sex was interrupted. There was no silent treatment or grumpy "payback" tone in his voice. The day after I would have to "stop in the middle," he was tender and loving, asking me if I was okay and hugging me more than usual. When I brought up the subject, we would speak of it; otherwise it was never mentioned.

When I asked him why he never brought it up, his answer was always the same: "Honey, I never think about *that*. I don't look at you that way. To me you're my beautiful wife. You're not an incest victim! Sweetheart, you are the woman I love; God gave you to me and I never think of you in any other way. The awful things you went through are never on my mind. When I look at you, I see the prettiest woman I know—the love of my life."

My response was typically sarcastic, "God gave you the raw end of that deal, didn't He?" I couldn't believe how he could just love me—how he didn't see me as ugly, dirty, and shameful. When I looked at myself in the mirror, I thought about it. I saw an incest victim; why didn't he? *One day he'll have had enough and he'll be gone*, I thought.

From 1966 to 1970, my flashback episodes and nightmares increased. Talking about it could no longer console me. I still had to talk—but I was convinced that this torture was never going to end. My brother Willie had put me in prison. He hadn't touched me in ten years, but he imprisoned me just the same. The number of days that I would stay depressed multiplied with each incident. Bill wearied of having to talk about it; but he persevered, sensing that I needed to. It must have been awful for him to keep hearing the rehashed stories of Willie's attacks, but he endured them for my sake. There were nights when we wanted to make love but I was too scared.

Bill would pray for both of us: "God, we need your help here. We would like to make love tonight, but we're scared—would you please just help us?"

We had to bring Jesus into our marriage bed out of sheer necessity. That taught us to trust God with the most intimate details of our lives. It isn't common to pray before sex; but we had to. Many times after making love, Bill and I would lay in bed and thank God out loud for the privilege of expressing our love to each other without incident. We couldn't take making love for granted.

Gradually something else happened that I found even more disturbing. Where once the nightmares and flashbacks were triggered by seeing Willie, or anyone drunk, now I began to have these terrifying incidents on days when those triggers didn't happen. I began to notice that emotional turmoil, little fights or arguments during the day with Bill, harsh words said between us—normal disputes in any other marriage—these became triggers. Anything that played on my self-esteem, insecurity, or fear of rejection became a possible trigger to trouble in the bedroom. Even financial pressures drove my subconscious mind back to the feelings I had as a child. While I was awake, I could control what I thought about; but once asleep, all the emotional anxieties I felt as a kid returned and sparked nightmares.

For most women, making love begins in the morning. When the man you love is soft and tender and treats you like his princess, the evening comes and you feel wonderfully romantic. You are in the mood and you want nothing more than to give yourself to him. For me there had to be no turmoil at all, and not just for that day but for several days before. If Bill had been the least bit inattentive to me—not cruel or angry, but just quiet—then sex would be a problem. If he read the paper or did a crossword puzzle to unwind before bed, I couldn't make love with him. If I tried, many times he would become Willie and we would have to stop. I had felt like Willie's prostitute for all of those years; inattention, insecurity, and emotional stress took me right back to feeling like that ten-year-old hooker.

In less than three years, my utopian life had become a mess. All of the lousy things that I left behind at the wedding altar had returned and intensified. When I realized that marrying to escape my 17 Sherbourne Street hell hadn't worked, the disappointment was overwhelming. I had been duped. Marriage had only delayed the insanity that I was cursed to live. I was free from 17 Sherbourne Street, but a prisoner no matter where I lived. My paradise had been sabotaged, and I felt betrayed by God a second time. I served Him, but I was afraid of Him—afraid of what He would do to me next. The best I could hope for was to endure the torment. I had to try to live through it, survive it. I began to realize that Willie's legacy would haunt me for life. I came to believe there would be no escape from my prison, except in death.

But God knew different.

Margaret, age one

Margaret, age four, with Mom

Margaret, age four

Margaret, age four, with Father

Margaret (far right) with
neighborhood children

Dad and Mom Davidson

Dad and Mom Hiebert

Mom, Ben, Dave, and Margaret, 1960

Margaret on brother Ben's
motorcycle, 1960

Brother Willie, age eighteen

Left to right: David (youngest brother) and Willie

Wonderful sister, Tina, and her husband, Murray

Margaret, Mom, and Tina, 1994 (four years before Mom passed away)

Bill and Margaret, 1962

Bill and Margaret, 1962

Bill and Margaret, 1963—the day I married
my best friend

Bill, Margaret, and our first miracle
baby girl, Shawn Marie, 1964

Bill, Blake, Heather, Shawn Marie, and
Margaret at our first home, 1973.

Daughter Heather, age 5, 1975

Blake, age eight, 1975

Shawn Marie, age eighteen, 1982

Left to right: Heather, Bill, Margaret, Shawn,
and Blake at Pigeon Lake

My entire family at Pigeon Lake

Margaret, Heather, and Shawn at
Banff, Alberta, Canada

Bill and Margaret, 1996

Shawn, Craig, and Danny

Blake & Christine's family: (back row) Jade, Blake, and Christine; (front row) Katie, Abbey, Margaret, and Chase

Heather, Al, Dylan, and Brooke

Nana (Margaret) with her wonderful grandsons, Dylan and Chase

Nana (Margaret) with newest grandson,
Danny

Papa and Danny

Blake and Margaret

Margaret and Rev. Peggy Kennedy, who spoke
God's Word over my life

CHAPTER 12

Ben and June

Even with Bill working at General Motors, we felt financial pressure. On top of our old debts, I wasn't working and, with two
children, there was little left for extras. So, when Bill was offered
overtime, he took it. If no overtime was available at the plant, Bill
worked at Pelissero's chicken farm, cleaning cages or catching
chickens. It was our intention to save any extra money, putting it
toward the down payment for a house. As time moved along, however, it always went for something else. Bill and I were not good at
handling our money. Saving seemed nearly impossible. God was
not yet Master of our finances. We didn't tithe consistently, and we
didn't give offerings over and above—we gave when we had it. In
this area, we hadn't yet learned to fully trust Him. It was easier to
owe God than our creditors.

After Blake was born, I got so depressed that Bill suggested we
spend our down payment savings on our first vacation. A house
seemed so far into the future, and a holiday, while it would use up
all of our existing savings, was perhaps just what I needed to get out
of the doldrums. Until my honeymoon, I had never been on a holiday; so I readily sacrificed the paltry amount set aside for a house
and left with Bill and our young family on my second-ever vacation.
With Blake just a couple of months old and Shawn not quite two,
we traveled three hours north of St. Catharines to Elim Lodge (a

Christian resort near Peterborough, Ontario, not associated with our church). I was in seventh heaven. We stayed in the lodge, which was like a big inn, and Bill splurged on the "meal package." We ate in the dining hall and maids made up the beds—it was great for me. I didn't have to lift a finger. Bill, always generous, loved showering me with things. He took pride in pampering me. The holiday cost a whole month's salary, but we didn't care. We had a blast!

Shortly after getting home, we received a call from the Pelisseros. Harry Pelissero had gotten to know Bill well while he worked on the farm. They wanted to know if Bill and I would superintend a small twelve-unit apartment building they owned. It was located on Barton Street, directly behind General Motors' Plant Number One, where Bill worked. With our rent paid for keeping the building clean and in good repair, we would be able to save for that elusive mortgage deposit. Living paycheck to paycheck was taking its toll, and this seemed like a terrific opportunity. We moved for the fourth time in four years.

Blake was about six months old when we moved into the apartment at Barton Street, and we lived there until he was three-and-a-half.

Reverend Earl Williams, who married Bill and me in 1963, had been the pastor of Elim Tabernacle for ten years. He was a kind and stately man. Incredibly organized, he carried himself with a stiff posture and a self-respect that exuded confidence. Making it a point to visit every family in the church at least once during the year, Earl Williams shepherded his flock with efficiency. He even visited Andy, Bill's brother, who hadn't been out to a service in years, exemplifying the custodial nature and chaplain-like style that made him loved by the St. Catharines' congregation. He was strong on integrity and character, and Bill learned much from him about taking responsibility, being on time, and letting your word be your bond.

When he left for another parish in 1968, the pulpit committee settled on a young, but powerful preacher named Gerald Morgan. He was everything that Earl Williams wasn't—not better or worse, just different. It was easy to see his ambition, and he picked up the pace, beginning from where Pastor Williams finished. Elim's congregation was growing, and the old church on Queenston Street didn't have the facilities for a proper Sunday school that was rapidly expanding. In addition to the space problem inside, there was virtually no parking outside. Members had to park on nearby side streets and walk to the little church in all kinds of weather. With no room to expand and no viable parking solution, the congregation decided to buy land and relocate. The church bought land on Scott Street in the north end of the city and initiated plans for a new church building. It fell upon the shoulders of the new pastor, a man of about thirty-eight or thirty-nine years, to raise the funds and begin construction of the new building.

Gerald Morgan was equal to the task. He had an affable personality and a strong presence in the pulpit. He was a large man—not so much tall, but barrel-chested—and he filled the pulpit when he preached. Where Earl Williams was measured and cautious, Gerald Morgan was dramatic and inspiring. Gerald Morgan never delivered a sermon without giving himself wholly, emotionally, and physically to its delivery. He didn't care about time and he worried little about dissenters—he wanted to see God move! Pastor Morgan had great faith and, when we left the service, we had faith; we felt God could do anything. He emphasized worship, sometimes failing to preach, saying that God wanted to move in our lives and that the Holy Spirit could do more in a person's heart through worship, than could be accomplished in a month of sermons. Some mused that he took those particular services in that direction merely because he wasn't prepared to preach that week, but it didn't seem contrived to Bill and me. Here was a man, only ten or twelve years older than us, with so much faith, so much energy, and such a great love for God that we couldn't help but grow under his ministry.

Then Pastor Morgan began to teach about money. He referred to being a steward of all that God has blessed us with, giving the tithe (the required ten percent) and giving to the poor. Then he encouraged giving offerings over and above the tithe to bless God's kingdom. We sat in those services convicted, knowing that in the area of finances God really wasn't Lord and Master. We were constantly broke. We had no money for our down payment. We refinanced and consolidated debt *ad infinitum*. A house was a million miles away and, even with no rent required at Barton Street, we reverted to living paycheck to paycheck, without any semblance of a household budget. It suddenly dawned on us that God couldn't bless us because we were living in disobedience to His Word. Bill and I resolved to be regular tithers and asked the Lord to forgive our past dalliances.

We started giving ten percent of our income on a regular basis, and Bill promptly got laid off. It felt like a test. Would we still be faithful to God, to the commitment we had made to faithfully give Him our tithes? In the past when Bill was laid off or on strike, we pared back our giving to nothing; then when he went back to work we started over, telling ourselves that God understood our predicament. The universality of God's laws about sowing and reaping, giving and blessing, were just hitting us. It was like a revelation. We decided this time when Bill wasn't working we would continue to be faithful in our giving and let God take care of our needs. It was liberating. Suddenly we felt justified praying to God for our needs, knowing that we were holding nothing back; we had confidence in the promises of God. He would supply all of our needs according to His riches in Christ Jesus. For the first time in our marriage, financial pressure eased. I no longer worried about it all the time.

Bill gave up leadership of the young people's group and started teaching the twelve-year-old boys' Sunday school class. I was occupied with two small children and, with Bill's shift work, Friday evenings had become too unpredictable. We were gaining consistency in our walk with God and were generally very pleased with things at church; then Pastor Morgan took things to a whole new level.

The hole for the new church basement had just been dug on the Scott Street property, and Pastor Morgan made a presentation the following Sunday morning to raise the rest of the funds for the building. In a sermon entitled, "How to Raise the Money to Build Our New Church," he laid down the gauntlet to every family at Elim Tabernacle: regardless of financial status, if they called Elim their home church, they were to trust God to help them give at least one thousand dollars in an offering to be collected in two weeks—and the money was to be given over and above regular tithes and offerings!

"Now, many of you will be like me," he explained. "I'll have to go to the bank and borrow that money. I don't have a thousand dollars. But I believe if we all take this on, that God will give us the money we need to get that new building up!" His voice was thunderous and full of convicting enthusiasm as usual; but this time Bill's blood pressure was rising.

All the way home from church, Bill muttered to himself. "The nerve of that preacher! He just thinks we can all go out and borrow a thousand dollars like it's nothing. The bank would be thrilled to give it to you! Borrow a thousand dollars, humph! Easy for him to say, he's only got one kid! What about the people who don't even have their own house?" Bill was seething.

The next Sunday there was a guest speaker at church and nothing was said about the pastor's challenge; but even though there was someone else in the pulpit, Bill couldn't get Pastor Morgan's previous week's sermon out of his mind.

Too honorable to gossip about the pastor, Bill held his anger in—except around me. "I can't get over the nerve of that guy— telling everyone to go borrow a thousand dollars!" he said again as we got in the car after the service. (A thousand dollars in 1968 was the equivalent of ten thousand dollars in the year 2000—ten weeks' pay.)

"Well what do you think we *should* do?" I asked quietly. "It *is* our church. Our kids' lives are going to be blessed for years to come in that new building. We should do something," I gently pushed.

I could tell that God was working on Bill's heart, but he wasn't giving any indication of that to me. "Margaret," he said in a low tone, trying not to give full vent to his anger, "I earn the bacon in this family, you just fry it, okay?"

Not knowing always when to shut my mouth, I opened it one last time. "Well, we have to do something!" Bill glared at me, but said nothing.

As Bill walked into the Canadian Imperial Bank of Commerce on the corner of Niagara and Scott the next morning, he was thinking out loud, "I'll show Margaret! I'll walk right into that loan officer's office and ask for that one thousand dollars. When he refuses a loan to an unemployed, debt-ridden GM worker with no collateral, I'll endure the laughter, walk out humiliated, and be able to tell Margaret, "Honey, I did the best I could. They won't loan me the money, so we can't give it." Up until that time, we had never gotten a loan when I didn't have to sign for it as well—usually they pushed for a cosigner too, and we had no one in our lives willing to do that! We couldn't even think of a person who might have such resources—there was no one to ask. Bill knew he didn't have a hope of securing that loan; he didn't even bother to tell me he was going to the bank that day.

"Can I help you, Mr. Davidson?" The bank manager was cordial. He knew Bill and me well enough. They were used to speaking to us; whenever there were insufficient funds in our account and a check was supposed to clear, they would graciously telephone us. Many times I would rush down to the bank, with the two kids in tow, having to make a quick deposit to cover the amount. It saved us the NSF charge, but it was embarrassing.

"Well, I need a loan!" Bill stuttered. "A thousand dollars."

"Okay. For a car?"

At this point Bill was tempted to lie. But what was the use? He would have to have the serial number, make, and model for collateral anyway.

"No, not for a car." Bill took a deep breath as the bank manager looked at him for an explanation. "I need the money...I want to give it to my church." There, he said it! He got it out and, to his amazement, the bank manager wasn't laughing.

"What church did you say that was?"

"Oh! I hadn't. It's the one a mile-and-a-half down the road—you know, they just recently dug the hole and poured the foundation. Right on Scott Street."

The bank manager looked across his desk at Bill, peering intently into his eyes. There was a small silence, an awkward moment when Bill figured he was choosing his words carefully. He put his pen down on the desk, leaned back in his swivel chair and said, "Okay. You can pick up the check tomorrow. Is that soon enough?"

"Sure! Sure! Tomorrow's good. I'll pick it up tomorrow!" Bill didn't know what else to say, he just wanted to get out of there fast, before the manager had a chance to change his mind.

Holding himself to a brisk walk while inside the bank, Bill ran to the car. He had to get home to tell me the news. "Margaret, not only did they give me the loan when I'm laid off, they didn't even ask for a cosigner! Wow! God is incredible!" Bill went into the bank looking for a way to weasel out of the guilty feeling in his heart, but instead God made a way for him to do what He was asking of him. We were learning that God blesses us when we are

196

faithful to Him. We had tithed this time, given when it hurt, and God was making a way for us to do something impossible: give away a thousand dollars.

Bill finished the paperwork and deposited the check into our account. He didn't even wait until the next Sunday to make out our personal check—payable to Elim Tabernacle. On Sunday morning the greatest thrill of our lives was to give that check for a thousand dollars to the building fund. Our loan was to be paid back at forty-eight dollars per month, over a two-year period—saving for a down payment would have to wait, again.

In the late Sixties and early Seventies, it was common to hear speakers like Oral Roberts sharing a "seed-faith" doctrine on television. We heard many testimonies of God working miracles in the lives of people who obediently gave to the Lord's work. Listening to these speakers, we felt positive that some mystery person was going to walk into our lives with a check for a thousand dollars so we could pay that loan off early. We kept looking for this well-dressed stranger, but we never met him. There were no "knights in shining armor" dropping off checks, eradicating loans; but, God did work mysteriously.

Before the first loan payment was due, the phone rang. It was Bill's eldest brother Bob. "Bill, how are you doin'?"

"Fine, Bob. And you?" Bill had seven brothers and, except for Andy, we weren't in contact with them a lot. We had a couple of family reunions each year, but the rest of the time everyone was quite busy. They weren't the kind of brothers to call just to see how you were doing.

"Good, Bill. Listen, I'm extremely busy with my own business ventures now, and I'm really not able to haul the sawdust anymore." For years, a ten-ton dump truck their father owned was loaded by hand at a sawmill near Fort Erie and then delivered to a factory in Niagara Falls, where they still used it as fuel in their furnaces. "Are you interested in doing it?"

"Well, what does it pay?"

"Ten bucks a load."

"Ten bucks? Bob, it's been ten dollars for years. Get them to up it to twelve dollars and I'll do it." I could see the wheels turning in Bill's mind. Four Saturdays per month, at twelve dollars per load, was forty-eight dollars per month. Four times in a year there would be an extra Saturday—forty-eight dollars extra money.

"Okay, I'll try to get them to up it, Bill." Bob hung up the phone.

The next day the phone rang again—it was Bob. "Bill, they said okay! They'll raise it to twelve dollars per load."

Bill started driving to the sawmill every Saturday morning with his father's old red, panel dump truck. He loaded eight tons of sawdust with a long-handled number ten shovel—in about three hours. Rain or shine, cold winter or blazing summer day, he was out there loading that truck. It was hard work, but he made nearly a day's wages in three hours. God had provided a way to make the loan payments. The best part was that General Motors called him back soon afterward; all of our needs were met, and more. God was showing us how we could trust Him; but, He was just getting started.

In late spring of 1969, we were living in the white apartment building on Barton Street, still doing the repairs and maintenance. Shawn was four-and-a-half years old and Blake had just turned three. We had a large paved parking lot adjacent to the building. On the other side and at the back there was grass. Shawn liked to play outside more often than I could watch her, and sometimes I would let her play for a few minutes while I tended to a small task. If I left her, or let her go out ahead of me, I always reminded her of the rules: "Shawn, if Mommy isn't with you, you have to stay away from the parking lot and the street. You can play at the side or at the back on the grass, okay?"

She knew the rules well and I never had a problem. One day it was particularly pleasant. The sun was out and it seemed more like summer than spring. Shawn wanted to go outside and play in the afternoon, so I let her, telling her that I would be right out. We went over the rules and she went into the back yard. I got delayed and took longer than usual before I went to check on her—I was inside about ten or fifteen minutes after Shawn left. When I went outside, she was gone. I couldn't see her anywhere. I raced around to the side of the building. She wasn't there. I checked the parking lot and the front. I went down the whole side street calling her name. No answer. She wasn't anywhere.

I rushed into the house to get Bill.

"Bill! Bill! Shawn's gone! I can't find her anywhere! Bill, she's gone...I don't where she is! I left her for a few minutes...in the back yard...she's not there! Oh, God! Oh, God, where is she?"

"Okay. Calm down. We'll find her—let's go." Bill was alarmed but calm. He assured me that she was all right, and we both went outside to search for her. We searched the street and called her name for half an hour. She didn't answer.

Panic was beginning to set in. Barton was a side street; but our building was on the corner of Barton and a busier through street. Across the through street was a steep embankment that led to the Sixteen Mile Creek. It was called a creek, but it was as wide as most rivers. Where we lived the creek narrowed and there were rapids with a severe undertow.

"What if she fell in the creek? Oh, God! Bill, what if she...?" I couldn't say what I was thinking. I was crying—I knew for sure I had lost her.

If this had have occurred nowadays, my first thought would probably have been abduction. We lived in more innocent times in the Sixties, and that thought didn't even enter my head. Instead I worried she had been hit by a car, had gotten lost, or had fallen in the creek and drowned.

We searched up and down Barton Street again; we checked across the road by the ravine—nothing! By this time she had been gone an hour. As we were heading back to the apartment building to call the police, we saw something. Way down the block, a little girl was walking toward us. We ran to her! It was Shawn, and she started running our direction when she saw us, crying the whole way. I took her into my arms and hugged her so tight I could have hurt her. Then I noticed she was bleeding—her hands and fingers had been cut.

Once we calmed her down we got the full story. "Mommy, I just wanted a pet," she stammered. She had seen a butterfly in the back yard of the apartment building and took it upon herself to go back inside to the storage room. There she found a glass Mason jar used for canning. She was going to catch the butterfly and keep it for a pet.

Shawn had a tender spot in her heart for animals. She wanted a pet more than anything and often asked for a puppy or a kitten. We used to tell her, "We can't have a pet in the apartment building,

Honey. Some day we'll have a house, and when we have a house, you can have a pet."

By the time she got back outside, the butterfly was gone. She went around the front of the apartment building and saw it again. By the time she caught up to the butterfly, she was two streets over from Barton and in the driveway of a lady she didn't know. The butterfly landed, and when Shawn went to place the jar over it, she hit the pavement too hard. The jar broke. The butterfly got away and the noise brought the lady out of her front door screaming.

"What are you doing? Look what you did! You broke this glass all over my driveway! Now I'm going to get a flat tire—you rotten little kid! Get out of here! Go home!" She was so angry, Shawn ran away terrified. She had cut herself on some of the shards of glass, but was crying more from fear of the screaming lady. She had gotten lost on the way home and that just added to her distraught state.

Bill and I were so glad she was safe, we couldn't even discipline her for leaving the yard.

Later that night, all we could think about was Shawn's pathetic little voice: "Mommy, I just wanted a pet. I didn't mean to break the jar! I just wanted a pet!"

I prayed that night, "Oh, God! Aren't we *ever* going to have a home of our own—where our kids can have pets?" I didn't know God answered desperate little prayers like that; but He does.

Because we were superintendents of the apartment building, we took applications from potential tenants, giving us the opportunity to help out friends and family members from time to time. An apartment became vacant and we rented it to my brother Ben and his wife, June. Ben was a tradesman at General Motors, and though Bill and Ben had been casual friends growing up, they had gotten closer working at the same place. Ben and June didn't have any children yet, and were looking for a place where they could save to buy a house. They had been married since the fall of 1963 and they already owned some property outside St. Catharines—ten acres in the country. They lived as our neighbors for about a year, and while they did, Ben built a big two-story, four-bedroom house on their country property. It was hard not to be jealous.

When Ben and June came over for a visit one evening after

moving, it wasn't anything unusual; we had been used to seeing a lot of them while they lived in the building.

"Bill," Ben started the conversation with a serious look on his face, "If I could sever my ten acres into two lots, five acres each, would you be interested in building a house on the other five acres?"

"Well, I don't know, Ben," Bill answered, almost embarrassed, "I don't think I could get a mortgage. I don't even have money for a down payment."

"That's just it! I'd sell you the five-acre partition for a dollar—to make it all legal—and you could use the equity in the land as a down payment to get a mortgage. Somewhere down the road, when you have the money, you could pay me back. Nothing on paper—just between you and me. You pay me for the land at today's prices whenever you've got it in the future."

Bill and I couldn't believe Ben and June's generosity. It was overwhelming.

The first difficulty came, however, when Ben applied to Lincoln County to sever the land. It was farmland, and the county didn't want it reduced to suburbs for city-dwellers who wanted to move to the country. Things got more complicated when several wealthy neighbors in the vicinity of Ben's house showed up at the county meeting and opposed the plan. We made it a matter of prayer between the four of us and, miraculously, the county's office approved it. It was miraculous because Ben, June, Bill, and I left for that public meeting knowing we were in for the fight of our lives— everyone in the area was against us. Lincoln County had no reason to approve the severance; they just did. We thanked God, knowing that His hand was in the midst of all of these circumstances.

With that, Bill and I had the title to five acres of land. We went from having no assets to being landowners in a week. Armed with that title we set about finding a mortgage—we were going to build our own house, just like Ben did. It was a dream come true. Unfortunately, the banks didn't share our enthusiasm.

We got our income tax refund and used all of it to dig the hole. The foundation and basement of our new home was ready to go in, all we needed was a mortgage. Bill went shopping for one. He thought because we owned the land a mortgage would be a slam dunk; but things were in a downturn economically in 1969, and

201

banks were calling in loans, not giving them out. Interest rates were rising higher than they had ever been before, and everyone was nervous.

Everywhere Bill went he got the same answer.

"Mr. Davidson, you have quite a bit of other debt and your credit rating could be better."

"What about the fact that I hold title to the land?" Bill would plead.

"Well, the land—the land just isn't worth that much; and owner-built houses tend not to be finished. People incur cost overruns and then they don't finish them. Banks don't like unfinished projects, Mr. Davidson. Sorry. Maybe if you were buying from an established builder, or if someone cosigned…"

Even the bank that had given us the loan for the church building fund refused us. No one wanted to give us a mortgage.

Bill was determined to build the house himself. He thought he could work a steady nightshift at the plant, come home from work at seven o'clock in the morning and work on the house until four in the afternoon. He would eat supper and go to bed until ten at night, then get up and go back to work. That was the plan. Ben promised to help him whenever he wasn't working himself, and Ben and June offered to let us live with them while we were building. They had four bedrooms—plenty of room for both families—and were a mere walk through the woods from where we would build. All of this seemed wonderful. God had to be in it; but bank managers couldn't seem to get on board. We began to wonder if we could even begin work on the house. Without a mortgage, all we had was a hole in the ground.

"Bill, we need eggs. Do you feel like going to Pelissero's to buy a couple dozen?" I asked Bill one morning.

"Okay," he answered and headed toward the farm where he used to work. Harry Pelissero had been a great help to Bill and me and, when there was no overtime or Bill was laid off, he always hired Bill to work on the farm. We had to drive across town to get eggs, but we wouldn't think of going anywhere else. It's funny how doing something as small and ordinary as buying eggs can change your life—but it did.

Harry came out to meet Bill when he arrived. "Bill, how goes the mortgage hunt? Have you got one yet?" We had been so excited about the prospect of building our own house, we had told anyone who would listen about how God was blessing us.

"Not too good, Harry," Bill replied. "Can't get anyone to give me a mortgage. I've got the hole dug and I'm ready to lay the cement blocks, but I don't have any money to buy them. It's getting pretty frustrating."

"Have you tried Canada Trust, Bill?"

"Yeah, I went there yesterday. They wouldn't even let me fill out an application. They said I owed too much."

"Isn't that something?" Harry didn't say anything more; he just said goodbye to Bill and thanked him for his business. Bill went home and didn't give it another thought.

That night we were eating the eggs for supper that Bill bought that morning, when the phone rang. Bill had been depressed about the whole mortgage situation all day, but despite his demeanor, he answered the phone.

"Mr. Davidson? Canada Trust calling, sir. Were you in yesterday seeing about a mortgage for a house you'd like to build?"

"Yes, that was me."

"Well sir, we've reconsidered and would like you to come in and fill out the mortgage application...that is, if you're still interested," the voice on the other end offered. "Are you free tomorrow morning?"

"I'll be there at nine o'clock!" Bill answered enthusiastically.

"We don't open until ten," the voice said.

"Oh! Okay. Well, I'll see you then." Bill realized he probably sounded overly anxious, but, in truth, he was holding back his emotions as it was. He couldn't believe what he was hearing.

The next morning Bill walked out of the trust company having secured a mortgage of fifteen thousand dollars. Canada Trust structured the loan into three equal amounts of $5,000 each, and agreed to pay out each amount as that part of the construction was completed. They wanted regular reports and the privilege of inspecting the progress of the house before forwarding each scheduled portion of the mortgage. The only other stipulation they made was that it had to be a brick home. Bill had wanted to build a clapboard house—it was cheaper than brick, and we could have carried a smaller mortgage. The trust company insisted that the house be built with a brick exterior, however, to ensure that it would exceed the value of the outstanding mortgage. We agreed to their terms and they willingly lent us the money.

Bill never asked at the time why they had a change of heart at Canada Trust. He figured, "Don't ask too many questions. Get out with the loan and leave well enough alone." Five years later, when it came time to renew, Bill found out why. Harry Pelissero called up the manager of the trust company and asked him to make that phone call to Bill. He offered to cosign our mortgage, on the condition we not be told. After five years, we had made all of our payments, the bank considered us a good risk, and the property value had doubled with a house on it. We no longer needed a cosigner; but God used Harry when we really needed help. When Bill learned of it, he went to Harry to thank him. Harry was upset that we had found out, but he said, "Bill, it wasn't a risk. I knew who I was signing for." It was a great compliment to Bill, and he was grateful that he hadn't slacked off while cleaning chicken coops for all those years. God had honored Bill's faithfulness, and in so doing showed us that He is no man's debtor.

By the end of June, the four of us moved into Ben and June's house, rent-free, so that we could save some money and be close to the site of our new house. In the meantime, Ben and June had been able to adopt a baby boy. The three of them took two bedrooms, and the four of us took the other two. We shared the groceries and ate together when we could. We stayed there five months—as long as it took to complete construction. Ben and June invited us into their home for no other reason than to help us out. The whole time we were there, they treated us like guests and never once made us feel uncomfortable. When Ben was able, about two weeks per month, he helped Bill with the building. Ben was so humble and gracious about the whole arrangement that he didn't even claim that the idea to help us came from God; but we knew it had.

What we didn't account for was another surprise pregnancy. I hadn't even entertained the possibility that I could have a third child. My heart and mind were set on two kids—Shawn and Blake. I didn't go to the doctor in June to confirm it, but I missed my second period in July; and I was sick. (Nothing is as recognizable as morning sickness, once you've had it. I knew the feeling and I knew I was pregnant, but I didn't want to hear a doctor say the words.) We moved into Ben and June's and I was sick every day. It was awful.

I complained to God constantly: "How dare You let me get pregnant! We can't afford another child! You know it and still You allowed me to have this accident!"

I was angry with God. I was only twenty-six years old, but I thought my family was complete. Blake was three and things were just staring to get easier with the children. I didn't want to go through another pregnancy, and I didn't want the "baby" stage all over again. I had a terrible attitude.

When complaining to God didn't give me the satisfaction I craved, I turned to Bill. "Why is God doing this to us? We just get the opportunity to build a house, we're trying to save money, we're living with relatives, and I go and get pregnant! The timing couldn't be worse! I don't want another baby—I'm too old!"

Bill half laughed, "You're too old? You're only twenty-six. Lots of people aren't even married at twenty-six."

"We can't afford another baby, Bill—not with the house and everything else," I shot back.

"Afford a baby? When have we ever been able to afford one? We couldn't afford to have Shawn or Blake when we had them either, but we've always made it in the past; we'll find a way to make it this time. We always get by."

Bill's intention was to reassure me, but I didn't want to accept this pregnancy. The more he tried to reason with me, the angrier I got.

"Well, I don't want to just make it—and I don't want this baby," I snapped.

"Margaret, what are you going to do about it now? Just face the facts and go to the doctor. Get a pregnancy test and make sure. Maybe you're upset about all this and you're not even pregnant." That was a pipe dream! I was sick. I didn't need a doctor to tell me I was pregnant. But Bill was right; there was nothing I could do but accept it. I just wanted to be angry for a while first.

As July came to a close, Andy and Jeanette wanted to go away together the first long weekend of August, and they asked us if we would come stay at their place and babysit for the weekend. We had already lived with Ben and June for a month. Figuring we would give them a break, we took our two kids over to Andy and Jeanette's house and added them to their five. It was August, and it was hot! All of July had been hot, but August was even hotter. The air was thick with humidity. It was rare for anyone then to have central air conditioning, and all nine of us were jammed together under one roof for the weekend. As we sat down on the Saturday evening for supper, I was sweltering, pregnant, sick—and miserable about all of it. Two of my nieces started fooling around, pinching each other beneath the table.

"Girls, stop it!" I yelled. "I'm not in the mood for your games tonight! Sit at the table properly and eat your supper. Any more shenanigans and I'm going to give it to both of you!"

As I turned away, the older of the two reached under the table and gave her younger sister one last pinch. She let out a yelp like she had been stabbed. I jumped out of my chair on the other side of the table and moved toward them as quickly as I could; but they were too fast. The perpetrator popped up and raced down the hall with her younger sister on her heels. The hardwood hallway had a carpet runner loosely laid down the center and buckled at the far end. As I ran after the screaming girls, I tripped over the buckle and flew through the air at full speed. I landed on a twelve- by thirty-inch grate that covered the cold air return. It ran parallel to the hallway to the right of the runner, and I slid across its entire length on my knee. The steel grate tore off all the flesh from my kneecap, shredding it like paper. I looked down and saw my knee bleeding profusely, bone and tendons exposed.

Now everyone felt bad. The girls were upset and burst into tears, convinced they were the cause of the accident. I was crying too— but not just from the pain of a torn-up knee. In that moment after falling, thoughts of guilt swept over me because I had been angry about being pregnant. Suddenly this previously unwanted baby meant more to me than anything. I started praying, "Oh, God. Please forgive me for not wanting this pregnancy! You gave it to me. Lord—make sure nothing's wrong. I want to have the baby. Please protect him or her." At once I realized the life inside me *was* important to me—extremely important!

For the rest of the night I was consumed, not with how my knee was going to be, but with the safety of that little baby in my womb. I thought I was going to miscarry as a result of the trauma. Bill wanted to take me to Emergency that night, but I refused to go. I was petrified of needles, and I knew that to stitch my wound they would have to numb the knee with local anesthetic. I was in no state to be argued with, so Bill relented. (I can be quite difficult when I've made up my mind, and Bill didn't want to fight with me when I was so firmly entrenched.) We tried to wrap the knee in a bandage, but it was too painful. I lay down with my leg elevated and tried to go to sleep. The pain was incredible, and just the movement of the air on my ravaged knee sent shivers up and down my spine. I didn't sleep at all that night. When morning came, Bill called the doctor's office.

"Try to put some ice on it. If she won't go to the hospital, bring her here to the office and I'll stitch her up," he told Bill.

Somehow Bill got me into the car and we took the fifteen-minute ride from the country to the west end of the city. It was too painful for me to put up with the ice; I was in agony and ready for whatever they had to do to get me fixed up. Not only did I have to have an injection, but then the doctor also had to try to stretch the now curled and dried skin back over the knee cap to stitch it together again. It took six injections to get the knee sufficiently numbed and thirty-five stitches to hold the mangled skin in place.

"You'll have a difficult time walking for the foreseeable future, Margaret; and with the amount of scar tissue that will form, you may never be able to kneel down on that knee. In addition, the range of motion and flexibility of the knee could..." The doctor wanted to go on, but I cut him off.

"No! No! None of that matters. That's not the question I need answered. I'm sure I'm pregnant! I've missed two periods—is my baby going to be okay? That's the question!"

"Margaret, I'm sure you'll be fine. Do you remember what you went through when you were first pregnant with Shawn—all the bleeding? You stick like glue. I'm sure you and the baby will be all right; but let's get that pregnancy test done to confirm you are indeed going to have another baby." I felt better that my doctor didn't seem to be alarmed.

It took six weeks to be able to walk without pain. I nursed my knee back to health, willingly put up with the inevitable morning sickness, and thought about how much I wanted another baby.

CB

Bill picked up the cement blocks for our house's foundation with his father's dump truck. He loaded and unloaded them by hand back at our property. In order to save money, he did the work himself, including mixing the mortar and laying the blocks. A perfectionist, Bill made sure they were laid straight and even. It took him five times longer than a mason, but his labor was free. From July 1969 until December 18 of the same year, Bill worked the night shift at General Motors and worked all day on the house. I lived alone. When Bill was home, he slept. It was a sacrifice, but we endured it cheerfully, realizing that in the end, we would have our own home. He would go to bed at about four in the afternoon and wake up around 9:30 or 10:00 in the evening. I would fix him some supper and we would have a few moments to talk before he would go back in for the eleven-to-seven shift. Saturdays Bill loaded the dump truck with sawdust and delivered it, before working on the house until evening, but Sundays were ours. We didn't work on the house or anything else on Sundays; we went to church twice, napped in the afternoon and enjoyed an occasional picnic, but nobody worked. Sundays got us through the rest of the week.

Although we saw each other during the week, we didn't have much time together. I went over to the new house often, nearly every day, to take him lunch at the construction site. We would eat together and dream about the finished product; how wonderful it would be to live in our very own house. Bill was making progress and our little bungalow was taking shape. The best part of it was we were saving money.

Once a third of the house was built and we were ready for our second mortgage draw from Canada Trust, Bill sent me into the Canadian Imperial Bank of Commerce—the bank that had given us the loan for the church, but who had refused us a mortgage. With Bill picking up the construction supplies in his father's dump truck, building most of the house himself and earning the money from the Saturday sawdust deliveries, we had enough left over from our first mortgage draw to pay off the entire balance of our church building fund loan. What was supposed to take two years, took six months.

I went into the bank with cash, and I plunked it on the counter for the loan officer.

"It's all there—everything we owe you! The rest of our loan—the seven hundred and change!" I said enthusiastically.

"But, Mrs. Davidson, there's no problem with your loan. You've made all the payments; you certainly don't have to pay it all off. You haven't even been late one time. No need to strain yourself to pay it off so soon."

The loan officer was clearly taken aback. (He was more accustomed to reassuring me things would be all right regarding an NSF check.)

"Well it's no strain…Bill even bought a tractor and disk plow for the farm before coming here. He's done all the work on the house himself, and we saved so much from our first mortgage draw—from the other bank—that we want to pay back the total balance. Thank you very much, sir."

The sweetest feeling in the world was paying back that final amount to the very bank that wouldn't even consider us for a mortgage. It felt like poetic justice.

It was hard work, but God was showing us that we could trust Him with our finances. If we put Him first, He would look after everything from a mortgage cosigner to a tractor for the farm. God was blessing us since we had made him Lord of our finances less than nine months previously. The scriptural law of reciprocity was at work in our lives: we reap what we sow. (See Galatians 6:7–8.)

The house construction continued with the second mortgage draw, and Bill roughed in the plumbing and electrical work. He left some of the intricate electrical work, the finish carpentry, and the outside brick-laying to professionals; the rest he did with Ben's help or by himself. Though I was in my seventh month of pregnancy by December, even I got into the action. I helped Bill lay the hardwood, sand, stain, and polyurethane all of it; then I painted the interior walls. On December 18, 1969, we moved into our new home on Moyer Street. It was a neat little white-brick bungalow, set back from the road about seventy-five yards and surrounded by forest. Driving by in the springtime, you could only catch a glimpse of the house behind the trees. It was cute, it was private, and it was ours! We were thrilled.

We thanked God for all of His goodness, but He was just getting started. I was about to learn that taking care of us financially was nothing; He was about to perform the greatest miracle I could imagine, and once again it would involve Ben and June.

Chapter 13

The Road to Freedom

The five months we lived at Ben and June's were nightmare-free. Building the house took so much of our time and energy that we flopped into bed at night and instantly fell into deep sleep. Things improved for the last trimester of the pregnancy, too. I felt better, and was enamored of our new bungalow. I spent my time cleaning and decorating the house. I was careful not to complain about cleaning; I was so grateful to have a house of my own.

On March 9, 1970, I went into labor. On the way to the hospital, we dropped off the children at Andy and Jeanette's. God blessed us with another girl and we named her Heather—a beautiful flower. I loved her instantly. The delivery, however, was difficult. My cervix dropped out of my body along with the placenta, so the doctors had to spend extra time putting me back together. Once again I realized how fortunate Bill and I were to have any child, let alone three beautiful, healthy ones.

I wasn't home two weeks when post-partum depression hit me again. Thirty years ago there was less awareness of hormonal changes during and following pregnancies. As a result, I didn't know that my doldrums were chemical and physiological, I just felt down. I thought I had no reason to be depressed, and thinking about that loaded more guilt upon my conscience. I felt bad about feeling bad. I was incredibly hard on myself. My expectations about the kind of mother I was going to be, and how I was going to be so different with my children than Mom was with me, put me in a place where I could only fail. To be unhappy and depressed was in itself a failure. I was sure I was supposed to be in control, composed and generally cheerful with my kids all of the time. Instead I was sullen and quiet, and the kids always seemed to be on my nerves. Feelings of anger flared into flagrant outbursts at the slightest provocation. I always felt guilty afterward for not allowing the children to be kids.

When outside the walls of our little bungalow, I hid my dark mood. On weekends I mustered every bit of resolve and determination I could and presented a Margaret Davidson to the world that others expected: a happy homemaker with three darling children and a hardworking husband, living her dream in her new home. During the week I sank into a quagmire of despair. With the depression came the return of nightmares and flashbacks. The shock I felt at their return was exacerbated by the fact that for almost a year—since the construction of our house had begun—I had been free of them. I felt betrayed, as if the nightmares owned me. They had teased me, pretending to disappear, letting me think that they had left for good; then, once life promised a little joy with my new baby girl, they doubled back and ambushed me. I felt lost in my hopelessness.

Living in the country was a mixed blessing. I did feel safer, in that Willie didn't know where I lived. (I always thought he would come back for me; that he would find me and rape me again.) But the *thought* of Willie still rendered me powerless. I had now lived as long without being traumatized by him as I had under his tyranny, yet emotionally I was as vulnerable as ever. His hold on my psyche was greater fourteen years later than when I lay gagged and tied on his bed. None of it made any sense to me and I was powerless to do anything about it.

The other problem was, although I felt safer in the country when *inside* my house, to get there I still had to drive through vacant land and forested areas, with miles between houses, on dirt roads without streetlights.

Part of the charade was appearing confident...and confident people are involved. So, I joined the choir at church. Every Tuesday evening I drove the twelve miles to Central Gospel Temple (Elim's new name) by myself. (Bill has many gifts, but singing isn't one of them—so it wasn't like I could get him to come to choir; besides, someone had to look after the children.)

The drive to church was in daylight; after practice, two to three hours later, I drove home in the dark, white-knuckled, clenching the steering wheel so tightly my nails dug into the palms of my hands. Before leaving the church I locked all of the car doors, then I would check them several times on the way home, never quite remembering if I had locked them—maybe I just *thought* I locked them.

I was petrified of stopping the car. *Keep moving, Margaret*, I would tell myself. *No one can jump into a moving car!* I just knew someone was lurking behind every mailbox or shrub, lying in wait for the right opportunity to jump into my car and attack me. At intersections I would only slow down, never stopping completely. If a traffic light was red or a car was coming, I would always turn right, then turn around at the first empty parking lot. By nine or ten o'clock at night, the streets weren't that busy, and I could often pull to the shoulder and make a u-turn—anything to avoid stopping the car.

The longer I was in the car driving home, the more intense my panic. I would think of every bad scenario, every terrible consequence. My greatest fear was a mechanical breakdown; our cars were always at least ten years old and unreliable. I would pray, "God, please let this car get me all the way home!" I always took the same route to church and back. On the way there I would study the houses I drove by. Those that looked cute and homey, and that kept their porch lights on, became "markers" for me. I had it all planned out: if I would get in any trouble, I would run to those houses. My "marker homes" were well spaced and I knew when the next one was coming. I would look for it, and when I passed it, I would focus on the next one, relieved I was that much closer to home. The people in those houses will never know how vital they were to me and how I desperately depended on their nightly habit of turning on their porch lights.

Many nights I would get June to go to choir practice with me, in *my* car. Once every month we traveled to women's ministries meetings at church. I appreciated June's company more than she ever knew. It was coming home from one of those women's ministries

213

meetings in the winter that I realized how much God was looking out for us. The meeting had gone late and afterward we went for coffee with a few of the other ladies. Just before midnight we turned off Effingham Road, the last paved road near our farmhouse, onto Sawmill, the dirt road that led to Moyer Street where we lived. Still about three miles from home and in the part of the drive where houses were now more than a quarter mile apart, we lost our traction and the car slid into a snow bank. I tried to back out, but the tires just spun, turning the snow beneath into ice.

We were only a couple of hundred yards from one of my marker homes and, as we walked toward it, I looked for the outside light. It was on! Fortunately the people who lived there were just preparing to go to bed. They came to the door and thought nothing of helping us. They fetched their shovels and some sand from their garage, and dug us out. Inside of ten minutes we were on our way, grateful that our porch-light neighbors were as warm and friendly as we had presumed. As I dropped June at her house around the corner from mine, all I could think about was, *What if June hadn't been with me? What if I had gotten stuck in that snow bank and I had been by myself? Oh, God, you have to protect me!* I would never have had the courage to knock on someone's door if I was by myself. I decided just to thank God that I wasn't alone this time, and resolved not to think about what might take place in the future. Whenever I could, I would ride with June—that was the only solution that gave me any kind of comfort.

I told no one about my fears, pretending all was well. I always went to choir practice and to women's ministries without complaint, because the only thing more terrifying than potential car trouble was the thought of telling someone why I was so afraid. I didn't want anyone to think less of me. I protected the secret and feigned normalcy, but the stress of going out and driving alone was almost unbearable. Each night that I would arrive safely at home, I would go in the front door and collapse, exhausted from the nervous tension.

Fear did not manifest itself only in long car rides from the city to the country. I was afraid of men. All men. Nothing made me more uncomfortable than to find myself alone in a room with a man. If a man put his arm around me or placed his hand on my shoulder, I cringed and found a way to weasel out. It didn't matter who the man was—he could have been a pastor or a deacon; if he touched me I was repulsed. While other men made me paranoid, a man who had been drinking absolutely paralyzed me with fear. I wouldn't be able to move; all I would think about was how to get out of there.

Heather had been born in March, and two months later, in the midst of my depression, Pastor Morgan telephoned me. "Margaret, it's Pastor Morgan. How are you doing today?"

"Fine, Pastor!" I lied.

"Margaret, as you know the elections for women's ministries are scheduled for tonight, and I'd like to know if you'd let your name stand for women's ministries president."

I started laughing. "I don't think so, Pastor. There's no way I can do that job. The mere idea of speaking in public scares me!"

"Well, I understand that there is a group of ladies praying and fasting today for the women's ministries leadership and elections," he continued, as though he hadn't heard me flat-out refuse him.

"Yes, that's true," I said.

"And you know, don't you, what a fragile state our women's ministries are in at present, and that if no one takes a leadership role, we might have to shut the whole ministry down?" (The problem with the women's ministries was generational. The women had traditionally met to make quilts and care packages for missionaries. There was nothing wrong with that, but the younger women in the church weren't coming out; they were hungry for something deeper, but the older ladies were resisting any change.)

"Yes, Pastor, I'm aware of the problems."

"Well, could I be so bold as to ask if you are one of those ladies fasting and praying for women's ministries leadership?"

"Um, well, yes, I happen to be," I answered nervously, feeling those words were about to ensnare me.

"Well, fasting and praying is good, Margaret, but in fasting and praying today, maybe you should also be willing to do what you can do. Maybe God would want to use *you* to help solve the leadership problem. You know we need the young married ladies to step up and take on more active positions."

Pastor Morgan was loving, but he was definitely pushing me. And it wasn't only him. In some secret place inside of me, I was eager to make a difference, to be used by God—I just didn't have any confidence. Pastor Morgan was expressing a belief in me, and I liked how it felt.

"I don't know, Pastor Morgan," I confessed, "I can't imagine that anybody would even vote for me."

"Look, Margaret, I'm just asking you to be part of the process. We need a pool of names from which to vote, some ladies to let their names stand, so that we can have a legitimate election. You probably won't even be elected, especially on the first ballot; no one gets elected on the first ballot."

That night I walked out of women's ministries as its new president. I was sick with fear. *God, what have you gotten me into?*

I was frantic when I got home and told Bill what happened. "I don't know the first thing about leadership or organizing women's events. Bill, they've made a terrible mistake. They've elected the wrong person!"

I was devastated...and angry. Angry with Pastor Morgan for tricking me, and angry with myself for foolishly agreeing to let my name stand for election.

I was battling an emotionally crippling depression that no one knew about; I was a fake, a caricature of a strong Christian woman, and now I was facing the pressure of being the new women's ministries president at a time when the whole thing was a powder keg. It was my job to unite the older women with the younger women and create an atmosphere where we could grow. That was the mandate. All of that and I had never been the leader of anything in my life. I was overwhelmed.

Bill encouraged me. "You'll do fine, Margaret. You're a good organizer. Look at how you organized our whole wedding! You'll be the best women's ministries president they've ever had. God and those other ladies see your potential, you just have to trust them."

"Bill, our wedding was eight years ago—and planning that certainly doesn't qualify me to be women's ministries president!"

My problem was shame. I couldn't believe in anything good happening to me, or that I could do anything of value, because all I felt when I thought about myself was shame. Twenty years later I would hear a radio speaker talk about it. He was the keynote speaker at a conference I attended, and he was talking about how victims of sexual abuse feel about themselves.

"Victims of sexual abuse feel like a giant pile of garbage," he said. "They're a heap of shame; a manure pile."

It was the first time in my life that I heard someone so aptly describe how I had felt about myself. It was as though he opened up my head and saw how I felt! It couldn't have been truer; I had *always* felt like a heap of garbage. It was refreshing to hear someone put it into words. He went on to explain how shame is a big lie and that, with God, we are saved from our shame as well as from our sin. We don't have to believe how we feel about ourselves—or more accurately, how satan tries to make us feel. By the time I heard the conference speaker in 1990, I had already learned what he was talking about; and much of that learning took place because I had accepted the job as women's ministries president in 1970. I had put myself in position for God to help me. I didn't realize it then, but God had a plan and it was rapidly unfolding.

Joan Jewel had also been a nominee for women's ministries president. Once I accepted my election, she was quickly installed as vice-president. June Hiebert was elected secretary/treasurer. I was surrounded with ladies that I could trust, and we built a great team. The Lord helped me every step of the way, and slowly we changed the structure of a women's ministries meeting from a social time centered on making quilts and bandages, to a worship time followed by ladies' testimonies and a devotional time in the Bible. The young ladies of the church loved the new format and started to come out. God gave me incredible wisdom, and the older ladies saw the value of reaching the younger ones. He had given us wonderful unity. Twenty months into my two-year term, things were going great at women's ministries.

Not so with its leader.

You could dress me up and make me look wonderful, but inside I was still a heap of shame. To me, the success I had enjoyed with the ladies was a house of cards waiting to collapse as soon as people found out the truth about the pretender atop its leadership team. At home I was a mess. Bill was becoming less patient with me. I was frequently miserable and depressed, getting up for services on Sunday and for the monthly women's meeting, but being a depressed, sullen troll the rest of the time. It was a challenge to do even simple things with me. Going out to a restaurant would complicate my life. To get me to go out someplace nice or to attend a public function, especially if those functions involved a secular crowd, was a battle. Once I was there, the sight of someone drinking alcohol would ruin the night. I would immediately want to leave.

"Bill, let's go! Get me out of here!" I would say gritting my teeth.

"Why, Margaret? We just got here."

"I don't care! I don't want to be here! Let's go." In an instant I was incorrigible. Being with drunk and semi-drunk people transported me back to the manure pile. I became again that heap of shame—dressed up maybe, but a pile of garbage just the same. I would be so uptight that we would have to leave. Then I would insist on verbalizing self-loathing thoughts, intent on pushing Bill away.

"You shouldn't have even married me. Why do you stay with me? Bill, you could do so much better than me. Just leave me. Go ahead and get someone better! I'm giving you permission!"

"I don't want anybody else, Honey. I love you." Bill always said the same thing. But I was inconsolable for several days afterward, while the depression demons drove me even deeper into the abyss.

One night in the spring of 1972, the executive committee went to Joan Jewel's house for coffee after a women's ministries meeting. Judy Pymont, a newly saved Christian friend, joined us. The four of us were becoming quite close. (After leading a women's meeting I always felt somewhat vulnerable, having given out everything within me. The times we spent over coffee afterward always recharged my batteries and encouraged me.) We were sitting at the table talking about the excitement among the women, how the ladies were worshiping and learning to pray together, and how the generational problem of nearly two years earlier had all but disappeared. The conversation shifted slightly, and Joan and Judy began talking about their lives before they knew Christ as Savior. Both of them had become Christians as adults, while June had been the daughter of a pastor.

"What a thrill it is now to know Jesus. Life was so hard before Christ," Judy said.

"Yeah, my life before was so awful, so sad—and now the Lord is filling me with such joy…I'm writing songs! It's so great to be saved, " Joan added.

While they conversed, I grew noticeably quiet. They were all talking about the joy they had since they had come to Christ. None of them suspected that I spent my days crying. I felt like a fraud. The shame of being a phony, on top of all my other shame, moved over me like a cloud. If I could have left right then, I would have— but I hadn't had one sip of my freshly poured coffee. I couldn't leave without making a bad excuse, and that would have made me feel even phonier; so I just sat there. Despite how I felt, I was afraid of being vulnerable, of showing any kind of weakness. I perpetuated the myth that was Margaret Davidson, but I was barely holding it together.

"Margaret, you and June don't know how lucky you are! You've been in the church since you were both kids. It must be great to have known the Lord for so long and not to have had to go through the ravages of the world!"

I had heard Joan speaking to me, but her words had stung me with such twisted irony, I was dumbfounded. I couldn't respond.

"Marg, why are you so quiet? You should be so thankful! You were raised in a Christian home, and you've never fallen away from the Lord—you don't have any of the problems we have."

Her last statement was more than I could handle. I lost it. I slumped to a heap on the floor in a flood of tears. For half an hour I wept uncontrollably. I cried the tears of twenty-five years of pain and torment, making tortuous groans as my sobs thrust themselves from the depths of my broken heart.

They think I've had a sheltered life! What do they know about me? I thought, as I cried so hard no words could form. They don't know a thing about me! They know a Margaret that has herself all together; my life is a mess! I'm such a fraud!

I was pummeling myself with insults in my mind. The ladies around me didn't know what they had said. How could they know? They tried for thirty minutes to get me to talk, to tell them what was the matter—but I couldn't speak for groaning in anguish.

I was still taking responsibility for Willie's rapes, still bearing the shame—Willie's shame! I wasn't mad at Willie or at Mom, I was angry with myself. I hated myself. It was my fault. I didn't do anything about it! I *let* Willie rape me! I didn't stop him. He paid me a quarter. I took it. It was all my fault, and that's why God hated me.

219

God hated me! He hated me, and He was punishing me. He had turned His back on me and had forgotten that He even made me, and I deserved it. I thought I was the only person who had ever gone through sexual abuse. I didn't even know the word *incest*. Sexual abuse had never been talked about. I had never heard of another case of it, especially in the church. I was convinced there was not another Christian woman in the world who had been forced into sex by a member of her own family. I was isolated, and in the solitude of my despair, satan had free reign.

Suddenly I no longer cared about keeping the secret. The secret was destroying me, and I wanted to tell—I wanted to tell everything! My inner anguish had reached its apex, and I no longer cared what those three women, or anyone else, thought. I wanted that secret out! I spilled my guts that night. For the first time in thirteen or fourteen years, I told someone besides Bill about Willie. I told about being tied up and raped hundreds of times. I told them about my shame, about how I wasn't really who they thought I was. I confessed to those three ladies the fraud that I had been, and how my life was filled with tears and emotional upheaval. Then I told them about the dreams and nightmares, and the mess I was making of my marriage and my home life. For an hour, I emptied my soul.

June was shocked. She hadn't known a thing. Ben had never suspected; they had no idea this was going on at 17 Sherbourne Street. "Margaret, we're so close. You didn't feel you could tell me?"

"June, I haven't told anyone—not Tina, not anyone. Only Ruby and Bill, and a little to Ruth before I got married. I...I haven't been able to trust anyone. I didn't want anyone to know this about me," I stammered.

When I had said all that was in my heart, Joan Jewel said something that would forever change my life. "Margaret, you don't have to put up with that kind of abuse. *Jesus can heal you!*" The words were a revelation.

Heal me? I'm not sick, I thought. It's funny to say it now, but the whole time I was tormented in my mind, I never thought of myself as sick. Wicked, yes—sick, no! In twenty years of going to church, no one had ever said such a thing to me. I never knew my memory could be healed.

Joan continued, "Just as Jesus can heal your body, He can heal your mind of its painful memories. I think Jesus wants to touch your mind tonight. Let's go into the living room and we'll pray for you."

She led me by the hand and I knelt on the floor of her living room. The three ladies placed their hands on my shoulders, and then Joan prayed the simplest, most beautiful prayer I had ever heard: "Jesus, we've been listening to each other give testimonies tonight of how much you've done for all of us. Now, Lord, would you please heal Margaret? Lord, you really want to use her, but it's hard now with all that she's feeling. Please, Lord Jesus, would you just heal her of all this pain? We agree together and believe that you will heal her memory. Thank you, Lord. Amen."

I got up from the prayer and sat on the sofa. Instantly, I felt better. For years I had heard newly saved Christians talk about coming to Jesus and feeling a load of guilt lifting off their shoulders. For the first time in my life, I could relate. Though *my* guilt had been lifted from me years earlier when I committed my life to Christ, that night *Willie's* guilt lifted from me. I sighed. I just felt like sighing. I sighed the biggest, most liberating sighs. The relief was palpable. An incredible peace settled over me—a peace that I had never felt in my life before. I was so conscious of Jesus' love for me; I felt safe. I felt safe and normal.

We continued to talk until the wee hours of the morning. I agreed that I would hold myself accountable to those three women, and if the flashbacks or nightmares returned, I was to tell them. They would get together with me again and pray. I agreed to call for prayer if I needed to, and I got my things together and headed home. June had come to women's ministries in her own car that night, not being able to go as early as I needed to, and so we each drove home alone.

Though it was well after midnight, I wasn't afraid. There was a resolute calm in the car. I felt secure and safe, like I had never felt before. The peace that had come over me at Joan's house was still with me. It occurred to me that this was no temporary peace, but rather something fundamental that had changed. This peace was Jesus' peace. It was "the peace that passes understanding." (See Philippians 4:7).

221

"God, I feel great!" I said out loud. "This is amazing!"

Normally at this time of night, driving home alone in the country, I would be gripped by fear. That night everything was different. I didn't feel my heart pounding beneath my blouse and, for the first time, I hadn't looked for my marker houses. I arrived at home before I knew it, without once checking out my progress by my special porch-light friends. I went in the house feeling like angels had carried me home.

Bill woke up as I entered the bedroom. He looked at the alarm clock on the night table. "Where have you been?" he mumbled.

"At a meeting," I whispered excitedly, "a very important meeting! I'll tell you all about it tomorrow."

"Okay. Good-night," Bill whispered back, and he rolled over and went back to sleep. I wanted to tell him what happened, but I restrained myself. Bill was on the day shift and had to be up in three hours. I wanted him to get his sleep. He was used to me coming home late from women's ministries, so he hadn't been worried or angry.

I could hardly wait to talk to Bill when he got home from work on Tuesday afternoon. I told him about the ladies at coffee, about my meltdown, and then about what Joan Jewel said. I told him how they prayed for me, and how we all believed that God had healed my bad memories.

"Wow! You told those ladies? What did you tell them?" Bill was in shock, as much from my exhilarant mood as from the news I was giving him.

"Everything! About Willie, the abuse, the nightmares, the flashbacks—everything!"

"And they prayed?"

"They prayed!"

"Wow! Well, how do you feel?"

"I don't know what happened, Bill, but I drove home last night from St. Catharines with the most peace I've ever had. I don't even remember the drive. And the peace—it's lasted all day! Bill, I have never in my life felt as free as I do now!"

I was talking excitedly and, as I rambled, my words began to register in Bill's mind. He welled up with tears; we held each other and cried.

"Oh, Honey, this isn't a time for crying," I said to him as I held his face in my hands. "It's a time to be happy." I looked into his eyes. "Bill, I'm really going to believe with those girls that the nightmares are gone—because they prayed that way—that all the nightmares will be gone forever. I'm really going to believe, okay?"

"Okay, Sweetheart. Okay. Me too! I'm going to believe too!"

The rest of the week was great. I was on cloud nine, and I didn't have to get myself "up" for Sunday; I couldn't wait to get to church. That Sunday we had a special speaker, Ferne Olson. (She had been the evangelist at Braeside Camp eighteen years earlier, on the night when most of Bill's family got saved.) The title of her message on that Sunday evening in 1972 was, "The Healing of Our Memories." I couldn't believe what I was hearing! God was reinforcing what I had just learned six days before, and now He was showing me through His Word that what happened to me was legitimate and biblical. She spoke with great authority that day, and I believed God was a God who healed memories.

Following the message there was a time for prayer at the altar. Ferne invited those who needed their memories healed to come up and be prayed for. I didn't go—Jesus had healed me already. (I thought at the time that Jesus had totally healed me. That was true with respect to nightmares, flashbacks, and living in fear; the road to complete recovery, however, which required modifying my behaviors and learning about forgiveness, was a road I would slowly travel for another thirty-five years.) Then I noticed someone else at the altar, and my heart jumped through my chest. It was my niece!

I was feeling so free myself that I wanted everyone to experience the same freedom. I had been looking for someone to pray with at the altar, just as Joan and the ladies had done with me. When I spotted her, I immediately sensed why she needed healing: Willie had gotten to her too!

She had been coming to church lately with Mom because her parents didn't attend. She had been searching and had seemed especially hungry for the things of God. I went up to the altar behind her kneeling frame, put my arm around her and whispered in her ear: "Sweetheart, it's Auntie Marg. I know why you're up here. I know the things you've been through. I know who did those things to you—I know because he did the same things to me."

She had been crying, and when I spoke she was startled by what I said. "Who? How did you know?"

"I know," I answered, "because…well,.I think the Lord just told me; and I'd like to pray with you. Let me tell you what Jesus has just done for me."

That was the first time I shared openly about my abuse, and I shared in order to help someone else. I was starting to figure out why God allowed this evil into my life: He wanted to heal me so completely, so miraculously, that I could help others who had experienced the same nightmare. There was some purpose to my pain—God was going to use me to help others.

I soon realized how hard God had been working to get through to me. He had been trying to reach out to me, trying to teach me—I just hadn't been listening. Now that He had set His peace in my heart, I was beginning to learn the lessons I needed to not just survive, but thrive.

Two Sundays after the prayer for my deliverance at Joan's place, Pastor Morgan began a series of messages he had announced ahead of time. I thought little of it when the series was being announced, but after that special Monday evening, everything I was being taught in church seemed to apply specifically to me. The series was called "Practicing the Presence of God." The fundamental point of the series was that we could bring the presence of God into every part of our lives. I had always reserved worship and praise for Sundays, where there were instruments and singers and where the worship leader led me in songs. Pastor Morgan was teaching us instead to be worshipers in every moment of our lives; to be "instant in season, out of season" (2 Tim. 4:2).

The practical application of what I was learning radically changed my life. I could practice the presence of God as I was doing laundry, folding diapers, cleaning the house, even driving the car; I could *train* my mind to focus on God. The mundane things that a mom does around the house each day, the chores that are done on autopilot with little thought or effort, provide opportunity to praise and worship God. I didn't have to be in church or assume the kneeling position in my prayer closet; I could talk to God in the coming and going of my life. Previously

I had held a puritanical view on worship—I had to be all primped and preened, in my Sunday best, in order to praise God. This view must have trickled down from my Mom's legalistic heritage and somewhere along the line, I took ownership of it.

I used to get upset at Bill. He would stand in the shower and sing and praise God, sometimes even speaking in tongues. I thought it sacrilegious; but when I would mention it he would say, "Marg, it's within me. I can begin to praise the Lord in an instant. I can use the prayer language God gave me, anytime—can't you? What's the matter with you? You're wound up too tight. You've been baptized in the Holy Spirit—you should be able to speak it out."

But I couldn't. I couldn't praise the Lord whenever and wherever I was. Maybe I had been filled with the Holy Spirit, but the evidence seemed weak. I received one little phrase in tongues and nothing more. I was so embarrassed by only being able to say a few words in my heavenly language that I hardly used it. Unless I was deep in prayer, unless I was by myself, I would restrict myself to English. Bill had been trying to get me to be more free in my personal worship, but I couldn't. Until I was set free from the guilt, shame, and fear of the past, I had been a "worship paralytic." Now, two weeks after my prayer of deliverance, I was hearing and understanding that God wanted me to be a worshiper in every moment of the day. I was finally ready to hear.

In the winter of 1971, just before I had my meltdown, I read a book called *Prison to Praise*.[1] While I listened to Pastor Morgan preach about the presence of God, the Holy Spirit brought it back to my mind. The author, Merlin Carothers, told how he had gone from stealing a car while AWOL from the army to becoming a chaplain. Along the way to his encounter with God, he was filled with the Holy Spirit, which changed his life and gave him a joy he had never known. One of the most disturbing parts of the book was his contention that we are to give thanks *in* everything and *for* everything; that God is in charge and nothing gets past Him. When we thank God for every situation, every predicament, we put Him back in control and He is free to work miracles on our behalf. The verse that changed his life was, "in everything give

[1] Merlin Carothers, *Prison to Praise* (Merlin R. Carothers, 1972).

thanks: for this is the will of God in Christ Jesus concerning you" (1 Thess. 5:18). Quoting this verse throughout his book, he cited example after example of people thanking God for their trouble and then told how God came through, helping them overcome.

At the time, I was in the depth of my personal despondency and trying to climb out of it under my own strength. The more I read of Merlin Carothers, the more I hated him. If I didn't hate the man, I hated what he was saying. I was certainly mad at him.

Thank God for my childhood? Yeah, right! I thought. I'm supposed to thank God for the fact that my "pervert" brother raped me! This Merlin guy doesn't know me! He doesn't have a clue what I've been through. He's been in jail—big deal! He hasn't had to live my life. This whole "rejoice in the Lord always" thing might work for him; he's never been tortured and brutalized. (See Philippians 4:4, NIV.) If he were me, I would like to see whether he would be thanking and praising and letting all his joy out!

My understanding had been totally closed off. I was unwilling to listen to God's voice when He was trying to get through to me. I needed first to understand that He could heal my memories, but I also needed to learn how to thwart satan's attacks on my mind; how to keep my mind "stayed on him" (Isa. 26:3).

As I listened to Pastor Morgan talk about the ever-present Spirit of God, I remembered Merlin Carothers's book. God had planted a seed as I read, and now it started to sprout inside my heart, where it had been lying dormant. Hope was growing inside of me. God was showing me that if I thanked Him in and for all things, that He could take the awful evil done to me and turn it around for my good and His glory. God was showing me that "all things work together for good to them that love God, to them who are the called according to His purpose" (Rom. 8:28). I had been called. God had formed me. I wasn't a mistake. In fact, He had a divine purpose and plan for my life that I was only now realizing. What the devil meant for evil, God could turn around for something good and wholesome. My shame could become His honor!

"O, God," I prayed, "help me to submit to Your plan. I realize that You have always been with me, waiting for me to turn to You for help. God, I'm turning to You now. Turn the ugliness that is my life into something beautiful. Work things out in my life for good, for your glory and purpose." I prayed the verse in Isaiah, "Give me 'beauty for ashes, the oil of joy for mourning,' and 'the garment of praise for the spirit of heaviness'" (Isa. 61:3).

God did want to make something beautiful of my life, but it wouldn't happen instantly; He had to show me all kinds of areas that needed work.

When God takes something out of our lives, He immediately replaces it with more of Himself. I began to praise the Lord as I did laundry, to worship and sing choruses around the house. It didn't matter what I was doing; I was learning to train my mind to think on things above. Jesus spoke of a person who had been delivered of a demon—his house was clean and swept, Jesus said, but empty. When the demon saw that there was nothing filling the house, it came back with a vengeance and occupied that house again; but this time it brought seven other worse spirits along. (See Luke 11:24–26.) God delivered me of the spirits of fear, condemnation, guilt, and shame that night at Joan Jewel's, but He needed to fill me up with Himself. I needed to live in the constant presence of God! I needed Him to fill the evil space that He had emptied with the person of the Holy Spirit.

As He was working this out in my life, He came across an obstacle.

I worked like crazy to get my housework done in the mornings so that I could put the kids to bed in the afternoons and watch my favorite soap operas. I loved the soaps. Soon after God replaced my anguish with His joy and peace, He began to convict me about what I was putting into my mind. God had been so gracious and loving, taking my fear and degradation away, and in essence I was fighting Him every afternoon, filling my mind with love triangles, deception, marital strife, and adultery. Originally the soaps had been a much-needed escape from the hell of my own reality; I fantasized and placed myself in that unreal world. I enjoyed going there because, while in that world, I didn't have to think about my own pathetic existence. Each day I pined for my retreat. I would exit my depression and the drudgery of motherhood, distracted by a world of fantasy.

Television soaps became my "broken cistern" (Jer. 2:13). They promised distraction and escape from my troubles, but they were only a fraud. As soon as the television was off, I was slammed back onto the ground of the real world. I longed for things that weren't of God. I compared my life to the imaginary lives of actors playing parts, but there was nothing real about them so my fantasies always crash-landed. Jesus had offered me water from His well; water which, if I drank of it, would keep me from ever thirsting again. Yet I would leave His well, the wellspring of the Spirit of God, and I would drink from my own broken cistern—a cistern that promised what it could never deliver. Instead of pure, clean, refreshing water, I was settling for polluted, unsanitary, life-threatening water. I would start the day singing praises and worshiping God, only to find myself distracted—hurrying the presence of the Lord along, so I could spend time with my soaps. I knew that if Jesus' presence was going to stay, the soaps had to go.

But I had become addicted to them. I decided that, during the day, I would not turn on the television at all. If I turned it on, even for company, I would watch what I shouldn't, and the presence of God would be chased away. To help me with my commitment, I made myself accountable to Judy Pymont. Being vulnerable with the ladies in my women's ministries executive had become a lot easier since the night in Joan Jewel's living room. Judy enjoyed the soaps as well and agreed to be a partner with me—we would quit them together. We asked each other at church each week whether or not we had watched them, and sometimes in the afternoons we phoned each other to talk. Sometimes we read the Bible together and prayed on the phone. The partnership worked; I was able to pry myself from the grip of the placebo and take hold of the genuine cure. God was transforming my mind.

For the next couple of years I praised my way through each day. I thought about God, about His wholesomeness, His truth and love for me. I thought about His plans and purposes and I sang songs. I might not be a great singer in the eyes of this world, but singing worship songs and choruses makes me a great singer in God's estimation. I would "enter his gates with thanksgiving and his courts with praise," in the morning, and I would sing myself to sleep at night. (See Psalm 100:4, NIV). I would bookend my days with praising God, and in the middle I would worship Him every moment I could. I didn't worry about being interrupted—if I was, I would take care of whatever was demanding my attention, then return to praising Him. I decided that God wanted to be a part of

228

my whole day and He understood when I would have to take care of the kids or run an errand. I was invigorated, practicing the presence of God.

In 1974, Bill and I needed a weekend away. Full Gospel Businessmen's Fellowship International, known by most as FGBMFI, was hugely popular. They were having a conference in Washington, D.C., and their keynote speaker was to be Rev. Merlin Carothers. We leapt at the chance to go. As Carothers spoke, he told us of the difference in his life once he received the baptism of the Holy Spirit. I had been raised in Pentecost; I knew all about being filled with the Spirit, yet I hardly used the gift I was given and doubted the Holy Spirit's work in me. Merlin spoke about a new joy that flooded into his life—a joy unconnected to circumstances. He said that the Holy Spirit not only led him into thanking God for every circumstance, but also to rejoice in everything.

God, not only do you want me to thank You for everything in my life, You want me to rejoice in my abuse? Lord, how can I rejoice about being sexually abused? I was troubled by what he was saying, yet I wanted the superceding joy Carothers was talking about—the kind that transcended problems and trials.

I genuinely wanted to "rejoice in the Lord always" (Phil. 4:4, NKJV). The thing that struck me about Merlin Carothers was that he always just quoted the Word of God. He didn't expand upon it much; he just quoted it. It was simple, forthright, and authoritative. I was learning how powerful the Word of God really is when you obey it.

Sometimes during the day, even while I praised the Lord, my mind would drift, and I would catch myself thinking about the nightmares I used to have. I learned to quote and pray words from the Bible: "In the name of Jesus, I command that thought, that dream to leave my mind." I learned never to play around with thoughts; instead I took them captive, and cast them out of my mind. (See 2 Corinthians 10:4–6, NIV.) After a short prayer I would start singing again, and my mind would return to the safety of God. I submitted my mind and my thoughts to Him. In place of those attacking thoughts came the presence of God. I always prayed my "rebuking" prayer out loud. If it didn't convince the devil of God's authority, it certainly convinced me. Hearing myself say the name of Jesus instantly brought His peace. I heard years later that the enemy cannot read our minds—he doesn't know our innermost thoughts; only God does. To rebuke him we must let him hear it. That certainly makes sense to me.

After rebuking the devil for his mental attack, I would often throw my deliverance back in his face by praying so he could hear, "Lord Jesus, I'm so thankful for what you did for me in Joan's living room. Please purify my mind, remove any evil thoughts, those thoughts not from You, and help me to meditate on Your goodness for the rest of the day. Amen."

After the prayer at Joan's house—except for one brief period (the result of my own disobedience), I never again had a flashback; I didn't have trouble making love to Bill and, after two years, I still hadn't had a returning nightmare. But I was still afraid to go to sleep every night. I would lie in bed wondering if this would be the night the nightmares would return. I knew it had been two years since I had one, but I dreaded waking up in that cold sweat.

"Jesus, I know that I have to train my mind to think on your Word and positive things—and I can do that during the day; but, Lord, I don't have any power over my subconscious mind. I can't control what I dream about! How can I go to sleep every night confident that I won't have a nightmare?" I pleaded with the Lord one night, and He spoke to my heart.

"Margaret," He whispered gently into my spirit, "if the last thing that you think about when you fall asleep at night is Me, I'll protect your thoughts while you sleep. Your dreams will be My responsibility."

"But, Lord, how am I going to remember to do that *every* night? And what if I forget? Lord, I'm afraid I'll forget and then the nightmare will come!"

He spoke again. "This is how you will remember: do you know the little song I taught you when you were a small girl?"

The Spirit of God sang it to me that night: "Jesus loves me! This I know, for the Bible tells me so. Little ones to Him belong; they are weak, but He is strong. Yes, Jesus loves me! Yes, Jesus loves me..."

"Margaret," the Lord continued, "Sing My song. That's how you'll remember."

For thirty years, from 1974 until this writing, I have gone to sleep singing that childhood song, "Jesus Loves Me."[2] Except for one six-week period, which I will talk about in the next chapter, I have not had one nightmare. I have been free of flashbacks, cold sweats, depression, and nightmares for almost thirty years, all because of the prayers of three faithful ladies, the power of God's Holy Spirit and that little children's song. Every night I turn my head on my pillow and, just before falling asleep, I hear the Lord gently remind me, "Sing to Me Margaret; sing to Me." Then, across the screen of my mind, roll the words, "Jesus loves me! This I know…"

There have been many mornings over the course of those twenty-seven years when Bill has said something like, "I woke up in the middle of the night again, Honey—you were singing your song. You were sleeping, but you were singing 'Jesus loves me…'" I believe it's in those moments, deep in the middle of the night, that satan comes to attack me with his sadistic dreams, but Jesus stops him, with me singing my little song.

I'm certainly not perfect, and there are days when I have sinned. I've spoken harshly, treated someone wrongly, or have been selfish and miserable; but I dare not go to sleep without singing my song to Jesus. At those times when I'm convicted of my wrongful behavior, I ask God to forgive me, promise to work on reconciliation the next day, and then I sing. I have to sing.

In 1975, Bill and I were sitting in church when an usher came and got me out of the service. "There's an urgent phone call for you," he reported. My heart thumped as I went to the phone, supposing there was some kind of family emergency.

Bill and I had been working with a couple, just recently saved. They were having marital trouble and had committed adultery against each other. When I got to the phone it was the husband. He was frantic. He had found his wife in the bedroom. She had taken some sleeping pills—he didn't know how many—and he wanted me to come over right away. I quickly wrote a note for Bill to take the kids home after church, and I took a taxi to their house.

Upon entering their bedroom, I saw my friend lying on the bed, and I asked if I could talk to her alone. Her husband left, and I felt

[2] Ann B. Warner, "Jesus Loves Me." Public Domain.

more at ease. She had had a rough life and an even rougher marriage. Many times she had appeared at my door, bruised and bleeding. Her husband beat her on a regular basis. (What a difference twenty years makes. Now we know not to send battered women back into marriages where the abuser remains untreated and uncounseled; but in 1975, we thought God could work things out without a separation. The truth is that abusive behavior needs to be arrested, and the victim must be removed from the threat of the offender before counseling has a hope of being effective.) She had cheated on him, and he constantly threw it back in her face, never forgiving her. His many dalliances notwithstanding, she couldn't forgive herself for stepping out on her husband.

As she lay there, groggy but not totally unconscious, I began to encourage her. "You know, Jesus loves you. Whatever you've done, He forgives. God has set me free from my past and He can heal your bad memories too."

"Whadda you know? Whadda you know about bad memories? You—you always lithed a good lithe," she mumbled back to me. It took me a moment to understand her garbled words; then it hit me. She thought my life had been wonderful—a good life!

Suddenly I heard myself telling my story to her. After sharing what I had been through, the Holy Spirit gave me incredible things to say. It was as though I was listening to someone else talk.

"God allowed that abuse to happen to me," I continued, "He didn't cause it, but He let it happen to me just the same—and He did that so I could Help others who are in pain. The pain I was in is all gone; He took it all away. If He could heal the pain of my memories, I know He can heal yours. My story is awful, so when I tell people how I was set free, they believe He can do the same for them. You see, I didn't understand it for a long time, but this is what He wants me to do with my life. My shame has become my glory—in Christ. God turned my ashes into beauty, and now I've become the planting of the Lord—solid like a tree—that He might be glorified in my healing."

Then I said the most profound thing, not realizing its impact until I thought about it later. I said her name and then looked into her eyes. "All my pain, all those bad memories—they're just scars now, like the scar on my knee. I hurt it five years ago and when it happened it hurt like crazy; but now when I look at my knee, all I see is the scar. I can see the scar, I remember what happened, but it's just a scar now—and scars don't hurt." It sounded so profound, I said it again, "Scars don't hurt. Jesus can make your painful memories into a scar. He'll take the pain away. He did it for me; let Him do it for you."

When I left her bedside I had a full revelation of God's purpose in my life: I was to help bring recovery to those who had been scarred by the enemy. God wanted me to tell my story to other hurting women and bring the hope of healing to their lives. I was such a free person now; God wanted me to help others realize that same freedom. I began sharing my story with select people and, every time I did, I told them that I had a scar, but it didn't hurt anymore. I could talk about the scar, touch the scar, expose it to the light—it didn't matter; it was just a scar, and scars don't hurt.

Before I would tell my story, I would pray and ask God if the listener would benefit from it. Afterward I felt wonderful. I was telling people I was a victim of rape and incest, and I felt wonderful doing it. Jesus had taken away all of the shame and degradation. I felt as though I was talking about someone else. I knew it all happened to me, but my healing and restoration was so complete, and I was so disconnected from the person I used to be, that the former Margaret Davidson seemed a stranger to me. The shame had been centered on a secret. Now the secret was out—God was using it like a banner of truth—and there wasn't any shame. I finally got to the place where I could thank God—like Merlin Carothers—that He let me go through the pain; because the joy, the elation I knew now from being healed, was so much more intense than the suffering I endured. The psalmist is so right, "Weeping may endure for a night, but joy comes in the morning" (Ps. 30:5, NKJV). With God, suffering is only temporary. His joy and peace make the difference.

That joy was finally made perfect in one after-service altar time at church. Pastor Morgan had been teaching us how to spend time in audible worship, making it a part of every service. He was encouraging us to worship joyfully and expressively. Bill and I had been entering in, experiencing greater fullness in worship and an increased comfort praising the Lord. We had had a beautiful worship service one Sunday morning and, following the sermon, we were invited to pray for our unsaved loved ones—those in our families who needed Jesus. Funny as it seemed, I started praying for my dad. I felt especially burdened for him that day, but didn't have the words to express it to the Lord in prayer. I decided to speak in tongues and let the Holy Spirit pray through me—at first just that one little phrase, those few words that He had given me. (See Romans 8:26–27, NIV.) Abruptly, as if a dam burst, I began speaking a plethora of words I had never learned. I was fluent in a heavenly language and full of the Holy Spirit. With the flood of tongues came a freedom I hadn't felt before. I was finally free to let the Spirit of God flow through me unabated, undeterred. Now I knew firsthand what it meant to have "joy unspeakable and full of glory" (1 Pet. 1:8).

The fullness I experienced in the Holy Spirit was integral to my recovery. He allows me to rise above circumstances and to rejoice in Jesus. I am not able, in my own strength, to give thanks in everything or to rejoice in the Lord always. It is the power of the Holy Spirit that enables me to do what is otherwise impossible. I know that not everyone holds to this same theology; all I know is once I was bound and now I'm free. The Holy Spirit, and the blessings that come from communing with Him, are the mainstay of my life. He has brought me out of the darkness and into Jesus' marvelous light, and I never want to go back. (See Peter 2:9.) I cannot tell my story without sharing the Holy Spirit's wonderful work in my life.

❧

God didn't do it all at once, but I can see His hand working at every stage of my life. The husband he gave me, getting me to trust Him for our finances, Pastor Williams and Pastor Morgan, Merlin Carothers and *Prison to Praise*, women's ministries, Ben and June, Joan Jewel and Judy Pymont, learning to worship, practicing the presence of God, the baptism in the Holy Spirit—all of this was God showing me He loved me. He was always reaching out to me, working things out for my good and His glory. I'm forever in His debt.

CHAPTER 14

Bumps in the Road

God had placed me on the road to freedom, but He knew (though I didn't) that there would be bumps in that road. It wouldn't be a smooth or easy journey. In the years immediately following my healing and deliverance, I didn't see the other areas in my character and personality that still needed to change. I was delighted just to have joy and freedom, to be free of nightmares and flashbacks. I had changed so dramatically that I was instantly a better person to be around. I hardly ever got depressed or down. My sense of humor flourished, and I had a new love of life.

Though it is difficult to believe, the nightmares had been worse for me to endure than the actual physical and sexual abuse. While being sexually assaulted, I forced my mind to go elsewhere, to dissociate from what was occurring. It gave me a measure of control to transport myself somewhere else mentally.

But no one can escape a nightmare. I was trapped inside until I woke up. I was destined to experience the whole thing until *it* decided I could wake up, and by then my soul was ravaged. If someone had asked me, while in the midst of my nightmares, which I could more easily endure—a repeat of the sexual trauma, or the endless torture inside my dream—I would certainly have said the former. The nightmare was that horrific. My psychological and emotional agony was magnified beyond the physical pain of rape.

For those who have never been through sexual assault, this doesn't make sense; but what violence does to the mind and soul is more severe, more long lasting, than what it does to the body.

With my newfound strength, I handled all the big things well—it was the little frustrations of everyday life that caused more grief. From the time the ladies prayed for me and my life started to drastically improve, I had God's peace and joy in my life. But God hadn't yet dealt with me about surrendering my deeply rooted anger and bitterness, the hidden enclaves of unforgiveness, or the rough edges of my nature—all of which still existed beneath the surface. Few people noticed these because things were infinitely better—but we can't retain all that garbage in our lives and avoid damaging ourselves and other people. To God, I was a lifelong mission, not a quick fix.

One of the first things I had to learn was daily dependence upon Jesus, through God's Word. I wanted to coast on the fuel of my deliverance, and God wanted me to daily pick up my cross and follow Him. I thought I could live in the ecstasy of the moment, that my joy and peace would always be there now that the oppressive evil wasn't. But God's Word says, "As thy days, so shall thy strength be" (Deut. 33:25).

That was just it. I had never learned to depend upon a daily portion of the Bible, the bread of life. Just as I needed to eat physically each day, God was showing me that I needed to be nourished spiritually from the Bible in the same way—daily. In the Old Testament, the children of Israel were fed manna. It was their sustenance, and God provided it for every person in the camp. He provided it for forty years with one condition: *Each day*, families had to go out early in the morning, when the manna fell, and collect enough for themselves and their servants for that day. They couldn't collect enough for a week and store it. Manna had a shelf life of one day—if anyone tried to eat day-old manna, it would turn rancid and poison those who ate it.

Perhaps some Israelites thought that their plan was more efficient: they would gather enough manna to last the whole week. God's ways hardly ever make sense to us humans; nonetheless, they always prevail. God wanted me to rely on His strength moment by moment, to receive His word and to allow Him to tweak my character a little each day. I learned this lesson in a unique way.

236

Ben and June decided to take a missions trip to Brazil in the summer of 1972. They were to be gone six weeks, and Bill and I offered to take care of their two boys until they returned. (After Heather was born, they adopted a second boy.) The older boy was four years old and his younger brother was the same age as Heather, two. Shawn was seven and Blake was six. For six uninterrupted weeks in an extremely hot summer, I had charge of five children under age eight!

Ben and June had been wonderfully generous toward us, helping us buy our house and waiting five years for us to remortgage before accepting any payment for the land; and even then, discounting the costs. Babysitting was a tangible way we could bless them—but I was unprepared for what six weeks of sibling rivalry and peer competition could be like. Our kids were constantly fighting with their cousins. They resented the way their world had changed and were not eager to share their mother. Then there was the heat. Like most people in the early Seventies, we did not have central air conditioning. Everyone was irritable and lethargic, and the smallest of irritations threatened the peace. I went from one catastrophe to the next all day long, and by nightfall I would collapse on my bed. I would desperately want to sleep, and yet I was so hot and uncomfortable that sleep wouldn't come. I lay there in my misery, knowing that I would be wiped out the next day, unable to cope. By the third week I was at my lowest point.

I fell into a heap one evening and cried to God. "God, I can't take this anymore!" Bill was working the afternoon shift, and he had the chores for all of the cattle to do in the mornings—the ones he and Ben normally shared—so I was alone with the kids, fighting for my emotional survival.

I saw my Bible on the mantle and decided that maybe God would have something positive to say about my situation. I'm not the type of person that gets a direct message from God every day, and I wouldn't suggest this method to others, but I randomly flipped my thumb through the pages allowing the Bible to fall open arbitrarily. That day God showed me that His Word is alive and vital. I opened my Bible to Isaiah and read, "When thou passest through the waters, I will be with thee; and through the rivers, they shall not overflow thee: when thou walkest through the fire, thou shall not be burned; neither shall the flame kindle upon thee" (Isa. 43:2). I turned back a few pages and came across, "Behold, the former things are come to pass, and new things do I declare…" (Isa. 42:9). Instantly, peace came to me. In that moment God's Word had spoken to my heart and brought to mind what I needed to know. The Spirit of God used the Word of God and brought hope in my moment of need. I had never seen the Bible in this light before. I knew I needed to read it, even study it; but what I didn't know was that in a moment, when I needed an answer or a word of encouragement, the Spirit of God would be there to help me with something He had inspired someone to write, hundreds and thousands of years before. If I read and memorized Scripture, I discovered, the Holy Spirit would bring it back to remembrance and minister to me. The Spirit of Truth uses the Word of Truth. My pain was caused by my failure to know and believe what was true.

In my experience, I cannot separate the Word of God from the work of the Holy Spirit; the former is the tool of the latter. He uses everything I put into my mind from God's Word and makes it come alive to me, speaking to me in personal situations. When I had come to the end of myself with those five children, God showed me that His principles were just what I needed. They weren't only right and proper for the ancients, but His Word was necessary and relevant for daily living. God brought me freedom through the Holy Spirit, based on truths written in the Bible. The two are inextricably linked. God was showing me that I needed to look into His "perfect law of liberty," *every* day. (See James 1:25.) It had to become my manna, my sustenance. God's Spirit would take what I read and nourish my soul. Just as I needed to eat each day, I was learning that I needed spiritual food. In my Christian walk, I had been eating week-old, rancid manna. I was trying to get by gorging myself once or twice per week, and my ability to cope had dissipated. I was sick spiritually.

"Sorry, Lord," I prayed. "I know that I need to read Your Word and commune with You daily. Please forgive me for thinking that I am strong enough in myself. I confess to You that You are my God in my weakness, and I must totally rely on You for everything."

My prayer was liberating! The pressure was off. God would always help me, even in the smallest of details. I had learned the secret of going to God when I am weak, just as my little song says, "I am weak, but He is strong. Yes, Jesus loves me…"

Margaret Davidson had always tried to be strong, to handle everything on her own. In reality I had just ignored problems and suppressed things. I hadn't dealt with them at all. God was showing me that I needed to be weak, to *need* Him; then He could be strong on my behalf. After that summer, God's Word became the source for my life. I intended to know it, to memorize it, to be regular in my study of it; every day I would take time to let God speak to me through His Word. When I read God's Word I found instant peace, joy, and freedom, and those good feelings would replace the angst in my spirit—but only temporarily.

There was unforgiveness in my heart, and it stirred up trouble whenever I demonstrated the least sign of spiritual weakness. If I entertained my flesh in the slightest, the peace and joy would be overcome by anger. Anger was the fruit of my unforgiveness. That's why I didn't recognize it. Anger masked the ill will I still held in my heart. Whenever I thought of Willie, or when someone mentioned him, my blood boiled.

Though the pain of my past no longer hurt and the memories were healed, I was not a whole person. I was in the process of becoming whole, but that process would take another fifteen years. Everything that I had learned up until 1975 had come as a result of trusting God and submitting to Him. When I didn't understand what He was doing, I still had to learn to submit, especially in circumstances beyond me. Submission and obedience, to one who has been controlled and dominated by another, does not come easily. I had submitted to God in worship, finances, practicing the presence of God, leadership, and in praying with spiritual authority; but as soon as I would hand God one area of my life, the search light of the Holy Spirit quickly revealed another. I was fast learning how little I really trusted God.

I began to look for ways to submit to God. I wanted to be obedient, to follow His Word as closely as possible. While reading the Bible in my personal devotions, the Holy Spirit suddenly highlighted water baptism. I grew up in the church. I was a confessed Christian from the time I was a little girl—yet I had no memory of being baptized. No one had ever asked me about it. I guess people just assumed that at some time in the past I had been baptized. I realized from Scripture that Jesus commanded those who believe in Him and confess Him as Lord and Savior to be baptized in water. Here I was, the women's ministries president, thirty-one years old and trying to lead others, feeling like a hypocrite. I made an appointment with Pastor Morgan.

"Pastor, I have no memory of ever being baptized in water. I don't know if it's because I was so young when it took place, or because it never happened. I asked my mom and brothers if they knew—no one seems to remember it," I explained.

"Well, if you did get baptized and you don't remember, it isn't doing you any good, Margaret. Quit beating yourself up about it and come to the baptismal seminar next Sunday evening." Pastor Morgan was so reassuring. I was relieved and agreed to be baptized.

While in the tank on the following Sunday, the pastor merely explained that I had no recollection of being baptized in water, that I wanted to know that I was following Christ with full obedience and that, if it was indeed a second baptism, it came only out of a heart desiring to please Jesus. Many in our church were shocked that night, including Blake and Shawn who were old enough by then to know what was taking place. Though it meant little to others, it meant the world to me. It was one more area in which God asked me to obey Him. When I came up from the water after being immersed, I felt like a new believer. I was pleased I had obeyed the Holy Spirit's promptings.

Though my whole life had been dysfunctional and I was a walking reservoir of insecurity, few people realized it. Most people, because of my extroverted personality, assumed I had things together. Humbling myself before the people of our congregation, being publicly baptized after everyone assumed I had been, was scary; but it was an important step in becoming authentic before God and others. I had been proud of my church persona—I wanted desperately to be the person that always had everything together. Instead I was slowly learning that God doesn't require perfection, just honest submission to Him.

Both Bill and I wanted to be more involved in church. When there were special meetings, we wanted to be there. Teaching Sunday school and women's ministries, singing in the choir, ensuring our kids would go to the youth group…all of these things became priorities;

but living out in the country made all of it difficult. Bill loved his little "hobby farm." He and Ben raised fifteen to twenty head of cattle, had them butchered, then sold the meat. The whole process barely paid for itself, but still Bill loved it. We had a couple of ponies, and a little pasture and lived in the quiet of the country, away from the city, in a picturesque little world. Several times every year Bill would bring his twelve-year-old boys' Sunday school class to the farm. They would go hiking in the bush, have a big cookout and bonfire, and play a game of touch football out in the field. The city boys really loved it. We were glad to have them, and while some of what we were able to do brought us joy, inviting people out after church services, or being involved in discipling new Christians, was restricted by the half-hour drive. More and more, our hearts were being pulled from the country into the city.

In the spring of 1974, we pulled out of our parking spot at Central Gospel Temple. As we waited at the end of the church driveway for the traffic to pass, Bill noticed a house for sale directly across the street.

"We're at the church so much, we should probably buy that house!" Bill said, half joking—but that little comment started us thinking. For the rest of the day we talked about moving off the farm and getting a house in the city. We discussed the subject over the next several weeks and, before we knew it, we were investigating listings in St. Catharines.

"There would be a lot less driving," Bill would say.

"Yeah, and Shawn and Blake are just a couple of years away from being in the youth group," I would answer, adding fuel to the growing impulse to move. "We could definitely be more involved."

"That's really it, Margaret. I mean, the question really is, what is God requiring us to do? We live on the farm and we enjoy it, but as far as God's kingdom goes, what are we really accomplishing? Are we just going to live our lives and do our own thing, or is there something greater for God that we could be doing? It might be that we are limiting ourselves, living out in the country."

Our desires were changing. Within the five years since we had moved into our first house, God had been drawing us to Himself in incredible ways. What used to matter to us, mattered less than ever, and all we wanted to do was be more active in ministry for Jesus.

As we moved toward summer the conversation grew more resolute. "Margaret, I don't think I want to be heaving bails of hay into the barn loft when I'm fifty, or pitching manure when the Rapture happens. I think we should see if the farm will sell—see if God is really at the heart of all of this talk."

After listing the house, we borrowed a tent trailer and went camping with several of our friends at a nearby campground.

The real estate agent suggested we list our five-acre farm for $49,900. Both Bill and I thought this was low and that if God was in this move He would bless us; so we listed it at $69,900. After only a couple of days at the campground, our agent contacted us, "An offer's come in. We need to get together."

Within one week our country farmhouse sold for $62,900. We were ecstatic.

Though Bill and I were enamored of moving into the city, our children weren't. All they could remember was country life. They didn't see the benefits of living in the city, and they didn't care about how it would make ministry, and involvement in church, easier. They rode the school bus every day, had friends they didn't want to leave and Blake especially lived to be out in the forest with his good friend from the farm down the road. The two boys had been inseparable for the last two years—always on some adventure in the bush, fishing, hiking, or chasing raccoons up trees. Country life for them was sheer freedom. The city seemed like a jail sentence.

We found a house in the north end of St. Catharines, near Lake Ontario, about a twenty-minute walk from the church. As soon as we saw this place, we knew living there would soften the blow of moving for the children. The house was nothing special—a bungalow similar to the one we lived in on the farm, only older—but the backyard was amazing. It had won "backyard of the year" in the region for its incredible landscaping and had an eight-foot-deep in-ground pool. Flowing into the large pool was a smaller kidney-shaped wading pool about eighteen inches deep. In the corner of the wading pool stood a three-foot waterfall. Part of the water returning from the filter filled a reservoir tucked behind jagged rocks, held together with mortar, providing a miniature cascade. When the reservoir filled, it ran over the rocks at the front and into the wading pool. Around the pool there were gardens with shrubs, plants and small trees. White stones filled the gardens bordering a cement patio that stretched from the rear fence to the back of the house. A lattice canopy supporting honeysuckle and wisteria vines covered a third of the patio. Separating the front and back yards were other rock gardens and a wooden privacy fence.

The poured patio consisted of dyed cement, and the yellow and clay pieces—four-feet square and bordered by chestnut colored wood trim—created a checkerboard look. A five-foot tall chain-link fence surrounded the patio area, separating it from the other parts of the backyard. Outside of the gated pool and patio, at the rear of the property, there was a concrete fishpond. It too was kidney-shaped and had a seven-foot-long concrete bridge across its narrowest part. The pond was stocked with huge goldfish and small carp that swam to the bridge whenever someone walked across, breaking the plane of the water, mouths gaping open, hoping to be fed. Behind the fishpond were two small wooden changing rooms for guests: one for men and one for ladies. To the left of the fishpond and changing rooms, one-third of the backyard remained. It had a beautifully manicured lawn surrounded by more rock gardens and small trees. Finally, at the very edge of the property, there was a dog run and kennel hidden among five evergreen trees that were at least twenty-five feet high, shielding us completely from the neighbors at the back.

We put in our offer and it was accepted—$45,000. We moved into the city and had a mortgage of only ten thousand dollars. God was again blessing us. We felt as though we were honoring Him, and because we were putting Him in a more prominent place in our lives, He provided us with this great place to raise our kids.

We moved in on the last weekend of August 1974. The children loved it and got about three weeks of swimming in before the weather turned cool. At first Blake didn't give us the satisfaction of enjoying the new surroundings—he missed the bush—but by the time the next summer rolled around, he had learned to swim and had friends over every day. It took him a year, but he ultimately accepted city life. Our house became the center of the neighborhood from June through September.

Bill and I were in a good place in our marriage. We made decent money, had a wonderful house and backyard, we were involved and growing at church, and I thought my life was set. I didn't want anything to change, but despite what I wanted, everything would.

In 1975 Bill and I decided to visit Jack and Dinah in Tucson, Arizona, where they had moved years before because of their son's severe asthma. We left the kids with my sister, Tina, and looked forward to getting away together. Jack had gone into business for himself as an insurance broker, selling health, auto, home, and life insurance. As he talked to Bill about the business, I could see Bill's interest growing. On the way home on the plane, a salesman sat beside us and Bill picked up where he had left off with Jack.

"You know, you'd be really good in sales," he said to Bill.

"Do you really think so?"

"Sure. A career in sales is full of opportunities. You're limited only by your own imagination." The man was trying to encourage Bill to dream—and while that boosted Bill's ego, it scared me half to death. I didn't want him to dream: I wanted him to work hard—at General Motors. I wanted him to go into work every day, to be on time, and bring home a steady paycheck. I certainly did not want our lifestyle threatened. I didn't care if he hated GM or not. I didn't like changing dirty diapers—he didn't have to like what he did for a living. I didn't even want to discuss the possibility of Bill becoming a salesman. I despised salesmen and certainly didn't want to be married to one!

Back home, Bill began speaking frequently with Marinus Brouwer at church. Marinus sold life insurance and loved telling Bill about its rewards, both for the people he was serving and for himself. Bill wanted to discuss the possibility of studying for the life insurance license, to see if he could pass the exams. I didn't want to hear anything about it.

"As far as I'm concerned, Bill, you hate the job that *God* gave you. You hate the very job that is looking after our family and buying food and clothes for our kids. I just don't think that's right. You should learn to be content with what you have. You don't have to enjoy your work, Bill—enjoy the paychecks."

"Honey, it's not about the paychecks. It's about doing something more important with my life. I go into the plant every day and my brain turns off. I do the same thing five hundred times and then I leave. If I don't get out of there, I'm going to go crazy!" Bill was trying to get me to understand.

"Well, I don't think that you should risk this family's future just so that you can like what you're doing!" I had learned the art of guilt-tripping well from Mom.

"Look, I don't even know if I can pass the exams. I just want to study to *see* if I pass."

Bill was laid off in the winter of 1975, and he began to study for his life insurance license. (During lay-offs, workers received about ninety percent of their normal paycheck through a special arrangement between GM and the Unemployment Insurance Office. Guys enjoyed the lay-off, looking forward to the paid rest.) Instead of just lying around the house waiting to be called back, Bill decided he would take the time to study.

I pretended that it really didn't matter if Bill studied for the life insurance industry, GM would soon phone and Bill would go back to work like he always had. He would see the folly of chasing dreams, come to his senses, and take the guaranteed, easy money. *Besides,* I told myself, *He probably won't pass the exams anyway. He's a high school dropout and most people in financial services have university degrees. I won't spoil his dreams prematurely. When he doesn't pass the exams, I'll be there to pick up the pieces and send him back to the factory.*

As the lay-off continued, Bill kept studying. He met with Marinus's manager at Northern Life Assurance Company of Canada, a man named Peter Vassarins. Bill was being groomed to be a new sales agent—something he could be proud of. But he failed the company's aptitude test. Peter told him his personality type wasn't suited for sales; that he was too laid back and not nearly aggressive enough. That news didn't faze Bill a bit. He just continued to study.

"All right," said Peter Vassarins, "Let's see how you do on the exams. Then we'll make a decision."

Bill passed all of the exams—with flying colors.

He went into GM and asked for a three-month leave of absence. He wanted to try out the life insurance business and, should he fail, return to his old job. General Motors was anticipating a slowing economy, and they weren't looking to do favors for employees who were laid off. Bill got his answer: if he wanted to pursue the life insurance business, he would be walking the tightrope without a net; there would be no leave.

Bill decided to take the risk and called up Peter before giving General Motors his notice. That was the Tuesday after Easter, 1975.

I was convinced that before Bill actually began at Northern Life, General Motors would call and Bill would come to his senses; but the lay-off dragged on. There was no call and there was no "coming to his senses." On Good Friday it suddenly hit me: Bill was going to tell GM he was through in just in three days. He was about to kiss good-bye his guaranteed paycheck, all of his benefits, and all of my security—for a guarantee of nothing. He would be one-hundred percent on commission. I felt doomed!

I finally said out loud what I had been thinking for months. "GM is going to call you back, Bill—you just need to wait a little longer."

"Margaret, I don't want to wait, I want to *quit*! I don't ever want to go back! Even if they call me, I don't want to go—I want to quit!"

Reality set in. Bill had made the decision. Once Tuesday came, nothing could be reversed! The whole time Bill had been studying, he had been talking about his prospects, but I hadn't been listening. I had been pretending—pretending that it would all just go away. Now I knew it wasn't going away, and I was inconsolable.

Fear swept over me. In that moment, every insecurity I had ever felt in my life gathered together and bombarded me in one organized assault. I was totally unprepared for the feelings of despair that rushed into my mind. Wave after wave of fear and doubt thrashed against my brain. Suddenly all reason and sanity vanished. I began to cry.

"Why? For what? For commission and no security?" I screamed the questions at him in rapid succession. He tried to explain, but I was through listening. "I'm leaving!" I went for my coat and moved toward the door. "I can't take any more of this!" Bill blocked my path. "Get out of my way, Bill! I'm leaving! You can go do your life insurance thing without me! Now let me out!"

"Honey, where are you going to go? It's midnight. Let's sit down and talk about this." His voice was calm and he was trying to appeal to me rationally, but rationality had left me. The truth was that I had nowhere to go; I just wanted to manipulate him. If he thought that I would leave him over this, maybe he would rescind his decision. I was struggling for control!

I couldn't get past him at the door, so I turned around violently and headed across the kitchen, screaming and crying. I rushed into the bathroom and slammed the door shut behind me; then I locked it. Outside the door Bill pleaded with me to come to reason. But in that moment there was nothing reasonable about me. Inside that bathroom was a little girl—a little girl who had been deprived and lied to, abused and threatened—and there was no way she was unlocking that door and letting him in.

"Go away! Just go away! You don't love me! If you did you wouldn't do this to me! You don't care about me and you don't care about our marriage! Go away! I'm just going to kill myself." As I yelled through my tears, I yanked open the medicine cabinet. I was in a frenzy, somewhere between madness and rage, and I grabbed a bottle of sleeping pills. I flipped the lid off the bottle and had at least fifty pills in my clenched fist.

"If you don't let me in, Margaret, I'll kick this door down! Now let me in there!" Bill's voice was firm and he was serious. Unlike me, he was totally in control.

After several minutes of arguing through the bathroom door, I was convinced he was going to break it down. I sat on the edge of the tub, the pills in one hand and a glass of water in the other, sobbing. Bill picked the lock from the other side of the handle and burst in. He grabbed my hand and forced me to throw the pills in the toilet. I collapsed into a heap. Bill picked me up and held me. For the longest time no one said anything.

"Come on, Honey, everything's going to be all right. Let's go into the bedroom. We'll talk it through." His voice was soft and reassuring, and I let him lead me into the bedroom. I was so broken I couldn't speak for almost half an hour. Bill just held me—like he always did—and I cried.

While I was trying to calm down, I realized that this whole thing was about me, not Bill.

"Margaret, I don't have to take the job. I can stay at General Motors. If this scares you too much...I mean, you're more important than any job...I didn't know you felt this strongly about it. I'll call Peter tomorrow. I'll take the books back to him and forget the whole thing. You mean more to me than any job ever could."

Here was my husband letting go of his dreams because of me, because of my fears. It was always about me! Margaret the victim! I had to have things *my* way. I had to be in control. I was insisting on having the right to crush my husband's dream. Suddenly I knew what I had to do. "No, Bill. I'm holding you back. You take this job. I don't have the right to take this decision away from you." It must have been God, in that moment, helping me come to my senses. Within the space of half an hour I had gone from being suicidal to total submission.

"Honey, I really believe I can do this," Bill reassured. "I'm sure God will take care of us. He always has in the past. Maybe we should pray about this. Would you pray with me right now?" After all of the emotional storm I had just put him through, it was incredible that he wanted to pray with me; but he did.

There in the quietness, after the biggest storm of our marriage, the peace of Jesus came into that bedroom; and just as Jesus calmed the storm on the Sea of Galilee, he whispered, "Peace, be still," into my heart that night—and peace came in. The decision was made. Bill was leaving General Motors.

Peace had entered our bedroom. What I didn't know until years later was that the storm was still raging in another room of the house—the one right beside the bathroom. It had never occurred to me as I yelled and screamed at Bill that one of our children was awake. If I had known, I don't know whether I would have cared; I was so self-absorbed in that moment. As I had slammed the bathroom door, I awakened Blake. He heard me threaten to kill myself; he heard me say that his Dad didn't love me. He heard it all.

Years later, when he felt comfortable, Blake told me the content of that argument. He told me how he lay crying on his pillow—a nine-year-old little boy—thinking for sure that his family, his world, was breaking apart. My children felt much of my pain and insecurity during their childhoods, without my realizing it. Blake said nothing for twenty-five years.

That Tuesday in April, the day after Easter Monday, Bill went into General Motors and did what he had imagined doing a thousand times: he quit. As he said good-bye to his many friends on the line, he endured their comments.

"Bill, you are one crazy guy!"

"You know that once you leave you won't get back in here—it's too bad you couldn't get a leave of absence."

No one believed he would last in the life insurance business; but they didn't know Bill like I did. He was thirty-three years old and starting a brand new chapter of his life. Every day he went into an office downtown, wearing a suit, feeling good about himself. He had passed all of the entrance exams, despite the personality and aptitude tests. Bill could never be pushy; he would have to win the confidence of potential clients by letting them see how he would place their interests ahead of his own. His Christian perspective made it easy to believe he was truly helping people, preparing them for the risk of losing a provider. He loved the feeling he had, knowing that he had provided security to families, that in the wake of personal tragedy, at least their finances would be stable. Bill believed in life insurance, and people found it easy to believe in Bill. God blessed his first year in the business. He was runner-up, just missing being the "rookie of the year" across all of Canada. He had never felt better about himself.

In April 1975, Bill started in the insurance business. Three years later, in July of 1978, my father died.

Dad and Mom had reconciled in 1973 and Dad moved back in. They decided to live in an apartment directly behind Central Gospel Temple, selling 17 Sherbourne Street. Mom had never believed in divorce, so when Dad tired of all of his dalliances he knew Mom would still be there. They lived more as roommates than lovers, however, each with a separate bedroom; but for the most part they got along. Dad promised not to drink in the apartment and he had to go out on the balcony to smoke. He agreed to go with Mom to church every Sunday, and to drive her to her various doctor appointments and errands. With these few concessions, Mom took him back. She was lonely and hated to be by herself. Dad's company was better than *no* company. They still had their verbal sparring matches, but the sting was gone from their words; they seemed more like reluctant, grumpy friends who would never admit to it, but were fond of each other just the same.

Dad had been diagnosed in the early Seventies with diabetes and gave himself injections every day. He wasn't supposed to drink and was given a strict diet to follow, but failed in both areas. The rest of the family didn't know much about the disease. We thought Dad just needed to be careful and reduce his sugar intake. We had no idea how he should have been eating. When we would have him over to our house for dinner, I would offer him a second piece of lemon meringue pie. He would look tempted and then say, "No. I'd better not." It never occurred to me that I was hurting him with the first piece. Back then insulin diabetics used was synthesized from pork or beef; it was long-acting and didn't react well to sudden increases in blood sugar. Dad should have been on a nearly sugar-free low-carbohydrate diet. I realized years later that Dad must have felt awful—suffering headaches, fatigue, and sharp mood swings most of the time. He barely understood the magnitude of his disease, and the rest of us didn't understand it at all.

Mom was always sick. She had had thirteen operations, many stomach ailments and various other illnesses, both real and imagined. Always convinced that she had the worst health, Dad couldn't take her to the doctor enough. At the beginning of July 1978, both were in the hospital—different hospitals. Dad was in St. Catharines General and Mom was in Hotel Dieu, the Catholic hospital. I was running back and forth from one hospital to the other, trying to meet the needs that the nursing staffs couldn't. Tina and Murray spent most of their summers up north at their cottage and, with the rest of my siblings working, much of the hospital care fell to me.

Those times alone with Dad had been good for our relationship. For the prior four years, we had spent each Sunday afternoon at their apartment having a snack—buns and jam followed by homemade molasses cookies—but I was still not drawn to my father. We spoke little. He had hurt me too many times, and the cuts were deep.

Things had begun to change for me around the altar at church. When I would go to pray after a service, I would pray in the wonderful prayer language that God had given me and, often, I would be burdened for the unsaved members of my family. I would be overcome with emotion and intercede earnestly for their salvation. This was happening more frequently than ever where Dad was concerned. Though he went to church each Sunday morning with Mom, he wouldn't go Sunday night, and there was never a clear indication of whether or not he had given his life to the Lord. His was an ambiguous Church experience. He could talk as though he knew the Lord, but somehow I couldn't bring myself to trust what he said—he had been conning everyone his whole life.

On July 3, I raced over from visiting Mom at Hotel Dieu and arrived at St. Catharines General by five o'clock in the afternoon. Dad hadn't been eating very well and I wanted to be there to help him eat his supper. (The nurses just didn't have the time to force him to eat.) I was concerned about him. They were doing all kinds of tests to determine why he was losing weight and felt so weak. As I was feeding him, we talked.

"You know, Margaret, I'm ready to go," he said.

"What do you mean, Dad? You're going to be fine. I'm sure the doctors will find out what's the matter and you'll be home before you know it," I said encouragingly.

"Maybe, maybe not; but I'm ready to go." He had never assured me of his relationship with God before, and it made me a little uncomfortable now. I was concerned he was giving up, but I was also intrigued that he might be telling me he was ready to go to meet God. I wanted to make sure I understood him, so I pressed him further.

"Are you telling me everything is right between you and God? You've asked him to forgive your sins and to come into your life?"

I wanted to make him say it.

"Yes."

"Well, Dad, what about the Mickey beside your bed at home?"

To me drinking cancelled out any authentic relationship with God, and I knew he still had a bottle stashed in his night table.

"Margaret, I don't drink anymore, really—I just take a little nip to get to sleep. I need it just to fall asleep." He really wanted me to believe that he and God were on good terms.

"Okay, Dad, okay," I said. "Now eat the rest of your supper for me."

As he ate, I mused over the incredible conversation we had just shared. A wonderful peace settled over us, and suddenly I didn't mind being with him. The hospital visit, the feeding—none of it felt like a chore anymore. The bond between us had strengthened, and, strangely, I felt like we had always been close, that he was my daddy and that he had never hurt me. I wondered why he had chosen to share what he did, but another part of me didn't care why; I was just glad he had.

The next afternoon around three thirty, the phone rang. "Hello, Mrs. Davidson?"

"Yes."

"Mrs. Davidson, I have some very bad news. Your father has just passed away."

I put the receiver down and instantly my eyes filled with tears. Bill was across the street talking to our neighbors. I ran outside crying, "Bill! Bill come home quick! Bill I need you!" I could hardly call him, for crying. I had had the most incredible moment of my life with my Dad the night before, and now he was gone. Just when there was some hope for a real relationship, he died. I never imagined he was that close to death.

Blake was at the house beside ours, just finishing the last of his newspaper deliveries as I rushed outside to get Bill. Upset that I was crying, Blake started to cry too, and rushed over. Bill ran across the street thinking there had been an accident—that someone had been hurt. He arrived at the same time as Blake.

"Dad died, Bill! The hospital just called! Dad's dead." I fell into Bill's arms and cried like a baby. It actually surprised me how grieved I was. Dad and I had had a good five years and an even better two weeks while he had been in the hospital—the relationship that I had always wanted with my father had shown promise, and then he was taken from me. The disappointment was overwhelming.

Dad died on Ike's birthday, July fourth, and the funeral was three days later. Mom would have to come home from Hotel Dieu and live alone—again. She hadn't even had the chance to say goodbye.

By November 1978, Mom was living with us.

She didn't do well in the month after she had come home from the hospital. While Dad was there, she had to make meals and take care of him. Now that she was alone, she wouldn't even cook for herself. I caught her several times opening a can of peas, cold, and eating them with a spoon right from the can. Most days I would go and pick her up and let her stay with me; that way at least I knew she was eating something. I didn't think she would bother to take care of herself, so I talked to my siblings about what to do. Bill seemed open to the idea of her coming to live with us, and it would be a more difficult adjustment for my sisters-in-law to have Mom in their homes. Tina and Murray were near retirement age and wanted to be free to travel. As it was, she was over at our place most of the time—it just made sense to have Mom with us.

We remortgaged the house to finish the rest of the basement and Shawn moved from her bedroom upstairs to the basement with Blake. (We had built a room for him about a year earlier, giving each of our children his or her own bedroom—fulfilling the dream we had had years earlier when we lived in the apartment on Barton Street.) Mom moved into Shawn's old bedroom upstairs. Now I had four children.

At seventy years of age, Mom was quite willing to be looked after; it communicated love to her to be doted upon. She followed me around the house like a puppy. Not only did she not want to live alone—she didn't want to be in a room by herself. It struck me one day that Bill's prophecy of fifteen years earlier had come true: "You might live with me one day, but I'm never going to live with you."

It might have been better for Mom to come live with us, but it had its repercussions on our family.

I was hard pressed to find any time for myself. Wherever I was, Mom was. Shawn, although we didn't know it at the time, was entering a very critical time—ninth grade. She hid it well, but was increasingly rebellious. Living downstairs provided her the perfect opportunity to live without accountability. She gained an instant freedom that she had never had before. The television was in the rec room, just outside her bedroom, and she started staying up late watching whatever she liked. Soon her interest in boys peaked. She would go to their place, or parties, without our knowledge. She became proficient at lying, spinning webs of deceit that Bill and I willingly entered with unmitigated trust.

In retrospect, I should have been more available during that time in Shawn's life. When I should have known what was going on in her life, I didn't. Sales required Bill to be away on calls most evenings, Mom exacted more and more of my time and care, and I was overly involved at the church—singing in the choir, going to Bible study on Wednesdays, and carrying on my duties as women's ministries president. Though everything seemed fine at home, I wasn't there to see whether or not Shawn was in any trouble. She had always been a polite and caring little girl. In my mind she had had the perfect Christian home environment. Unlike me, she had no reason to get into trouble—her life had been picture perfect. The only problem was, I didn't stop long enough to check whether what I assumed was true or not. It turned out that the only place where things were perfect with my kids was in my mind.

Over-involved and under-rested, by January 1979, I was losing weight. At first I reveled in the weight loss. I wasn't overweight to begin with but, like most women, I though, being slimmer was a good thing. My thin figure notwithstanding, I wasn't feeling well. I was constantly tired and I couldn't seem to concentrate and finish tasks. By February I was skin and bones. Then things became more stressful.

I was over at the house of my neighbor across the street. Judy and I had become fairly close friends, and she was easily accessible to me when I needed a quick respite from Mom. Mom had been angry with me and went to bed early to sulk. It was the evening of Valentine's Day. I had made little valentine notes to all of my children and sent them in their lunches to school. Around the supper table that night, the children thanked me and talked about how they were surprised and amused by the little cards. It was then that Mom realized I hadn't given her a valentine. As if she were one of my own children, she became hurt and jealous. It was not an intentional slight on my part, I hadn't thought of her as I was making the notes for my kids; they were valentine cards for children. Mom took great offense, however, and stormed off to bed. This was the woman who refused to wrap my Christmas gifts or let me play with the ones I got; the woman who threw out birthday and Christmas cards as soon as those who gave them left. This woman was offended because I didn't give her a children's valentine card. I had to get to Judy's!

Shawn was babysitting, Bill was working, and Heather and Blake were in bed. At about eleven o'clock, Mom woke up and decided to make herself a cup of instant coffee. She felt light-headed and woozy and, as she picked up the kettle, she suffered a minor heart attack and collapsed. As she hit the kitchen floor she broke a couple of vertebrae in her back. When she came to, she couldn't move.

254

"Bawlake! Bawlake! Help, Bawlake! Help me! Bawlake!" She moaned for some fifteen minutes before Blake heard her. In a very real sense, it was a miracle he heard her at all. Blake's room in the basement was on the south side of the house. There were no windows in his room and, with the door shut, it was pitch black. He called his bedroom the "tomb" because it was so cold and dark he could sleep until noon and not know it was daytime. Blake was a deep sleeper. Every morning I would call him five or six times, and he would swear he never heard me the first time. Somehow that night he heard his grandmother's soft groaning and his name being repeated over and over, and he went up to the kitchen to investigate.

"I fell. I fell and I can't get up," was all Mom could say to him. A sick gray pallor painted her face. She was sweating profusely. Somehow Blake helped her up and walked her slowly to her bed at the end of the hall, taking about fifteen minutes to go thirty feet. Soon after he got her back to bed, I came home and he told me what happened.

The next morning Mom couldn't get out of bed and we called an ambulance. After tests to figure out why she fell in the first place, doctors discovered she had had her third heart attack. Now she was just where she wanted to be: in the hospital with a real health problem, conveniently brought on by me. I hadn't given her a valentine. When she stormed off to bed upset, I didn't calm her down or check to see how she was. She was so upset, she had a heart attack, fell and broke her back; and because I was having coffee with a friend, she had to lie there for God knows how long, before getting any help. She had me right where she wanted me. I was in the scope, lined up perfectly in the crosshairs of her guilt gun, and she was firing like it was a semi-automatic assault rifle.

To get over the guilt of being a terrible daughter, I was running up to the hospital two to three times every day and seeing to her needs. Once I got there it was a steady stream of accusations and guilt trips. I would stay as long as I dared, then rush home to get meals for my family and do the laundry that was piling up. I wasn't eating properly. I felt terribly tired and depressed, and I was drinking huge amounts of water. When I would get to Mom's hospital room, I would willingly endure the onslaught of verbal abuse just to get at her pitcher of water. Inside of an hour I would drink the entire pitcher, and before I got home I would be thirsty again. During this time I had a continuous yeast infection, but I didn't think anything of it. (I often had problems with yeast and bladder infections, due, I thought, to the damage Willie had done to me as a little girl.)

My doctor had been running tests for six weeks—everything from gall bladder and thyroid tests to those for ulcers. Finally at the beginning of March he addressed what he thought was the problem. "How's your marriage? Are you and Bill doing okay?"

I blew a gasket! "You doctors are all the same! You can't find out what's really wrong, so you blame it on nerves, or stress, or marital problems! Bill and I are doing fine! Something is the matter with me physically! I'm always tired, always thirsty, and I have a chronic yeast infection! Do some more blood tests! Something, anything! But please find out what's wrong with me!"

❦

Two years before this I had had a hysterectomy. I was thirty-two years old and was bleeding three out of four weeks per month. My uterus and cervix had gone through all they could take and, though they didn't want to remove them because of my age, the doctors were left with no choice. (It would have been dangerous for me to become pregnant a fourth time anyway.) Recovery from that kind of abdominal surgery was difficult in those days, and for six weeks I could lift nothing heavier than a toothbrush. Due to my age, doctors decided to leave my ovaries intact, not wanting me to be on hormone replacement drugs for the next forty years.

After that surgery the doctors began to suspect that my problems were related to what I had gone through as a child. Dr. Wood performed the hysterectomy and my family doctor assisted. While I was in post-surgery recovery, Dr. Wood came in. "How many children did you tell me you've had?"

"Three."

He stood at the end of my bed looking at me and shaking his head in disbelief. "Do you believe in miracles, Margaret?"

"Yes—why?"

"Because you have three miracle children. The uterus that you had should never have supported one pregnancy, let alone three.

Whatever you have been through has totally ravaged your reproductive organs. Thank God for your kids!" Shaking his head he left the room.

When the penis of a fully mature man penetrates the vagina of a four-year-old girl, it can only do so with great tearing. Willie had damaged my cervix at the end of my vagina and, pressing past that, he had actually entered my tiny uterus. Repeated tearing and subsequent scarring should have rendered me childless. My premature hysterectomy was most certainly a consequence of all the rapes. Twenty years later I was still living out the effects of Willie's attacks. I was angry.

I am quite sure my family doctor and Dr. Wood consulted together about my case afterward, and it's possible that he thought my current problems were psychological in nature, that my symptoms were further consequences of abuse. That's why he questioned me about my marriage. It was a reasonable assumption; especially because of the chronic urinary tract infections I endured. I had a continuous renewal on antibiotic suppositories because of it. Many nights I would awaken in such discomfort that I had to sit in a tub of hot water and baking soda just to get enough relief to sleep. He didn't say it in so many words, but I knew my doctor believed my chronic urinary tract infection recurred for the same reasons. For once I wanted an illness to be just that, an illness—and not because of Willie's abuse.

One week before that particular visit to the doctor, I had been washing dishes. I didn't know there was a broken cup in the sink and I cut the knuckle on the middle finger of my right hand. It bled and bled and wouldn't stop. When Bill came home I opened up the bandage to show him the cut. It was still bleeding.

"You need stitches. Go to the hospital and let them close that up or it will never heal," he insisted.

"I'll go to the hospital, but I am not going to let them stitch it up," I shot back. "If I get stitches, they'll have to give me a needle, and I don't want any needles!"

Bill went out to his business appointment that night and I went to the emergency room.

"Well, what's the verdict, Doc?" I asked the young attending physician.

"I have to stitch it up."

"Yeah? What's plan B?"

"Plan B?" he asked.

"You know…if stitches aren't an option."

"I don't understand," he said, confused. "Why wouldn't stitches be an option?"

"Because I'm not letting you anywhere near me with a needle, that's why! I hate needles! They scare me and I don't want to let you stick me with one to numb my finger! So what's plan B?"

"Well, I guess we'll just have to tape it closed. But you'll have to be careful with it."

"Tape away, Doc," I said, relieved that there was another option.

"But if I tape it, you have to keep it dry. No washing dishes or anything—got it?"

"No problem. I'll keep it out of the water."

I went home and showed Bill, thrilled that I didn't have to have an injection.

Besides frequent urinating—that I blamed on the urinary tract infection—I craved carbohydrates and sweets. One day I sat down and ate eleven homemade dinner rolls with peanut butter and jam on each of them. I couldn't believe I ate eleven in one sitting. But I didn't gain an ounce. I was still losing weight.

After noticing that the cut on my knuckle was still very raw, Bill once again voiced his concern. "You know, Margaret, I have to ask people every day about their blood sugar levels, and when they buy insurance they have to have a glucose blood test; I think you're showing signs of high blood sugar. Why don't you get your doctor to check *that* out? I mean…your dad was diabetic."

"That's not hereditary," I said, as though it were a fact. I didn't even want to think of the possibility of being diabetic—that would mean injections, lots of them, every day for the rest of my life. I was mortified at the thought of one needle, let alone several every day; but I eventually gave in to Bill's prodding. I was there asking the doctor to check for diabetes when he asked me about my marriage.

CB

"Okay. We'll take a blood sample and send it to the lab. They'll call you with the results later this afternoon," he assured me. All I was thinking was that I had to let him prick me for a blood sample.

I went home from the doctor's office and turned the phone off. If I had diabetes, I certainly didn't want to know about it. I lay down on the couch and took a nap. I was always so tired. Before the kids got home from school, I woke up and baked a chocolate cake for dessert that night; then I prepared supper. As I was getting supper ready, the phone rang. (It was still turned off, but Shawn, sitting right beneath the wall-mounted phone in the kitchen, heard the faint ring and picked up the receiver before I could stop her.)

It was my doctor. "Is this Margaret Davidson?"

"No. It's Shawn."

"Listen, Shawn, is your Mom there? It's really important that I speak with her!"

"Okay. It's someone for you, Mom! He says it's important."

"Hello," I said, nervous about who was on the other end.

"Margaret, you have to go to the hospital, and you have to go right now, even as I'm talking to you!" he said, sounding frantic. "The lab and I have been trying to get ahold of you all afternoon!"

"Forget it! I'm in the middle of supper here! I'm not going to any hospital!"

"You have to!"

"Why? Tell me why?" I was incorrigible.

"Because your blood-sugar is dangerously high! You could go into a coma at any moment! You have to get to the hospital—now!"

"Well, great! When I'm in a coma you can take me anywhere you like—but until then I'm not going! Treat me at home! I've just gotten my mom home from the hospital with a back brace on, my kids are here and Bill isn't even home!"

Just then Bill walked in.

"Margaret! If you're not in the hospital tomorrow morning by nine o'clock when I check in, I'm going to send an ambulance for you; they will sedate you if necessary!" Clearly my doctor was losing patience with me. I hung up the phone as quickly as I could, but

Bill had already heard too much; and what he hadn't heard, the kids filled in.

We argued about it the whole evening, but the next morning, after arranging for Tina to come by to watch the children and Mom, I was on my way to the hospital. They admitted me immediately. An older nurse, together with a student, came into my room moments after I arrived. In their hands they had syringes, and a vial of insulin.

"What do you think you're going to do with those?" I asked in a surly tone.

"We're going to give you an insulin injection."

"Well, I'm not taking any needles, so you can just forget about that!"

"Mrs. Davidson, your blood sugar levels are really high and the doctor ordered that we administer this insulin right away." The older nurse was trying to be understanding, but it was clear that my fear of needles was a just a silly distraction to her, preventing her from doing her job. The young student nurse looked dumbfounded—and at a total loss as to how to deal with such a difficult patient.

"Look! I haven't seen my doctor, and when I did talk to him, he didn't mention any of this. I'm not prepared to get stuck with a bunch of needles on your say-so. Until I see him, you are not giving me any needles! My doctor is in the hospital. I heard his name paged. Get him in here. I want to talk to him."

I am easily agitated at the best of times; with my blood sugar elevated to five times the normal level, I was a bear. I didn't want to face the fact that I needed to have injections for the rest of my life. If I never started, maybe I wouldn't need to depend on them. There had to be a way to control the diabetes with a strict diet—I would avoid taking needles at any cost!

"Fine, Mrs. Davidson. We'll get your doctor up here to speak with you," the older nurse huffed patronizingly. The truth was, I didn't deserve any kindness. I made sure that their morning began with the nastiest patient they would have to see all day.

Moments later I heard my doctor paged once again, on the hospital intercom. When he entered the room he knew with whom he was dealing. "What's the problem, Margaret?"

"I don't want to take needles. I hate needles and I don't want to take them! Find a different way to deal with this!"

"Margaret, there is no other way to deal with this. Your pancreas has stopped producing insulin and pills won't start it up again. You need to have insulin injections every day for the rest of your life. Now, the sooner you learn how to care for this disease and give yourself injections, the sooner you can go home!"

He was patient but firm; and he said the magic word: *Home*. I hadn't thought I would be in the hospital overnight; yet he was telling me I couldn't go home until I not only learned how to deal with needles, but learned to give them to myself. I had my sister looking after the kids, and Mom was at home in a back brace; all I could think about was getting home.

One week after I was in the emergency room, talking the young doctor into fixing my bleeding knuckle without stitches, I was using a needle on an orange, getting ready to give one to myself. I couldn't believe it. For the rest of my life, I would be starting out each day with a syringe full of insulin. Getting home depended upon the hospital's assessment of my progress. I had to show them I understood the basics of nutrition, food types and "exchanges," and I had to be doing my own monitoring and injecting. Fortunately, once I took over giving myself the needle, the fear left. I was in control of when, and how, that needle went in, and that removed the fear. I still didn't like taking them, but I was coping.

My doctor explained that a weakness or predisposition to diabetes is an inherited trait, but that full-blown diabetes surfaces during an infection or acute stress. Bill was a little less than five years into his new career, and no longer getting company draws or advances; he was on full commission, and if he didn't sell, or his sales were delayed in getting issued, we had no money. The economy was slipping into recession and interest rates were on the rise. My father had died six months earlier, Mom was living with us (having heart attacks and breaking vertebra), Shawn was starting high school—now I had diabetes! I had enough stress in my life for ten people.

The month before my stay in the hospital, my eyesight had deteriorated to the extent that, even with my glasses on, I couldn't make out faces. I had always had poor eyesight and thought I just needed a new prescription. It took a full month, but once on insulin, I could read perfectly with my glasses on and felt comfortable driving. In 1979 there were no glucometers for diabetics to monitor their blood sugar levels; so at least twice each day I had to go into a washroom and urinate on a test strip, then wait for the color to emerge, indicating whether the sugar in my blood was high, low, or normal. Extreme highs and lows produce the same symptoms. I could feel low and believe I needed something to eat, when in reality I was high and eating would only exacerbate the whole situation. By the time sugar registers in the urine, it is extremely high in the bloodstream—but back then, a urine test strip was the only gauge available. Only slow, long-acting insulin, taken in the morning and meant to last the entire day, was available. It took eight hours to peak and stayed in my system for twenty-four. If my sugar was high, I just had to ride it out.

Keeping my sugars in the normal range required a very strict, sugar-free diet. I had to start measuring food portions into carefully defined exchanges; eating just enough to match the amount of insulin I took that morning. Carrying food with me became a must. I had to eat three meals and three snacks every day, whether I felt like it or not. If I did more physical activity one day than I did the previous day, I had to eat more to compensate. If I didn't eat enough, I wouldn't have enough sugar in my blood and I would go into insulin reaction. Doctors told me I needed to employ the same exercise regimen every day, and they recommended walking. Where would I find a half-hour in my busy day to go for a walk?

An impulsive person from birth, now my whole day had to be measured and planned. I had to decide how hungry I would be for supper before I injected myself at seven in the morning. If I took the amount of insulin needed to break down a typical supper, and I arrived at the table and wasn't hungry, I had to force myself to eat an amount proportional to the insulin I had taken ten hours earlier. I would complain out loud, "How do I know at breakfast how hungry I'm going to be at supper?" Diabetes is still a disease of guesswork—but was even more so in 1979. Eating became unenjoyable, a military routine. I had always enjoyed baking, but now that I couldn't share in it, I didn't feel like baking anymore.

No matter how conscientiously I planned my nutrition, there were times when the temptation to cheat pushed everything else out of my mind. After eating a couple of chocolate bars on a binge, or sneaking some of the cookies I packed into the kids' lunches, I would have to suffer the consequences of high sugar—irritability, headaches, fatigue, and lethargy. If I failed to eat as much as I was supposed to, the resultant low put me in a drunken-like stupor—complete with spaghetti legs, slurred speech, and the fear that I could lapse into unconsciousness at any moment. To prevent lapsing into a coma, I would have to force-feed myself something loaded with sugar—the last thing on earth I wanted and at a time when my mind couldn't think clearly. Given my volatile nature and propensity for needing to be in control, the lows were something my family soon began to dread. They would try to get me to eat, and, in my confused stupor, I would feel as if they were telling me what to do. I would rebel and flat-out refuse to eat, boldly dancing up to the edge of the precipice of consciousness, the whole time being intolerable and nasty.

Diabetes was not just an adjustment for *me*; it was a burden for everyone that had to live with me.

The doctors required me to keep a journal of all my blood sugar levels, the urine tests, the amount of insulin I took each day and how much I ate. I even had to write down how vigorously I exercised or if I didn't at all. Amid everything else in my life, now I had a new full-time job: diabetes! And each morning I had to wake up to that blasted needle—a refrigerated surge of Lente (synthesized pork insulin), flowing from the syringe into the rolled up fatty tissue on my tummy, thighs or backside, injected with small, measured pushes of the plunger, so I could bear the stinging.

CHAPTER 15

Potholes

Sometime our travels take us on beautifully paved highways, smooth with recent asphalt and freshly painted centerlines; and it is sheer pleasure to drive down them. Other roads are relatively smooth, though somewhat worn from years of use; they are still paved, but frost, weather, and traffic have caused the pavement to heave in some places. The heaving has left bumps, necessitating that drivers slow down in order to avoid sudden and violent jolts. And occasionally, we drive down roads where the pavement is gone or never existed in the first place—roads that are neither smooth nor well marked. Water has washed away parts of the surface, leaving giant potholes. If we drive too quickly down these roads, we cannot see where the road is washed away or where the potholes are until it is too late. The very next instant we hit a giant pothole at an ungodly speed. Our car stops dead, sustaining damage to the whole undercarriage, smashing the springs and shocks, blowing out the tires and leaving us stranded in unfamiliar territory. Looking around, we find that the countryside is sparsely populated, and we are left with no idea of how to get home.

My road to freedom began as a beautifully paved highway, but somehow I had turned down an old country road and I wasn't slowing down. I was speeding through my life, not considering its course, fraught with dangers. I was about to hit not just bumps but potholes, some of them so large as to be considered craters. The jarring, sudden stop would leave me shaken and disillusioned, doubting that I had ever really been on the road to freedom at all.

Shawn sat cross-legged at the head of her bed clutching her pillow for support. I was sitting on the bedside facing her, determined to make eye contact as we spoke. We were having a typical "mother-daughter" conversation. Shawn was fourteen and about to finish her first year of high school.

The conversation inevitably turned to boys—liking them, being liked, and how awful it felt to be rejected. Sensing that we were in the midst of a teachable moment, I began to admonish her, as I often did, about the value of being a virgin until she was married, about rejecting the pressure to have sex. I wanted her to have a right view of sex—that it belonged inside the safety of a loving marriage and that, outside of those bounds, it was often scary and damaging, especially to teenagers. I was trying hard to help her see the importance of a good reputation, that girls should be careful not to be considered "loose" by boys.

"Mom, you wouldn't understand about boys today. You would never understand about sex before marriage and things. You've been a Christian your whole life. Mom, at school there are hardly any Christians, and lots of kids are having sex! It's a different world now than when you grew up."

Shawn was trying her best not to patronize as she spoke, but was failing miserably. She was convinced I didn't have a clue what her high school was like and that if I *were* to understand, *she* would have to explain it to me.

The truth was that she was right. Here I was talking to my daughter, whom I thought I knew, but whom I didn't know in the least. Within a couple of months I would begin to discover how troubled she really was. Even as I was having this heart-to-heart, mother-daughter moment, Shawn was skipping classes and failing courses. She was hanging out with older guys at school—even sneaking out in the middle of the night through her bedroom window to be with them, and making it back undetected before daylight (though I wouldn't discover this for a couple of years). I thought I was having a preventative talk with my innocent ninth-grade daughter about the evils of being overly boy-crazy. The truth was she was involved

266

with boys to a much greater extent than I could have imagined. She was not the naïve little girl I had presumed.

After I had gone on with my lecture for some time, she interrupted. "Mom! What do you know about teenage sex anyway?"

I felt the sharpness of her tone and the lack of respect for anything I knew or had experienced. Justifiably indignant, I answered, "Do you really want to know what I know? Here's what I know!"

Then I told her. I told my daughter about Willie's attacks of terror. It felt strange…different than when telling someone outside the family. She knew who her Uncle Willie was—although she had very little to do with him and hadn't seen him for years. She was my daughter, and now she knew that her mother was raped and forced into sex, not just as a teen, but even as a little girl. As I spoke, I wondered what she would think of me and how her opinion of me would change—yet I felt compelled to continue.

"Shawn, Willie abused me! I know how bad a sexual experience can be, and I know how wonderful sex is inside of marriage. Now I know that making love as a teenager wouldn't be like what I went through, but it can leave you scarred and hurt. God invented sex. It's great when it's experienced with a loving man who's made vows to love you for the rest of your life; but people in their rebellion against God have twisted it into something God never intended—hurt and shame."

I was passionate. I wanted to spare her the pain associated with a sexual experience she wasn't ready for. While it was scary to be so open with my own daughter, I hoped my vulnerability would show how much I cared for her.

She exhibited little reaction as I uncovered my secret. She just sat there on the bed and took it in. I assumed she needed to process everything I told her and she would have more questions for me in the future. What I could not have known was that she was summarily dismissing most of what I said. She wasn't denying that it happened; just that it had any relevance to her. In her mind, sex as a teenager was bad for me, because it happened in the context of rape. My experience with sex as a teenager was traumatic because it was forced. Everything I said about sex scarring emotions when it doesn't happen in the context of a loving marriage, she translated as "Mom's experience was bad—but it doesn't have to be that way with me." She bottled up and didn't respond because she already had too much in her life she didn't want me to know.

I left her with explicit instructions not to reveal our conversation with anyone, especially to Gramma, as she didn't know any of this had taken place.

When once I had worried about what my children would think about me if they ever found out about my secret, after telling Shawn, I felt a great relief. At least I had been the one to tell her. She hadn't heard a rumor or gossip from someone else, and I felt inexplicably closer to her. I thought the bond between mother and daughter was stronger.

Shawn and Blake were the best of friends. They told each other everything, made easier by the convenience of living side by side in the basement. I didn't want Shawn put in the position where something could slip out. It was clear to me within a few days that I had to have the same conversation with Blake. Suddenly it was not a question of protecting my children from hearing about my secret and knowing what happened to me; it was now imperative that they hear about it *from* me.

Within a few days of my conversation with Shawn, Blake and I were alone in the evening. I was washing the dishes and he was drying. We were talking about how different things were in our family, different than how I had grown up; how God had blessed us and provided for us, and that we weren't poor like I had been as a kid. Blake started to ask questions about what things were like when I was growing up, and I knew I had to seize the opportunity.

"Blake, there is something that I told Shawn and I need to tell you too—but you need to keep it a secret. You can't talk about it with anyone else but me. Okay?"

"Okay, Mom."

Telling Blake was very different from telling Shawn. Aside from the obvious difference of divulging such sensitive details to my son instead of my daughter, their personalities were completely different. While I spoke to Shawn she was quiet—just taking it all in. Blake has never been quiet, never without questions. Long after the dishes were done he sat on the kitchen counter, firing one query after another. He wanted to know how I survived and why God would let that happen. "Did Dad know about all this? What does he think about it? Doesn't he want to kill Uncle Willie when he sees him? Why didn't you tell Gramma? How could she not have known? When did it all stop? How did you get over it?" The questions went on for over an hour and then, though visibly shaken, he seemed to be satisfied.

I wondered if he was old enough to handle it. He was only twelve at the time, but I wanted him to hear about it from me.

CB

Starting in 1978 and continuing into the Eighties, God really used Rich Beuhler's radio ministry to teach me about forgiveness. Though I thought I had forgiven Willie, I learned I hadn't. I felt I had because I could talk about what he had done to me and it didn't hurt—my experience seemed just a scar to me. I felt quite detached from it all, almost as though it happened to someone else and I was just telling the story. I no longer felt hatred for Willie. I felt ambivalence. I didn't want to kill him; I just wanted nothing to do with him. Avoiding him was my priority. Of course, when given the opportunity, I had told everyone that God had healed me—and He had, emotionally. Spiritually however, there was more growing and healing to be done. I started to see the areas in my life where I refused to forgive. I was beginning to see what forgiveness really meant. I knew that there was unresolved bitterness in my heart because I still feared inadvertently running into Willie, and I couldn't stand the thought of being near him. These thoughts produced fear. Rich taught that "perfect love casts out fear," and I began to desire God's perfect love to be at work in my life; but I didn't know how to go about it. (See 1 John 4:18, NKJV.) For me the first step was identifying unforgiveness.

Forgiving a rapist is a foreign concept in the world; it offends most people's sense of justice. Society thinks only in terms of fairness. The perpetrator must be punished, and that alone will bring closure and healing to the victim. This revenge-justice solution, however, does not deal with the hurt and pain in a victim's soul. Though I wished nothing but a hard life for Willie, I got no pleasure from knowing he had it. Willie's alcoholism and the loss of everything meaningful in his life gave me no satisfaction. Knowing

269

he "got what he deserved" brought no warmth and comfort to my life. To willfully remain in a state of unforgiveness required that I hold on to everything that had taken place. I wouldn't let it go and, as a result, it was always with me. Even though it didn't hurt any longer, anger was still present—anger that showed itself in unrelated parts of my life. I was an angry person, easily set off. That anger is what indicated I had not truly forgiven.

At some point, we get tired of being angry.

My coping method for fifteen years had been avoidance. I was still running away, still acting like a victim. Willie was a trigger to bad memories. If I didn't see him, I didn't think about him; the abuse, the alcoholism—I didn't think about any of it. Rich Beuhler started me thinking about willfully forgiving, but putting it into practice would take the next twenty years. I learned that forgiving is a process with many advances and nearly as many setbacks. It is a lifestyle based on a decision to forgive—an act of the will. Frankly, the feeling of justified resentment felt better—but God was softening my heart. Slowly.

ౠ

In the spring of 1981, we were able to arrange for Mom to move into Linhaven Seniors Residence. Mom had lived with us for three years. During that time she had a heart attack and broke her back, her shoulder, her collarbone, and her arm. It had gotten to the place where we couldn't leave her alone without constant worry. We were insisting that Shawn or Blake stay home to "babysit" whenever we had to be out. The kids were good about it, but they were teenagers and often had to alter their weekends just to stay home with her. Bill and I spoke to my brothers and to Tina, and we all agreed that the time had come to get Mom on a seniors facility's waiting list. Her next accident or illness might make her an invalid, and I was not prepared to take care of a bedridden person twenty-four hours a day.

The only problem with this perfect plan was that, to Mom, being sent into a home was the same thing as being buried alive.

"You don't love me!" she complained. "If you put me into dat ol'-folks' home, you don't love me! You just vant to put me vhere I von't bodder you. You can forget about me and dat's vhat you vant."

270

She was awful to deal with, and each day that passed without news from Linhaven took me deeper into guilt. No one has ever been as oppressive as Katarina Hiebert when she wants to lay down a guilt-trip. She expressed no thanks or gratitude for the three years she had spent living with us—with all of the health problems I had already nursed her through; instead, all she said was that her daughter hated her and wanted to get rid of her.

Linhaven did call, and Mom moved in to her new room in March—just after her birthday. She was seventy-three years old.

In 1980, I met a young lady who helped out at our church's summer camp. We struck up a friendship as she headed for Bible college. During the Christmas break and reading week in 1981, she stayed with our family.

As I continued to write to her at Bible school, I realized that she had no place to go when the term ended in April. She needed a place to board for the summer. Bill and I talked it over, then we spoke to the kids; and since we already had the extra bedroom, everyone thought it was a great idea to help her out. As she moved in, she carved out a special place in our hearts and, without knowing it, thrust me into another phase of my healing.

CS

Raising children properly when you haven't been raised well yourself is a constantly unfolding mystery. I knew what I didn't want to be, but I couldn't always see what I had become. I was easily angered, and it wasn't just controlled displeasure either—I frequently lost it. I knew that I was excitable, but I put that down to genetics. I thought I inherited my temper, and that was a good excuse for a long time to do nothing about it. But God was about to show me that anger is not inherited; it is a learned behavior, and one that He can modify. (See Proverbs 22:24–25, NIV.) My problem was that it felt good to let it go. Losing my temper let out the "pressure" from my pressure cooker and made me feel better. No one else felt better, but I did.

Most of the time I would justify my anger: someone caused me to blow my stack. As a result, my husband and children were raised in an environment of insecurity. When they were around me, they walked on eggshells, trying at all costs not to upset me. This situation produced indirect communication and masked emotions. The kids wouldn't often express how they felt about an issue—deferring comments, avoiding honesty—just so that I wouldn't unleash a capricious tirade. Of course I didn't know this at the time, but my anger was driving my children and my husband away. They were not free to have an open and honest discussion with me; they refused to be transparent and real. Instead they became accustomed to sugarcoating everything, telling me what they thought I wanted to hear. Whether it was true or not was not the issue; the goal was to keep me calm at all costs. I had no idea at the time that the root of my anger and my controlling nature lay in the bitterness and unforgiveness I still harbored in my heart.

In my mind I had a right to be angry—every time. It was always justified. I thought other people were always at fault and they caused me to vent. In reality, my anger always lay so close to the surface that the least little comment could uncover it. I was dealing with anger in the same way I had my bad memories years earlier—I smothered it beneath a plethora of other emotions and intentional denial. Before God could work on my anger, He had to expose it. I would not have admitted it then, but I had never dealt with my anger because I had never come to grips with what caused it—unforgiveness. I started to read in Proverbs that losing my temper was foolish. (See Proverbs 29:11, NIV.) I no longer wanted to drive away the people closest to me, but anger was like a drug; I couldn't stop. I could not control my temper!

I tried desperately to control everything else—other people's lives, their decisions and actions; but when things invariably strayed from what I mapped out, I got angry and lashed out. I wanted Bill to be accountable to me. I wanted to know where he was. If he took longer running an errand than he indicated before he left, I would stew; and when he got home, he would experience my full fury. Innocently engaged in conversation with someone he bumped into, Bill would think nothing of taking an extra hour to get home. But when he would come through the front door, I would give him the third degree.

"Just once, Bill, just once, I'd like for you to go to the store and come home right away, without yakking away half the day with some client. Business, business! I'm so sick of hearing about business! You've always gotta talk business—well maybe I had plans. Maybe your wife wants some of your day too! Did you ever think of that?" My words dripped with the same load of guilt I had always resented in my mother.

After venting, I would usually stomp off in another direction, leaving Bill alone, trying to figure out the evil he had committed. The truth was that I was just jealous. I wanted to control his free time—I didn't want him to have any free time that didn't include me. In my mind I would create the perfect scenarios and get disappointed if things turned out differently. This applied to special events, family birthdays, even Christmas mornings. Things had to be done my way or there would be trouble. These sorry episodes were all too common; and an hour or too later I would be filled with grief.

While unleashing my fury on Bill or the kids, it seemed as though I was "outside myself." I watched myself say the most hurtful things—but once I was started, I didn't want to be stopped. The dam was open and, until the reservoir was empty, it was futile for anyone to try and shut the gate. The rush of temper was too strong. If people tried to calm me down, I would invariably become more incensed. I would take it as someone trying to control me. I had been controlled enough as a child, and I was determined to control myself! I wanted to say what I wanted to say, and nobody was going to deny me. Ironically, losing my temper made me feel like I was in control, when the exact opposite was true. I wanted to be in control so badly, I wouldn't even let the Holy Spirit quiet me. I would push down His gentle urgings, choosing instead the gratification that comes from letting someone have it. Only later did His conviction have any impact. By then usually several hurtful things had been said, and I had gone through a couple hours of moping and feeling sorry for myself. *Why do people make me get so angry?* I would think to myself.

"If you don't forgive, *you* become bitter," I heard Rich Beuhler say on the radio. Though I had heard that before, this was the first time I felt the full meaning of those words.

I'm bitter, I thought. All my life I had in some strange way been proud of my sarcastic wit, my acid tongue. It allowed me to be quite funny—at least to anyone outside my sights. That day, listening to Rich Beuhler on the radio, was the first time I connected my vicious sarcasm with unforgiveness. I decided I didn't want to be bitter. I longed to be sweet.

I began to say little S.O.S. prayers as I felt my temperature rise. *God, please, please help me to keep my big mouth shut! When Bill gets home, help me just to welcome him and be pleasant,* I would pray in my mind. *Holy Spirit, prick my mind with your convicting voice. Let me know when I am about to lose my temper and help me to walk away.*

Those brief little prayers began to revolutionize my life. I would lose my temper less often and began feeling proud of myself. With greater gaps of time between fits of rage, I thought everyone should be as proud of me as I was; but I found that the people I loved didn't care that I lost my temper less often—they only cared that I continued to hurt them. They simply wanted my angry words to stop.

Though angry less often, I still wasn't dealing with the source of all that rage. I didn't know how. I thought I had forgiven Willie and my father—and my mother, for that matter. I thought forgiving meant dismissing offenses, pretending that they never happened. Forgive and forget. That's what I did. I pretended that what they had done to me hadn't really hurt. And because I no longer felt nauseous when Willie's name was mentioned, believing I had forgiven him, I embraced the resulting numbness, exchanging it for real peace. I prayed for his soul, but it was a somewhat half-hearted prayer. I would have argued then that numbness and ambivalence were better than he deserved from me.

God had healed me from my bad memories and nightmares, but more was needed. I came to realize this only through a terrifying experience.

That first Christmas, though she had little money, our student boarder wanted to get gifts for Shawn, Blake, and Heather. She bought Shawn a romance novel and, although she purchased it from the campus bookstore, I wanted to preview the book beforehand. I didn't want Shawn reading material that was too explicit for a fourteen-year-old girl. The book seemed to be aimed at adults, not teenagers and, being protective, I wanted to make sure she could handle the book's content.

274

The story followed two men in the air force and the two women they had met. It was written well, and before long I was enthralled. Even for a non-reader like myself, the book captivated me and I hung on every word. About halfway through the novel, the two young men ended up at the house of the two girls they had persuaded to date them. They started to make out and were pushing the girls to go further sexually. The girls became uncomfortable and resisted their advances.

At that very moment, I stopped reading. I felt uneasy. My attention was being forced away from the book, and my mind was filled with another voice. It sounded just like my voice, but it was so strong and persistent, I knew it was the Holy Spirit. "Margaret, you shouldn't be reading this book." That's all He said, but it was a strong impression.

"O, yeah, Lord," I said out loud, "I know—but I've been healed of those memories. I'll be fine."

With that, I forced my eyes back down on the page and continued reading. The words became more detailed as the author graphically described how these two lovely young ladies were raped. Suddenly I was transported back in time emotionally. The pathos and empathy most readers would've experienced as they read about the trauma described by the author would've been intense; for me those feelings were not imagined—I knew them. I felt everything the author described as though it was happening to me.

I was white and pasty, and my heart was thumping in fear. I had to put the book down. But where would I put it? I didn't want anyone else to know I was reading this book; yet secretly I wanted to continue reading later. *I just needed a break*, I told myself. I went into my bedroom and slipped the paperback between the mattress and box spring of my bed. I knew no one would find it there.

The next day, I waited for Bill to go to work and the kids to go to school before I stole into the bedroom to retrieve the book. I sat in the living room and read on. Two more times I heard the strong impression from the Holy Spirit within me, warning me not to go on, to put the book down. Two more times I ignored Him.

Once I reached the last chapter, I understood how the book could have been sold at a Christian bookstore. Out of the deep pain they were in, the two ladies who were raped ended up finding Jesus as their Savior. But for me the book had little redeeming value. What stuck in my mind were the emotional connections I made with the victims. For me this book's only purpose was my personal entertainment.

And that was the problem.

I finished the book and placed it back in its hiding place in my bed, convinced that the book was too graphic, the subject matter too advanced, for Shawn to read. I explained this to our Christmas guest, who by this time was back in her second semester of Bible college. Then I forgot about the whole thing.

Within two weeks, the thing I dreaded most happened: my nightmares returned. I woke up in a terrified cold sweat, shaking and crying. For the first time in more than ten years I had a nightmare about being raped. Unlike my earlier nightmares, where I would wake up just before being raped, now I didn't wake up. I wasn't myself in the dream—I was me, but I was inside the bodies of the two girls from the novel. The two airmen would rape me repeatedly as described in the book, but the experience was more familiar than that. The men would do the things Willie did, but they wouldn't be Willie. I was in the bodies of the two young ladies, and Willie, though I couldn't see him, was somehow in the bodies of the two rapists.

Every night I was getting raped again. Bill tried to understand why the demons returned. He encouraged me to read the Bible, thinking that I had let my spiritual disciplines slip and satan was attacking me. I told him that I was reading the Word—and I was—so that couldn't be it. Before long I was in the throes of the worst depression of my life, oppressed by nightmares every night and gripped by fear and despair every day. Thoughts of suicide consumed me. I became frigid in bed; for six weeks we had no sex life, no intimacy at all.

I didn't think to blame this on the book I had read. Since there had been a two-week delay between my finishing the novel and the start of my trouble, I didn't connect the dots.

Sundays were the worst for me. I didn't feel like going to church, but I had to. I was married to a Davidson—a deacon at that—and it wouldn't do to miss church for any reason other than cancer or a serious car accident. I would sit through the services reeling, rushing out at the end and talking to no one. I wanted to be alone. I was depressed and angry with God for letting the nightmares come back into my life. I would get the car from the parking spot, drive around to the church entrance and pick up the rest of the family. Bill and the kids would pile in and, after they got out of the car at home, I would throw the gearshift in reverse and take off. Bill and the kids didn't have a clue as to where I was going. Bill thought I was losing my mind. I had completely shut down. I wasn't talking. All he could do was pray for me.

I ran away like this for three Sundays in a row, racing down to the Welland Canal. I would go to the end of Welland Avenue, where there were no barriers erected between the road and the edge of the water. I would point my idling car at the canal and inch toward the water, waiting for the courage to tromp on the accelerator. The first two Sundays, I couldn't do it; but on the third Sunday things were easier. Voices inside my head told me that my pain would all go. *Just end it all right here*, they assured, *and you won't be in torment.* This time I had the courage. I remember the adrenalin pumping as I turned toward the water's edge. The car was idling a little faster and I was determined to do it. But, before I could step on the gas, something caught my attention. Every other time I had been all alone; no cars and no pedestrians. But this time a man was there...and he was walking toward my car! As he approached I put on the brake. I couldn't believe my eyes. He looked for all the world like *Willie!*

My adrenalin level, already building up as I planned to drive into the canal, went through the roof. Instead of being excited that I was about to end my pain in the icy February water, fear gripped me by the throat. I slapped the gearshift into reverse and spun the tires on the gravel shoulder. I threw the transmission into drive and peeled away, leaving long tire marks on the pavement as my tires squealed. I didn't even look in the rearview mirror. I needed to get out of there. I was in a panic!

When I got home I rushed into the house and went straight to the bedroom. I needed to calm down. For the rest of the day I acted as if I wasn't feeling well and stayed in the bedroom.

Bill kept trying to talk to me. He was stubbornly sticking to his theory that all of this trouble was coming upon me for a spiritual reason—that all I needed to do was read more of God's Word and it would go away. The odd part was, I had been reading my Bible. The whole six weeks I was depressed, I read my Bible. I knew it couldn't be that I just needed to read more; but I was so desperate that on the Monday after my attempt to drive into the canal, I resolved to spend the whole day seeking God. Everyone was at work or school, and I remember falling down on my face before God on the living room carpet. I cried out to Him, but He felt a million miles away.

I took the Bible in my hands and read the story of Samson. To this day I don't know why I started reading in Judges, of all places, but that's where I read. I saw that after Samson lied three times to Delilah about the source of his strength, he finally gave in to the temptation and revealed the secret: his long hair. Delilah cut his hair while he slept. When she woke him, telling him that the enemy was in the room, Samson tried to fight them off as before, but he had lost all of his supernatural might. "He did not know that the LORD [his strength] had left him" (Judg. 16:20; see also verses 4–21). His enemies easily put him in chains and poked out his eyes. He worked for the rest of his days as a slave and only gained honor in his death.

"That's it, Lord! That's it! I've lost my strength! You healed me and I've been living in your supernatural strength for all these years," I sobbed. "But I lost it, God. Somehow I lost my strength. You removed your protection from me! Why? Why have I lost the strength and protection from You? Why?"

I was heartbroken. I felt just like Samson. I knew that somehow I had disobeyed God and I was reaping the consequences.

I lay there on the carpet for the longest time, sobbing until I had no more ability to cry. As the crying subsided into quietness, my mind began to clear and I heard this: "Remember the book, Margaret?"

I jumped up off the floor and ran to the bedroom. I grabbed the book from between the mattress and box spring, held it out in front of me with both hands and rushed down the stairs. We had an airtight wood stove in the corner of the recreation room that we kept burning twenty-four hours a day in the winter, to help heat the house. I opened the door of the stove and heaved that book as hard as I could into the fire. Then I shut the stove and slumped to the floor.

Instantly the peace of God returned to my troubled spirit. The demons of depression that I had been fighting left—I felt them leave. I was in the presence of God in that basement and I knew I was going to be all right. Joy that I hadn't felt since the night at Joan Jewel's, years earlier, engulfed me. I felt like laughing and crying at the same time.

I knew it. I knew that the secret of my strength was God. I knew that I wasn't to take that for granted ever again. I knew that I was not to trivialize His power or play with my deliverance carelessly ever again—I was determined to obey the voice of the Holy Spirit whenever He was directing me. Without Him I was nothing. With Him I could be whole and accomplish everything He had planned for me. All of this I knew in a moment; and this knowledge was wrapped in the peace and assurance He brought to my soul.

"God help me never to disobey your voice again."

Something else came to my attention that day: though God had healed me of my memories and His power kept me safe from the nightmares and flashbacks, there was still some unfinished business He and I had to attend to. God still required that I submit to Him some areas that I controlled. I began to learn more about forgiveness—what I didn't know was that it would take the next fifteen years for me to fully grasp it.

I started to realize that I was a terrible forgiver. My unforgiveness and need to control everything were linked. The more I let go of anger and bitterness, the less I needed to have everything go perfectly. I began to see how my kids felt about me. They felt like they weren't allowed to make mistakes. I would pounce on everything that was different than the way I had envisioned it in my mind. I wrongly assumed that their upbringing was so radically different than mine, that their advantages were so much better, that they would be perfect—perfect children, perfect teenagers, and ultimately perfect adults. I believed they would always be dedicated Christians and passionately follow Christ. I wanted to be proud of everything they did and everything they didn't do. This seemed reasonable to me because of the advantages they had that I didn't. When they inevitably rebelled or disobeyed, it hurt. I took it personally.

Ridiculous as it sounds in words, I expected perfection. My own character deficiencies, I presumed, were a result of what I had endured as a child. My children had none of the negative experiences I lived through and, therefore, had no reason to disobey or fail. I wouldn't let them fail. I was disappointed in them if they messed up. I took it as a reflection on my own ability to parent. It was as though I failed every time the children erred. *I must be a rotten mother*, I would always think; and sometimes I would say out loud, "If that's the way my kids are going to act, then that must mean I'm doing a lousy job." It's what I believed. I thought that if my children didn't serve God, if they rebelled and didn't represent me well, then it was my fault. It made perfect sense to me. If I could serve Jesus, coming through abuse, poverty, and alcoholism, certainly God would judge me severely, if my kids, having every advantage of a Christian home, were not model Christians. The behavior of my children was linked to my own self-esteem—it was all about whether or not I was a good mom.

Being hard on my children when they screwed up was really me being hard on me. Because I beat myself up, because I had to be the "perfect mom," they received the brunt of what I visited upon myself. I had trouble forgiving even normal childhood and teenage indiscretions and lapses in judgment. I couldn't stand irresponsibility and I expected adult behavior from them, even when, much of the time, I didn't demonstrate it. I finally began to see how immature I really was and realized that, if I wanted to grow up spiritually, I needed to learn how to forgive—starting with my own husband and children. I acknowledged that there were things I couldn't control, including the behavior of others, and that if other people made mistakes, it wasn't necessarily my fault. I had to stop volunteering to be responsible for everybody else's mistakes.

ॐ

Just as I was venturing down this new road and learning how to forgive, Veneta Wills approached me in the church foyer one Sunday. Veneta was my successor at women's ministries. (I had stepped down when Mom came to live with us.) "Margaret, we're asking certain ladies to give their testimony over the next several months, and we would like you to be one of those ladies. Would you share your story with us?"

"You don't know what you're asking," I said. The invitation shocked me, so I said what every believer says when scared and unsure of how to respond: "I'll pray about it."

I went home and talked to Bill.

There were complications. I had promised God that if He healed my memories, I would never refuse to tell my story to help somebody. "Somebody," in my mind, meant individual people; I would tell my story to individuals to help them. The one-to-one picture I had in my mind had suddenly become public speaking to a room full of people who had known me since I was in Sunday school.

And yet, I thought, *they don't really know me.* All of those women would be expecting a nice, tightly wrapped tale of what it means to grow up in the church, to know Jesus from childhood; what I would have to deliver, if I was faithful to my promise to God, would blow apart those expectations.

Then there was Mom. She was living at Linhaven, but she was very much alive. I wondered what would happen if someone heard my testimony and then went to visit her. I didn't want to hurt her needlessly. I didn't know how I could share my story with a hundred ladies and expect them all to keep it a secret from Mom.

Besides Mom, Heather still didn't know. She was only eleven years old. To make matters worse, the night I was to give my testimony was to be a "mother and daughter" night. I would have to uncover my secret before my own daughter and the daughters of my friends. It would be excruciating. Always concerned with appearances and how others saw me, the thought of publicly revealing incest was incredibly scary. I was in a tough spot. If I didn't share my story honestly and openly, then I would be breaking my promise to God. If I broke my promise to Him, would He ever trust me again? Would I sink back into what was my old life? Would refusing to tell my story be equivalent to refusing to give God the credit He so richly deserved? The result of reading the book God told me not to was fresh in my memory. I did not want God to lift His protective hand from my life ever again.

"Why don't you talk about what God has done in other areas of your life? Just don't mention the abuse," Bill suggested, trying to save me the anguish of being that transparent and vulnerable before the whole church.

"I could do that—but isn't my whole life really about what God has done to heal me and make me who I am? How do I tell my story and leave out the essence of it? I think that would be cheating God. He knew what I meant when I promised Him I would share. I don't want to be phony. I don't see how I can refuse this request, and I don't see how I can skirt the whole issue of abuse. I guess I'll just have to trust God with what I can't control."

I asked people to pray for me and prepared myself by asking God for the wisdom to share my story as sensitively as possible. I warned Veneta not to promote it as something it wasn't, and told her that parts of my talk would be disturbing and emotionally upsetting. Then I turned my attention to Heather.

Heather was the last person in our family to hear what I had been through. Without much detail, sharing only what I needed to, I explained how I had grown up. For an eleven-year-old, she was exceptionally mature and handled the whole discussion well. Then she did something that the other children hadn't: she thanked me for trusting her enough to tell her. She told me how sorry she was that I had to go through all of that, and she hugged me.

03

The night of the talk arrived. Standing at the front of the fellowship hall in the basement of the church, I was introduced by Veneta. All the eyes in the place were fixed on me.

"Before I share my life's journey following Jesus, I have a favor to ask everyone here. If you ever visit my mother, Mrs. Hiebert, at Linhaven Seniors Residence, and I know many of you know her, please don't tell her I gave my testimony here tonight or tell her anything I am about to say. She knows nothing about what I'm preparing to share. Most of you would have no way of knowing this, but I am a survivor of childhood sexual abuse. I was a victim of incest."

I continued talking about living in an alcoholic household. I told about the abject poverty, the insecurity and the shame I had experienced, and then what Jesus had done for me. Insisting on being vulnerable, I shared with them my struggle to forgive those who had hurt me. My greatest joy was sharing how I learned to practice the presence of God, to praise and worship my way through assaults on my mind by the enemy. I told them how God had been so kind and compassionate to me, that He is faithful and is there to pull us out of whatever trouble satan inflicts upon us. Feeling the presence of God as I spoke that night, I felt no shame—just pride. I was proud of my God; proud of what He had done and of the lengths to which He had gone to rescue a hurt little girl. I told those ladies that if God had done all of this for me, He would do the same for them. Afterward I prayed with several ladies, delighted that I had honored my promise to God.

During my testimony the room was silent. I'm sure that I shocked ladies who had known me for years, but as I told of God's wonderful work in my life, they hung on every word. Many were crying. I saw my old Sunday school teachers shaking their heads, doubtlessly wondering how they could not have known. Several women came up to me afterward and thanked me for being so open with them. They said my story had encouraged them and helped them see how awesome God is.

One hundred ladies attended the meeting that night, and one hundred ladies kept my confidence. Mom lived another seventeen years and, though many from our church visited her in Linhaven, no one ever told her what I shared that night. God honored my obedience and willingness to share what He had done for me, and He kept my Mom from any more pain. He is such a caring God!

While God was doing wonderful things spiritually for me, the situation was tough on the home front. Bill had been in the life insurance business for six years and most of that time he had done quite well. He was runner-up as rookie of the year for all of Canada in his first year, and the second year he exceeded expectations. While he worked fifty to sixty hours per week, and every night of the week except Fridays, he also took university courses, endeavoring to become a chartered life underwriter—a designation in the insurance industry that would allow him to be in the top ten percent of agents. He wanted to help people with their whole financial portfolios—life insurance, retirement savings, investments, mutual and segregated funds, and estate planning. Over the next number of years, Bill would complete more than fifteen university credits and obtain three financial planning designations. I was so proud of him.

He hadn't finished high school and he fought through a speech impediment, yet he was successful in one of the toughest businesses in the marketplace. Selling one policy for every five interviews was the industry norm; Bill sold one for nearly every two interviews.

In 1981, however, interest rates hit twenty-three percent, while inflation was in double-digits. Canada was plunged into the worst recession since the Great Depression of the 1930s.

People started losing their houses and letting their policies lapse. Anything deemed non-essential to survival was cut from family budgets. There was no money for extras, and many considered insurance an extra. Bill's company faired better than most—coming up with a high coverage, low-cost product—but with little savings and cash value in the policies, Bill had to work especially hard for low commissions. In addition to lower commissions and older business that went off the books when people could no longer afford their premiums, the company cut the bonus and commission rates on new business. Bill was working harder than ever—for less. Both Shawn and Blake were in high school, and Bill wasn't around the house much. Sometimes he got discouraged and the Lord used me, ironically, to encourage him.

After supper most nights, Bill would force himself back into the office to make prospecting calls. He would call referrals, often perfect strangers, trying to book sales appointments. That would scare most people; but when you stutter, talking on the phone is crippling. Bill hated it. He would go to the office and I would slip into the bedroom and pray. I was so confident that God was our source—He had done so much for us—that many days I found it easier to trust God than Bill did. God brought us through that recession meeting all of our needs, with our faith firmer than it ever was before. Knowing I didn't want Bill to go into the business in the first place, he found it amusing that I was now his biggest booster.

Whatever potholes I had hit, whatever collateral damage I had sustained, God pulled me, and my family, through it. He always found a way to right my vehicle and face it in the correct direction—placing me precisely where I belonged, back on the road to freedom. I couldn't imagine encountering anything bigger than what He had already brought us through; but that's the great thing about God—He doesn't share with us what we are not yet ready to hear.

CHAPTER 16

Willie's Demons

D arkness is never so dark as in the place where no light has ever shone. I had a secret. I kept it in a vault for a lot of years, but now light was seeping in. That light brought forgiveness, freedom from shame and guilt, and a hope that promised tomorrow would be better than today. But I wasn't the only one with a secret.

The door to Willie's vault was impregnable—steel, two feet thick and bolted shut with several foolproof locks. Any cracks around the edges of the vault door were sealed in a layer of alcohol thick enough to prevent any truth and light to shine in. The awful things he did to his little sister were safely locked inside. If he kept moving, taking a drink with each movement, he would never have to look inside that vault. Occasionally the seal would wear thin, and when a little daylight broke through, revealing just the outline of the evil inside, the pain became excruciating. It was more than any human being could bear. Willie's memories haunted him. They wouldn't allow him to exist in a sober state, for then the real Willie existed in all of his vileness. To look on himself with sober introspection meant coming to grips with who he was and what he had done. It was much easier to bring in the black cloud, to shut the door and seal it. Looking at the outside of the vault, especially through a drunken stupor, allowed him to cope. There might have been a hint from the outside, that something was deeply wrong inside, but the

285

true nature of that demon was shrouded by the blackness. It seemed better for others, and better for Willie, to speculate about the pain that constrained him to drink; better to guess than to know. The drunkenness was easier to gaze upon, than the intrinsic evil that drove him to it. Willie lived to make himself numb.

When I was nineteen and newly married, Willie moved back into 17 Sherbourne Street. Divorce from Claudette was immanent. Willie had a high paying job for someone relatively unskilled and unschooled. He drove a cement mixer and was part of a powerful union. At that time he controlled his drinking enough that it didn't interfere with his work. He showed up at work each day and did his job. Like his father, Willie could hold his liquor. While others might be wasted, Willie's body had adjusted to the heavy amount of alcohol he consumed. He could function normally, even with several drinks in his system.

Just before he turned thirty-one years old, Willie slipped from the top of his cement truck and fell fifteen feet to the ground, breaking his back. He would never work again.

Besides the obvious physical pain involved in his recovery, depression set in. Willie had been a hard worker. He had always had the money he needed. Now he couldn't work. Any sense of worth he attached to himself, vanished. His wife left him and he couldn't stand the pain of seeing his kids—it was easier to pretend that his children didn't exist. They pretended the same thing: Willie didn't exist to them.

Now, instead of the light seeping in to Willie's vault, the demons inside were oozing out. All he could do for months was lie in bed—and think. As soon as he could get up and make his way around with a cane, he would set his sights on the bar. Mom wouldn't allow Willie to bring booze into the house, so he spent all of his time out drinking. At the end of each day a buddy would drive him home. Sometimes he made it into the house. Sometimes he lay where he fell.

Occasionally Mom would tire of Willie, or he would get frustrated at the rules, and he would move into a place of his own; but soon his rent money would be gone, spent on drinking, and he would land back at Sherbourne Street. This was a continuous cycle for four or five years. Workman's compensation settled his injury claim and Willie received a monthly pension. It wasn't a lot of money, but certainly more than it cost to keep him going. He never supported his wife and kids; to him they no longer existed. After a few years, Claudette remarried.

His friends were friends until Willie had too much to drink. Once drunk, the formerly quiet and unassuming Willie became loud and obnoxious. Some people become emotional when drinking; Willie got angry. He was a mean drunk. Until he passed out, the best option was to leave him by himself. So Willie drank alone, even in a room full of people. (He was so angry and so antisocial that it crossed my mind that Willie might have been a victim of sexual abuse himself. When the family first moved here from Saskatchewan, they lived with their neighbors and relatives in that one-room house together. It is entirely possible that some adult molested him. Where else could he have learned the things that he inflicted upon me? How else could he have become so engrossed in sexual violence, especially by the age of fourteen?)

From the time Willie was thirty until he was sixty-five, I saw him less than a dozen times, thought about him as little as possible, and avoided accidental encounters. It never occurred to me then to care about Willie or the reasons he stole my innocence. I didn't care if he was in pain; if he was, he deserved to be.

If he had other victims amongst my siblings, I didn't know about it. The fact that I was the only girl younger than him—the rest of his siblings being brothers—made me an easy mark. Until I gave my testimony at women's ministries, I doubt my brothers ever knew. Even after I made my childhood abuse public, my brothers never brought the subject up with me. They only spoke about it when I raised it. I've come to realize that they felt so bad about what happened to me, they found it difficult to talk about. Deep inside they believe they should have known; they should have been there to prevent it and to keep me safe. Speaking of it only compounded their feelings of regret. In reality, by the time my siblings knew, there was nothing anyone could do.

As time went along, Willie became more and more alienated from the rest of the family. Though Pete and Hank were heavy drinkers, they considered Willie a flat-out drunk. He embarrassed the other alcoholics in our family. No one wanted to be seen with Willie, let alone drink with him. Even Dad, who started Willie drinking in the first place, wanted nothing to do with him by the time Willie was forty years old. Willie only came around to "borrow" money. He never asked his parents or siblings for a handout—it was always just a loan. It didn't matter that it was only five or ten dollars, always accompanied by a disingenuous promise to pay it back.

For a brief period after he turned forty, Willie lived with a woman named Delores. A needy woman, Delores possessed little self-esteem. The two of them kept each other from being alone for about five years. Willie became too much for even Delores, and once she left, Willie never had another woman in his life. His love affair was with the bottle, and he would devote the rest of his years, the best of his life, to her. Willie lived for the next drink. He remained in Welland, a community about twenty miles south of St. Catharines, where he and Delores had lived. Welland became Willie's haunt.

Because all that mattered was his next drink, nothing else did. Within fifteen years, Willie slid from a being a functioning, working alcoholic, to an indigent street person. Willie soon cared little about his appearance and adopted a lifestyle of filth; he didn't bathe or care that he hadn't. It didn't bother him to wear the same clothes until they were literally rags. He wore most of what he owned, regardless of whether it was winter or summer, all at the same time. Willie's hair was generally long and unkempt, greasy and rarely washed. He didn't like shaving and wore a long goatee. What teeth he had, he never brushed, so by the time he was forty-five he had none left. His pension paid for false teeth, but when he lost them vomiting into a toilet; he never bothered to replace them.

He moved from rooming house to rooming house until back rent or problems cohabitating with others caught up with him. There were times when he had no place to live; a park bench in the summer or a men's shelter if the weather was cold, fit the bill. My oldest brother, Ike, was the one in the family who kept in touch with him the most. Once Dad died, Willie didn't come around to borrow money as often, so Ike would travel to Welland to check on him—for Mom's sake. Willie disgusted Dad, but Mom pitied him. She felt sorry for him and blamed the booze, not Willie, for destroying his life.

288

Three or four times per year Ike traveled the 406 Highway to Welland, to find Willie. When he did, he would always take him for something to eat, slip him some money, and talk to him. Ike was a wonderfully compassionate man and we all loved him, even those who wanted nothing to do with Jesus. He wasn't condemning or legalistic—Ike cared. Whenever he could, he would tell Willie that Jesus loved him and that he could forgive him for his sins. Willie would always listen. (It was worth listening to Ike's speech to get the money.) Occasionally Ike would go early in the morning on a weekday and find Willie sober enough to bring back to St. Catharines to visit Mom. He would never tell her in advance that he was going, in case Willie wasn't in good enough shape to bring back. Too often, however, all Ike could do was help Willie make it back to his room—he would be too drunk or sick from a hangover to bring to Mom.

Once or twice during Mom's stay at our house, Willie took a bus from Welland to St. Catharines to visit her. The visit curried favor from Mom and translated into a few dollars; she would reward his initiative. On those days, the kids or Bill were usually home, and I felt comfortable enough to let him in to visit, for Mom's sake. When he made the trip to St. Catharines himself, it was always in good weather, and he and Mom would sit out in the backyard. It always eased Mom's fears to see Willie. Whatever he was to the rest of the world, he was her son and she loved him. She grew concerned when it turned cold outside. She feared for his life, knowing he didn't take care of himself. After visiting with Willie, despite the fact it invariably cost her money, she would be in a really good mood; the son she worried about the most was safe. Strange as it sounds, I was glad when he occasionally dropped in—it temporarily made Mom easier to live with.

Sometimes in winter, Ike wouldn't be able to find Willie. Often the police had picked him out of a snow bank and taken him to the county lock-up to get warm and sober. He got to be known around town, and he liked the notoriety. Many of the flophouses in Welland were located two to three miles from downtown, and most days Willie would walk from his room to the business section, to panhandle for extra money. The merchants there called him "Boxcar Willie," taken from the country music song. He took to the name because he liked country music, even referring to himself using the moniker. Ike thought it made him feel important. Willie walked thousands of miles in his lifetime. He had lost his driver's license years before and preferred saving the bus fare for something to drink. While he walked, it was not uncommon to see him, dressed in everything he owned, carrying a loaf of bread and a stick of bologna. He wasn't a fussy eater—bologna or wieners would suffice...anything soft enough to eat without teeth.

Once he turned fifty-five, Willie threw himself on the mercy of Mr. Blackbeard, a businessman in town who owned many of the rooming houses. Blackbeard controlled whole blocks of storefronts, apartment buildings, and rundown houses. He wasn't a classy, respected type of businessman; his money came from being able to collect from those down on their luck. Mr. Blackbeard's formula worked well for Willie. He took Willie to the bank and opened an account—one in which they shared signing authority. At the beginning of each month, Willie's pension check came and was automatically deposited in the shared account. Mr. Blackbeard would then take Willie's rent and food tab for the month. (He ate at a little greasy-spoon restaurant across the street from his room.) This ensured that Willie could have a couple of meals every day and a roof over his head at night. In addition, Willie received enough money to buy one bottle a day. If he wanted to drink more, he would have to get the money from begging on the street. All of this was administered by Mr. Blackbeard's right-hand man, Ted.[1] He was the closest thing Mr. Blackbeard had to a building superintendent, but he liked to think of himself as Willie's caretaker— his guardian.

Willie had few friends. Instead he had people that were useful to him. There was a local minister who would give him money or a hot meal from time to time, and a doctor he would visit if someone forced him into it. To these useful associates, he never mentioned his family. No one in Welland knew Willie even had siblings. He often spoke of his mom and how much she loved him, but he never spoke of anyone else. It wasn't prudent to mention family when being alone in the world could illicit more sympathy. Willie was a

[1] Name changed to protect privacy.

master manipulator and revealing only an ailing mother, who lived in a different city, was better motivation to those he panhandled than the truth. Being alone in the world raises empathy in the coldest of hearts. Willie was alone in the world, but he was alone because he wanted it that way. He wanted to forget everything that he had ever lived, everything about his family—unless he needed cash; then he would recover enough of his memory to pay someone a visit.

In his mind, he wasn't an alcoholic. No one could help him; he didn't need help. He "might have had too much to drink once in awhile," but he was no alcoholic! Willie tried reality but he didn't like it—it hurt too much. Drunkenness was not the problem, sobriety was. Inebriation allowed him to be the person he wanted to be. No longer inhibited, he did as he pleased; and because he could not recall the evil he did, it was as though he hadn't done it at all. While drunk, Willie never had to think of all he had lost—his marriage, his children, his extended family, and his dignity. Drinking made him feel as though he still had it all; the bottle was his surrogate life, replacing all he had lost. To stop drinking was much too scary. Facing the real Willie in the mirror every day would be insufferable.

Most of what I know about Willie's life I've gleaned only in the last few years. From the time I was twenty-one-years old until I was fifty, I had as little contact with him as possible. Ike and George sought him out from time to time, but I never inquired after him. Mom would try to talk about him after he had visited her; she wanted to tell me how he was doing. I would listen for a minute or so and then say, "Mom, I'm really not interested in Willie's life. Let's talk about something else." I always said it quickly, dismissing the subject. It made me feel uncomfortable.

"Vell, maybe you don't care about your brodder. But I do. He is still my son and your brodder! And you shouldn't be so cruel to him!" Mom's response was predictable; but I would rather listen to her scold me than talk about Willie.

Willie's lifestyle never embarrassed Mom—she pitied him, which to her was the same thing as loving him. To Mom, if someone felt sorry for you, they must really care. This is why Mom often accused me of not loving her. I wouldn't pity her. I don't know what it was within me, but I couldn't let myself feel sorry for Mom. It might be because I knew that's what she wanted more than any-

291

thing else, and I didn't want to give her the satisfaction. I wanted to feel genuine love and approval from her, and she wanted to be pitied by me. Neither of us got what we wanted. I loved Mom, but I was never going to let her wallow in pity. I couldn't stand it.

"Villie is just like Dad," she would say. "Da booze—dat awful, awful drinkin'—dat's vhat makes dem like dat!"

Whatever "made them like that," I didn't care about. I only wanted to live my life away from them—away from alcohol and the strife it invariably brought.

ೞ

By 1985 I was studying to join Bill in the life insurance business. As the day approached to write my exams, I felt awful—but there was no way I was staying home. I didn't know it then, but I had an acute infection and cysts on my kidneys. I wrote the exams with a high fever, and then went to the hospital. (Bill had challenged me to enter the business. He believed I could do it and I didn't want to disappoint him. Though I only had part of a remedial grade nine education, I studied and studied. There was no way I was going to skip the tests.) My condition was serious given my diabetes, and for a time the medical community wasn't sure I was going to recover; but I responded to the antibiotics in the hospital and pulled through.

I needed to pass the two exams at a seventy percent level. I passed one and failed the other—by just one percent. Bill was thrilled and promised me that if I could come that close with a high fever and cysts on my kidneys, I would certainly pass the rewrite when healthy. At the first opportunity, I rewrote the exam. This time I passed. Bill and I were in business together.

We worked well as a team and God blessed us. I worked alongside Bill for the next four or five years, and, because I was out of the house and in business, God was able to show me that, though my healing had begun, it was incomplete. My entry into the business world would bring me closer to God's ultimate plan for my life. I was to learn a crucial lesson one day while out picking up a check from one of our clients.

I thought nothing of it at the time. I had been working in the office with Bill for about ten years. On this particular day, Bill asked me to travel to Welland. We had a client there who had a check for us to invest. Bill and I built our business on service, and it was commonplace for us to make every effort to get new business. If someone wanted to invest with us, we would make it easy. It never dawned on me at the time, that I would be entering Boxcar Willie's territory.

Being a businesswomen had done wonders for my confidence. I dressed up every day and headed to the office. I sold life insurance policies and helped with clients' financial investments. I felt great about myself. I hardly ever had a thought about Willie and, since I resolved to be careful about the books I read, I hadn't had any nightmares or flashbacks. If you had asked me then, I would have said that I had totally forgiven what was done to me as a child; God had wonderfully healed me.

I headed out to Welland by myself. I remember looking forward to the half-hour ride, musing that it would be a welcome respite from the frenetic pace of the office. I had picked up our client's check in downtown Welland, and was returning to my car parked on the street, when I looked up. I froze. I couldn't believe what I was seeing. There he was—Willie—walking down the sidewalk toward me. For a moment all I could do was stare. He was dressed in what looked like army surplus clothes that he had slept in for several days. His hair was greasy and longer than I had remembered; but it was Willie. He was occupied checking pay phones and parking meters for coins, and he hadn't recognized me. At once, fear gripped me. I didn't want him to see me. What would he say? Would he make a scene? Would he corner me into taking him for a ride somewhere? I would never get into a car alone with him! Never!

I lowered my head and looked the other way before brushing past him. As soon as he was behind me, I ducked into the Christian book store, my heart pounding and my face ashen.

"Are you alright, ma'am?" the store clerk asked me. "You look like you've seen a ghost!"

"Huh? Oh. Well—I just ran into someone I didn't expect to see! That's all! Can I just wait here for a moment?" I had seen a ghost; a ghost from the past, and he had brought with him the feelings of danger he always had.

I waited in the store for five more minutes then raced back to where I was parked, fumbling with the key in the car door and hoping that Willie hadn't turned around. After what seemed like ten minutes, I got the car door open and I locked myself inside. The car started. I was moving. I started breathing again. As I got about a mile from the downtown core, my mind focused on the radio that was playing. I began to hear the words the singer on the local Christian radio station, was singing:

"I am the Lord, that healeth thee, I am the Lord that healeth thee, I am the Lord that healeth thee."

"God! You are the Lord that heals me! Why don't I feel healed? What are you saying? Is there more? Do I need more healing? God, show me what I need to do!"

"I am the Lord, that healeth thee, I am the Lord that healeth thee, I am the Lord that healeth thee..." the singer went on.

I rushed back to the office and told Bill everything that happened, unsure of what God was about to do in my life.

捣

From 1965 to the mid-nineties, my other family members chose the courses their lives would take.

Hank started out well. He got married and had a supervisor's job at General Motors. At one point he and Ike went into business together and opened up a gas station. But as he approached his thirties, the bottle caught up with him too. Hank was quiet and shy, but when he drank he became gregarious, the life of the party. He liked how he felt when he drank: confidant, as if he could take on all comers. Soon his world collapsed around him, and the lies that alcohol tells its victims no longer stood up in the real one. He may have felt confident and sociable, but really he wasn't making it. After his second daughter was born, his relationship with his wife deteriorated, and they separated. Devastated by the breakup of his marriage and hurting from not seeing his daughters, Hank drank to escape.

Hank never visited his kids. He said it hurt too much; his heart couldn't bear it. He went from one menial job to the next, earning just enough to keep a roof over his head and beer in the fridge. For the last twenty years of his life he subsisted on welfare. He moved out West, away from everything and everyone that reminded him of what his life could have been. Several months after I contacted a pastor in

British Columbia to look up Hank and see if he was doing okay, we got a call: Hank had been found dead in his room. He died of alcohol poisoning at fifty-nine years old. Hank drank himself to death.

His body was cremated and his ashes were sent back to St. Catharines, where his family gathered for a small memorial service. His children didn't come.

Of all my brothers, Hank was very special. I never knew of a time when he ever committed his life to Christ. Though the rest of my siblings prayed and asked Jesus to be their Savior as children, Hank always resisted. He said that he didn't need to give his life to Christ, that if he followed the Ten Commandments it would be good enough. Hank was sensitive and kind, and I truly believe he felt being kind to others was enough—but it wasn't enough to heal his pain or restore the broken relationship with his daughters; that would have only come through Jesus. I don't know if Hank had the opportunity late in his life to call out to God—I know that his mother prayed for him, earnestly and faithfully. I know that I did too. I have hope in that.

෫

Mom had her faults, but in one area she excelled—Mom could pray! She would always tell my brothers, "Every night, every night, I pray for you!" And she did. When she lived with us, I would often walk into her bedroom as she prepared to go to sleep; she would have her eyes closed and her lips would be moving. She was praying. She prayed for her kids, and she prayed for their wives or girlfriends. She prayed for them by name, and she prayed that they would come to know Jesus.

Mom had a difficult life. She didn't always respond in the right ways. She treated her sons and daughters unequally, and the enormous expectations that she placed upon her children seemed unfair and often selfish; but the one way that we experienced Mom's love was that she prayed for us. She prayed for her children and her grandchildren. She prayed for us by name too. Mom never told me she loved me—that was foreign to her—but she always told me she was praying for me. Later in life, I took the latter phrase to mean the former. Mom was praying for me because she loved me. She knew of no other way to show it.

To some it might have seemed that prayer was just another legalistic way for Katarina Hiebert to be holy; but if you *knew* her, you would know it was a labor of love. She loved to talk to God. She talked to God about the people she loved—and the people she loved knew it. Willie often told the pastor-friend he had in Welland, "I have a mother who prays for me. Yeah, she loves me and I love her—and she prays every day for me."

Despite all that Mom missed while raising me, despite every guilt-trip and manipulation she concocted to get her own way, and regardless of how distant and disapproving she was, I'm glad she prayed for her children. The rest can be forgiven; and once it is, what stands out is that she might have failed, but she never failed to pray. Much of who I am and what I have been able to accomplish and to recover from, I owe to Mom, because she prayed for me. She prayed for me when she didn't even know what I needed; but God did and He used her prayers to pull me through!

೦೩

Pete married and had three children. He lived around the corner from Mom in the old neighborhood, and our two families saw much more of each other for just that reason. On Sunday afternoons, Pete and his wife would often come to 17 Sherbourne Street to visit with the rest of us who were there to see Mom. Pete's children went to Sunday school with their Grandma, enabling our children to get to know their cousins at church. I had a special relationship with both of Pete's daughters—Christine, whom I babysat when Bill and I were first married; and Brenda, who had a special place in her heart for Christ. Brenda was the only member of Pete's family who faithfully went to church. Mom was especially vigilant with Pete's kids, constantly calling them, making sure they went to Sunday school with her.

Pete chose the bottle too, but for most of his life he managed to remain a functional alcoholic. He had a violent temper and lost more jobs for that reason than for drinking; but when he drank, Pete became even more violent. He liked to fight, and barroom brawls were a way of life for him. I experienced Pete's mean streak as a child and was always wary of him, making sure I wasn't around when he had been drinking. He might have been a functioning alcoholic, in that he always showed up for work and did a good job, but nobody truly functions as an alcoholic. Alcohol gets in the way of relationships. It wasn't long before Pete and his wife were having marital difficulties; amid the philandering and violence, divorce became the logical end.

After their divorce, Pete had several girlfriends whom he lived with for a period of time, but he never remarried. All of the boys who weren't Christians smoked as well as drank, and it caught up with them. Hank had his larynx removed four years before he died, and Pete battled cirrhosis of the liver from his mid-forties on. Still Pete continued to smoke and drink—he couldn't kick either habit. Pete met a horrible fate three years before Hank died.

He had been drinking at a neighbor's house. When it was time to go home, Pete decided to take a shortcut through a patch of forest and across a field. It was winter, but because he wasn't far from his place, he had dressed only in a light jacket. It was dusk when Pete left the neighbor's house drunk. Cutting through the woods, he tried to amble over a barbed wire fence, became entangled and passed out. When he came to, about twelve hours later, he had had been out in the elements for a long time and had lost a lot of blood. By this time he had sobered up, but he didn't have strength to free himself from the barbed wire. He lay there in the snow for another day-and-a-half before being found. He lived two more days in the hospital before succumbing to pneumonia. Before he died, however, he received a visit from Dave Topping, one of the ministers on staff at Central Gospel Temple. On his deathbed, Pete gave his heart to Christ. Mom had the comfort of knowing that her son had experienced the love and forgiveness of Jesus before he died.

☙

David, my younger brother, initially followed a path similar to the one chosen by Hank and Pete. When he was a teenager he got into some trouble with the law, and by the late Sixties, drugs came into the scene. His heart was not as hard as some of his older brothers, though, so Dave had seasons when he would return to following Christ. During those times, he was always driving trucks and was away from his wife and children. He found it difficult to get to church regularly or to grow in his faith. Alcohol, the ever-present menace in my family, was always there to make the fall complete, and Dave would struggle for a few more years. This cycle continued until Dave was in his forties. In the end, though he lost his first marriage, David sincerely committed his life to Christ and married a lovely Christian woman. Today they attend a church in St. Catharines and are part of a nurturing Christian community.

Ike and George always served Jesus. Once they committed themselves to Christ, they rose to the level of leadership. George was involved as a head usher for many years at Central Gospel Temple, and Ike served on the deacon board. They raised their children in the church and were a terrific example to Bill and me.

Tina committed her life to Christ after her own battle with drinking. She attends a little country church and has developed an authentic love of Jesus.

Ben and June retired early, spending most of their time helping on the mission field or in fledgling churches. They even spent fifteen years as part-time pastors, while Ben worked a full-time job.

I am convinced that, without Jesus, each of us would most certainly have lived troubled lives like Willie, Hank, and Pete—battling the demons in a bottle. By God's grace and intervention, our stories will end differently and our legacy will be one God fashions for His glory.

ೞ

The darkness is pitch black. The light is pure white light. Everything hides in the darkness. Everything is exposed in the light.

The demons that consumed Willie lived in that pitch black, surfacing from the long neck of a bottle every time he went for a sip. They hid everything of beauty and made his life a mere existence, barely tolerable by most and loathsome to him. Those same demons traveled from their dark netherworld, through the bottle, to Hank and Pete; and they nearly tore David to shreds. But the white light of truth and grace sealed me from their wretched schemes, while opening up my vault, forcing me to look at what was really inside.

The white light is Jesus.

CHAPTER 17

Wayward Kids

Though I was functioning at a very high level outwardly, the run-in with Willie in Welland signaled all was not well inside; my healing was still incomplete. Others might have thought everything in my life was normal, if not fantastic—but I knew different; and being close to normal was not good enough. I was still not that well-adjusted, overcoming woman I longed to be, but I could see her from where I was. I wanted to be so complete a person that no connection to my experiences as a child could be made by casual observers. I wanted to be the woman who had never been victimized—confident and whole. I knew if God could heal my memories, He could heal the residual effects of the resentment I had harbored my whole adult life; but first I would have to admit it. The initial healing was instantaneous; that prayer in Joan's living room brought it home immediately. The complete lesson of forgiveness, however, became a journey of several years. I had to learn things about my own nature—dark things, ugly things—things I did not want to have to admit to, things for which I was responsible. My ordeal somehow justified the responses I had fashioned, yet those responses now threatened everything I wanted to become. The ugliness that had attached itself to my personality and was evident in my comportment, would only come to light as I lost all power over the circumstances and people I had so desperately tried to control—starting with my children.

Bill and I were proud of our children. My childhood was screwed-up, but I was proud of the kids we had raised. When they were small, strangers commented on their politeness and manners. As they grew older, the three of them became involved in church activities, did well in school, and by all accounts were ambitious, independent, and mature. I appreciated this, but felt God owed it to me. I held to my penance theory: because I had suffered so much pain and injustice, there was no way God would let anything bad happen in my family. It was as though I had drawn up an agreement with God: *I'll get better and grow despite all of the crud I've been through, but You keep anything damaging from happening to my kids.* I had signed off on this presumed deal, I just had not bothered to make sure God's signature was on the document. Why would He not have agreed? It was only reasonable.

Throughout Shawn's high school years, I thought she was serving God. She said all the right things, was involved in the youth group at church, and sang in an ensemble. Most of those four years, however, she lived a double life. With a room in the basement, she stayed up until the rest of the house was asleep and then slipped out with her friends. Her practice of crawling out the basement window had been going on for a year before we found out.

One night I heard a bang and woke up Bill to investigate. He went downstairs into Shawn's room. It was empty. The window, which hung from two hinges, was swinging, banging on the bottom frame in the breeze. Bill threw on his clothes and rushed out to the front yard. A block down the street, he could barely make out two silhouettes.

"Shawn! Is that you? Shawn!" He yelled after the pair. Immediately the boy took off running. Shawn stood there frozen. Bill raced up to where she stood motionless.

"What are you doing? Who was that guy? It's one o'clock in the morning! What on earth are you doing?" The questions were coming fast and furious.

Bill was not expecting any answers and Shawn did not have any to give. She just stood there, crying, trying to hide herself in the darkness.

300

Rarely has Bill been as angry. He pulled her by the arm, "Get home—while I try to figure out what I'm going to do to you!"

Down in Shawn's room, Bill and I talked with a girl we didn't know—someone who had been masquerading as our obedient and responsible daughter. We never thought her capable of such deception. After the initial shock wore off, Bill was strangely calm; but I was livid. I didn't believe Shawn was sorry for what she had done, or even felt badly about it. She was upset that she was caught in the act. I was in danger of losing all control. I walked out of the room, and left Bill to deal with her. Shawn had few answers and claimed it was the only time she had ever crawled out the window. (Of course that wasn't true. It had been her routine; she crawled out of that window two or three times a week.) She made it sound as though it was unarranged and spontaneous. Her friend, this boy that liked her, had knocked on the window and woke her up. She said she didn't know why, she just went with him. She was sorry. After expressing his sincere disappointment and spelling out how hurt, betrayed, and deceived we both felt, Bill meted out the punishment.

Bill and I went to bed and cried.

Shawn was used to living a lie and became very good at it. After the night she got caught sneaking out of the house, her lifestyle seemed to improve. She even wrote me a note one Sunday soon afterward, on the back of a church-offering envelope. I still have the original envelope. It read, *"Dear Mom, thanks for getting me through the times when 'I was once so lost.' I love and appreciate you sooooo much. Please always be there for me. I love you. Love, Shawn. P.S. It is my desire to live for Jesus."*

I thought that was it. The Lord had awakened me that night to find Shawn running out of the house in order to stop her—to get her to turn around and change the direction her life was heading. Unbeknownst to me, though, Shawn continued to struggle. She says now that serving God was her desire even then, but she couldn't seem to follow through.

As she began the eleventh grade, she began dating a very nice young man from church. He and Blake were good friends. They double and triple-dated with other teenagers we knew well from the youth group. I believed Shawn had really straightened her life out. She talked like it.

Approaching the end of her senior year, Shawn discussed with Bill and me what she wanted to do.

"Mom, Dad. I'd like to work for a year, you know, get a job, earn some money and then...well, then I'd like to go to Bible college." Bill and I couldn't believe what we were hearing. We were ecstatic.

"Okay. Great. Are you sure that's what you want to do?"

"Yep. That's it. It's what I want to do," she reaffirmed.

"Well, you work then. We'll help you out as much as we can...you know—if you're short," Bill assured.

Shawn was telling us what we wanted to hear. We didn't know it at the time, but she didn't know what to do coming out of high school. She did know that it would thrill us to hear she wanted to go to Bible college, and she so badly wanted to please us—she wanted our approval—that she said it. If "getting us off her back" was what she wanted, telling us *that* did the trick. All of the deceit of the past was forgotten. Our oldest girl wanted to go to Bible college! We gave her all the space she needed. She applied to Eastern Pentecostal Bible College, the official college of the eastern districts of the Pentecostal Assemblies of Canada, and was accepted. After working at a department store for a year and earning her tuition, we sent her off to Peterborough, thrilled at all the progress she had made.

Shawn enrolled at Eastern in September and, in October, Bill, Heather, and I went to Arizona to visit Bill's brother Jack. Blake was in his senior year of high school. Shawn had been in Bible college for six weeks. We thought Shawn probably would appreciate a weekend at home, so, the first weekend we were away, we made arrangements for her to come home and stay with Blake. She was excited and asked if she could bring a friend from school with her. Bill and I felt perfectly at ease with the whole arrangement. Blake had proven to be trustworthy—we never worried about him. He seemed to make good decisions and was mature beyond his years. He was involved in several ministries at church and demonstrated excellent leadership skills. He was determined to enter the ministry as a pastor, and was finishing his last two semesters at high school before attending the same school as Shawn. We took off from Toronto International Airport with Heather, and never gave the situation another thought—we had great kids and we trusted them implicitly.

We returned from Arizona within a week. The day after we arrived, Shawn called from school. "Daddy? Can you come pick me up? I've been asked to leave. I'll explain everything when I get home."

"Are you all right? I mean you're not sick or anything, are you?"

"No, Daddy—it's nothing like that. I don't want to talk about it over the phone. Just come and get me, okay?" Shawn really seemed anxious to get off the phone. Bill agreed to go get her and hung up the receiver.

The two-hour drive to Peterborough was quiet. Bill and I wondered what could have happened. We wondered what could have taken place that would necessitate Shawn leaving school. We felt the knots form in our stomachs, sick at what was about to transpire.

The president of the school, Rev. Robert Taitinger, met with us. He explained that they had reliable information about Shawn's weekend home, that she had spent the night with a former boyfriend and that, when confronted with it, Shawn confessed. As a result she was being expelled from Eastern Pentecostal Bible College.

On the way home Shawn filled in the details. Shawn and her friend had gone out with Shawn's boyfriend from church on the Saturday evening. He had dropped them both back at the house at about eleven o'clock. The friend from Bible college still wanted to have some fun. After a brief phone call they decided to go to a party at the house of an old friend from high school. Once there, Shawn hooked up with Mike[2], one of the people whom she frequently sneaked out of the house to be with during her sophomore and junior years. She spent the night with him while her friend from Bible college went elsewhere. Within a week of returning to school, the college administration became aware of what happened, and Shawn was expelled.

I couldn't believe what I was hearing. My daughter had lost her reputation, her virginity, and her future in one night of incredibly poor judgment, marked by a lack of integrity and totally out of the character she had displayed in the previous two years. All of the

[2] Name changed to protect privacy.

trust we had rebuilt since she was caught running off in the night, was once again dashed to pieces. Who was this girl? I didn't know my own daughter!

We had been strict parents. We had talked about the preciousness of holding onto virginity until marriage. She had always had a curfew. With what I had gone through, I couldn't have imagined, given the choice, giving up my virginity in a flippant one-night-stand. My virginity was stolen from me. It wasn't possible for me to give it to my husband on my wedding night. How could Shawn just throw hers away? And what of her boyfriend from church? How could she betray his trust? They had been dating for over two years. I couldn't understand why she would do such a thing.

I was ashamed and embarrassed. My "perfect little family" was embroiled in scandal. We tried to keep Shawn's homecoming from college secret, but that lasted only a week and then we felt disapproval from the leering eyes at church. People didn't say anything, but I knew what they were thinking and took it personally. *How could she have done this to us?* I thought about how much I had boasted about my kids while in Arizona. We were so proud of them. As embarrassed and disappointed as I was with Shawn's behavior, I defended her. It made me angry that others were gossiping and backbiting. I wanted to protect her from the shame that she inevitably felt. I was as disappointed at the loss of my perfect-family fantasy as I was of the reality of Shawn's loss. She had lost her innocence and I lost the dream of her innocence. The whole thing knocked the emotional wind out of me.

Though disappointed, Bill was stoic as usual. "People fail, Margaret," he would say. "People make mistakes, but God forgives. We'll get through it, and we have to get Shawn through it; that's the important thing."

After Shawn was expelled from Bible college, we grew even further apart. I was angry and hurt, and she felt as though I withdrew my love. Without realizing it, I failed to express my love to her. I didn't stop telling Shawn I loved her, but emotional uneasiness and distance defined our relationship. I hardly noticed it—but it was obvious to Shawn: don't disappoint Mom or you'll lose that "loving feeling."

Shawn drifted. She was rapidly losing her dream, her purpose. Shawn had always wanted to find a nice guy, someone who wanted to be a pastor, and become his wife. She thought that this would make me proud. The fiasco at Eastern left her bitter. Shawn knew she deserved expulsion; still, she was hurt and angry. She took back her old job at Zellers Department Store and spoke increasingly of moving out. All the while the rift between us grew. Shawn broke every house rule, ignored her curfew, and was intent on doing things as she saw fit. Her relationship with the young man from church disintegrated under the weight of her betrayal, and she ran into the open arms of Mike, the only one who "understood" her. For a while there was the pretense of going to church, but that dissipated once it was clear we weren't impressed; we were determined not to warm up to Mike. Shawn insisted on bringing him over to the house for Christmas, barely two months after she had come home. The whole family was tense and treated him with polite contempt. Naturally, Shawn was responsible for her own choices, but she was my daughter. It was easier blaming Mike than Shawn, and I needed someone upon whom to unleash my fury.

Looking back, I wish I could have shown Mike genuine Christian love and acceptance. I know that to him I did not represent Christ well; but I was so full of my own pain and hurt, cold disdain was all I could muster.

Shawn and I fought constantly. Finally she went to her dad and told him she was moving out. Bill convinced me to help her find an apartment so that, at the very least, she would be somewhere safe. I agreed, and in the spring of 1984 Shawn moved out. It wasn't how I had pictured sending my daughter into adulthood.

For the six months after being expelled from Bible College, the conflicts with Shawn took center stage and I failed to notice circumstances changing in Heather's life. She began to hang around a rougher crowd and started smoking. Heather was acting out, but I didn't even notice. I didn't want to think of the possibility that another one of my children was in trouble.

In February, just after that stressful Christmas, Blake took a position with a traveling ministry. It meant delaying his Bible school plans, but it offered a world of experience and he leapt at the opportunity. Our boarder turned twenty-one and moved to Toronto to accept a job. By March, Heather was really the only one home, and within five months even she would be gone. I went from a house full of kids to an empty nest inside of a year.

In the summer of 1984, Braeside again figured prominently in our family. Heather had gone to youth camp and, while there, rededicated her life to the Lord. She came home telling Bill and me that she really wanted to live a consistent Christian life, but was worried about going to high school surrounded by her old friends. We knew the peer pressure would be daunting. We decided that a year in private Christian School might give Heather the solid foundation she needed to make her strong in the face of adversity. She agreed, and we enrolled her in Niagara Christian College in Fort Erie, about an hour's drive from our house. She lived on campus during the week and was able to come home for weekends. It was hard raising the tuition, but God helped us as we determined to give Heather every opportunity to succeed in her commitment to Christ. (Years later, Heather told us she agreed to go to Niagara Christian College merely to get away from us; she did, however, benefit from the experience.)

Very quickly in that fall of 1984, Bill and I were living alone in that empty nest. Blake maintained a bedroom at home, but was gone ministering six to eight weeks at a time with just two or three days of rest in between. Heather was home on the weekends, but during the week, with Shawn living elsewhere, Bill and I were left trying to fill our five-bedroom home. It was depressing. With my family gone and barely forty years old, I felt old before my time. The years at home with my kids had come and gone too quickly. It was a rough period to get through. For several months I cried a lot.

In June of that year, at barely eighteen years old, Blake got engaged. He came to us with the idea of marrying Christine, whom he had been dating for three years. She was a lovely girl and fit in as though she was my own daughter, and somehow, despite their tender ages, it seemed reasonable for them to marry. Blake had no guarantee of a job after the wedding, planned for the following July in 1985, but he had always been ambitious and self-motivated, and we believed that he would find work. Ultimately he planned to go into the ministry, and though both he and Christine were young, they were mature. We figured they would work toward that goal as a team. Blake was not one to make decisions lightly, and somehow, we trusted that his marrying Christine was a good decision (though now it is hard to imagine how we ever gave our blessing to two teenagers). Blake and Christine's wedding was an elaborate affair with 250 guests, and Bill and I were in our glory.

After the summer wedding, Heather returned home from her Christian boarding school experience and resumed her high school career in the public system. She appreciated our home-life after spending a year away and, though she was in and out of mischief during her year at Niagara, there was a new maturity about her. She and I developed a closer relationship over the next four years, as in many ways she became an only child. Heather and I got closer; Shawn and I, however, drifted further apart.

Shawn entered and left relationships with guys quickly. The same was true of jobs; she didn't seem settled in the least. Leaving retail and entering the hotel industry, she began waitressing. Within a few days she met a man. They began to date and within a couple of weeks were living together—of course I found out about all of this much later. Shawn wanted to be carefree, but couldn't deal with my disapproval—so she lied and misled us. Soon the pressure of that duplicity would be too much to bear, but for the moment it kept the peace. Shawn was willing to live a lie. Peace at all costs. She came home at least weekly for visits and hugs. She needed lots of hugs. We seemed to get along together better, but it was a superficial peace. If I didn't ask too many questions or probe into her personal life, our relationship was bearable.

In December of 1985, she introduced her boyfriend to our family. We didn't warm up to him immediately but were happy to have Mike out of the picture. This fellow was funny, had a job, and dreamed of opening his own business. Besides that, he liked our family and enjoyed hanging around the house. He had come to family dinners, and he had a terrific sense of humor. We soon figured out that they were living common-law, but we decided to make him our missionary project. They began attending church with us and soon he said he believed in Jesus, said the sinner's prayer, and committed his life to Christ. At once they felt pressured to make their relationship legitimate. All we could see was his conversion, and we were glad when he proposed marriage. But Shawn had doubts about his sincerity. Her doubts were confirmed the evening before the wedding when he confessed to her face that he didn't love her. Shawn told me later she was relieved when she saw him arrive on the morning of the wedding.

Shawn wrote the ceremony and Blake assisted in the wedding. It was a great day; Bill and I were so proud of her and she felt accepted. Marriage had won her the approval of her parents. As displeased as we had been with her previous living arrangements, we were equally thrilled now. She smiled her way through the whole day; never once letting on that her heart had been ripped open. She has confided to me since that she thought if she just married him, she would win him over; she would please him so much that he would learn to love her.

No one knew her pain. There was lots of fighting, and after the first year of warfare, Shawn left. She was determined to remain separated—and would have, except for me. I was convinced her husband was changing, that God needed more time to shape him into His image. I talked Shawn into going back to him.

Though Shawn returned, the trust never did, and underlying suspicion sabotaged their relationship for the next five years. Shawn's self-esteem was plummeting, and the rest of us knew nothing of it. She looked for love and affection elsewhere, and throughout those years had repeated affairs, though she never admitted to them. She and her husband fought and argued constantly, and in her heart she justified what she did.

Shawn's sense of humor disappeared. The usual jokes and laughter she was known for departed as she tried to fit the mold of the expectations she assumed her husband had for her—yet never reached the place where she was confident in his love.

As a way to bring extra money into the home, Shawn marketed herself as a business consultant and reorganized several medical offices. While working for a chiropractic clinic, she got the opportunity to attend a business convention in Banff, Alberta. She was ripe for another affair. She met someone there, and he became her escape. He made her feel important and attractive and, after having searched in vain for her husband's approval throughout her troubled six-year marriage, she found the acceptance she longed for in one night from a complete stranger, 3,000 miles from home. At least that's what she thought.

308

She came home, announced she was leaving her husband, and moved to Banff inside of two months. Our family was devastated. Having been separated for a couple of months, five years earlier, we thought that she would come back again this time. She didn't. All she wanted to do was run away—away from her husband, away from her unhappy life, away from her demanding family, and away from church. If she didn't have to deal with it, then she could manage.

Upon moving out West, she moved in with another man whom she had met at the Banff Springs Hotel. She didn't even ask her husband for a share of the finances, and settled for next to nothing. She wanted it done. Over with. She wanted out.

All Bill and I could do was pray for her. At first I tried to do more. Whenever Shawn called I tried to talk some sense into her. I told her how she was ruining her life and how we disapproved of what she was doing. That only alienated her. She soon announced that she didn't believe in Jesus at all. She believed that, "everyone has a god within them and that we just have to let that god within develop. Everyone has to find God—whatever that might be—for themselves," she would say.

She wanted to hear nothing of Christianity. She called the way she was raised, "a bunch of rules." Everything Bill and I had done to raise her in Christ had been for nothing; now our oldest daughter was embracing the New Age Movement and flat-out rejected the Bible and God's authority. I couldn't help myself, every time she called I told her I was praying for her. Each time I said it, I could feel her moving away from me. I was trying to move closer, telling her I loved her enough to pray for her, and she resented it, thinking that my love was connected to my approval of her.

"Mom you are disappointed in me. You don't approve of my life and that means you don't love me," she would say. "I'm tired of living a lie, Mom! Either you're going to love me the way I am, or not; but either way, I'm living my life, my way!"

Her words cut deep. I would call Blake, who by this time was pastoring a newly planted church in Oakville, some forty miles away. Blake and Shawn had been close their whole lives. He had the ability to talk to her without the fighting and arguing that defined my relationship with her.

"Mom, you gotta let her go," he would scold. "You aren't going to win her back by pressuring her. Shawn knows deep down in her heart the things that you and Dad have taught her. She knows the truth and she'll come back to it. Trust God, Mom—and stop telling her every two minutes you're praying for her. She puts off talking to you because when she does all you do is guilt-trip her. Mom, you gotta do your beggin' on your knees. No one is so far from God that He can't reach them."

Blake was right of course, but I didn't want to hear it—my child was lecturing me.

When he told me I was giving Shawn a guilt-trip while I thought I was saying the things that expressed my love to her, all I could think about was my Mom. *I've become my mother!* I thought.

"Oh, God," I cried, "Shawn resents me like I did my Mom! Oh, God, forgive me. Help me not to place guilt on Shawn. Help her to come back to Jesus, and please don't let me stand in the way."

It was the hardest thing I ever had to do, but when Shawn called I refused to bring up the "God" subject. I started asking about her life and what was important to her, shuddering at her responses. She loved this new freedom to talk openly without guilt and disapproval coming from me. So much of her life had been hidden and hypocritical, that now she longed to have everything out in the open. I had to hear about her drinking and carousing lifestyle. She traveled back from Banff with Charles to introduce him to us. Unfortunately, I responded terribly. I was so hurt. I couldn't believe the promiscuous lifestyle she was leading. I wanted her and her husband to reconcile, and I couldn't bear to meet this new fellow. After a couple of days, and lots of pressure from the rest of my kids, I relented and suffered through a steely introduction to her new "live-in."

Our daughter was ruining her life and we had to stand by the roadside, saying nothing and watching the carnage. Blake's words rang in my ears, "Shut-up to Shawn, Mom. Do your talking to God."

God felt a million miles away, my daughter was out-of-control, wrecking her life, and I wasn't allowed to do anything. I was used to controlling things! I was angry with God, too. How could He let this happen to my perfect little family? He owed me! I had gone through all the trials! God owed it to me to keep my children from getting ravaged by the world. I wanted to shake Shawn—to shake her and shake her until I could get through to her. I was scared to death. I thought she would die, that I would get some call from the police: "I'm sorry to be calling you, Mrs. Davidson, but there's been an accident. Your daughter was drinking and, well, I'm sorry to have to tell you this, but your daughter is…"

I couldn't even finish those thoughts. I would shake my head and cry out to God in frustration. "God, spare her life. Don't let her die without knowing you. God, if she has to ruin her life and go through all of this pain, okay, but spare her life! Spare her life until she can come back to you!"

Just before all of the upheaval began in Shawn's life, things had been very positive. In 1988 Blake and Christine had their first child. Her name was Jade, and Bill and I were grandparents for the first time. The very next year, our second granddaughter, Katerina, arrived in the spring. Two months later Heather married a nice young man from church and the two of them moved to Peterborough.

It was 1992.

At church we had survived a congregational split and the bitter removal of our senior pastor. Bill was serving on the board through it all. The church needed to heal, and Pastor Jack Counsell came back for a second term at Central. He was such a good teacher. As he expounded from the Word, the congregation soaked it up, licking its wounds. He spoke a lot about forgiveness. At the same time Rich Beuhler's radio show was emphasizing the same things. I specifically remember one program entitled, "Forgive Your Accusers." Buehler described the kind of forgiveness commanded by Jesus. We, as His followers, are to forgive and pray for those who despitefully use us, forgiving the people who hate us—whom we've hated.

Around that time, Heather and Blake began the healing in *their* relationship. Blake felt hindered in his pastoral ministry because of things that had occurred between Heather and him. As close as Blake had been to Shawn, his relationship to Heather had always been strained. Seeking Heather's forgiveness, Blake traveled down to St. Catharines to talk to his sister. During that conversation,

Heather said she had forgiven him, but six years later, the deep resentments she held toward him surfaced. It was then that she realized giving lip service to forgiveness and truly forgiving are entirely different things. Blake broke down crying and apologized to Heather for mistreating her, for hurting her, and undermining her self-esteem throughout her childhood. He explained to Heather that his prayer life had been blocked, that he couldn't be close to God without dealing with this, and that he needed to humble himself, asking her to forgive him. They had several open and honest talks over the next couple of years, and a once terribly volatile relationship was healed. Heather decided to truly forgive Blake, and the reconciliation began.

In the dark, as parents often are, Bill and I knew nothing of this. We knew Heather and Blake weren't close, but we had no idea why. When we found out the nature of the rift between them, we were shocked at its severity, and yet took solace in how God was working it out. The four of us spent a few sessions together with a Christian counselor, and our hurt and disappointments faded as we dealt with things in the light.

After coming to grips with forgiving Blake, Heather began to talk to me about the unforgiveness in my heart. She treasured the look of relief on Blake's face when she offered him her forgiveness, how the guilt and pain left his troubled spirit when she simply said, "It's okay, Blake. I forgive you." She thought much about how, without her forgiveness, Blake felt he couldn't go on in his ministry, that he was a hypocrite and a fraud. She thought about what a difference it made in his life just to know he was forgiven, about the confidence it gave him and how their relationship was normal now—stronger than it could ever have been without her decision to forgive.

One day over a cup of coffee she said, "Mom, have you ever thought that Uncle Willie is living the way he is because he thinks that you can never forgive him? Have you ever thought about going to him and telling him that you've forgiven him?"

Her question floored me. I thought for sure that I had completely forgiven Willie; but, by not telling him, I held onto a sense of power. I was in control of my forgiveness. It was up to me when and if he would know about it. It was the ace in my hand. I knew he was forgiven, but he didn't. I felt he didn't deserve to know.

The whole thing began to bother me. I knew that I was forgiven; Jesus went to great lengths to let me know it. He put myriad reminders of His forgiveness all through His Word. Whenever I prayed and asked Him to forgive me, I knew He had. He would let me know. That sweet, holy presence and comfort would seep into my soul after my prayers of confession. He loved me enough to constantly reassure me that I was a forgiven child of His. I didn't tell anyone, but I began to ache for Willie—for his hurt, for his soul, and for the condemnation he lived beneath.

On the outside I resisted the idea of an encounter with Willie—I had spent my whole life avoiding him. Even if I had an inkling to talk to him, Bill quashed it.

"Heather says maybe I should go and talk to Willie and tell him I've forgiven him," I said, testing the waters. "What do you think?"

"No," Bill said flatly, "you definitely should not. Heather doesn't know what that would do to you—I do! You don't need to put yourself through that!" Then as if to justify his answer he said, "God doesn't expect you to put yourself through that to prove you've forgiven him. It's too big a risk! It could open up old wounds needlessly and cause a lot of damage. It's not up to you to tell Willie he's forgiven—that's God's job, if Willie asks Him!"

The truth, though, was that Heather was on to something. The timing was not yet right, but she planted a seed in my mind, and though it would take several years, that meeting was destined to take place. God was merely preparing me for the possibility. Not much more was said about it for the next six years—but the thought of Willie going through his whole life feeling and living like an animal, disturbed me. I hoped he would call out to God. I knew that if God could help me forgive him, Willie needed to know God would forgive him, too. But it was not only me that God would have to work on; Bill's mind was set in stone.

Throughout our marriage, Bill and I had always been of a mind to work out problems. We would tell our married children, "If you had to argue all night, that's fine; but don't come home—stay and work it out!"

It wasn't that we would have locked our kids out if they were in trouble, but all of our children knew it would be seen as a failure to give up on a marriage. During the struggles our daughter endured in her marriage and the subsequent break-up, we mistakenly sided with her husband. Our son-in-law looked like a victim of an unstable woman. Shawn, without seeking help or telling us there was much wrong, took drastic steps to get out of a situation in which she felt trapped. I've learned since that we were blinded by our own expectations and denial. Knowing our strong views, Shawn hadn't said anything negative to us about her husband. Instead, she chose to put up with things until they reached intolerable levels; and then took the fastest and most desperate way out.

Neither her solution nor ours was a mature or spiritual response. We concluded that our daughter must have been drifting from the Lord for some time to act out like she did. While it's true her actions were not typically Christian, for the first few months we didn't see how culpable all the people involved were. We regret not seeing the problems earlier on and helping our girl find other routes to take. But then, nobody else saw it coming, either.

By 1996, Shawn was separated from her husband, living with another man, and divorce proceedings were pending.

While all of this was taking place, I began to get concerned for Heather. After moving back to St. Catharines from Peterborough, she seemed to drift. Her worldview became very liberal, and she felt drawn to experiment with things she had left alone in her teenage years. She'd had children young, a daughter, Brooke, and a son, Dylan, and at twenty-five tried to recapture a life she thought she'd missed. Always outgoing and social, Heather coasted away from her marriage commitment.

Once again, Bill and I were clueless. Heather never indicated that she was lonely and hurting inside. In January 1997 she went out West to visit Shawn. After five days there, she came home, packed up, and left with the kids. For the second time in five years, one of our children's marriages was breaking up. Heather stopped coming to church after the breakup, and she stopped talking. She felt like a failure and a villain, and said "if we refused to support her without knowing all of the facts" that was fine with her. Bill and I were reeling.

Through their break-ups, our relationship with both of our daughters was strained. They were angry with us. They accused us of being legalistic and judgmental—and we were. We couldn't believe they took the actions they did to solve their problems. If there was one thing that we stressed as we raised our kids, it was to persevere. Marriage was worth fighting for, and it certainly looked as if they had given up too quickly. What we did not know was the severity of the verbal and mental sparring each of them endured. By the time they left, each of them was suffering an all-time low in terms of self-esteem. They were ripe for the picking. Anyone who was kind to them, who treated them with a modicum of respect, became their ticket out of Hades. When Shawn and Heather left their marriages, they did so dramatically. When they made up their minds to leave their husbands, they had given up hope—they just wanted out! The only thing they could see was an exit sign.

With reconciliation removed as a possibility, Heather also refused to call herself a Christian. She was estranged from us— although we still spoke—for a couple of years. She blamed much of what took place in her life, as did Shawn, on the way they were raised. God was about rules that didn't work; none of them had much of a picture of grace. They both believed they were too messed up to be called Christians, yet were too miserable and desperate to stay in their hurtful relationships.

I felt like a complete failure. I found out that even Blake was not nearly the perfect son I thought he was, that there was much in his life that was hurtful and disappointing; things he had been very careful to keep secret, but that found their way to the light. My daughters both rejected faith in Jesus (though Heather never said she didn't believe in God, just that she couldn't serve Him), and two of my six grandchildren were facing the hurt of divorce and the prospect of being raised in a broken home. I thought God had abandoned me. He had definitely broken the deal we had to give me a perfect life. I had suffered through separation; I had lived without my Dad; I knew the pain of rejection—and God was supposed to keep all of that from happening to my kids! The devil heaped thoughts of degradation upon me. I thought I had been a terrible mother and that God was punishing me for my pride.

The "deacon's family" was a mess and I knew it was my fault. The devil pounded me with condemnation and I took it. I thought I deserved it. I was inconsolable.

Through all of it, though, Bill was steady. He hurt—but he never lost faith. We decided to join a special Tuesday morning prayer meeting where parents of adult children who were not serving God gathered to pray for their prodigal children. We took comfort from the others in that room. There was no judging. We were all in the same boat: we raised our kids to love God, and our kids refused. We did the best we could. We weren't perfect, but we loved our children; and yet none of the ones we were praying for were currently following Christ. At seven o'clock on Tuesday mornings, we wrapped our arms around each other and called upon God to intervene in our kids' lives. We shed tears. We bared our souls. We honestly admitted our weaknesses and shortcomings, and we confessed an absolute dependence upon God because we had no answers left. If God was going to save our kids, God was going to have to do it. They were no longer listening to their parents. Blake's words rang in my ears, "You're gonna have to do your beggin' on your knees." That's where I was—I was on my knees, and I was begging God to reach my girls.

That prayer meeting sustained us over the next six months—and then, God began to move.

CHAPTER 18

Brutal Honesty

Truth. Everyone says they want it, but I was learning how brutal truth could be. It's raw and cutting. In my world, the world inside my mind, truth had always been limited. I didn't mind the truth expressed about others, but I certainly did not embrace honesty directed toward me—especially when it revealed something negative. Instead of listening to truth that hurt, I avoided it. I refused to consider or discuss anything in relationships that could hurt me. My children, convinced that I couldn't handle the truth (that I would blow up in anger or retreat from it), carried on pseudo-relationships with me. After years of relating this way, they had it down to a science. *Tell Mom only what she wants to hear. Make her happy. Keep the peace. Hide your true lifestyle. Don't disappoint her.* These were the unspoken mottos my girls lived by. Things between us were best when kept on the surface, but I wasn't satisfied with that. I longed for deep and meaningful relationships with my daughters. Our casual, phony interaction held no intimacy, but I didn't know how to change things; I didn't know how to be real. I presumed that they had the problem and that we couldn't really be close emotionally until they moved closer toward me. I was waiting for them to move.

My whole life, I had trouble with forgiveness. I found it difficult, nearly impossible, to forgive people when they disappointed me.

317

Ultimately I would end up pardoning the indiscretion—but it would take time. It was soothing to stew in my anger and disappointment, letting people really know how much they hurt me. Once they felt my pain, once they were in the throes of guilt, then slowly I would begin to forgive them. I would forgive in bits, managing the relationship frugally, giving back only as much approval as was absolutely necessary, teasing them and making them pay for days or weeks until full relationship privileges could be restored. It wasn't conscious on my part. It was just the way I reacted to people hurting my feelings. It never mattered whether or not what they said was true; I couldn't get past the offense to consider its validity. It hurt, therefore, it was wrong.

In the latter part of the Eighties, my attitude about forgiveness began to change. Pastor Counsell preached a message from the Old Testament, centered upon the bitter waters of Marah. (See Exodus 15:22–27.) The people of Israel were dying because the water was polluted. Moses, under God's direction, performed a miracle to purify the bitter water. Our pastor likened that bitter water to a spiritual condition of unforgiveness that we allow to exist in our lives. Unforgiveness that we refuse to give to Christ becomes a cesspool—a poisonous stench that slowly kills others. I was deeply convicted about the cesspools I had allowed to fester in my life.

Within a few weeks, he preached a second sermon on forgiveness from Matthew. I had read Jesus' words before, but somehow their impact had been lost on me. "For if you forgive men when they sin against you, your heavenly Father will also forgive you. But if you do not forgive men their sins, your Father will not forgive your sins" (Matt. 6:14–15, NIV). The words jumped off the page! I had to show Bill.

"Have you ever seen this in the Bible before?" I asked excitedly.

"Sure, lots of times," he replied matter-of-factly, as if it were common knowledge.

"I guess I just haven't seen it before," I said sheepishly. "I really need to make sure I forgive people. I don't think I am a very good 'forgiver.'"

I began to examine all the little grudges I held against others. I didn't want anything to block God's forgiveness to me, so how could I refuse to forgive others? It all made such beautiful sense. I

318

started looking at my emotions more closely, searching for signs of grudges and judgmental attitudes. It was the first taste I had of being honest with myself. I decided I would ask the Holy Spirit to search my heart for the truth I had so often ignored. I began to desire truth in my "inward parts"—my soul. (See Psalm 51:6.)

A few days later, I saw this same principle in the Lord's Prayer. (See Luke 11:2–4.) I couldn't believe it. I had recited that prayer hundreds of times but had never realized my forgiveness from God rested upon my willingness to forgive those that had sinned against me. I brought it up to Bill again.

"Bill, this means Willie! I really have to forgive Willie!" I asserted.

"But haven't you forgiven him?" Bill asked.

"I've said I've forgiven him, and God has honored my intention—you know by healing my memory—but sometimes feelings of real hate come back into my mind. I just kind of ignore them, but I really feel them. I guess I've been thinking of forgiveness as a one-time thing, and I'm seeing that in the Lord's Prayer, it's a continuous action, 'forgive me my trespasses, as I forgive those that trespass against me.' I think it's not just a one-time thing, Bill; I have to keep forgiving. Every time a thought of unforgiveness or hate comes into my mind, I have to exercise my will again—right then! I have to admit that I'm feeling unforgiveness and ask God to help me forgive it. It's like unforgiveness is always trying to get back into my heart. Forgiving is a constant process—I have to keep on doing it!"

The revelation was incredible. Bill looked at me as though everyone knew this; but to me it was new truth, and it was liberating.

From then on, each time I would have a bad thought about Willie (or someone else I had already made a decision to forgive), I would say a prayer and refuse to let that unforgiveness back into my heart. "Lord, you know that I've already forgiven him, so I take that "unforgiveness" thought captive and present it to you. It's against what I know to be true. I repent from it and bring it into captivity, casting it out of my mind." (See 2 Corinthians 10:4–5.)

Whenever I did this, instant peace replaced the angst I had felt only moments earlier.

All of this caused me to look at others differently. I saw homeless people and those with psychological problems in a new light.

"God," I often prayed, "that's who I would be if you didn't help me to forgive. I know it's you who has kept me sane. Thank You, Lord, for helping me."

I knew that my ability to live a normal life, to stay out of the mental institution, rested with God's supernatural forgiveness. I could not do it on my own, but with God's help I could forgive—and keep on forgiving, whenever the need arose.

Five or six years later, however, when the marriages and lives of my daughters started falling apart, I failed to see that my disappointment in them was a form of unforgiveness. I was overwhelmed with grief at the way they were living. Without consciously realizing it, I began to treat my girls differently.

The prayer meetings with those few other couples ended. Tuesday mornings had become inconvenient for most, and we couldn't find an alternative time to meet. We agreed to keep praying for each other's children regardless, resolving to stay in touch. The closeness and community that I had found so vital for the past six months, was gone, leaving a gaping hole in my spiritual life. Realizing I needed others to help me trust God for my kids, I joined a women's small group Bible study, led by others in my church.

❧

It was 1997 and, in addition to all of my family problems, my doctor had just shut me down. After several EKGs and various other procedures, it had been determined that my heart had lost twenty percent of its strength. I was having trouble breathing while lying down, and a distinctive gurgling in my chest, caused by excess fluid in my lungs, scared me half to death. Bill was extremely concerned. The cardiac specialist diagnosed me with "silent heart disease" and told me that, without notice, I could have suffered a massive coronary. I didn't have any pain, but the doctor explained that a certain percentage of heart-disease patients were like that. There would be no warning signs other than shortness of breath; I could just collapse and die.

The news was devastating. Though I had had diabetes for twenty years, I had led a very active life. I was only fifty-three years old and this doctor was telling me my life was effectively over. Within one week I had to drop everything. I had walked four or five miles every day for twenty years—that had to stop. The cardiac specialist told Bill I wasn't to go by myself, and that when I did walk, I had to take it easy; instead of walking four or five miles in an hour, I must only walk one or two in that time. He suggested that I quit work, too. I was to stay home. All stress had to be reduced. That meant the singles ministry that Bill and I had built up to fifty people over the previous four years was out, too. I had to quit everything, cold turkey. I was alone, at home, involved in nothing, contributing nothing, and utterly depressed. If all of this was supposed to reduce the stress in my life, it failed miserably. I was used to being busy. I felt incapacitated and worthless. I sat at home trying unsuccessfully to keep myself occupied. Once again, I was angry with God. "Lord! I'm fifty-three and my life is over! How can all of this be happening to me?"

∽

"All of this" included other unresolved issues with God. I still hadn't gotten over our business failure five years earlier. In 1992, just before all of the personal troubles began with Shawn and Heather, the business Bill and I had worked together to build up over a twenty-year period, crashed. For the first time in Canadian history, a Life Assurance Company had been declared insolvent by the federal government. We arrived at our office a few days before Christmas to find the sheriff present and all the doors locked. For the next nine months we went without any income. All of our savings and retirement investments disappeared as we tried to keep our heads above water. Just when things were going so wonderfully, and Bill and I were making the best money in our lives, it was all taken from us. At forty-eight years of age, we were starting over financially.

My security was stripped from me, and I felt exactly like the little girl on Sherbourne Street when the hydro was cut off and there weren't enough groceries to eat. By the time our major underwriter was purchased out of receivership, we had nothing left. We made the difficult decision to stand by our clients, refusing to jump ship. We thought that was the right decision. We put our clients first, but some of them left anyway—too scared to wait for a resolution. By

August of 1993, Bill and I had a condo, mortgaged to the maximum, and nothing else. We had lost everything.

❧

Now, in 1997, the only activities reserved for me were church services and my ladies' small group Bible study. In that circle of ladies, I could unburden myself—and that I did. I'm so grateful for all of those ladies! They went through one of the darkest periods of my life with me, and gave me hope that God would answer prayer and things would change. It seemed to me that I had lost my "Christian" family (they weren't dead physically, but most of them were spiritually), Bill and I had lost our reasonably affluent lifestyle and our financial security, and, now, I had lost my health. I literally felt like a modern version of Job. The topic of study during that spring in the ladies group was "Experiencing God"—and at that point, He was all I had; all else was lost. There were no more distractions. If I couldn't experience God now, I never could.

When I complained to Blake, he kept saying things I didn't want to hear. "Mom, I know it's hard, but use this time to slow down—get to know God more deeply. You can learn a lot in solitude." I resented most of what Blake said to me then. He was very much like his father—always trying to get me to see some lesson or learn some principle. The truth was that I didn't want to slow down, I didn't want to get quiet before God, and I didn't want to learn some grand lesson in the solitude. I wanted my life back!

One morning in the fall of 1997, a fleeting thought flashed across my mind. I was having my personal devotion time with God and I thought, *Wouldn't it be nice to go visit Shawn?* I didn't think much of it at the time; it was just one of the hundred random thoughts that leap into our minds throughout a day.

We had never gone to visit Shawn, who was living in Alberta. She had lived in Canmore, near Banff, for over three years. At first she lived with the man she had met at the Banff Springs Hotel; then, when that relationship broke down, she quickly moved in with another. We spoke on the phone, but even then our talks were strained. At some point in every conversation one of us would sabotage the phone call. The way that she was living bothered me. She was so liberal—without morals. She talked of her involvement in things I couldn't conceive of; things that I purposefully stayed a million miles away from: drinking and partying. I hated how she wanted to be so honest with me, telling me what was going on in her life. I would listen up to a certain point, holding my tongue, but then say something—something I shouldn't have. I couldn't help myself.

I told myself it was because I cared so much about her; that I couldn't stand to see her lost, without Christ and living for every lustful desire she had. But truthfully, I couldn't believe she had traded in every value we had ever taught her. It hurt when she told me her god was different. I would end up saying something that Shawn would take as judgmental. She would react defensively, telling me I could have a relationship accepting her as she was or I could have no relationship at all—the choice was mine. I don't know if I hijacked our conversations on purpose, feeling better if I wasn't too close to her, or if my heart was just so broken, I couldn't control my emotions. Either way the result was the same: Shawn and I lived three thousand miles apart; but that was relatively close, compared to the emotional and relational distance between us. When I tried to care, and share how I felt, Shawn felt judged and unloved. I thought that if I showed too much love to her, if she felt too comfortable in a relationship with me, then she would take it as approval. If there was one thing I did not want to communicate to Shawn, it was approval of the way she was living. I pulled back. I loved from a distance, with words—but not the right ones. Shawn felt pushed away. I felt hurt. We spoke mostly in safe terms, about safe things, as though we were strangers.

As a result, the thought of going to visit Shawn, staying in the same house as her and her commonlaw husband, was ludicrous. It was ridiculous. Shawn and I would fight the whole time. It would be nasty. Besides, the man she was living with didn't even believe in God. And they were living together, though Shawn wasn't even divorced from her husband. The whole thing was an unmitigated disaster. How could Bill and I stay there and condone what was going on?

In spite of all the reasons to the contrary, I thought of visiting her.

Shawn called in October, the week before our Canadian Thanksgiving holiday. "Mom, I've been thinking it would be real

323

nice for you and Daddy if you could come to Canmore and spend Christmas with me."

"Funny," I replied, "the other day I had the same thought. Let me talk to Dad, and we'll see if we can get there."

I got off the phone and instantly worried I had made the wrong decision. I thought that if we stayed with her and her boyfriend, we would be giving our blessing to their common-law relationship.

Bill didn't agree. He thought we just had to go and visit our daughter—that she was living with him regardless of whether we visited or not. Our visit could not possibly make the situation any worse, and it might just improve things. When we told some of our friends from church and some Christian family members, it became obvious where my thinking had come from.

People told us we would be sanctioning their unholy union. They thought that Bill and I would be incredibly uncomfortable sleeping in the next room, and that our assumed approval would prevent Shawn from coming back to the Lord. Some quoted scripture and became adamant that we were making a decision we would come to regret. Bill and I were of one mind however, and Blake reassured us that we were doing the right thing—reaching out to have relationship with Shawn regardless of her lifestyle. He reminded me that Jesus did the same thing, and He was criticized for it too—by the religious establishment of His day.

As we prepared to go, Blake gave his usual speech to me: "Mom, just go and have a really great time with your daughter. Don't try to talk about the Lord. Just love her and make a memory. Okay?" He always wanted me to agree with him.

"Okay. I'll try my best. Pray for Dad and me. We don't really know if we're doing the right thing."

"Trust me! You're doing the right thing. You'll be happy you went. Say hello to Shawn for me."

Blake always spoke with confidence, like he was always right. He isn't always right, but he always sounds as though he is. But Bill and I had peace about the visit, and we determined to show God's unconditional love to our daughter.

Shawn has told me since that she didn't think we would actually come when she casually raised the subject of a visit.

During the two months leading up to Christmas, Rich Beuhler's radio show dealt with the subject of unconditional love. He described people who love, but don't show it—he was describing me. I loved Shawn, but I was realizing that she didn't feel it. My love to her was based on her performance, not her person. When she did things that hurt and disappointed me, I instinctively withdrew my love. It wasn't that I didn't love her; I just couldn't show it in the face of my grave disappointment. It hurt too much. With regard to wayward kids and family members, Rich said something I'll never forget: "Love must be unconditional, and when it is, it will win them back." At that moment I became focused, determined to win back my daughter by loving her.

We arrived for a ten-day visit over Christmas and New Year's and had the time of our lives. Bill and I decided we wouldn't even say grace out loud; we would bow our heads and quietly thank God for our own plates of food. Shawn, however, wanted to honor us and began asking Dad to pray before meals. We played cards, went sightseeing, and talked endlessly and easily. Shawn's boyfriend seemed like a nice young man. He was kind and courteous, and seemed to genuinely enjoy our time together. We sat around each evening and reminisced about our times together as a family—and we laughed. Whenever we had been together as a family in the past, there had always been laughter. We have always teased and joked and been mercilessly sarcastic with each other. That sense of humor can only be present, however, when everybody is secure and knows they're loved. The laughter that was missing in our relationship since Shawn moved to Alberta, returned during those ten days.

It wasn't as though Bill and I compromised. I got up each morning, just as I always did, and read my Bible. For me, devotional time had forever been a morning ritual. A few days into our visit, Shawn awoke earlier than usual and saw me reading my Bible.

"Oh, wow! That brings back memories," she remarked.

"What does?" I asked, lifting my eyes from the page.

"You know…just how it used to be—waking up, seeing you read the Bible like that," she said with a nostalgic look. "Some things never change."

"Sit down. Join me," I invited.

"No. No! I can't go there, Mom."

"Okay, I've read enough anyway," I said as I placed my Bible down and closed it. It was the only time in the whole ten days that anything about God was discussed. I put my Bible down and chose to talk to my daughter. I didn't think it was any big deal at the time, but it was significant to Shawn. She felt that I was accepting her as she was for the first time. That I would put the Bible down to spend time with her had more impact than I could have imagined. Shawn, after refusing to be a part of my devotions and relationship with Christ, was still loved and received. There was no disappointment showing on my face, and no guilt-laden comments came from my mouth. Putting the Bible down and engaging my daughter in conversation seemed to me to be the perfect thing to do—and it was.

Bill and I returned home. We had had a great time. There were no fights, no arguments, and no discussions about faith. As far as we knew, nothing had really changed. Shawn was no closer to giving her life to Christ. The only difference was that we had had ten days of letting each other know how important and loved they were. Shawn felt no obligation to be anyone but who she was at that time. She was being open and honest in the state in which she was living, and my response was not to judge her. Shawn and I had begun a real and authentic relationship.

Three weeks after we returned home, I received a card from Shawn thanking me for loving her—and then she added as a postscript: "I'm talking about Jesus' love, Mom."

The fact that I hadn't mentioned Jesus was, in itself, an expression of His love to her. All of the forced conversations I had had about God in the past drove her from Him. I had to stop talking about God and just love like He does.

Unlike Blake, who almost always told me what he thought of my behavior, the girls never wanted to rock the boat. Shawn spent her teenage years, and even the first few years after she was married, putting on the image she thought I wanted to see. She masqueraded as a "good girl" every time I was around. She didn't argue with me if she could avoid it—anything to keep the peace. It was her way of managing my anger and disappointment in her. She wanted me to love her so much that she presented herself to me as someone I would find easy to love; but her life was a house of cards. When it all fell down and there was no image left to keep up, I had rejected her. I hadn't done it purposely, but I had been so disappointed in her behavior—the affairs, the divorce, and the promiscuity—that I had unknowingly removed the expressions of love from our relationship.

In talking to Blake about my relationship with Shawn back then, he revealed that, while referencing me, Shawn would often sing that pop song from mid-sixties: "You've Lost That Lovin' Feeling." The phoniness between us had just gotten easier to deal with. We both contributed to it. It was easier to be cordial and distant than real, truthful, and close. The trip to Canmore that Christmas began to change all that.

It began with me. I needed to forgive Shawn for not being the perfect daughter I had demanded—one who served God unswervingly; who had impeccable morals and a chaste, godly lifestyle. She was the daughter who failed to live up to my expectations, and I decided to love, accept, and forgive her anyway.

I began to reflect on my relationships with my other children. Despite the fact of Blake being in the ministry, I consciously thought about his shortcomings, failures and the ways he had disappointed me. I asked God to help me to forgive him too.

☙

When Heather's marriage failed, it strained the relationship between her and me. She drifted for the next six months, occasionally finding comfort in a bar, where she was well liked and where nobody judged her. One Saturday night as Heather sat in the bar she looked around at the people. She summed up in her mind how lost each of them were, and how no one in that room had anything to offer her or her children...and she decided she wouldn't go back. The next day she took her kids to the beach.

Though she refused to hang out in bars, she had no interest in going to church either, so she went to the beach instead. That afternoon she noticed a nice man with his son on the towel next to hers. She watched him for some time. He seemed to be so attentive to his boy—talking to him, playing with him. She decided to strike up a conversation with him. He was quiet and gentle, and real—not like most of the guys she met while drinking. She learned he was separated from his wife. The boy he was with was his stepson, yet they seemed quite close. Heather was impressed with his kindness and sense of responsibility.

The following Sunday Heather returned to the beach with her kids, hoping Al would once again be there. After a short search she spotted him and started up the conversation where they had left off the previous week. They began dating soon after and quickly fell in love, though neither of them was yet divorced.

Upon meeting Al, Bill and I immediately liked him. Although we had been hoping for a healing and reconciliation of Heather's marriagel, we accepted Al. We tried our best not to be judgmental of Heather and her situation, but sometimes our best efforts didn't cover our disappointment. Though Heather visited more often, we weren't close and usually ended up offending one another. Our relationship was formal and polite, but distant. Heather felt the undercurrent of our disapproval, though we said nothing. An unstated tension kept everyone in line, saying the safe things while steering clear of anything that might set the other off.

Within nine months Heather and Al bought a house and moved in together. Like Shawn, Heather was going her own way. We couldn't believe that our children had strayed so far from the way they had been raised, but this was another test. Would I love Heather authentically? Would I put aside the way she was living in order to have a real relationship with her? I decided I must.

Through all of this Heather was quite bitter and angry. She had decided that much of her troubles had been the fault of her parents and the way we brought her up. She was constantly saying that Bill and I had been too strict, that we didn't give her choices growing up, and that we were legalistic and judgmental. It hurt to hear her say it, but much of what she said was true…and God was working in us. Despite the progress I had made with Shawn, I still had to work to be accepting when things didn't please me. It was so much easier to judge than love.

"God, help me to forgive Heather. Help me to love her unconditionally too—and not just her, but Al as well," I prayed.

I determined that I would not wait until my adult kids were perfect in my eyes before I would love them—and show it. The huge burden of anger, frustration, and disappointment began to lift from me as I learned to love my kids all over again.

Heather was hurting financially around the same time my health was deteriorating. Because the doctor had told me to reduce my workload, Bill and I were looking for part-time help in the office. We had been interviewing, looking for the right person to take on secretarial and office management duties, when a colleague got our attention. His suggestion would make all the difference to the relationship between Heather and me.

He asked, "Why would you hire a stranger when your own daughter needs a job?" Neither Bill nor I had an answer. We knew the answer; we just didn't want to say it.

Things were hanging by a thread between us. Bringing Heather into the office as a subordinate seemed risky. We could lose the little we had that was positive. What if she didn't work out? What kind of atmosphere would it create in the office to have all of us working together? Bill and I didn't mention it to Heather right away because we were terrified of the consequences should the experiment fail.

Our friend's words lingered in our minds. Feeling convicted by God for not helping our daughter when it was in our power to do so, we offered Heather the position. She was thrilled. Though she slowly warmed up to Bill and me, she didn't want to hear anything about church, or God, or the Bible. She sounded angry and hard whenever these subjects were raised. Bill and I tried not to push the envelope and worked at being loving and accepting—and things improved.

Nothing had really changed, and yet *everything* had. The bitterness and unforgiveness, the blame and guilt that I had unwittingly pressed upon my kids were gone. I was able to love them and express that love, and they didn't feel as though they needed to earn it. God was loving my wayward kids through me. I felt invigorated and hopeful of our future, whether or not any of them returned to following Jesus.

ଔ

Four months after the Christmas trip to Canmore, in March of 1998, Shawn called Blake. She was upset over several things, but the central issue was a dying friend. "I know what she needs to hear, Blake," Shawn said. "She's facing death; she's scared and I know what could give her peace—but I can't tell her! I'm not living it. She needs hope and I can't give it to her!"

She continued to pour her heart out to her brother, who had always been a close friend and confidante. "Blake, I'm sick of the way I'm living—sick of it! I can't be faithful in relationships, my whole life is a lie, and I'm miserable!" By now tears were flowing and she was so broken she could hardly get the words out.

"Shawn," Blake offered quietly, "Shawn, you know what you need to do, don't you?"

"Yeah, I know," she stammered, "I know." With that admission she hung up the phone.

Two days later she phoned Blake back. This time her voice was totally different. She was excited and enthusiastic. There was no sign of the despair and tears present only two days before. "I did it!" She exclaimed. "Blake, I did it! I got saved!"

"When? How?"

The other night, you know, when I got off the phone with you. I did what you said. I just told God I was sick of the way I was living and asked Him to forgive me and to come into my life. I asked God to take over the mess my life is in. He did! He really did! And I've been to church already too. I went to a Bible study the other night. Blake, this time I'm serious with God. I really want to grow."

Stunned, Blake listened on the other end of the phone as Shawn told him that a big part of her decision came as a result of our visit a few months previous.

"Mom and Dad came and just loved me, Blake. Ever since then I've just wanted to stop the way I'm living. They showed me real love—Jesus' love! I just knew that Jesus could love me and forgive me if Mom and Dad could."

Blake congratulated her and hung up the phone. She was about to call me and tell me the news. In the moments after her call, Blake prayed that this decision would stick. He had seen Shawn go through many ups and downs over the years when it came to a relationship with Christ. He hoped and prayed this time was real—but he was skeptical.

Shawn grew quickly. Six months after she got saved, she moved back to Ontario to live with Bill and me. She realized that her common-law relationship was beyond repair, and, as a baby Christian, she knew she needed to take some time to learn to put God first. She urgently wanted to be alone with God. Her goal was to read the Bible through seven times, attend Bible studies, and pray. She wanted to devote her life to God, and when He would let her, she would go back to Canmore—only then.

During the six months before she moved home, a blossoming friendship began to take shape with Craig, a business associate, who had come to her little church shortly after she had. He had committed his life to Christ as well, but, apprehensive that their friendship might become romantic, Shawn came home. She wanted to develop a closeness with Jesus, before doing so with any other man.

Our commitment to Shawn was open-ended. She didn't know when she would be strong enough to return to Alberta, and she wanted Craig, the friend she truly cared for, to have his own relationship with God, independent of hers. If he meant business with God, he would continue to grow while they were apart. If there was a future for them as a couple, God would have to work that out. Right then, Shawn's priority was to get close to God.

Bill and I fixed up the spare bedroom at the condo and allowed our thirty-four-year-old daughter, who hadn't lived with us for sixteen years, back into our home. It wasn't easy. Shawn had lived a very self-indulgent life, and no one would ever accuse her of being a neat freak. I had to learn, over the next seven months, to let the little things go and to support her in her quest to become a disciplined, committed follower of Christ. I didn't always succeed.

The seven months Shawn lived with us during her sabbatical were as much a time of growth and change for me as they were for Shawn. She absolutely refused to be phony. Shawn had lived lies for years and she would only stand for truth between us. She was learning to "speak the truth in love," and I was chosen to be the major recipient. (See Ephesians 4:15, NIV.) Repeatedly, she would point out my manipulative and controlling tendencies. When I justified the way I treated people because they hurt me, she called me on it. When I would want to sulk and give people the silent treatment, she pushed me to talk. She was growing, but I was miserable. I started to see how God was using my own newly saved daughter to teach me things I had refused to learn.

During those seven months, Shawn went through a time of complete deliverance. She had believed all kinds of lies her whole life, and she needed to expunge them from her mind. She had believed she was worthless, and that her life of promiscuity and sexuality couldn't be helped—that it was "who she was." As she exposed the lies she had believed, then renounced the things that perpetuated them, freedom came. The things that had entangled her for years no longer bound her, and she was in no mood to put up with anything judgmental or legalistic, especially from me. If there wasn't a scriptural basis for a belief, she wouldn't accept it. Shawn was teaching me to let go of the things by which I judged others. I began to discover that I was not the spiritually mature person I thought I was. Shawn felt free to speak truth into my life—daily.

It hurt. I didn't want to face much of what she saw in me. We hadn't lived together for years, and I hadn't been close to her, yet because Jesus was overcoming so much in her life, I forced myself to take what she was telling me. I had failed to see my controlling and manipulative nature and how self-absorbed I had become.

Everything in my mind was centered on me. How could God let all of this happen to me? How could he take away our business? How could my health be failing? These were the questions I constantly asked. Even the fact that my children rebelled against God and rejected the way they were raised was somehow all about me. How could my girls rebel and do this to their mother? The truth is, it wasn't about me at all. They had to find Christ for themselves. They were not intentionally trying to hurt me. I had made it a personal insult, not them. I had been mad at God, mad at them, and mostly mad at myself. I told myself that I hadn't been a godly enough mother, that I was a poor example. I heaped all of this upon myself, as though it were up to me to save my girls. God was showing me that all these thoughts stemmed from pride, and He was requiring me to repent from it.

I had to realize that God doesn't have grandchildren. My children needed a personal revelation of God for themselves. They had to come to the end of their own might and strength and admit that they needed Jesus. It wasn't about me at all. The circumstances of their lives formed the journey for them to discover the wonders of

God's grace. I had to let God, in His sovereignty, pursue my children His way.

As much as I hated to admit it, I had taken on many of Mom's manipulative ways. She loved it when she got her way, and when she didn't, she manipulated. I didn't feign illnesses like she did, I simply punished people with silence or guilt-trips. When others hurt me, I wanted them to feel my pain, so I stopped demonstrating my love. I had become a manipulator of love. If you pleased me, I expressed my love. If you didn't, I withheld love. I would either withdraw or, worse, lash out.

These are the things Shawn began to show me. She suddenly cared more that I knew the truth than whether or not there were good feelings between us. Shawn began to value truth and authenticity more than peace. Once I saw how I was truly behaving, real healing and closeness in our relationship returned.

I would arrive at home and Shawn would be reading the Bible. Hardly ever did I arrive unexpectedly that I didn't find her fervently reading, studying. For as long as I could remember, Shawn had been a television addict. Now all she wanted to do was fill herself up with God's wisdom and insight. In our many discussions she would quote the Bible to back up her opinions, and she accepted nothing without a scriptural basis. She challenged her traditions and everything she had been taught. If I had only a traditional explanation or cultural reason for thinking in a certain way, Shawn challenged me on that too, asking where that belief came from in the Bible.

Shawn found it essential to be open about everything. She had led a very promiscuous life for twenty years. As she healed, she wanted to talk to both Bill and me about the lies she had believed and how God was teaching her truth. The details were hard to hear, and Bill and I would have to force ourselves to listen, knowing that she needed to purge herself of everything she had done in secret and under the cloak of a lie. No subject between Shawn and me was taboo. She felt new freedom and was determined to live in it.

As with me, healing was complete within Shawn as she opened up to the Holy Spirit. Praise and worship became a central part of her life. She renewed her acquaintance with the Holy Spirit and coveted His infilling. When she worshiped at home or at church, it was with unconscious abandon and she was full of love and adoration to Jesus. It reminded me of Mary Magdelene, to whom Jesus referred when he said, "Her many sins have been forgiven—for she loved much. But he who has been forgiven little loves little." (See Luke 7:47, NIV.) Shawn had found much forgiveness and she loved Jesus with all of her heart. All Shawn wanted to talk about was God, the Bible, and new truth she was learning. God was busy transforming her before my eyes; and through her, He was demanding much more of me.

The emotional upheaval was grueling. The constant self-analysis tired me out. It was a good thing I couldn't be as busy as before, because I needed all of my strength just to deal with what God was trying to change in me. I thought all of this turmoil would hurt my newfound relationship with Shawn, but instead we were closer than ever. Many times I took a few days to accept the things she told me, fighting the ever-present desire to withdraw and give up on the whole idea of being close to her—but somehow I didn't. We became the best of friends. God was pruning; our relationship was getting healthier. I discovered Shawn loved me regardless of the warts on my personality. I loved her, too. I admired her for pursuing God with such unmitigated urgency. Living with Shawn brought back an excitement to my walk with God. Like her, I wanted truth more than ever.

Lying had always been a part of my life. Sometimes I didn't even know it was there—I just exaggerated. Feeling so poorly about my home, my family, and the abuse I had been through, it had always been easier to lie my way through it. Pretending things were different had been the way I coped with circumstances I didn't like. God began to deal with me about my exaggerating. I decided to make myself accountable to Shawn and to Bill. I asked them to correct my accounts of events that were inaccurate, and to tell me when I wasn't being truthful. I was surprised at the frequency of their admonitions, but it started to change my view of myself.

I was becoming a truthful person—the real Margaret Davidson—and learning to like who she was. Brutal honesty was shaping me into the person God wanted me to be; healing me and making me whole. At last I was embracing truth.

334

છ

In May of 1999, Shawn—a mature and beautiful woman of God—returned to Canmore and married Craig. (Their relationship had developed through long-distance phone calls while she lived with us.) Craig had secretly made the wedding arrangements and Shawn was not to know the day or time. Just as in Middle Eastern weddings when Jesus walked the earth, the wedding day would be a surprise. Craig gave Shawn enough notice to make herself ready, and then they traveled up into the Alberta mountains with their pastor and a few friends. In a mountain lake, both of them were baptized in water and then married in a simple ceremony. It was the second marriage for both of them, and they wanted it to be based in Christ. Shawn phoned us afterward. She was as happy and excited as she had ever been. God was blessing her and restoring what the enemy had robbed her of for so many years.

A month after Shawn went home to Canmore, we embarked upon our annual four-week-long vacation at the cottage. While there, Heather and Al, Blake and Christine and all of the kids spent time together; and although Heather and Al were still living together unmarried, we welcomed them to stay with us. Bill and I decided to stop trying to play God and judge. Instead, we viewed the cottage vacation as a time to love them and build family relationships.

Rudy and Karen Krulik came to visit as well, and we spent nearly a week together with our best friends. They were preparing to go on a motorcycle trip to the east coast of the United States with three other couples. "Marg, you and Bill should get a bike. It would be fun for you guys to come with us next time!" Karen said.

"I don't think so," I joked, "At our age that would be asking to go to heaven early."

"Yeah, but what a way to go!" Karen quipped back.

We were barely home a week when the phone rang. I couldn't believe what I was hearing. My pastor was on the line. "Margaret, I have some bad news. Karen and Rudy have been involved in a motorcycle accident in Maine. Rudy is badly injured. He's lost his leg—he isn't expected to make it—and Karen is dead. I'm trying to get hold of their children; they don't know yet."

I was in shock and couldn't believe this was happening. We had just seen them a week before!

After hanging up with the pastor, I phoned Blake and Christine in Oakville, then called Heather.

"Heather, Honey, I have unbelievable news," my voice was broken and she knew something terrible was coming. "Honey, Uncle Rudy and Aunt Karen had a motorcycle accident. Uncle Rudy is hurt badly and Aunt Karen didn't make it. Honey, she died." Suddenly the situation was more than I could bare and I burst into tears. Heather joined me on the other end and we cried for a few moments. "I'm not sure Susan knows yet, and they're having a hard time getting a hold of Neal at work. I'm going to head over to Susan's and see if I can be of some help."

"I want to go too, Mom. I'll meet you over there." Heather and Susan had been friends since they were kids, and Blake and Neal were still close. Heather and I arrived moments after Susan heard the news, and we stayed with her most of that evening.

Doctors initially kept Rudy in a hospital in Maine, but after five days he was sufficiently stable to be flown home to a hospital in St. Catharines. He had lost his leg and suffered multiple broken bones, but his prognosis had changed and now he was expected to recover fully.

Karen's funeral was eight days later in our home church in St. Catharines. Rudy insisted on coming to the funeral and was to arrive by ambulance. The Kruliks had led a worldwide ministry and were well known all over North America. As a result the church was full—friends gathered at the church until more than 1,200 people were present

While waiting for Rudy to arrive from the hospital, our pastor's wife played hymns softly on the piano. After about fifteen minutes, it became obvious to all there that Rudy was having difficulty getting to the church. Quietly at first, a small group of people at the back of the church began to sing the hymns. There was no song leader; people just began to sing. Within minutes the whole place was singing by heart the words to the great old hymns of the church. The presence of the Holy Spirit descended in that place that day. The volume of praise reached levels uncommon on a Sunday morning, and twelve hundred people worshiped God for an hour-and-a-half, without interruption, until Rudy arrived by ambulance.

Rudy came into his wife's funeral amid the sounds of a congregational choir singing. While we all worshiped, a real and tangible joy filled that place. If you were a Christian, you could sense hope and overcoming victory. Karen may have died, but she was in heaven, and everyone in the room knew it.

Blake sat beside me. Next to him sat my daughter-in-law, Christine, and finally, Heather. From the moment the singing started, Heather was shaken. She had lost someone closer than most of her relatives. Heather, along with the rest of our children, had always addressed her as "Aunt Karen." The room was full of praise and hope, and yet inside of Heather's heart there was none. These people were crushed; their pain was great, and yet they sang with real joy and peace. Heather had no peace. She was far from God and she felt wrenching anguish at Karen's death. In those moments she thought about sitting at her own mother's funeral. *What if it had been her mom who had died? What if she were in Susan's place?* She thought about her life, how her own family had broken up and how she had run from God. Longing to know and experience the peace she witnessed that day, she resolved in that hour-and-a-half of spontaneous worship to change the way she was living.

The whole funeral was one of the most beautiful services I have ever attended. Rudy was helped onto the platform and spoke about God's sustaining power and victory, despite experiencing the greatest personal loss in his life. Bill, as Rudy's best buddy for forty years, eulogized Karen and honored our friendship. But the most moving moment came as Neal, Karen's son, sang a tribute to his mom. Incredibly, Neal kept his composure while everyone else in the church cried. When he finished, the whole place erupted in tearful praise. Hope was not lost that day; but rather, confirmed—for Heather, too.

It had taken the death of my best friend—Heather's "Aunt Karen"—to bring Heather back to full relationship with Jesus. Over the next couple of years she continued to grow in Christ and, in October of 2001, while she and Al were visiting Blake's church in Oakville, Al walked the aisle and committed his life to Christ. What made this even more special was that Al did so as Rudy Krulik, who was guest speaking that day, gave the invitation.

337

Heather and Al, married since December 2000, were now united in Christ as well as marriage. God was answering our prayers.

Since then, both Shawn and Heather have expressed how important our unconditional love was to them while their lives were in turmoil. Heather told us how much it meant to her when we hired her in the midst of her most desperate financial hardship. What felt so risky at the time became God's toolbox, enabling me to rebuild my relationship with my daughter. The same thing was true of visiting Shawn before her conversion. God was teaching me to love my own daughters in spite of their immoral lifestyles, to accept them, and to build bonds with no strings attached. I had to do with Shawn and Heather what Jesus had done with me: love me. While I was a sinner and while still in my sinful state, He died, in order to draw me to Himself. (See Romans 5:8, NIV.)

None of these victories came without pain and hardship. Heather went through a crisis in her relationship with Al within a couple months of Karen's funeral, a cancer scare the following spring requiring a hysterectomy, and then the decision to get married, not knowing if Al would ever embrace faith in Christ. During those times, God allowed me to be her friend, to listen to her, to cry with her, and to share my undying support for her. Very quickly Heather came to know how special she was and how much her father and I loved her. Because of that, nothing else mattered.

God used my daughters and their brutal honesty with me—their insistence on being open and truthful—to conform me to the image of God's Son; but that was not His only device. During all of these turbulent times with Shawn and Heather, God was intent on creating something new out of another dysfunctional, unthinkable relationship—the worst relationship I had ever known with any living person. The beauty He created out of that ugliness is almost too mind-boggling to comprehend. Only God could have done it— because what He accomplished is impossible.

CHAPTER 19

Full Circle

I never forgot Heather's words to me after her reconciliation with Blake in 1992. Bill wished I would forget, but I couldn't get them out of my mind: *Somehow Willie needs to know that you have forgiven him.*

Even when my mind was elsewhere, her words would penetrate my thoughts and I couldn't shake them. I would go a few weeks without thinking about it, but then the words would break through again until nearly all I could think about was the awful guilt Willie had to live with. Then I would think a desperate, horrible thought: *What if Willie goes to hell because I refuse to show him the power of Jesus' forgiveness?*

While this battle waged daily in my thoughts, my brother Ike was nearing death from prostate cancer. It had been a four-year battle and, in November of 1994, three months after Pete died, Ike was entering his last month. I loved Ike, and whenever I could I went up to the hospital to try and relieve his wife Jackie. I would bring him drinks of water, cold cloths and anything else that helped reduce his suffering. He was in tremendous pain, but loved it when I would read the Bible to him and pray at his side. Some days were better than others. On one of his good days, we had a conversation about Willie.

"You know, Ike, you are really the only person in the family who keeps in regular contact with Willie," I started. "And now that you're too sick to go...well, I've been thinking...I know it sounds ridiculous...but I've been thinking of going to visit him."

"Really?"

"Well, yeah! I don't know what you think about that, but if I wanted to go see him, I'd need to know how to find him."

"What would you say to him when you found him?" Ike's curiosity was piqued because, in my whole life, I had hardly said a thing about Willie. Most of the time, when his name came up in conversation, I took it as my personal responsibility to change the subject.

"I've been thinking lately," I continued, "that Willie doesn't know I've forgiven him. If I could, I would like to tell him that. Bill doesn't think it is such a good idea to open healed wounds, but I don't want him to die without knowing I forgave him. You probably don't think it's a very good idea either," I commented defensively.

"No. No, I think it's a good idea—talking to Willie, that's a good thing. I think it would be good for him to hear it."

Ike was thinking of the effect such a visit would have on Willie, about how it might make the difference for him, helping him to reach out to God. Other than from Heather, his was the first positive response I had had on the subject. Bill wasn't thinking about Willie and what might be good for him. He was my husband, my protector, my knight in shining armor; he was intent on sparing me any more pain. Once Ike encouraged me however, I set my heart on going through with it.

Ike died in December of 1994. In January of 1995, I shared with Tina and Dave what was in my heart to do.

"I'll go with you if you want," Dave offered. "If it will make you feel better, a little safer, I'll go along."

"Okay, then," I accepted. But I had conditions. "Dave, I don't want you to say anything. You gotta let me do all the talking and not interfere!" Dave agreed.

(As usual, I wanted to be in complete control. Part of me thought God was only testing me to see if I would trust Him enough to go through with it. I honestly felt I would get to Willie and God would say, "Okay, Margaret, you were willing to do what I asked of you. You met with Willie—good girl! Now I'm letting you off the hook; you don't have to bring up the whole sexual-abuse thing!"

340

I thought God would do for me what He had done for Abraham when Abraham was prepared to offer up his son Isaac on the altar of sacrifice. (See Genesis 22:11–12, NIV.) Contacting Willie was my Isaac on the altar; surely, God would find another way. By controlling the conversation, I wouldn't have to bring up anything I didn't want to. I wanted to be able to hear God say, "That's enough, Margaret; you can go home now," and I didn't want to miss it because Dave was talking.

I went home and broached the subject with Bill.

He listened intently for a long time, without saying much. "You know how I feel about the whole thing," he said quietly, "but I won't stop you. If you feel this is something God wants you to do, then do it!" He paused for a moment, fighting his own reservations, and then said, "I'll support you." That was all I needed to hear.

Ike had suggested that I visit Willie at the end of a month. By then he would have drunk away all of his money for the month and the chances of finding him sober were much greater. I heeded his advice. Dave and I showed up at his rooming house in the last few days of January—unannounced. That morning I woke up with an amazing sense of peace; I wasn't at all apprehensive or nervous. The day before, Sunday, I hadn't felt well. I spent most of the day sleeping. But when it hit me that this was the day David and I agreed to go see Willie, I was strangely calm. It would have been nice to have spent Sunday in church, praying and preparing for this day, but, being sick, I missed that opportunity. Despite feeling less than ready, God overshadowed me with His presence, and I knew that I was in the center of His will.

Due to the cold, Willie wasn't out begging. I stayed in the car while Dave went up to his room to find him. He told Willie to get out of bed and get dressed, that he would like to take him for coffee. Willie, never one to miss an opportunity for a handout, obliged. Ike had been right. Willie wasn't feeling too well, but he was sober and coherent. When I saw Willie walking toward the car, sober, I thanked God that our trip to Welland hadn't been wasted.

It suddenly occurred to me, as the two of them approached, that Dave and I hadn't even prayed before he went up to Willie's room—and there he was. When I stepped out of the car, Willie had

341

a surprised look on his face. "What are *you* doing here?" was all he could say.

"Well," there was a pause as I thought about how much I would let him know right off the bat, "I have something to say to you; and at the rate my brothers are dying, I thought I'd better come and talk to you before *you* die!"

Willie hadn't gone to either of his brothers' funerals. It hurt too much, and he couldn't deal with that much reality. Instead, a drunken stupor dulled the pain.

"Yeah, Margaret, only the good die young," he responded with a sigh. His mind was surprisingly alert despite his obvious physical need for alcohol. The irony of his retort wasn't lost on me. Willie—the town drunk, an embarrassment to all who knew him, a man alone in the world—had outlived Ike—the gentle, compassionate church deacon and family man. When he said it, I could feel the contempt and derision in which he held himself. He clearly felt Ike should still be alive and he should be the one who was dead. Even as he spoke, pity welled up inside of me. I couldn't explain it, but I felt sorry for this despicable, evil man—the man I had spent most of my life hating.

"So whaddaya say? Can I buy you a coffee?" I asked.

"Sure. You can buy me a coffee," Willie awkwardly conceded. "I can always use a coffee."

We crossed the street to the diner where Willie was a regular and sat down in an out-of-the-way booth. The moment we sat down, I could feel all eyes fixed on us. Everyone there knew "Boxcar Willie," and despite Willie's ragged appearance, both Dave and I looked enough like him for strangers to see the family resemblance. Willie had talked about having a mother, but as far as everyone knew he had no other family. When diner regulars saw me—a well-dressed woman in a business suit—and Dave—a tall, neatly groomed young man—it was obvious they figured out we were all siblings. The visual contradiction was too much for most, and involuntary stares seized them. I could hear their thoughts, *Boxcar has a family?*

Dave left the booth momentarily to order at the counter and I started right in, not wanting to lose my nerve. "I have something to say to you, and I want you to let me get it out without interrupting me, OK?"

342

He nodded yes.

"Willie I…really…well for a long time now, I have wanted to come and tell you something."

I had begun—now I would have to finish.

"I want you to know…" I paused to take a deep breath and gather my thoughts. "I want you to know that Jesus has healed me from the abuse you put me through."

Instantly Willie's face changed. He threw up his hands as though he were stopping traffic and started shaking his head. He didn't want me to go on. I am sure he would have left the booth if he could have, but Dave had returned and was blocking his way. The calm of moments before turned to extreme discomfort, and he was clearly flustered. He mumbled several phrases without finishing them, as though he could no longer string his words together, and every time he tried, he was unsatisfied with the results. The disjointed fragments carried a common theme of denial, and with each unsuccessful attempt at it, I worried he would get violent.

慘

As I sat across from him watching his reaction, I caught Dave out of the corner of my eye. He was sitting there beside Willie like a statue. He hadn't moved. His arms were folded and his face stern. Willie's sudden agitation hadn't fazed David one bit, and I couldn't help but think he was ready to get physical if need be.

My mind flipped back ten years to the time I first told Dave about Willie's sexual assaults on me. When he heard it, he said, "I'll kill him!" (Dave could take care of himself—he always had—and killing might not have been out of the question.)

"You can't kill him if I've forgiven him!" I had said. It hadn't been long, at the time, since Dave had committed his life to the Lord. He calmed down, wanting to do the right thing; but I could tell then, and the same was true at the diner ten years later, he was prepared to do battle if required. I wondered if Dave hoped Willie would get violent—then he would have to pop him.

Willie's violence was what Bill was afraid of. I learned later that Bill was distracted all that morning, unable to keep his mind on his work. All he could think about was the further injury Willie could inflict on me. He warned me that this whole experiment could blow up in my face and send me reeling backwards, emotionally and psychologically. When I got back to the office, Bill told me all he could do the whole morning was pray for me.

ॐ

Willie's reaction momentarily caused me to doubt my resolve, but suddenly, out of the depths of my gut, I felt a boldness well up within me—a sheer refusal to be intimidated.

"Wil! Be quiet!" I scolded as though he was a little boy misbehaving. "You agreed to be quiet and let me finish—now, do what you said and be quiet! Let me finish!"

I was stern, not gentle in the least, but under perfect control. I spoke with authority, but without raising my voice. No one else in the restaurant would have known what was taking place in our booth. I think it shocked him.

Willie calmed down and said, "OK."

Though the whole episode took place in seconds, it played out in my mind in slow motion. I hadn't leaped into this encounter naively. I had read that 99 percent of perpetrators of abuse deny it, so Willie's reaction, though unnerving, was predictable and hadn't thrown me off course. This initiative was never about Willie and his reaction—it was about facing my abuser and telling him that I had forgiven him.

"Willie, I just wanted to tell you that Jesus healed my mind over twenty years ago of the pain that you caused by what you did to me; and I'm here to tell you that I forgive you for all the pain you caused in my life."

With that, Willie's face seemed to soften, and the tension that was evident moments earlier, vanished. A cloud of utter humiliation swept over his being. "Well...uh...did that...did that really happen?" As soon as he said it, he knew he was as good as confessing, and he quickly gave up the pretense of denial. "I mean...well you don't *remember* all of that!"

"Huh! I remember much more than I care to tell you!" I shot back, incredulous that he could possibly think I had forgot ten years of his weekly attacks. "I was there when it happened, and I guess I ought to know!"

Now he wasn't arguing or being defensive at all. He looked the part of a convicted felon immediately before sentencing: meek, unassuming, and resigned to his fate.

Despite the firmness of my words, all of this had taken place in barely audible tones. Dave could hear and Willie could hear, but no one else could. There was no scene. Willie looked visibly shaken and Dave remained an immutable statue. Onlookers might have known something was the matter, but the details of that trouble had been kept between the three of us in that booth. I had not come to publicly castigate Willie; I had come to offer clemency.

I did it. I had finally addressed my abuse with my abuser. For forty years, nothing that took place Saturdays at 17 Sherbourne Street had been mentioned between Willie and me; and while it was not spoken of, it did not exist—at least for Willie. Through all the years and all the drunken stupors, Willie had tried to convince himself that I hadn't remembered a thing. He had pushed it out of his mind with an alcohol-driven bulldozer and surmised I had done the same, with or without booze. This day, in this diner, I had jerked him violently back to the reality—the cold, hard, sober reality—of his crimes.

We sipped our coffee for a moment and then I continued. "Willie, I spent a large part of my life praying you'd go to hell, because I didn't want to go to heaven if you were there." I paused and made sure he was looking right at me. "I don't pray that way anymore. Willie, Jesus helped me to forgive you in order to show you He'll do the same for you. Jesus will forgive you, too. Why don't you ask Him to?"

"I'm too far gone for that Margaret—I'm too far gone for that," he said as he bowed his head.

"Willie, listen. You're never too far gone for Jesus to forgive you." In that moment, incredible pity flooded my heart. He was so lost. He was so hopeless. Pathetic.

Dave hadn't said a word. True to his promise, he hadn't so much as cleared his throat. I was proud of him—it's not an easy thing for a Hiebert to keep quiet. "I'm going to go see about the bill," he finally interjected, assuming we were nearly finished. He got up from the table and went to the cash register.

As soon as David went to the front counter, the most amazing thing happened. Willie whispered something. "Margaret—I think I should say something to you too."

I braced myself.

"I think I should ask you to forgive me."

"But I have, Willie!"

"No, I need to *ask* you to. I had no idea that you could remember those things—what happened—and I need to ask you to forgive me!"

My eyes welled up. "Willie," I said, my lips trembling, "Asking me to forgive you is way beyond anything I ever expected or dreamed you would say today!" I looked right into his eyes. "Thank you. Thank you, but believe me when I tell you, I have already forgiven you!"

"Yeah, I know," he stammered, "but I needed to ask."

Just then David returned to the table. He could tell more had been said, since I was nearly weeping, but he didn't pry. We just walked Willie back to his room, got in the car and headed home. On the way home we talked about how gracious God had been to me that day and how marvelously everything turned out.

૦૪

God gave me much more than I thought possible from Willie that day. God told me to go. He impressed it upon my heart to speak to Willie about His supernatural healing and forgiveness, and I had hoped for a ram in the thicket, for a substitute at the last moment.[1] How thankful I was that there was no thicket, no ram and no back-up plan. God required that I personally deliver a gift of forgiveness; and in return He gave me Willie's confession and appeal for pardon.

"Oh, thank you, Lord," I prayed. "Thank you that you gave me the strength to do what you asked of me. Thank you that you didn't let me chicken out!"

God could not have given me a greater gift—in fact there has never been a blessing, before or since, that equaled it—than to hear Willie say, "Margaret, forgive me." God didn't want me to hurt any more than I already had, or to wonder for the rest of my life whether Willie knew the things God had done for me. God wanted me to

[1] Genesis 22:13, KJV

experience His joy—the joy God feels each time someone asks Him to forgive him; each time a sinner confesses his sin, and He gets to say, "I forgive you!" I got a picture that day of how God feels at the very moment someone is redeemed, bought back from the realm of the damned. I was experiencing heaven's joy, the kind of joy that comes only when forgiveness knows completion.

"God, help me never to doubt You again. Help me to trust in You always. I know You will never hurt me! You are such an awesome God! You are my wonderful, loving Heavenly Father, and I love You with all of my heart!"

I couldn't stop praising Him, and I couldn't wait to get back to the office to tell Bill!

∛

Dave and I left Willie, promising to be in touch. As we drove toward St. Catharines, I felt as though someone had injected me with a thousand cc's of adrenalin. Though I wanted to get back to the office, we were hungry and stopped for lunch. By the time we got back to Bill, it was two hours later than we had planned, and Bill had been worried. Thoughts of my exposure and vulnerability to Willie had been more than he could bear. When I arrived he couldn't be excited for me until his feelings of angst subsided. Soon he was as thrilled as I was. We both saw how God was making the most ugly things beautiful.

Confronting Willie had empowered me. No longer was I under any kind of oppression. I had been able to face the thing I feared the most, stare it down and say what I needed to say. Sexual abuse hadn't destroyed me. The evil that Willie inflicted on me no longer held any power over me. If I thought I was free twenty years before, after praying in Joan Jewel's living room, it was only because I didn't know how free I could truly be. The emotional high lasted for three weeks. I told everyone I could find how great God was and how He knew that this last step, as I followed His direction, was the last key to free me.

As I reflected on that morning visit with Willie, the irony was overwhelming. When I had said good-bye to him, I had even given him a hug—unthinkable as little as a month before. I hugged the man I had despised for years.

True to my word and motivated by the fact that Ike was gone, I phoned Willie once a month to see how he was doing and to talk with him. For the next two years I visited him eight or nine times, lending him some money, but more importantly showing him that someone still cared about him. I always called Ted the rooming-house superintendent, before I went. I would ask him to tell Willie I was coming and that, if I visited, he was to be sober and prepared to see me. In all the times I visited, Willie was never drunk. I never went alone—I always took Tina or Dave with me—and Willie was always reasonably well behaved.

Ted fashioned himself the rooming-house caregiver and saw my visits as opportunities to extract a little extra remuneration. He always gave me a long sob story about how he cared for Willie and looked after him, cleaning him up when he was sick and making sure he ate. His stories included unbelievable details of his own subsidy of Willie, claiming money came from his own pocket to keep Willie alive. I don't know how much he really did for Willie, but a part of me was glad someone was at least looking out for him; besides, Ted had a phone and Willie didn't. I would throw a few dollars his way to keep him quiet until the next visit. He was an aggravating leech, but served as the only halfway dependable link to Willie; so I did what I had to, to keep him on the job.

Mom was approaching her ninetieth birthday in January of 1998 when she got the flu. She had been living in Linhaven Seniors Home for over sixteen years, and thriving—despite the fact that that home was always "going to kill her." I visited two to three times per week, sometimes more, and our relationship, always rocky, had been quite good of late. As the secrets of my life have been exposed to the light, the light hasn't always shone flatteringly upon Mom; however, she did possess positive attributes. Though she wallowed in self-pity and manipulated everyone around her through guilt, she never abandoned us. She worked seasonally whenever possible (in the canning factory or tying grapevines in the vineyards of Niagara), and I had grown to admire her tenacity. Though she had a difficult time expressing love in words, her actions and commitment to providing for her children, proved her character.

No one ever visited Mom without hearing her predict her impending demise. "I had a terrible night last night," she would say. "I didn't tink I vould make it 'til da morning. I'm glat you came to see me today, because I vill not be in dis vorlt much longer; I coult go tonight. Ohhhh, I feel just awful!" She had gotten to eighty-nine years old, telling everyone she was going to die "that night," almost every day of those eighty-nine years.

When I visited her that Saturday in January, she didn't utter her usual warning. She was extremely weak and the nurses had called to let me know she was not fighting this particular flu well; even so, I was able to speak to her several times that day and she responded. In one of those conversations, she said something she never had before. I was sitting by her side, wiping her forehead with a cold cloth. She looked up at me and said, "I love you, Margaret."

Mom often responded, "Me too," or "I love you too" after I said "I love you" to her, but on this day, when she was so sick and I was by her side, she said it of her own free will.

"I love you too, Mom," I said.

As a nurse walked by the open door to her room she said, "Katarina, I'm sorry you're so sick!"

Mom responded, "I'll be better tomorrow." There wasn't the usual "I'll be lucky to make it through the night" comment. Then she said it again: "I'll be better in the morning." It was totally out of character, and I thought it an odd thing at the time for her to say—but its significance became apparent later.

I had spent nearly the whole day Saturday at Lindhaven. Dave had been there as well, and George had come the day before. Tina and Murray were vacationing in Florida. When I went home for supper and told Bill how sick Mom was, he encouraged me to spend as much time with her that evening as I wished. Bill went with me when I returned after supper, and we could see she was having trouble breathing. Earlier in the day David had told me he thought she had pneumonia. We both could hear the gurgling in her lungs as she drew every breath. The last thing Bill and I did before going home was to pray with her. We told her how much we loved her, and then went home to bed. She was calm and resting, but I was worried for her; I felt as though I had seen my mother for the last time and said as much to Bill.

I awoke to the phone ringing at four o'clock Sunday morning. It was a nurse from Linhaven. "I'm sorry to have to tell you this, Mrs. Davidson, but your mom just passed away."

I put the phone down and cried. Mom wasn't perfect, but we had been linked together for fifty-four years, and I loved her. All at once I felt like an orphan in the world. As I sat there with Bill holding me, it hit me: it was morning and Mom *was* better—she was in the arms of Jesus. Her words from the previous afternoon had come true. I felt God's indescribable comfort in that moment.

❤

I phoned Ted and arranged to visit Willie. When I told him Mom died, he cried. He cried like a baby. Maybe he knew that the only person who had loved and cared for him without condition was gone. To Willie, Mom's prayers for him were the one tangible human expression that said he mattered. Everyone has a mother—and now his was gone. If I felt like an orphan, Willie felt like a helpless, hopeless orphan. Ted told me later that Willie's health spiraled downward from the moment he heard of Mom's death.

Mom died in January 1998.

Just over one year later, in March 1999, Shawn committed her life to Christ. By November of that year, she had returned home to live with Bill and me in order to grow in Christ; and from the moment she arrived she began talking about visiting her Uncle Willie. So great was her own personal sense of forgiveness and pardon, she hoped it would make a difference for Willie. If he heard how Jesus had forgiven her, maybe he could believe Jesus would forgive him too.

In May of 1999 I phoned Ted. "Ted, it's Margaret Davidson. How are you?"

"Pretty good, but Willie's taken a turn and it's costing me a lot of my own money to keep care of him, ya know! He ain't been even walkin' lately—ya know, bad circulation an' all." Everything was always about Ted and how hard-done-by he was. He was always asking for money.

"Yeah, Ted, so you're always telling me. Listen, I want to come and see Willie. Both Tina and I are coming, and I'm bringing my daughter, Willie's niece. Make sure Willie is presentable and sober OK? Don't give him a drop to drink before we get there! We'll be there tomorrow morning."

"Well, I don't know…he's been pretty sick lately and, ya know, I've been lookin' after 'im day and night! I don't know if I can get 'im up outta bed, but I'll try. Hey, when you come, you think you could bring a couple extra bucks for his expenses?"

"Look, Ted," I got stern, "just make sure he's ready to see us and I'll see what I can do about throwing a few dollars your way!" Doubtful that Ted had listened to a word I had said, I repeated myself. "Just make sure he knows we're coming,"

"Yeah, OK! I hear ya. You'll be here tomorrow—no booze—I got it."

When the three of us arrived, we had to go to his room. Ted had been unable to get Willie out of bed. He wasn't well. I went into the room to see if I could motivate him to get up and go for coffee, but he just lay there on his small, dirty single bed. He had lost forty or fifty pounds since the last time I had seen him.

The room itself was tiny—like a jail cell—with barely enough room for his bed and a small nightstand. One undersized, dirty window let in the smallest imaginable amount of light—a blessing on some level, because the room was so grungy; but frustrating on another. The filth and resulting smell assaulted my senses as I walked over to the side of the bed.

"Come on, Willie, get up!" I said in a drill sergeant tone. "Tina and I are here to see you, and we brought your niece Shawn."

"Who?" Willie mumbled weakly.

"My daughter! Your niece, Shawn."

"Oh." Willie just lay there, his eyes closed. He was shaking as if he was cold.

"C'mon, Willie, I'll help you finish getting dressed. We'll go get a bite to eat. C'mon let me help you."

I went to his closet and pulled out a dirty, wrinkled shirt. As Willie tried to stand up, his pants hit the floor in a crumpled heap. With that, the strength in his legs left him and he flopped back down on the bed. I leaned over and helped him get back up. His hair was thin and greasy, and I could tell he hadn't showered for days, if not weeks. Willie was wearing only a thin, soiled pair of underwear beneath his way-too-big pants. Tina couldn't believe I was going to so much trouble, even dressing the man, just to visit. The room, the whole scene, became too much for her and she decided she would wait outside. Shawn went with her. Willie leaned on me to keep his balance while I pulled up each leg of his pants. I got him to stand using me as his support, but he was really shaky.

"Hold up your pants, Willie, while I try to get your shirt on!" I directed. His pants were now four sizes too big and wouldn't stay up. He kept losing his balance and letting go of his pants to hold on to me. Each time he did, his pants hit the floor.

"Don't you have a belt?" I was getting a little frustrated now.

"Maybe in the closet," he muttered.

I left him to go look in the closet and Willie thumped back down on the bed.

There was so little light eking its way through the layer of grime on the window that I couldn't see anything in the dark closet. Finally I spotted some twine on the floor. I fed it through the loops of his pants, forming a makeshift belt.

Once he was dressed, Tina and Shawn came back into the room and the three of us helped him down the steps and out to the street. He could only walk with our support. He hadn't bathed in so long, not caring about personal hygiene, that the three of us were nearly overcome by his body odor. Shoving it out of our minds, we placed his arms around our shoulders and slowly made our way to the greasy spoon restaurant across the street. It was clear to me then that Willie was dying. His years of drinking all day every day had caught up with him, and his body, ravaged by alcohol, was succumbing to cirrhosis of the liver.

Willie wanted nothing to eat when we finally got to the diner—he had a glass of milk. The waitress looked at us and couldn't help herself. "Who are *you?*" she asked.

"I'm his sister," I said as though I owed her an explanation, "and this is his other sister; and this is my daughter, his niece." I almost sounded proud of it, as when someone is bragging about to whom they're related. It wasn't that I was proud Willie was the town drunk, but letting others know that he had siblings clothed him with some humanity. I wanted to give him that. He wasn't just a drunken freak. Willie was someone's child. He had grown up, wasted his life and done evil things, but he was one of God's lost creations.

I remember thinking how, in the past two years, he had changed from someone who gave me shudders to a person I cared about. I cared what happened to Willie Hiebert! Other than that God's love had overtaken my heart, there was no way I should care what happened, good or bad, to Willie. He should have been dead to me; yet there I was, concerned about keeping his dignity intact while being judged by a diner waitress. Maybe the way I had judged others in the past was suddenly revealed in the derisive tone she had used. Perhaps I was seeing just how ugly and indiscriminant human value judgments of others are. Maybe I was seeing how my own criticism and superiority looked to God whenever I attacked one of His other children so cruelly. The only difference between other homeless, drunken bums and this one, was that this one was my brother. Somehow in this moment, that really mattered.

The waitress didn't say anything more, but gave me the look I've seen in the eyes of teenagers a thousand times. It was as though her face screamed, *Whatever! If he were my brother—I wouldn't be telling the world!*

The three of us sat down at a table. Willie drank his milk. Tina, Shawn, and I sipped our coffee and we talked.

I started. "Willie, George tells me that you gave your heart to Jesus as a boy!" I said incredulously. "And that you even went to Braeside Camp. He said you were a "flaming evangelist," enthusiastic about winning the neighborhood boys to Christ! Is that true?"

Willie looked down at the table. "That was a long time ago."

"Whatever happened? What happened to you, Willie? Don't you know that it's not God's will for anybody to perish?"[2]

His face became very serious. I could tell he really wanted to answer the question truthfully. "I've just done too many bad things now," he finally said quietly.

"That's not true, Willie," I interrupted. "That's not true! Don't you know that verse in the Bible, 'God so loved the world that he gave his only begotten...'" When I got to the word "son,"

[2] 2 Peter 3:9, NIV

353

Willie joined with me and finished the verse from memory.

"Willie," I said as tenderly as I could, "all it takes is for you to ask Jesus to forgive you of all those bad things you mentioned, and He will!"

That was Shawn's cue to enter the conversation. She was determined to tell Uncle Willie about her life, about how Jesus forgave her. Her return to Alberta was imminent, and she had come to visit Willie with a purpose.

"Uncle Willie, I used to think that too. I've done so many things wrong. I cheated in my marriage, was unfaithful in every relationship I ever had, partied, lived for myself. I think I've broken every one of God's commandments except for murder. And I thought that God couldn't love me, couldn't accept me. I felt exactly how you feel now. I thought it was too late too. But then, I took a chance—one more chance. A year ago I gave my life to Jesus and just appealed to His compassion and forgiveness. Uncle Willie, He forgave me. He gave me such a wonderful sense of being pardoned. For the first time in twenty years, maybe my whole life, I felt clean and pure. In the year since, He's changed my life and given me more happiness than I ever had while I was running from Him and doing my own thing. Uncle Willie," she paused as if to indicate that what was to follow was the most significant thing she was going to say, "Jesus forgave me, so I know He'll forgive you too!"

"Nah, it's too late for me," Willie said resolutely. "I'm too bad."

In that moment I knew this to be the biggest lie that Willie believed. He had based his whole life on it. After he had driven him to such evil, the devil made sure Willie knew it. He made sure that he rode him hard about it every day. He filled Willie's mind with hopeless thoughts and pointed accusations, pulverizing him with the depth of his own evil—an evil so great, even God with all of His love, wouldn't be able to forgive it. I could tell by his eyes that Willie believed every word the enemy had whispered into his heart. It was his religion. Willie attended the first church of the damned, where there is no hope and no salvation. Its followers are cursed to live out their days in self-destructive behavior that prolongs their pain, but doesn't quite kill them, enabling any measure of relief; and the whole time they live, they feel the guilt of cowardice. They would kill themselves, but don't even have the nerve to do that. Haunted by what they've done, they feel their miserable existence will never come to an end. Damned they are. Damned to live as drunken robots, having black holes for souls—the videotapes of their evil acts played perpetually on the screens of their scarred memories.

I reached for the most heart-wrenching appeal I had: "Willie, why don't you answer Mom's prayers? Answer Ike's prayers! They want to see you in heaven, Willie. Okay—write off your life here on earth, but Willie, give your life to Christ, ask Him to forgive you and make it to heaven for Mom's sake and Ike's sake!"

"No," he said, not defiantly but resolutely. "No—I can't. I'm just a hopeless bum." He was reciting his mantra, his core belief. He knew it by heart. It was the one thing of which he was sure.

As we walked slowly back to his rooming house, I was struck by his frailty. He was so sick. He was sixty-six years old—although he looked much older—skin and bones, and he had nothing left to live for. As we got to his building he insisted on going up to the room by himself. We said good-bye and left, after a promise to return and visit soon.

"Thanks for coming," Willie called back to us.

"We'll be in touch!" I assured. Then we got in the car.

Shawn returned to Alberta the following week. She was glad she had had the opportunity to speak to Willie and prayed it would ultimately have a positive effect on him, though she had definitely hoped for a more immediate one.

☙

The Canadian holiday weekend in May is always the weekend before the twenty-fourth. It was raining early on the Saturday morning of the long weekend, and I was feeling a little disappointed that the weather was so nasty I wouldn't be able to be outside. I was sulking over a cup of coffee at the kitchen table when the phone rang. It was "rooming-house Ted."

"Margaret? Margaret Davidson?"

"Yes—yes, it's me!"

"Margaret, it's Ted, Willie's super. We had to put Willie in the hospital last night. He's pretty bad—bleeding internally, ya know? Anyway they gave 'im seven bags of blood last night and he's doin' a little better, but he's in rough shape. I thought you'd wanna know."

"Okay, Ted, thanks for calling."

The next day Tina and I made the trip to Welland to see him.

Upon arriving at the hospital, we expected to see Willie laid out on a gurney and near death. We were surprised when we saw him, not in his room, but sitting in a wheelchair at the nurses' station. There he sat in all his glory, with a big toothless grin, singing western songs to his captive audience. Boxcar at his best.

"Willie! How are you? I'm surprised you're up and about! I heard you were at death's door," I said as we interrupted his performance.

"Nah, not me! I feel great and I'll be gettin' outta here soon— maybe tomorrow. So I'll need a couple bucks. Have you got some you can loan me?"

The seven pints of blood had energized him and he was in good spirits. He felt better than he had in months. A few minutes later his doctor told us that he was still bleeding internally and that he was in the last stages of cirrhosis. Willie wouldn't be going home.

"Really, I'm broke! I need a loan," Willie reiterated as he read the look of incredulity on my face.

I slipped my hand into my pocket and pulled out a twonie—a Canadian two-dollar coin. Willie took the two bucks and said, "Dig a little deeper; I know there's more down there!"

"There's no more down there for you, that's for sure!" I shot back.

Tina and I wheeled him to his room.

"Can you put my twonie in the bank?" He gestured toward his shoe by the window, so I slipped the coin down into its toe.

"Do you want me to tell your daughter you're in the hospital?" I asked. He didn't often see her—but I did. She lived in St. Catharines and I knew where she worked. I had hooked up with her several times in the past few years. She and I renewed acquaintance and, though she didn't have much to do with Willie, she always asked after his health.

"Sure. You can tell her. That would be nice of you."

Soon the doctor came by and I went out into the hall to speak with him. He was surprised to learn Willie had any family.

"Oh, he's got family! He has lots of family—six brothers and two sisters! And his mom just died a couple of years ago," I told him.

As we spoke for a few minutes about Willie's condition, the doctor furrowed his brow and became very serious. "Your brother's

356

liver is about finished," he said, "and there's no more that we can do for him. See if you can get him to sign power of attorney over to you so that you can make decisions for him as he becomes incapacitated. I'm going to see about getting him into a convalescent hospital. He's losing blood continuously and we can't just keep giving him transfusions."

"Well, how much longer does he have?"

"Months. Weeks maybe."

When I went home and told Bill what Willie's doctor had said, he relieved me of any obligation at the office and said I could go to Welland as much as I desired. Nearly every day for the next two weeks, I made the twenty-five minute drive to Welland's hospital and cared for my dying brother. I had lost Pete, Ike and Hank, plus Mom, in the previous five years, and I knew Willie's time here was coming to a close. He agreed to sign the papers giving me power of attorney, and I spoke with the medical staff about his care. Near the end he was fading quickly, and some days he wasn't conscious at all. When I spoke to him he groaned and mumbled unintelligibly.

His ex-wife, Claudette, and his daughter came to see him in the first week, and he was able to talk on those days. It had been years since they had spoken, and I felt good that they had the chance to see each other. The following week I made arrangements with one of his old drinking buddies to come with me. Paul had become a Christian shortly after my brother Pete died and had even enrolled in Bible college. His whole life had turned around; he was engaged to be married and was preparing for the ministry. When he had heard of Willie's condition he wanted to come with me to talk to him. He had a heart for those whose lives had been ravaged by alcohol as his had been. Willie wasn't very well, however, and it had been years since Willie had seen Paul. On the day that he came to the hospital, Willie didn't even acknowledge his presence. As Paul sat on one side of Willie's bed, I took Willie's face into my hands and began to speak to him. I spoke, and Paul prayed.

"Willie," I said rather loudly, knowing he was in a drug-induced cloud, "Willie, can you hear me say I love you?" In the last couple of years, Willie had heard those words regularly from me. It was inconceivable, humanly speaking, and I was amazed to hear them come out of my mouth each time they did. I felt genuine, supernatural love for my brother, and I knew he needed to hear it. He probably hadn't heard those words from anyone for years, if ever; yet in the last two years of his life he heard them whenever he spoke to me.

He nodded yes, but his eyes remained closed.

"Your old friend Paul is here. He's on the other side of the bed." No response.

As I began to speak to him again, he reached out his hand and felt for mine. I held his hand tightly and said, "Willie, I want to let you know how *much* I love you!" First one eye opened and then the other, as though it was the most work he had done in his whole life. "Can I pray with you? I love you enough that I want to pray with you."

I prayed out loud as Paul interceded on the opposite side of the room. I prayed for his health and then I prayed for his soul. I prayed so that he could hear me ask God to bring him into relationship with Himself. I prayed that God would be merciful and draw Willie by His Spirit, and that Willie would respond affirmatively. I prayed that he would turn his life over to Jesus. The prayer was not long, but I wanted Willie to know that I loved him, and wanted him to go to heaven, and that God still loved him too.

There was no more movement from Willie. We had no assurance he even heard us. A few moments after the prayer ended, we left, disappointed. Paul had really believed for God to create a special moment where Willie would have been lucid enough to speak and respond to hearing God's good news one more time. God had so radically changed Paul that he wanted the opportunity to tell Willie about it. Willie knew that Paul was a drunk just like him, and not far removed from the predicament in which he had found himself; but what he hadn't known, what Paul hadn't had the chance to tell him, was that God had rescued him. He was no longer a hopeless drunk. God had made him a new person. Instead Paul had to leave the hospital that day with no opportunity, no special moment. Though it was unspoken, we were thinking that it was getting too late for Willie; he was running out of time.

On the thirteenth day after Willie entered the hospital, I once again made the trip to see him; but this time I was alone. Usually Tina or someone came with me, but no one was available, so I went alone. Willie was groggy, but more alert than he had been for a while, and able to respond weakly. The doctors had told me when I arrived that they had decided not to give him any more blood. He was bleeding so badly internally that giving him more blood was only going to prolong the agony, and ultimately wouldn't help him. I decided to take any opportunity I could to speak to him, not knowing how many more days he would be conscious.

"Willie. Willie, I want you to look at me!" Getting his attention had become more difficult, and I wanted to make sure he was focusing on what I was saying. "Willie, I've got something important to say to you. Have you got your ears on?" I usually spoke to him that way; half in jest, but as if I was his big sister telling him what to do. In many ways it was true. He had lived his whole life irresponsibly, reaping the consequences, and now he was the little kid and I was the grownup.

"Yeah," he said weakly.

I was feeling desperate. "Willie," I continued, unsure he was focused on my voice, "can you hear me?"

"Yeah."

"Willie—you're dying! You're not going home this time. You're dying. Now, where are you going to go? Are you going to go to heaven or are you going to go to hell? It's your choice!"

He started to speak, but he was getting weaker by the minute. His eyes were closed, but a horrible pained expression came over his face. He said, "I can't...I can't do it...I can't..."

"You can't do what Willie? You can't stop drinking? Is that it?" In that moment it was as if God was helping me read his mind. Willie only saw himself as a drunk. In his own mind he was hopeless; he couldn't stop drinking, so he couldn't ask God to forgive him. To Willie it would be like trying to fool God. The legalism of his Mennonite childhood prevented him from believing he could come to Christ in such an awful state. In a second I knew it. I knew everything he was feeling.

"Willie! Are you afraid that you'll ask Jesus to forgive you and the first thing you'll do if you get out of here is reach for another bottle?"

He nodded.

"Willie, I'm not talking about Mom's rules. God knows your weaknesses. You can come to Him just as you are—besides, Willie, you're not getting out of this hospital! You won't even have a chance to take another drink! You won't even have a chance to slip and fall or to go back on your word to God. But even if you did get out of here—Willie, even if God did a miracle and healed you, and in your weakness you had another drink—Willie, still then, God would forgive you. He loves you so much Willie, whenever you ask Him to He will forgive you!"

I was talking fast and furiously. As I spoke I was praying, *God give me the right words that change Willie's mind about you! Give me the right words.* Willie couldn't believe God would hear the words of a drunk; of a man who, given another opportunity, would drink again.

"Willie, Willie!" I had to keep his attention; by now I was almost yelling to make sure he could still hear me. I could tell his strength was fading. "It's not Mom's way. You get to heaven God's way, and He already paid the price for all your sins through Jesus. Jesus already paid the penalty for everything you've done wrong and He's paid that price whether you accept it or not. He went to the cross for your sins, Willie, and He wants you to believe that He went there for you. All you have to do is accept it!"

The whole time I was talking I held his face in my hands. "Can you accept that Jesus went to the cross for you, Willie? Can you accept that?" Unable to muster the strength to say any more, Willie just nodded his head, ever so slightly, up and down.

"Okay, Willie, OK. I'm going to pray, and I know you can't repeat the words out loud, but you say them in your heart, OK?"

Again he moved his head up and down.

"Jesus," I started, "Jesus, please forgive my sins." I waited as if he could say the words out loud. Then I continued, "I accept the fact that you died on the cross for my sins. Thank you for your love and forgiveness. Because you have forgiven me, I know that my eternal home is in heaven. Jesus, let me know in my heart that you have forgiven me and that I'll be with you when I die." After every few words I paused, giving him time to repeat them after me in his mind.

After I finished praying, I asked him, "Willie, did you pray that prayer in your heart while I prayed it out loud?"

He grunted something indiscernible. I wanted more assurance, so I let go of his face and grabbed his hand in mine. "I know you're really weak and tired Willie, but I'm going to ask you some questions and you squeeze my hand the number of times I tell you to and answer me—OK?"

"Willie, do you know that I love you and that I forgive you? If you do, squeeze my hand once."

Immediately he squeezed my hand.

"Okay, if you know Jesus loves you and He has forgiven you, squeeze my hand two times—really hard, Willie. Okay?"

I wanted to know for sure whether or not Willie prayed that prayer with me. I didn't want a "maybe" to linger in my mind for the rest of my life. I waited.

Willie squeezed my hand once. It was harder than the first squeeze, just like I asked him; then, a moment later, he squeezed it a second time. Joy flooded into my soul. He squeezed two times! I knew he had prayed with me!

I told him I loved him, that the decision he made was brave, that God would take him home to heaven to see Mom and Ike, and that he had nothing more to worry about. Then I left and went home.

The next morning the hospital personnel phoned. Willie was gone.

I couldn't believe God's timing. I felt amazing peace; Willie was in heaven. There are many people in the world who would wish someone like Willie only a spot in the hottest hell, but I am glad to know a God who will forgive sins as grave as Willie's. It gives me confidence that He'll forgive me. The greatest gift God has ever given me in my life is a healing so perfect, so miraculous and so complete, that I can rejoice that my abuser's been forgiven and that, when he died, he went to heaven.

God had brought me from incapacitated victim—having trouble coping with the smallest of tasks and the greatest of nightmares—to compassionate, overcoming sister, able to lead the brother who had taken so much from me, to Jesus, who had given me everything. It is wonderfully inconceivable to me, even today, to realize that God's help in forgiving and restoring me after Willie's abuse, became the catalyst for that same Willie to trust in Jesus to forgive him. God did His wonderful transforming work not only to heal, but also to reach one who was so lost that nothing else could reach him. My life had come full circle. What had started out as utter pain had been transformed into a thing of beauty. No more was my life about being out of control—or being in control, for that matter; it was about letting

God take control. In the end, everything was about salvaging eternal souls—mine, Willie's, and that of everyone else who has been touched and helped by my story.

I had seen the end from the beginning and now it made sense. My deep wounds were healed; mere scars now—scars that don't hurt—that serve as reminders to others that God heals all.

One of the most common questions asked of me is, "Where was God? Where was God when you were lying on that bed, tied up and gagged, naked and humiliated, being raped by Willie?"

Now I know the answer. He was *there*. He was right there in that room, crying with me and saying, "Hang in there, Margaret! Hang in there! I'm going to heal you of this. I'll use this for My glory. You watch, Margaret—I'll work all of this evil for your good! Just trust Me, Sweetheart. Just trust in Me."

He knew it all—the end from the beginning, the healing from the pain. He knew how He was going to take my mourning and turn it into dancing.[3] God knew Himself. He knew His own goodness. He knew that He is the God of the impossible, and if I would trust Him, follow Him, and allow Him to heal me, then He would use my life to heal others; and not just other victims, but the very one who had wounded me in the first place.

People cannot look at my life without seeing God: the great Emancipator and Healer, the God who is love incarnate.

For Willie's funeral we summoned a preacher from Toronto who was formerly stationed in Welland. He had known Willie and tried at various times to help him. As he was preparing for the funeral and visiting with the family, I told him the story of Willie and me. I leave you with his graveside words: "This man being buried today has hurt a lot of people! You can either forgive him, or he can keep hurting you for the rest of your life—you choose!"

I had made my decision.

[3] Psalm 30:11, KJV

Postscript from the Author:

Thank you for reading *Scars Don't Hurt* and for bringing my story into your life. If, like me, you are on your own journey to emotional and spiritual health and would like some help along that road or you desire some spiritual and counseling resources or guidance, please contact me at:

Margaret Davidson
Scars Don't Hurt Ministries
P.O. Box #23067
St. Catharines, ON Canada
L7R 7P6

Or

Logon to: www.scarsdonthurt.org and send me an email message.

I would love to hear from you. I pray that God wonderfully heals and restores you in the same way that He did for me.

God Bless,
Margaret